ESSENTIAL JAPANESE

Essential Japanese

AN INTRODUCTION TO THE STANDARD
COLLOQUIAL LANGUAGE

by
Samuel E. Martin

Associate Professor of Far Eastern Linguistics
Yale University

THIRD REVISED EDITION

CHARLES E. TUTTLE COMPANY
Rutland, Vermont & Tokyo, Japan

European Representatives
Continent: BOXERBOOKS, INC., Zurich
British Isles: PRENTICE-HALL INTERNATIONAL, INC., London

Published by the Charles E. Tuttle Company
of Rutland, Vermont & Tokyo, Japan
with editorial offices at No. 15 Edogawa-cho,
Bunkyo-ku, Tokyo

First edition, August 1954
Second edition (revised), April 1956
Eighth printing, 1962
Third edition (revised), 1962
Fourth printing, 1964

Library of Congress
Catalog Card No. 59–5072

Printed in Japan

CONTENTS

Introduction xi

Introduction to the Third Revised Edition xvii

LESSON 1

Basic Sentences: 'Saying the Right Thing' 1

Structure Notes 3

1. 1	Pronunciation	3	1. 6 Vowels in sequence	11
1. 2	Rhythm	4	1. 7 Consonants	14
1. 3	Syllables	5	1. 8 Flapped R	21
1. 4	Voicing	6	1. 9 Syllabic nasal	23
1. 5	Vowels	8	1.10 Accent	26

Exercises 32

Pronunciation Check Points 34

LESSON 2

Basic Sentences: 'What and Where?' 39

Structure Notes 41

2. 1	Nouns	41	2.11 Particle ni	47
2. 2	Prenouns	41	2.12 Words meaning 'is'	48
2. 3	Place words	41	2.13 Inflected words	49
2. 4	Copular noun.	42	2.14 Sentence types	50
2. 5	Untranslated English words	43	2.15 Words of related reference	50
2. 6	Particles	44	2.16 Words for restaurant and hotel	52
2. 7	Particle wa	44		
2. 8	Particle ga	44	2.17 Words for toilet ..	53
2. 9	Particle ka	46	2.18 The word for 'what'	53
2.10	Particle no	46		

Exercises 54

Comprehension 55

LESSON 3

Basic Sentences: 'Things To Do' 57

Structure Notes 59

3. 1 Time words 59
3. 2 Nouns with and without particles ... 61
3. 3 Particles **kara, máde, e** 62
3. 4 Particle **né** 64
3. 5 Particle **de** 65
3. 6 Particle **o** 66
3. 7 Particle **to** meaning 'with' and 'and' ... 67
3. 8 Expressions for accompaniment 69
3. 9 Verbs, polite moods 69
3.10 Uses of the gerund.. 71
3.11 Use of the imperfect, perfect, and tentative moods 73
3.12 Negatives 74
3.13 Words for 'work' .. 75
3.14 Verbal nouns 75
3.15 Going in vehicles .. 76
3.16 'As soon as' 76

Exercises 76

Comprehension 78

LESSON 4

Basic Sentences: 'The Weather' 80

Structure Notes 83

4. 1 Adjectives 83
4. 2 Plain and polite forms 85
4. 3 Shapes of the plain forms 86
4. 4 Learning the forms 90
4. 5 Irregular verbs 92
4. 6 Adjectives and the copula 94
4. 7 Uses of the plain imperfect and perfect . 96
4. 8 Uses of the infinitive 98
4. 9 The plain negative.. 102
4.10 The particle **mo** .. 103
4.11 Particle **to** meaning 'when' 103
4.12 Particle **kara** meaning 'since' and 'because' 105
4.13 Multiple particles .. 106
4.14 **Kotó** 108
4.15 **Tsumori** 111
4.16 More adverbs 112
4.17 More gerund expressions. Errands 113
4.18 Gerund$+$**iru** 115
4.19 **Asobu** 117

Exercises 117

Comprehension 120

LESSON 5

Basic Sentences: 'Business' 122

Structure Notes 127

5. 1	Modifiers 127	5.11	Plain negative 147
5. 2	Adjective modifier clauses 132	5.12	Negative infinitive .. 149
5. 3	Copula modifier clauses 135	5.13	Imperfect negative+ de 150
5. 4	Copular nouns in modifier clauses 135	5.14	Hazu 151
5. 5	The noun no 138	5.15	Tokoro 152
5. 6	No desu 139	5.16	Verbs for leaving .. 154
5. 7	Verb+deshō 141	5.17	Máe ni and áto de 155
5. 8	Ka nè 144	5.18	Máde and uchi 158
5. 9	No de 144	5.19	Verbs meaning 'knows' 159
5.10	No ni 145	5.20	Talking a language 161

Exercises 161

Comprehension 167

LESSON 6

Basic Sentences: 'Shopping' 169

Structure Notes 174

6. 1	Numerals and numbers 174	6.14	Names of the months 189
6. 2	Other quantity words 175	6.15	Giving dates 190
6. 3	Use of numbers and quantity words 176	6.16	Telling time 190
6. 4	Primary and second-ary numerals 177	6.17	Gurai and goro 191
6. 5	Primary numerals .. 178	6.18	Particle ya 191
6. 6	Arithmetic 179	6.19	Nádo, nánka 192
6. 7	Counters 180	6.20	Particle ka meaning 'or' 193
6. 8	Sound changes 182	6.21	Particles wa and o with Ikaga desu ka? 194
6. 9	Secondary numerals. 185	6.22	Hitotsu 194
6.10	Secondary counters . 186	6.23	'Only'—daké and shika 195
6.11	Counting people ... 186	6.24	Approximate num-bers 197
6.12	Counting birds 187	6.25	Fractions 198
6.13	Counting days 187		

6.26 Percentage 199   6.28 Zutsu 199
6.27 Multiples 199   6.29 Góto ni, óki ni 201
Exercises 201
Comprehension 204

LESSON 7

Basic Sentences: 'Life in Japan' 206
Structure Notes 212

7. 1 Quotations 212   7.14 Gerund+áru 241
7. 2 To iu 216   7.15 The noun hó 243
7. 3 The plain tentative. 219   7.16 Comparisons 244
7. 4 Tentative+to (ni)   7.17 Questions with com-
      suru 222   parisons 250
7. 5 Noun+to shite 223   7.18 Ichiban 251
7. 6 Gerund+míru 223   7.19 Ordinal numbers .. 252
7. 7 Desideratives 224   7.20 Particle hodo and
7. 8 Alternative questions 228   negative comparisons 252
7. 9 Yó 233   7.21 Naruhodo 254
7.10 Quoting requests .. 237   7.22 Bákari 254
7.11 Particle yo 239   7.23 Mamá 256
7.12 Miéru and kikoeru . 240   7.24 Onaji 256
7.13 Prenouns+ni 241   7.25 Clothing 257
Exercises 259
Comprehension 265

LESSON 8

Basic Sentences: 'Telephone Calls' 268
Structure Notes 274

8. 1 Interrogatives+ka   8. 7 Denial of permission
      and mo 274   =prohibition 292
8. 2 Gerund+mo 282   8. 8 Denial of obligation 293
8. 3 Interrogative+   8. 9 Obligation, prohibi-
      gerund+mo 284   tion, permission:
8. 4 The provisional mood 288   summary 294
8. 5 Obligation 291   8.10 The conditional
8. 6 Permission 292   mood: forms 297

8.11 The conditional
     mood: uses 299
8.12 Advice 305
8.13 'Had better' 307
8.14 The particle sáe .. 308
8.15 The explicit use of

     ni 311
8.16 'The more..
     ..the more' 313
8.17 The particle shi .. 314
8.18 Correlative com-
     pounds 317

Exercises 318
Comprehension 322

LESSON 9

Basic Sentences: 'A Polite Conversation' 324
Structure Notes 328

9. 1 Status words:
     humble, neutral,
     exalted 328
9. 2 Kinship terms 329
9. 3 Other nouns 330
9. 4 Honorific prefixes . 331
9. 5 Honorific suffixes .. 332
9. 6 Verbs: the honorific
     infinitive 332
9. 7 Special honorific
     verbs 335
9. 8 Mōshiageru 339
9. 9 Inflection of ir-
     regular exalted verbs 340
9.10 Special inflections of
     -másu 340

9.11 Use of humble verbs 341
9.12 Adjectives 343
9.13 Formation of the
     adjective honorific
     infinitive 345
9.14 Summary of
     honorific predicates. 347
9.15 Uses of gozáru 348
9.16 Uses of irassháru . 350
9.17 Oide 351
9.18 Verbs for giving .. 354
9.19 Favors 357
9.20 Requests 363
9.21 Answers to negative
     questions 364
9.22 The specific plural. 365

Exercises 367
Comprehension 370

LESSON 10

Basic Sentences: 'Womantalk' 373
Structure Notes 378

10. 1 Sò desu 378
10. 2 Bound form
      sō 'appearance' 379

10. 3 Rashíi 381
10. 4 Expressions
      meaning 'like' 383

10. 5   The alternative 383
10. 6   -nágara 385
10. 7   Áru with people .. 387
10. 8   Kotó ni suru.
        Kotó ni naru 388
10. 9   Shimau and oku .. 389
10.10   Wáke 390
10.11   Double negatives .. 391
10.12   Ni chigai nái 392
10.13   Ni tsúite and
        ni yotte 393
10.14   Causative, passive,
        and passive causative
        verbs 395
10.15   Use of the causative 397
10.16   Uses of the passive.. 400
10.17   Use of the passive
        causative 403
10.18   The potential 404
10.19   Ka mo shirenái ... 407
10.20   Ka shira 408
10.21   Desiderative verbs .. 409
10.22   Monó desu 410

Exercises 412

Comprehension 415

Appendix I.   Other Styles of Speech 418

    1.   The impersonal style 418
    2.   The plain style 420
    3.   The modern literary style 427

Appendix II. Accent Patterns 429

Key to Exercises 434

Additional Accent Practice 456

Index of Structure Notes 457

INTRODUCTION

This book was written for several types of student. It is intended primarily for the American living in Japan who wishes to acquire a good knowledge of spoken Japanese in a short time. Emphasis is focused on the STRUCTURE of the language; vocabulary is considered of secondary importance. Since English equivalents are provided for most sentences, there is no general vocabulary for the book. If the student runs across a word he doesn't know, he should underline it and later look it up in a dictionary or ask a Japanese for its meaning.

To make the most effective use of the book, the student should hire a native tutor to give him drill on the patterns provided in the lessons. During actual drill sessions, no English is to be spoken. Sometimes it is better to have a tutor who hesitates to speak English or doesn't even know the language. It should be made very clear to the tutor—directly or through an interpreter—that the student desires drill in talking Japanese naturally, just the way the tutor himself talks. The tutor must not slow down below a natural speed, or exaggerate the pronunciation, or break his sentences in places where he wouldn't naturally pause. Any distortion of the tutor's natural speech will hinder the student's progress. Nor should the tutor attempt to explain the structure of the language; that is the purpose of the textbook. Sometimes it is better to have a talkative person who is not too highly educated, since he will be less likely to produce bookish expressions

c

and wander off the drill path in attempting to give grammatical explanations. The tutor will have to provide some additional material besides what is in the book. He should use the patterns given here as a cue, and expand upon them, varying the words he uses. The student will hear words he does not know and, especially during the early stage, constructions he is not familiar with. If it is possible to find out the meanings of new words and constructions without slowing down the drill procedure, it is well to do so. But if finding out the meaning of everything you hear means continually interrupting the flow of Japanese, it is better to skip over new things and concentrate on the parts you do understand.

The book is arranged in ten lessons. If two or three hours a day, five days a week, are spent in drill, it should be possible to cover a lesson a week. If less time is available for drill work, the material will have to be covered at a slower pace. If more time is available, it is probably better to devote the extra hours to more thorough drill on constructions and to continuing review of earlier material, rather than to speeding up the covering of the lessons. The differences between the basic structure of Japanese and that of English are too many to cover in less than about three months, even for very bright students. At that, the student will need to continue reviewing structure points after he has finished the basic course and is expanding his vocabulary range in free conversation.

Each lesson contains four parts: Basic Sentences, Structure Notes, Exercises, and Comprehension. The student should memorize the Basic Sentences with the native tutor, having the tutor say each sentence over and over while repeating it after him, until the student can say the sentence all by himself to the tutor's satisfaction. While drilling, the student must not watch the book too closely; he should follow the lips of the tutor.   The language is not to be read, it is to be spoken.   This is true also when practicing away from the native tutor; use the book to jog your memory, not to take its place.

When the student first goes over the Basic Sentences, there are many points he does not understand about the words and how they are put together. He does not interrupt his memorizing drill to ask the tutor about the structure. Instead, after his first drill on the Basic Sentences, he reads through the Structure Notes. Later, he has the tutor drill him on the forms and additional examples given in each structure note.   The tutor should be able to expand on these patterns and give many additional examples.   After the Basic Sentences, there are notes on Vocabulary Items; here will be found the meanings of those words which are not obvious from the English equivalents of the Basic Sentences or from the Structure Notes, and also some words which do not appear in the Basic Sentences but occur in the additional examples of the Structure Notes or in the Comprehension material.

The Exercises are an attempt to check on how well the Structure Notes have been assimilated, and should not be attempted till the preceding material has been thoroly studied.   These exercises are more effective when they are done with the tutor, but if time does not permit, they may be used alone, since a Key is provided at the end of the book with appropriate answers.

The Comprehension material is intended to be suggestive. The student should not study this until it has been presented by the tutor; the tutor may feel free to expand, rephrase, or change the dialogs in any way he sees fit. He should try to avoid words and grammatical constructions not yet learned. After the Comprehension material has been presented, the tutor may ask questions to see whether the student has understood. Then the two may engage in free conversation within the vocabulary range available to them.

The student should not worry about memorizing individual words. If you learn a few hundred typical sentences, with different structure points embedded within them, you will find new words very easy to acquire from actual conversation instead of using dictionaries and textbooks. Always learn new words in phrases and sentences; remember them that way. This way you will learn more precisely just what they mean and how they are used. Also, you will find it easier to recall them. Do not expect every word to have a single simple English equivalent; languages do not overlap each other very neatly. Sometimes a single Japanese word will have several English equivalents and sometimes it will be the other way around. You may want to recall the word by an English tag, but remember that the tag is just a device, and not the whole story on what the word means or how it is used.

The Structure Notes for the first lesson are devoted entirely to pronunciation. A good pronunciation is made or lost at the very beginning. If you start off with poor habits, these reinforce themselves as you practice the sentences. The words given as examples for pronunciation practice need not be memorized. The Basic Sentences for the first lesson consist of common polite expressions you will be using all the time. Do not worry about the grammatical constructions involved in these sentences—they will become clear later. In place of Comprehension material, the first lesson has a list of Pronunciation Check Points. Here, in summary, are the key differences between American and Japanese pronunciation habits. These check points should be gone over at frequent intervals thruout the course.

After the student has finished this book, he may want more material to drill on. A very good collection of drill material can be found in the book *Spoken Japanese* by Bernard Bloch and Eleanor Harz Jorden (2 vols, Holt, New York, 1945). That material is in a different Romanization system from the one used in this book, but the differences are easy to learn. *Essential Japanese* uses the Hepburn Romanization, which is the sort you will find in most Japanese-English dictionaries and other study aids. The author himself prefers a structural orthography of the type used in *Spoken Japanese*—a modification of the **Kunrei-shiki** system which has been adopted by the Japanese Government. But since the Hepburn—**Hebon-shiki**—system is in such wide use among the people for whom this work is intended, that is the system employed here.

Students who wish to learn to read and write Japanese in the native orthography will find this book a valuable introduction to the language itself. About Lesson 6, they can start learning the *kana* letters, and about Lesson 8, they can begin the Naganuma readers (Naoe Naganuma, *Hyōjun Nihongo Tokuhon*: Revised Edition, Tokyo, 1948). It is unwise to undertake the study of the Japanese writing system before acquiring some fluency in the spoken language. The student will find the following volume an aid in learning the modern writing system: Elizabeth F. Gardner and Samuel E. Martin, *An Introduction to Modern Japanese Orthography—I. Kana:* Institute of Far Eastern Languages, Yale University, 1952.

The structural analysis on which the present work rests is primarily the work of Professor Bernard Bloch of Yale University. Contributions have also been made by Dr. Eleanor Harz Jorden, Professor Elizabeth F. Gardner, and the author. In addition to published and unpublished works of those mentioned, the Japanese-Japanese dictionary of Kyōsuke Kindaichi (*Meikai-kokugo-jiten*: Tokyo, 1942) and the accent dictionary compiled by the Japan Broadcasting Company (Nippon-hōsō-kyōkai, *Nihongo-akusento-jiten*: Tokyo, 1951) proved very helpful. The author is grateful to members of the Japanese tutorial staff of Yale University for giving aid in the form of examples and material: Mrs. Katherine Nakaso Fennessey, Mrs. Miyo Okada, Mr. Mikiso Hane, Mr. Kentaro Ikeda, and Mr. Senzo Usui. The responsibility for the choice and accuracy of the material is the author's, and reports of errors or misjudgments will be received with sincere appreciation.

SAMUEL E. MARTIN

INTRODUCTION TO THE THIRD
REVISED EDITION

When I first wrote ESSENTIAL JAPANESE, I did not anticipate the warm welcome it would receive. I wanted to design a short book of essential grammar for individual study, rather than for the schoolroom. But the book has won such wide acceptance as a class textbook that it seems well to add a few notes on how the material can best be adapted for the classroom. The "lessons" are, of course, much too long to be thought of as assignments. Depending on the time available, the teacher should break each lesson up into parts, somewhat in the following fashion: The Basic Sentences of each Lesson can be divided into three or four groups. Between each assignment of sentences, a group of Structure Notes are to be covered. The Exercises are best saved until the Structure Notes have been covered; then all the Basic Sentences can be reviewed before the Comprehension is presented. Some teachers have suggested reversing the order of Lessons 5 and 6, in order to present the numbers by the end of the first half of a divided course; this allows you to save the difficult modifier constructions of Lesson 5 for the second half of the course. I have left the order intact; but those who wish can easily reverse the two lessons as assignments. Students in America may wish to cover the numbers lightly (after all, who counts birds?); and everyone will probably find the coverage of honorifics in Lesson 9 more extensive than needed in a beginning course. The material can be shortened as the teacher sees fit.

This edition has been extensively revised; I have changed many sentences and added a number of points to the grammatical explanations and to the index. But I have retained the original format and page numbers so far as possible. Thanks are due to a number of people who have kindly called my attention to places that needed correction or improvement; in particular, I want to thank Roy Grey, Charles Terry, David Thomson, and Fumiko Watanabe for numerous suggestions. Hamako Itō Chaplin and Shirō Sugata were helpful in settling a number of questions of usage. I realize that there are still many places that could be improved and perhaps a number of errors that have passed unnoticed; I will be grateful for further suggestions for revision.

Tokyo 1961   S.E.M.

ESSENTIAL JAPANESE

Note to accompany following remarks on pronunciation: Many Japanese shorten a final long vowel in a word which already has one long vowel, or a double consonant, or n + a consonant: shóko for shôkō 'officer', gakko for gakkō 'school', sensé for senséi 'teacher', honto for hontō 'truly', benkyo for benkyō 'study'. You will also hear short vowels in certain phrases like mo ichido for mō ichido 'once more' and arígato for arígatō 'thanks'.

LESSON 1.

A. BASIC SENTENCES. 'Saying the Right Thing.'
1. Ohayō gozaimásu.   Good morning! [It is early.]
2. Konnichi wa.   Hello! [As for today...]
3. Komban wa.   Good evening! [As for this evening...]
4. Ogénki desu ka?   How are you?*
5. Okage-sama de (génki desu).   I'm fine, thank you.
6. Anáta wa?   [How about] you?
7. Aikawarazu (désu yo)!   Same as always.
8. Sayōnára. or Sayonára. or Sayonara!   Goodbye.
9. Hái. or É. or Só.   Yes. Yeah.
10. Iie. or Íya.   No. Nope.
11. Shitsúrei shimáshita.   Excuse me. [I have commited a discourtesy.]
12. Gomen nasái.   Please excuse me.
13. Chótto shitsúrei desu ga...   Excuse me, but... [I have a question or request].
14. Ohanashi-chū shitsúrei desu ga...   Excuse me for interrupting, but...
15. Onegai itashimásu. ⎫ Onegai shimásu. ⎬   Please [do so]. [I make a request of you.]
16. Osóre irimasu. ⎫ Sumimasén. ⎬   I'm sorry to trouble you.
17. Osóre irimashita. ⎫ Sumimasén deshita. ⎬   I'm sorry to have troubled you.

---

*Traditionally translated by **Ikága desu ka?** 'How is it?' or 'How about it?'; common as a proposition or invitation (such as a shopkeeper's invitation to make a purchase), the phrase sometimes means 'How are things?' or 'How do you feel?'

18. (Dŏ mo) arígatō go-
    zaimasu.
    (Dŏ mo) sumimasén.
Thank you (very much) [for what you are doing or will do].

19. Arígatō gozaimáshi-
    ta.
    Sumimasén deshita.
Thank you [for what you have done].

20. Dŏ itashimáshite.
Not at all. (You're welcome.)

21. (Iroiro) oséwa ni na-
    rimáshita.
Thank you for (all) your trouble.

22. Kashikomarimáshita.
Yes, sir. (I will do it.)

23. Gokúrō-sama deshi-
    ta.
Thank you [for doing some service expected of you].

24. Ojama désu ka.
    Ojama dé wa arima-
    sén ka?
Am I disturbing you?

25. Ojama itashimáshita.
    Ojama shimáshita.
Excuse me for having disturbed you.

26. Goenryo náku.
Don't stand on ceremony. [Make yourself at home. Help yourself. Speak right up. Tell the man what you want. Don't hesitate.]

27. Yóku irasshaimáshi-
    ta.
Hello, I'm glad you could come. [Welcome.]

28. Omachidō-sama dé-
    shita.
I'm sorry to have kept you waiting.

29. Dŏzo (osaki ni).
Please (go ahead–after you).

30. Osaki ni (shitsúrei
    shimásu).
Excuse me for going first.

31. Oagari kudasái.
Please come in (a Japanese house).

32.	**Ohairi kudasái.**	Please come in (a room, a Western house).
33.	**Dé wa** (or **Ja**), **shitsú-rei** (**ita**)**shimásu.**	Well, I'll say goodbye. [Excuse me.]
34.	**Ja, mata.**	So long! [Well, (see you) again!]
35.	**Mata dŏzo.**	Please [come] again.
36.	**Yukkúri** (**hanáshite kudasai**).	(Please talk) slowly.
37.	(**Dŏzo**) **mō ichido** (**it-te kudasái**).	(Please) (say it) again.
38.	**Chótto mátte** (**kuda-sai**).	Please wait a moment.
39.	**Móshi-moshi** or **Chótto!**	Hello! Hey! Say!
40.	**Oyasumi nasái.**	Good night. [Please rest well.]

NOTE: **Osaki ni** can mean either 'you go first' or '(excuse me for) going first', depending on the situation.

B. STRUCTURE NOTES.

1. 1. PRONUNCIATION. Every language has a system of sounds, and no two systems are exactly alike. The same organs are used in pronouncing the sounds of Japanese and those of English, but they are used in somewhat different ways. These organs are parts of the mouth, the tongue, the nose and the throat. You will find it helpful to learn a bit about how these organs are used to make the sounds of English and those of Japanese. Many of the sounds in these two languages are so similar that you

can use English sounds for the Japanese ones without being misunderstood, but there are some of your English
pronunciation habits which must be avoided if you are
to speak understandable Japanese. And if you don't
want your Japanese to have a marked American accent,
you will want to pay close attention to the slight differences between even those sounds which are most alike in
the two languages.

1. 2. RHYTHM. English is spoken in a SYNCOPATED
fashion—we bounce along, rushing syllables in between
heavy stresses, keeping an irregular rhythm and tempo
based on our stress system. Each normal English syllable
is spoken with one of four stresses—and there's even an extra one, especially loud, to show unusual emphasis. If
you listen to the word 'windshield-wiper' you will notice
that the first syllable (wind-) is more heavily pronounced
than the others; the last syllable (-er) is the weakest; and
for some speakers there is a difference in stress between
the remaining syllables (-shield- and -wipe-). Those Americans who hear no difference in stress between -shield- and
-wipe- may hear the somewhat stronger stress on the syllable 'new' in the phrase 'a new windshield-wiper' (with
the strongest stress still on the syllable wind-).

Japanese, on the other hand, speak in a METRO-
NOMIC fashion—as if there were a musician's metronome
evenly beating out each syllable. Instead of putting a
heavy stress on some syllables, and various weaker stresses
on the others, the Japanese gives each syllable a moderate,
even stress. And instead of rushing syllables in between
the heavy-stressed ones—speeding up the weaker syllables,

slowing down for the stronger ones—the Japanese allows about the same amount of time for each of his syllables, regardless of the apparent prominence of the syllable.

To the ears of an American, accustomed to hearing distinctive stresses, not all Japanese syllables are heard evenly strong. This is because not all Japanese syllables are equally PROMINENT. The prominence of a syllable is conditioned by a variety of factors, such as stress, vowel-color, pitch, voicing, etc. Of these factors, stress is the most important in English, but the least important in Japanese. Of course, those syllables which have voiceless or dropped vowels in Japanese will sound weakly stressed to an untrained American ear.

So the first English habit to overcome in speaking Japanese is syncopation. Try to time your Japanese syllables evenly, giving them an equal stress.

1. 3. SYLLABLES. Now, what is a Japanese syllable? An English syllable, as noted above, is a sound or group of sounds accompanied by one of four stresses. A Japanese syllable isn't that sort of thing at all. It's a sound or group of sounds which take up a certain relative space of time. In other words, one of those metronome beats. A Japanese syllable may consist of a SHORT VOWEL (é 'picture', ó 'tail'), or a CONSONANT + A SHORT VOWEL (té 'hand', tá 'field', yó 'world'), or a CONSONANT + Y + A SHORT VOWEL (the first syllable of kyónen 'last year'). [NOTE: The sounds sh, ch, ts are in each case single consonants even though we write them with two letters.]

In addition, a syllable may consist of a CONSONANT

WHEN FOLLOWED BY ANOTHER CONSONANT (OTHER THAN Y) OR A PAUSE—for example, the first k of yukkúri 'slowly', the first s [a spelling abbreviation for what is really sh] of irasshaimáshita '(you) came', the first n of kónnichi 'today', and both the m and the n of kómban 'this evening'.* The syllabic consonants are further discussed in notes 1.8 and 1.9.

Finally, a syllable may consist of EITHER HALF OF A LONG VOWEL. In other words, what we write as ā, ē, ō, ū are really just abbreviations for aa, ee, oo, uu,— two syllables each. Long vowels are further discussed in note 1.6.

Below are some of the words occurring in the Basic Sentences, with the syllable divisions indicated by hyphens.

ohayō gozaimásu	o-ha-yo-o-go-za-i-má-s
konnichi wa	ko-n-ni-chi-wa
komban wa	ko-m-ba-n-wa
chótto	chó-t-to
arígatō	a-rí-ga-to-o
goenryo náku	go-e-n-ryo-ná-ku
mátte kudasai	má-t-te-ku-da-sa-i
hái	há-i
iie	i-i-e
sayonára	sa-yo-ná-ra

1.4. VOICING. In the throat there are two pieces of muscular tissue which can be vibrated with a flow of air from the lungs like a couple of heavy rubber bands. When these vocal cords—as they are called—vibrate, we say

*In konnichi wa and komban wa the accent is lost.

the sound has VOICING or is VOICED. When these cords are somewhat relaxed at the sides of the throat, we say the sound is VOICELESS or UNVOICED. You can feel the vibration of the vocal cords by placing your hand on your throat. Or put your hands over your ears and you will notice a buzz whenever a sound is voiced.

In most languages, some of the sounds are typically voiced and others are typically voiceless. For instance, in English the initial sounds of these pairs differ in that the ones on the left (k, ch, t, s, p, f, th) are voiceless, and those on the right (g, j, d, z, b, v, th) are voiced:

VOICELESS	VOICED
Kay	gay
cheer	jeer
toe	dough
seal	zeal
pay	bay
fan	van
thin	then

There are similar pairs of voiced and voiceless sounds in Japanese:

VOICELESS		VOICED	
kín	'gold'	gín	'silver'
chi	'blood'	jí	'graphic character, letter'
tó	'ten'	dŏ	'how'
sŏ	'so, right'	zŏ	'elephant'
pán	'bread'	bán	'guard, watchman'

In English, the sounds we call VOWELS—those made

without any close contact between the tongue and top of
the mouth—are always voiced, unless we are softly whis-
pering. In Japanese, vowel sounds are often unvoiced
when they come between voiceless consonants. Virtually
every speaker of Japanese pronounces the vowels written
i and **u** as unvoiced between voiceless consonants, and some
drop these vowels completely. At the end of a word after
a voiceless consonant these vowels are also frequently unvoiced or dropped, so that the final syllable of **ohayō gozaimásu** 'good morning' and **génki desu** 'I'm fine' sound as
if there were no **u** there at all. The other vowels—those
we write **a, e, o**—are usually pronounced voiced. But
unaccented **ka** and **ko** at the beginning of a word are often
unvoiced when followed by the same syllable: **kakánai**
'does not write', **koko** 'here'. And **ha** and **ho** are often
unvoiced when followed by a voiceless consonant+the
same vowel: **haká** 'grave', **hokori** 'dust', **hosói** 'slender'.

1. 5. VOWELS. There is a striking difference between
the way a Japanese pronounces his vowels and the way
an American pronounces his. Japanese vowels seem to
stand still. English vowels often slide off from their starting points in one of three directions: with the tongue moving front and up (as in key, bay, shy, toy); with the tongue
moving back and up and the lips rounding (as in now,
know, who); with the tongue relaxing toward a central
position (as in yeah, ah, law, uh, huh; with many speakers
also in bad, bed, bid, bud; with some Southern and Western speakers also in bat, bet, bit, butt).

A vowel takes its characteristic color from the way the
tongue, mouth and lips are held. Vowels are often described in terms of the tongue's position in three top-to-

bottom levels (HIGH, MID, LOW) and three front-to-back positions (FRONT, CENTRAL, BACK). If we ignore the off-glides mentioned above, and think only about the points of departure, we can illustrate these positions for American vowels with such words as these:

	FRONT	CENTRAL	BACK
HIGH	be, bit, bid	'jist', 'pirty'[1]	woo, put, wood
MID	set, said	cut, mud	show, boy[2]
LOW	bat, bad	father, cot, nod	caught, gnawed[3], boy[2]

For many American speakers all nine possible positions are used. The Japanese, however, fills only five of the spaces as in the following words:

	FRONT	CENTRAL	BACK
HIGH	mimí 'ear'	——	tsuzuku 'continues'
MID	té 'hand'	——	momo 'peach'
LOW	——	anáta 'you'	——

In English, we spell the same vowel sound many different ways (dough, toe, slow, so, sew, etc.) and the same letter may indicate a number of different vowels (line, marine, inn, shirt). In Romanized Japanese the same symbol is normally used for each occurrence of the same vowel. You should learn these symbols and the sounds

---

1. As in 'jist fine' and 'pirty good'. Many American speakers from Southern states use this high central vowel instead of the high back vowel, especially after y.

2. For some speakers, the vowel of 'boy' begins mid, for others low.

3. Some speakers do not distinguish 'caught' from 'cot', 'gnawed' from 'nod'. For such speakers, this space (low back) may be blank.

they stand for, and not confuse this simple use of these letters with their many English uses. The use of the letters may be remembered as: i as in ski, e as in pet, a as in father, o as in so, u as in rhubarb.

In both English and Japanese, the lips are relaxed for vowels in the front and center of the mouth, and somewhat rounded for those in the back. Many Japanese round their lips very little, however, and you will probably notice that the Japanese u involves less of this lip-rounding than the American equivalent. (Actually, much of the American lip-rounding is part of the off-glide.) After the consonants s, ts, and z, the Japanese u is sometimes pronounced in a HIGH CENTRAL position (like the vowel in 'jist fine', 'pirty good' or the Southerner's 'oodles'). Notice the various u sounds in these words:

susumu	'advances'	tsuzuku	'continues'
kuruma	'wagon'	nusúmu	'steals, swipes'
kutsú	'shoes'	gyūnyū	'milk'

In ordinary conversation, when the Japanese syllable u comes before ma, me, or mo, it is often pronounced as if it were the syllable m:

umá [mma]	'horse'
umé [mme]	'plum'
umoregi [mmoregi]	'fossil-wood'

Notice that Japanese does not utilize the MID CENTRAL position on the vowel chart. This is one of the most common of English vowels; it is sometimes indicated by the phonetic symbol ə ('inverted e'). For many English speakers, this is the most common vowel in weak-stressed syllables; so the American who forgets that Japanese has no weak-stressed syllables tends to replace various Japanese vowels with this relaxed central vowel. For **anáta** 'you', many Americans will say **ənátə**, overstressing the syllable **ná** and sliding over the other syllables. Be careful to avoid weak stresses and you will not confuse the Japanese with this mid central vowel.

1. 6. VOWELS IN SEQUENCE. In Japanese, any vowel may be followed by any other vowel—each is pronounced in a short, clear, evenly stressed fashion. Here are some examples of vowel sequences:

hái	'yes'	**máe**	'front'
ue	'top'	**ié**	'house'
omóu	'thinks'	**taué**	'rice-planting'
aói	'is blue'	**guai**	'state, condition'

Note that there is a syllable—an even space of time—for each vowel: **o-mó-u, ta-u-é, a-ó-i, gu-a-i.**

Now in English we do not have vowels in sequence. Each vowel is followed either by a consonant or by one of those three off-glides mentioned in 1. 5: the y-glide in key, bay, by, boy; the w-glide in now, know, new; the h-glide in ah, yeah, law, huh. When we Americans hear a Japanese vowel sequence, we are apt to reinterpret this as one of our combinations of vowel + glide. We hear Japanese **hái** like English 'high' and Japanese **máe** like English 'my'. The difficulty is that English 'high' and 'my' rime, but Japanese **hái** and **máe** do not. The following chart will give you an idea of the difference in pro-

nunciation between the two English words on the one hand
and each of the Japanese words on the other:

FRONT   CENTRAL   BACK

HIGH   hái

high

MID   máe

LOW

[There are some Tokyo speakers who do sound their
ai's much like their **ae**'s. Such speakers rime the words
káeru 'return' and **háiru** 'enter'. Speakers of Standard
Japanese, however, try to keep these sequences distinct.]

Just as we hear Japanese **ai** and **ae** alike, we tend to
hear Japanese **au** and **ao** the same. Listen carefully to the
difference between these pairs:

kau	'buys'	**áu**	'meets'
kao	'face'	**áo**	'blue'

Offhand, both of the words on the left seem to sound
like English 'cow?' and those on the right like English
'ow!' The following chart will give you an idea of the
difference in pronunciation. As you can see, this **chart**
is a mirror image of the one above.

FRONT   CENTRAL   BACK

HIGH   kau

cow

MID   kao

LOW

Since any vowel can follow any other vowel in Japanese, it is natural that a vowel can follow itself. These double vowels are sometimes called LONG VOWELS—because, being two syllables, they take twice as long to pronounce as the short ones. In the Hepburn Romanization of Japanese, which this book uses, the double vowels are usually written with a macron (-) over the simple vowel, except in the case of i which is written double: ii. Instead of a macron, some people use a circumflex accent (∧ —like a small inverted V). In the **Kunrei-shiki** system, the circumflex is used.

It is extremely important to master the difference between the short (simple) vowels and the long (double) ones early in your study of Japanese. So many words are distinguished by vowel length alone that, unless you are careful with these distinctions, your Japanese will be like a faulty telephone connection, likely to break down at any moment. English vowels are neither long nor short, by Japanese standards, but they often SOUND long, because of the off-glides. Remember to make your SHORT vowels SHORTER and your LONG vowels LONGER than the equivalent English vowels. Here are some examples of long and short vowels:

tá	'field'	sǎ	[sá-a]	'well!'
é	'picture'	ě	[é-e]	'yes'
kí	'tree'	íi	[i-i]	'is good'
ho	'sail'	hō	[ho-o]	'law'
fú	'metropolitan prefecture'	fǔ	[fú-u]	'seal'

In ordinary conversation, most Japanese do not distinguish the vowel sequence **ei** from **ee** (=**ē**). In some parts of Japan, however, the distinction is still maintained. To an American ear, both sequences sound about like the vowel in 'bay'. You should practice making the **ē** sound clear and long without the off-glide of the equivalent English sound. Examples:

téinei	'polite'	**nĕsan**	'older sister'
keiei	'management'	**tēburu**	'table'

1.7. CONSONANTS. In the structural system of every language, a given sound is made in somewhat different ways, depending on what sounds precede and follow it. If you hold your hand very close to your mouth and say the word 'pan' clearly and naturally, you will feel a slight puff of breath; on the other hand, if you say 'span' or 'ban' you will not feel the puff of breath. A more effective demonstration is to light a match and hold it close. Those consonants with a puff of breath will put the match out, those without will merely make it flicker. This puff of breath is called ASPIRATION; consonants accompanied by it are said to be ASPIRATED. English p, t, ch, and k (often spelled with the letter c as in 'cat') are aspirated in initial position, but not after the consonant s—compare 'pin, spin; tick, stick; charge, dischárge; key, ski'. In final position, English p, t, and k may be either aspirated or unaspirated, or not released at all.

Now in Japanese, the consonants **p, t, ch,** and **k** are usually somewhat aspirated as in English, but the aspiration is not so heavy. The Japanese consonants are UN-ASPIRATED when they are double (that is, long). Since the corresponding English double consonants are aspirated—as in 'hip-pocket, part-time, night-chief, bookkeepers'—you should give special attention to suppressing the puff of breath when you make the Japanese double consonants.

Another characteristic of Japanese double consonants—including **ss, ssh,** as well as **pp, tt, tch, kk**—is the special TENSENESS with which they are pronounced. It's as if the Japanese tightened up his throat in order to hold on and get in that extra syllable represented by the first of the consonants.

Listen to the difference between the single and double consonants in the following examples, then imitate them, being very careful to hold the first of the double consonants for a full syllable's duration and then release it tight and clear with no puff of air.

pén	'pen'	**ippén**	'one time'
íto	'thread; silk'	**itto**	'a way, a course'
káko	'past'	**kákko**	'parentheses; brackets'
kásai	'fire'	**kassai**	'applause'
ísho	'will, testament'	**issho**	'together'
ichí	'one'	**itchi**	'accord, agreement, unity'

Just as the difference between long and short vowels is very important to make your Japanese understandable, so is the difference between long and short consonants.

One other point about aspiration. In English we do not aspirate a consonant after s. But in Japanese, when the syllable **su** is reduced to just a syllabic s (as in **Ikága desu** ka?), a following **p**, **t**, or **k** still has the slight aspiration it would have in initial position. Notice the difference in pronunciation between English 'ski'—one syllable, no aspiration—and Japanese **suki** 'likes'—two syllables, with **u** unvoiced or dropped, but with slight aspiration of **k.**

Consonants are usually described in terms of the WAY they are pronounced (voiced, voiceless; aspirated, unaspirated; etc.) and the PLACE they are pronounced. In general, Japanese uses about the same places in the mouth as English—**b**, **p**, and **m** are made with the lips, and **k** and **g** with the back of the tongue against the soft part of the roof of the mouth.

But **t**, **d**, and **n** are all made farther front than the English equivalents. For these sounds in English, most of us touch the front of the tongue or the tip (or both) against the ridge BEHIND the teeth, or even farther back than that. But in Japanese, the tongue is pushed forward against the teeth themselves. This gives the Japanese sounds—called DENTAL consonants—a sharper quality; the English sounds—called ALVEOLAR consonants (after the alveolar ridge behind the teeth)—sound dull and indistinct to a Japanese. Notice the difference between sounds in certain Japanese and English words:

ENGLISH (alveolar!)	JAPANESE (dental!)	
toe	tǒ	'ten'
dough	dǒ	'how'
no	nǒ	'Nō [Japanese classical ballet]'

The Japanese consonants **s**, **z**, **sh**, **ch**, and **j** are also pronounced somewhat more FRONT than many American speakers pronounce the English equivalents. Since the American sounds are farthest front in words like 'see, zeal, sheep, cheap, jeep' it may help to think of the sounds in these words. Some Japanese give the **j** a sound rather like that used by the French in 'Jacques' or by some Americans in 'azure, garage, rouge'.*

Be careful how you pronounce the Japanese **f**. English f is made with the lower lip against the upper teeth. The Japanese place both lips close together (as if about to make a **p** or a **b**—or as if about to whistle) and then let the air come out in a puff between. A Japanese **f**, then, is an F WITHOUT ANY TEETH. Occasionally you will hear a Japanese use an ordinary h instead of this **f**.

Japanese voiced consonants (**b, d, z, j, g, m, n**) are more fully voiced than English initial voiced consonants. In English we start off somewhat lazily with the voicing, giving our vocal cords an instant to warm up. It is only between vowels—'rabbit, lady, dizzy, tiger, coming, inning'— that we voice these sounds all the way thru. Japanese warm their vocal cords up an instant before they start to make the sound and this gives their voiced consonants a bit more prominence than ours.

The Japanese consonant g has two pronunciations. In Southern Japan it is usually pronounced like g in English 'go' (but of course never like g in 'gem' because that sound would be written **j**). In Northern Japan, many people pronounce the **g** always like the English sound in 'sing' or 'singer'. In Tokyo, there's a compromise. The general rule is: initial in a word, pronounce as in 'go'; within a

---

*And at the beginning of a word many Japanese pronounce z as if it were spelled "dz"; in slow over-precise speech, you may hear the "dz" version even in the middle of a word.

word, pronounce as in 'singer'. There are a few exceptions to this rule—the particle **ga** is always pronounced with the ng sound, and the element **go** meaning 'five' is usually pronounced like English 'go' even within a word—but these are of minor importance.

You may have trouble with this ng sound. It is made with the tongue in the same position as for **g**, but with the nasal passage open—the way it is for **m** or **n**. Notice that this is NOT the same sound as that used by most English speakers in the word 'finger'—that is, by those speakers who do not rime this word exactly with 'singer'. It is as if we should spell the former word 'fingger' to show that we make first the back nasal sound (ng) and then the back non-nasal sound (g). Since you are not used to using this ng sound at the beginning of a stressed syllable in English, you may want to practice it in the following way. Hold the tip of your tongue down with your finger or one of those flat tongue-depressers doctors use. Then try to say the sound n as in 'nine'. You will feel the tip of your tongue try to come up, but keep it down and make the back part of the tongue do the work. You have then made the ng sound. All you have to do after that is train the tip of your tongue so you won't have to hold it down with a tongue-depresser while making this sound. The Japanese **g** in the middle of a word, then, is an N MADE WITH THE BACK OF THE TONGUE. If you find this sound too difficult, just use your English g in all positions. You won't quite be talking Standard Japanese, but then neither do lots of Japanese!

Here are some examples of the two kinds of **g**:

	g— [g]		—g— [ng]
gakkŏ	'school'	shōgákkō	'primary school'
gín	'silver	kíngin	'gold and silver'
ga	'moth'	ga*	'but; [subject particle]'
jŭ-go*	'fifteen'	júgo	'non-combatant (status)'
			'behind the guns'
sén-go*	'1005'	séngo	'postwar'
		*Exceptions!	

The word **gógo** 'p.m., afternoon' shows both kinds: [gó-ngo].

Another sound which may cause you trouble is **ts**. Unlike Japanese **t** [dental!], this sound usually starts at the alveolar ridge like an English **t**. It normally occurs only before the vowel **u**, and between the **t** and the **u** there is a slight hiss represented by the **s**. This sound does not occur initially in English, except for a few rare words like 'tsetse-fly'. However, you sometimes hear it in rapid speech: 'ts cool today' (for 'it is cool today'), 'ts all right with me' (for 'it is all right with me'). You may tend to slide over the **t** and only pronounce the **s**; this will cause confusion, because **tsu** and **su** distinguish a number of words. Practice on these words for the distinction:

súmi	'inside-corner, angle'	tsúmi	'guilt'
suru	'does'	tsuru	'fishes'
súmu	'resides'	tsúmu	'spindle'
kásu	'dregs'	kátsu	'wins'
suzuki	'sea-bass'	tsuzuki	'continuing; sequel'

Notice that the vowel **u** gets unvoiced or dropped when there is a following voiceless consonant:

sukí [s-kí] 'likable'	tsukí [ts-kí] 'moon'
susumu [s-su-mu] 'advances'	tsutsúmu [ts-tsú-mu] 'wraps up'
susuki [s-su-ki] 'pampas-grass'	tsutsúki [ts-tsú-ki] 'pecking, biting'

After you have practiced on the difference between **tsu** and **su** for awhile, you might try these tongue-twisters:

susumi-tsuzukemáshita 'continued to advance'
tsutsumi-tsuzukemáshita 'continued to wrap up'

The thing to remember about the syllable **tsu** is—DON'T OMIT THE T.

In addition to the simple consonants, the combinations **ky, gy, py, by, my, ny, hy** occur. (There is also **ry,** for which see below, 1. 8.) These are pronounced somewhat as are the corresponding English sounds in 'cute', 'gewgaw' or 'regular', 'rebuke', 'music', and 'Hugh' (provided you distinguish 'Hugh' from 'you'). In English, these combinations are usually followed by a vowel corresponding to Japanese **u**, but in Japanese they are also followed by **a** and **o**.* Here are some examples:

kyakusha	[kya-ku-sha]	'passenger car'
yūbínkyoku	[yu-u-bí-ng-kyo-ku]	'postoffice'
kyūkō	[kyu-u-ko-o]	'express (train)'
gyaku	[gya-ku]	'reverse'
jitsugyōka	[ji-tsu-gyo-o-ka]	'businessman'
gyūniku	[gyu-u-ni-ku]	'beef'
happyaku	[ha-p-pya-ku]	'eight hundred'
happyō	[ha-p-pyo-o]	'publication'
pyú to	[pyú-u-to]	'with a hiss (like a bullet)'

*Listen to the difference between **byðin** [byo-o-i-n] 'hospital' and **biyðin** [bi-yó-o-i-n] 'beauty shop'.

sámbyaku	[sá-m-bya-ku]	'three hundred'
byōki	[byo-o-ki]	'ill'
byůrō	[byú-u-ro-o]	'bureau'
sammyaku	[sa-m-mya-ku]	'mountain range'
myǒban	[myó-o-ba-N]	'tomorrow evening'
myůzu	[myú-u-zu]	'muse'
nyǎ	[nyá-a]	'miaw'
nyáo	[nyá-o]	'miaw'
nyǒhachi	[nyó-o-ha-chi]	'cymbals'
gyūnyū	[gyu-u-nyu-u]	'milk'
hyakushǒ	[hya-ku-shó-o]	'farmer'
hyōjun	[hyo-o-ju-N]	'standard'
hyůzu	[hyú-u-zu]	'fuse'

1. 8. FLAPPED R. The sound which seems to cause Americans most distress is the Japanese r. This is a sound called a FLAP. You make it by lifting the tip of the tongue backwards, then quickly and decisively bringing it down with a brief flick against the alveolar ridge (behind the teeth). Many Americans have this sound in the middle of words like 'Betty, letter, latter, cottage'; some Englishmen use this sound for the r in 'very, merry, berry' (so that the Englishman's 'berry' often sounds like the American 'Betty'). This r will sound a little bit like a d to you. The difference between the Japanese r and d are primarily two: length—the r is brief, the d somewhat longer; and position of contact—the r is against the alveolar ridge with the very tip of the tongue, the d is against the teeth with somewhat more of the tongue. You might begin to practice this sound in medial position, being care-

ful not to make it like an American r—nor to trill it
lengthily like an Italian r—and at the same time keep it
distinct from the Japanese d:

Japanese d (TEETH!)	Japanese r (RIDGE! BRIEF!)	American r
háda 'skin, body'	hára 'field'	harakiri, horror
todokéru 'delivers'	torokéru 'is enchanted'	Tory
sode 'sleeve'	sore 'that'	Cory
——	ari 'ant'	sorry
——	suru 'does'	true

Be sure you are putting the r at the beginning of the
syllable: sórosoro [só-ro-so-ro] 'leisurely'. Once you have
acquired the sound, try practicing it initially:

Japanese d (TEETH!)	Japanese r (RIDGE! BRIEF!)	American r
daku 'embraces'	rakú 'comfort, pleasure'	rock
denchū 'telephone-pole'	renchū 'gang'	wrench
dokú 'poison'	rokú 'six'	rogue
——	ringo 'apple'	ring
——	rúsu 'absence'	roots

Once you're able to make the initial r, you're ready
to tackle the combination ry. This sound is made by
putting the back part of the tongue in position to make
the y sound, then very swiftly moving just the tip of the
tongue up to make the flap for the r. You might practice
the words first without the r, making the y good and strong;
then go over them inserting the r lightly, without damag-
ing the y. Do not make the r and then add an extra
syllable just to get the y in. Examples:

ryáku	[ryá-ku]	'abbreviation'
Ryūkyŭ	[ryu-u-kyú-u]	'Ryukyu (Islands)'

ryŏshin	[ryó-o-shi-N]	'parents'
shōryaku	[sho-o-rya-ku]	'abbreviation, omission'
jōryū	[jo-o-ryu-u]	'upper reaches (of a river)'
daitŏryō	[da-i-tó-o-ryo-o]	'President'

1. 9. SYLLABIC NASAL. There is one more sound which may cause you some trouble. This is the syllabic nasal. The Japanese write this sound with the same symbol, but it is pronounced in different ways, depending on the sounds around it. The Hepburn Romanization writes the syllabic nasal sometimes **m**, sometimes **n** and sometimes **n'** or **n-** (n followed by an apostrophe or a hyphen). The sound is written **m** if it is followed by **p, b,** or **m**—any lip sound other than **f** or **w**; it is written **n'** or **n-** if it is followed by a vowel (**a, e, i, o, u,**) or by **y**; and it is written just **n** before other consonants (including **f** and **w**) and at the end of a word.*

The pronunciation of the syllabic nasal varies according to its surroundings, but it is always pronounced with the nasal passage open and it ALWAYS TAKES A FULL SYLLABLE'S TIME. There are four main pronunciations:

1. Before **p, b, m**—a long (syllabic) **m**.
2. Before **t, ts, d, n, ch, j**—a long (syllabic) **n** [dental!]
3. Before **k, g**—a long (syllabic) **ng**.
4. Elsewhere (before vowel, **y, w, r. s, sh, z, h, f,** or at the end of a word)—long nasalization.

You will have little difficulty with the first two pronunciations. Just remember to hold the nasal for a full

---

*But often (as in Kenkyusha's Japanese-English Dictionary) **n** is written for **m: shinbun** instead of **shimbun.**

syllable's time.   Here are some examples:

1. **kembutsu**   [ke-m-bu-tsu]   'sightseeing'
   kimpatsu   [ki-m-pa-tsu]   'blond [hair]'
   sámmai   [sá-m-ma-i]   'three sheets [of paper]'
2. **chanto**   [cha-n-to]   'just, precisely'
   shintsū   [shi-n-tsu-u]   'anguish, heartache'
   kóndo   [kó-n-do]   'this time; next time'
   konnichi wa   [ko-n-ni-chi-wa]   'hello, good afternoon'
   kenchiku   [ke-n-chi-ku]   'construction, building'
   sánji   [sá-n-ji]   'three o'clock'

   The third pronunciation may cause you some difficulty. The combination **nk** is pronounced about as in banker, but the ng sound of the **n** is held for a full syllable. The combination written in the Hepburn Romanization as **ng** is pronounced with that ngg sound of fingger in some parts of Japan, but in the Standard Language it is pronounced like two ng sounds in a row: ngng, with the first held for a full syllable, and the second beginning the following syllable. Get out your tongue-depresser again, and keep the tongue tip down a little longer. Cf. **nangai** 'how many floors' and **nagái** 'is long'.

3. **génki**   [gé-ng-ki]   'good health'
   sánkaku   [sá-ng-ka-ku]   'triangle'
   inki   [i-ng-ki]   'ink'
   kongetsu   [ko-ng-nge-tsu]   'this month'

kíngyo	[kí-ng-ngyo]	'goldfish'
búngaku	[bú-ng-nga-ku]	'literature'
ringo	[ri-ng-ngo]	'apple'

The fourth pronunciation you will probably find the most difficult. The basic part of this sound is just nasalization—such as the French put on some of their vowels in words like *garçon, Lyons, on sait.* Some Americans use simple nasalization in place of the nt in words like 'plenty, twenty' [ple'y, twe'y]. If you like, you may think of this as an N WITH THE TONGUE NOT QUITE TOUCHING THE TOP OF THE MOUTH ANYWHERE. This sound is heard most distinctly at the end of a word:

4. pán	[pá-N]	'bread'
shimbun	[shi-m-bu-N]	'newspaper'
Nihón	[ni-hó-N]	'Japan'
kín	[kí-N]	'gold'
pén	[pé-N]	'pen'

It is also heard before s, sh, z, h, f, r:

4. kénsa	[ké-N-sa]	'investigation'
shinshiki	[shi-N-shi-ki]	'new style'
banzái	[ba-N-zá-i]	'hurrah!'
jikanhyō	[ji-ka-N-hyo-o]	'timetable'
mannénhitsu	[ma-n-né-N-hi-tsu]	'fountain-pen'
Nihonfū	[ni-ho-N-fu-u]	'Japanese style'
sánri	[sá-N-ri]	'three Japanese miles'
shinryaku	[shi-N-rya-ku]	'invasion'
goenryo	[go-e-N-ryo]	'reticence'

Before vowels, **y**, and **w**, the syllabic nasal takes on some of the color of the following sound. For example, in **hón-ya** [hó-N-ya] 'bookshop', the N sounds like a nasalized y, anticipating the following, non-nasal y. In **hón wa** [hó-N-wa] 'as for the book', the N sounds like a nasalized w, anticipating the following, non-nasal w. Before **i** or **e**, the syllabic nasal may also sound like a nasalized y: **Nihón e** [ni-hó-N-e] 'to Japan', **ten-in** [te-N-i-N] 'clerk'. Here are some more examples:

4.	**pán-ya**	[pá-N-ya]	'bakery, bakeshop'
	kon-yaku	[ko-N-ya-ku]	'engagement (to be married)'
	shinwa	[shi-N-wa]	'myth'
	denwa	[de-N-wa]	'telephone'
	kin-en	[ki-N-e-N]	'No Smoking'
	sen-en	[se-N-e-N]	'1000 Yen'
	kin-iro	[ki-N-i-ro]	'gold color'
	tán-i	[tá-N-i]	'unit'
	nan-ō	[na-N-o-o]	'Southern Europe'

Listen carefully for the difference between **mán-ichi** [má-N-i-chi] 'if' and **máinichi** [má-i-ni-chi] 'every day.'

1. 10. ACCENT. You have probably wondered about the little jiggers above certain vowels (**anáta, shitsúrei, kashikomarimáshita**). These are accent marks. In English, accent refers to the way in which the four levels of stress occur. In Japanese, the accent is the way in which PITCH LEVELS occur. When the vibrating vocal cords are drawn out long and tight, the pitch is high; when they are relaxed and shortened, the pitch is low. In English we use different pitch levels to indicate certain general types of phrases—like question [?], statement [.], suspension [...], continuation [,], and so forth. This use of pitch is called INTONATION. Japanese has intonation, too, but it is usually restricted to the last voiced syllable of a phrase. In this book, intonation is noted by question mark, period, comma, triple dots, and exclamation point—representing pitch changes not unlike those which would occur in English before such marks. Note that in English the intonation contour extends over much more of the phrase, but the Japanese intonation occurs only with the last syllable or two.

In addition to intonation, Japanese uses pitch to differentiate words and phrases from each other—much as we use stress in English. It is this use of pitch that we call accent.

In different parts of Japan there are different accent patterns. Over half the population of Japan speak with accent patterns rather like those of Standard Japanese— that is, the speech of Tokyo. The principal exception is Western Japan (Kyoto, Osaka, Kobe; also parts of Shikoku and southern Kyushu). There, the accent often seems just the opposite from that of Standard Japanese. Where the Tokyo speaker goes up in pitch, the Kyoto speaker often goes down. In some parts of Japan (places in northern Kyushu and in northeastern Honshu), the accent is not distinctive at all; all words have the same pattern.

If you are planning to talk Japanese in Western Japan, you can completely ignore the accent marks in this book. And even if you are going to talk Japanese in Tokyo, you will be fairly well understood, even without the accent distinctions. The Japanese of today are used to hearing their language spoken with a variety of accent patterns. The important thing is that you should always imitate the persons you hear speaking Japanese and mimic their accents, wherever you may be. However, if you wish to put the final polish on your knowledge of Standard Japanese, you may want to devote some attention to the accent. For this reason, the standard accent is marked in this book, and an Appendix provides a discussion of accent patterns in words and phrases. [A phrase is several words said together as if one word.]

What the accent mark represents in Standard Japanese is THE LAST SYLLABLE BEFORE A FALL IN PITCH. In sayōnára 'goodbye', there is a fall of pitch right after the syllable ná; in arígatō 'thanks', right after the syllable rí. In Tokyo speech EVERY SYLLABLE UP TO THE FALL OF PITCH IS HIGH EXCEPT THE FIRST OF THE PHRASE. The relative pitches in sayonára look like this:

Of course, if the first syllable is itself the last before the fall, it is high:

You will be able to hear this fall of pitch most clearly when it occurs on the first of a vowel sequence—like the long vowels ā, ē, ii, ō, ū, or the sequences ai, ei, oi, ui,— or when it occurs on a vowel followed by the syllabic nasal. This is because we tend to hear each of these double-syllables as just one syllable and we are used to hearing a fall of pitch WITHIN a syllable in English: He saw Jóhn. Look at the bóy. Sáy. Híl Mé. Nó. Yóu. Listen to these examples:

Dó itashimashite. dó-o-i-ta-shi-ma-sh-te	'Not at all.'
Kono chihó ni arimasu. ko-no-chi-hó-o-ni-a-ri-ma-s	'It's in this region.'
Nihón ni imasu. ni-hó-n-ni-i-ma-s	'He's in Japan.'
Íi tenki desu. i-i-te-n-ki-de-s	'It's nice weather.'
Warúi sō desu. wa-rú-i-so-o-de-s	'They say it's bad.'
Só desu ka. só-o-de-s-ka	'Oh, I see.'
Kyó desu. kyó-o-de-s	'It's today.'
Wakarimasén deshita. wa-ka-ri-ma-sé-n-de-sh-ta	'I didn't understand'
Aói kimono o kite imasu. a-ó-i-ki-mo-no-o-ki-te-i-ma-s	'She's wearing a blue kimono

The range of pitch is somewhat wider in English than in Japanese. When we have a fall, it descends from high er to lower pitches than the corresponding Japanese fall. To our ears, the Japanese rises and falls in pitch are very light and often difficult to catch. They are nonetheless an important part of Japanese speech.

In Standard Japanese there is just one accent—one fall of pitch—within a phrase. But a given sentence may either be broken up into a number of small phrases or read all in one big phrase. It's possible to say the sentence meaning 'Not at all; you're welcome' slowly and deliberately as two phrases: dó itashimáshite. It is more usual to say it as just one phrase: dó itashimashite. When two or more smaller phrases are said together as a larger phrase, the accent of the first phrase stays, but the accent of the later phrases disappears. In the lesson material of this book, the accent is usually marked as if each sentence were slowly and deliberately broken up with a maximum of phrases; but you will notice these phrases are often combined into larger units, with all accents except the first in the larger phrase disappearing. Instead of shitsúrei itashimáshita you will more often hear shitsúrei itashimashita 'excuse me', instead of arígatō gozaimásu you will hear arígatō gozaimasu 'thank you'.

Since the accent mark represents the last syllable before a FALL in pitch, it never occurs right before a pause. What happens is that a word with a final accent (such as otōtó in otōtó wa 'as for my younger brother') replaces that accent with an intonation before pause—otōto, ór otōto? or ▶tōto. or otōto! Before a pause, you can't tell whether a word has a final accent or no accent at all; when you add a particle (such as the topic particle wa) it immediately becomes clear:

Hana.	'Nose.'	**Hana wa...**	'As for the nose...'
Hana.	'Flower.'	**Haná wa...**	'As for the flower...'

When we cite final-accent words in isolation we put the mark on anyway, in order to show how the word behaves within a phrase: hana 'nose', haná 'flower'.

The term 'final accent' refers not only to an accent on the very last syllable, but also often to one on the next-to-last syllable, provided the last syllable is the second of a vowel sequence—like kinŏ [ki-nó-o] 'yesterday', chihŏ [chi-hó-o] 'region', senséi [se-n-sé-i] or [se-n-sé-e] 'teacher' kudasái [ku-da-sá-i] 'please (give)', or is the syllable nasal—like Nihón [ni-hó-n] 'Japan', hón [ho-n] 'book', issén [i-s-sé-n] 'one Sen'. In these cases, the intonation often extends over the last two syllables.

When a vowel becomes unvoiced or dropped (like u in arimásu 'something exists', désu 'something equals something', itashimásu 'I do'), the intonation usually covers the preceding syllable and the accent really disappears: arimasu [a-ri-ma-s]. The accent appears again, however, if the word is followed by another word: Arimásu ka? 'Are there any?' Arimásu ga... 'There are, but...' In this book, the accent is usually written on such words even at the end of a sentence.

Here are some examples of the accent on various syllables. Listen for the pitch falls. Remember the single phrases may be joined together into longer phrases and the later accents dropped.

Íi desu ka?	Is it all right?
Damé desu.	It's no good, it won't do.
Kékkō desu.	No, thank you.
Wasuremáshita.	I've forgotten (it).
Wakarimáshita ka?	Did you understand?
Sukí desu ka, kirai désu ka?	Do you like it or not?

Chótto kité kudasai.	
(Chótto kíte kudasai.)	Please come here a minute.
Chótto kite kudasai.	
Íkura desu ka?	'How much is it?'
Sore mo số desu ne.	'That's true, too.'
Mádo o akete kudasái.	'Please open the window.'
To o shímete kudasai.	'Please close the door.'
To o akete kudasái.	'Please open the door.'

Here are the names of some places in and around Japan. Notice the accents. The particle **wa** is added in parentheses after a final accent.

Kyúshū, Shikóku, Hónshū, Hokkáidō; Ryūkyǔ (wa), Okinawa; Shína or Chūgoku [China], Mánshū [Manchuria], Chōsén (wa) [Korea], Róshiya [Russia]; Tōkyō, Ōsaka, Kốbe, Kyốto, Nágoya, Yokohama, Kamakurá (wa), Séndai, Kanázawa, Niigata, Chíba, Shizúoka, Wakáyama, Okáyama, Hiroshima, Shimonóseki, Móji, Fukúoka, Nagásaki, Kagoshima, Kumamoto, Matsuyama, Tokushíma, Sapporo, Hakodate.

Turn to page 456 for additional practice on the accent of place names in Tokyo.

C. EXERCISES. Check on your learning of the Basic Sentences. For each of the following situations, pick the Japanese sentence which best fits.

    1. You step on someone's foot getting to your seat in a movie.

(a) **Shitsúrei itashimáshita.** (c) **Ja, shitsúrei itashimásu.**

(b) **Osóre irimashita.**   (d) **Kashikomarimáshita.**

2. You approach a stranger to ask the way to your hotel.

(a) Onegai itashimásu. (c) Goenryo náku.

(b) Chótto shitsúrei desu (d) Omachidō-sama déshita.
ga...

3. You don't quite understand what someone has just said.

(a) Yóku irasshaimáshita. (c) Gokúrō-sama deshita.

(b) Mō ichido itte kuda- (d) Iie.
sái.

4. The person is talking too fast for you to follow.

(a) Hái. (c) Dózo, yukkúri hanáshite kudasai.

(b) Ojama itashimáshita. (d) Mata dózo.

5. You want time to frame your reply to a question.

(a) Sayōnára. (c) Iroiro oséwa ni narimáshita.

(b) Chótto mátte kudasai. (d) Onegai itashimásu.

6. You come to your teacher's room with a problem.

(a) Arígatō gozaimáshita. (c) Oyasumi nasái.

(b) Ja, máta. (d) Ojama désu ka?

7. The teacher tells you to come into the room.

(a) Dózo osaki e. (c) Chótto mátte kudasai.

(b) Oagari kudasái. (d) Ohairi kudasái.

8. The teacher helps you with your problem. You say:

(a) Dó mo arígatō gozai- (c) Onegai itashimásu.
máshita.

(b) Móshi moshi. (d) Kashikomarimáshita.

Or, you may say:

(e) **Ohanashichū shitsúrei**   (g) **Yóku irasshaimáshita.**
    desu ga...

(f) **Osóre irimashita.**   (h) **Oyasumi nasái.**

9. On leaving the teacher's room, you might say:

(a) **Komban wa.**   (c) **Ojama itashimáshita.**
(b) **Màta dòzo.**   (d) **Mō ichido.**

10. The phone rings. You pick it up and say:

(a) **Konnichi wa.**   (c) **Móshi moshi.**
(b) **Hái.**   (d) **Ikága desu ka?**

11. Somebody ahead of you on the street has dropped a
    letter. You call to him.

(a) **Móshi moshi.**   (c) **É.**
(b) **Mata dòzo.**   (d) **Dòzo osaki ni.**

12. You are at a meeting, and have to leave early. You
    excuse yourself.

(a) **Ja, mata.**   (c) **Onegai shimásu.**
(b) **Gomen nasái. Ojama**   (d) **Osaki ni shitsúrei shi-**
    désu ka?   **másu.**

D. PRONUNCIATION CHECK POINTS.

1. LONG AND SHORT VOWELS, LONG AND SHORT CONSONANTS.

shóko	[shó-ko]	library
shōko	[sho-o-ko]	proof
shókō	[shó-o-ko-o]	commissioned officer

shókku	[shó-k-ku]	shock
koko	[ko-ko]	here
kókko	[kó-k-ko]	National Treasury
kokkō	[ko-k-ko-o]	diplomatic relations
kokō	[ko-ko-o]	the tiger's mouth; dangerous situation
kŏko	[kó-o-ko]	the study of antiquities
kŏkō	[kó-o-ko-o]	filial piety
yokka	[yo-k-ka]	four days
yōka	[yo-o-ka]	eight days

2. DOUBLE CONSONANTS [long! tense! no puff!]

kippu	ticket	issho	together
seppuku	harakiri	zasshi	magazine
chótto	just, a little	itchi	agreement
kissa	tea-shop	yukkúri	slowly
massúgu	straight ahead	gakkō	school

3. DOUBLE VOWELS [two syllables!]

depáto	department store	ōkíi	is big
má!	well! [surprise]	kōhíi	coffee
tēburu	table	Tōkyō	Tokyo
nésan	older sister	Ōsaka	Osaka
níisan	older brother	gyūnyū	milk
yoroshii	excellent	Ryūkyú	Ryukyu [Islands]

4. SHORT VOWELS [shorter than English! no off-glides!]

tá	field	mimi	ear
mata	again	ó	tail
é	picture	koko	here
té	hand	bú	part
kí	tree	kuruma	wagon

5. VOICELESS VOWELS [whisper the syllable!]

k(u)suri	medicine	k(o)kóro	heart, soul
k(i)ppu	ticket	k(i)té	coming
k(i)shá	train	k(i)tte	stamp

6. DROPPED VOWELS [keep tongue in position for the vowel, but make the consonant a full syllable!]

arimás(u)	there exists	ch(i)kái	is near
arimásh(i)ta	there existed	ts(u)kau	uses
s(u)kí des(u)	likes	h(i)tótsu	one
s(u)toráiki	strike	f(u)tatsú	two
ts(u)tsumi	package	ch(i)chí	father
h(i)kóki	airplane	sh(i)chí	seven
f(u)tsū	usually	h(i)to*	person
sh(i)ká	deer	sh(i)ta	bottomside, under

7. NO STRESS [even syllables! no mid central uh-vowel!]

Ikága desu ka?	How are you?
Aikawarazu.	Same as always.
Arígatō gozaimáshita.	Thank you.
Ano takái yamá wa nán to iimásu ka?	What is that tall mountain called?
Atatákakatta desu.	It was warm.

8. AU AND AO, AI AND AE.

áu	meets	mai, mái	dance
áo	blue	máe	front
taué	rice-planting	háiru	enters
taóru	breaks off, plucks	káeru	returns

*Before i and y Japanese h often sounds like the German ich-sound (a voiceless y with friction); in downtown Tokyo sh is often substituted, so that h(i)to sounds like shto.

9. DENTAL CONSONANTS [tongue against teeth!]

tatami	mat	déte	going out
té	hand	depáto	department store
Tōkyō	Tokyo	Nán desu ka?	What is it?
tadáima	just now	kóndo	this time, next time

10. F [no teeth!]

Fúji-san	Mt. Fuji	fukuró	bag
kangófu	nurse	futsū	usually

11. G [Nasal within a word!]

gógo	afternoon	géngo	language
gakusei	student	kagi	key
agó	chin	Chūgoku	China
kágu	furniture	Chūgoku-go	Chinese

12. TS [don't forget the t!]

tsugí	next	tsukau	uses
tsukúru	makes	tsuyu	dew
atsúi	is hot	tsutsumi	package

13. R [brief flap against the alveolar ridge!]

rainen	next year	rikúgun	army
rúsu	absence	Rengókuku	United Nations
ryokō	trip, travel	Róshiya	Russia
Ryūkyū	Ryukyu Islands	koréra	these
shōryaku	abbreviation		

14. SYLLABIC NASAL [sound varies with surroundings!]

shimbun	newspaper	Nihón e iku	goes to Japan
sensō	war	hón o yómu	reads a book
mannénhitsu	fountain-pen	wakarimasén ka?	don't you understand?
kin-yóbi	Friday	kóndo	this time, next time
pán wa	as for bread	hón-ya	bookshop

15. **ACCENT** [listen for the fall of pitch! don't expect the marked syllable to be any louder than the others!]

Atsui monó desu ka?	Is it a thick thing?
Atsúi monó desu ka?	Is it a hot thing?
Hana désu ka, haná de-su ka?	Is it a nose or a flower?
Zasshi o yónde imasu.	He's reading a magazine.
Kodomo o yonde imásu.	He's calling the child.
Ushi o kau hitó desu.	It's the man who buys cows.
Ushi o káu hito desu.	It's the man who raises cows.
Kaki ga sukí desu ka?	Do you like persimmons?
Káki ga sukí desu ka?	Do you like oysters?
Kórera wa damé desu.	Cholera is no good.
Koréra wa damé desu.	These are no good.

15. **UMA, UME, UMO** [often pronounced **mma, mme, mmo!**]

Umá desu ka?	Is it a horse?
Dóko de umaremáshita ka?	Where were you born?
Ume ga sukí desu ka?	Do you like plums?
Kore wa umoregi to ii-másu.	This is called fossil-wood.

16. **EI** [often pronounced **e-e** like **ē!**]

téinei	polite	kírei	pretty, neat
Beikoku	U.S.	Eikoku	England
Eigo	English	keiei	management

17. A tongue-twister: **Tōkyō tokkyo kyoká-kyoku** 'Tokyo Patent Office'.

LESSON 2.

A. BASIC SENTENCES.   'What and Where?'

1. Kore wa, nán desu   What is this?
    ka?
2. Sore wa, hón desu.   That's a book.
3. Anáta no hón desu   Is it your book?
    ka?
4. Hái, só desu.   Yes, it is.
5. Watakushi no hón   Which is my book?
    wa, dóre desu ka?
6. Are désu.   It's that one (over there).
7. Á, só desu ka?   Oh? [Is that so?]
8. Kono zasshi wa, dáre Whose is this magazine?
    no desu ka?
9. Anáta no desu ka,   Is it yours, or is it his?
    anó hito no desu
    ka?
10. Watakushi nó desu.   It's mine.
11. Ano tatémono wa,   Is that building a bank?
    ginkō désu ka?
12. Iie, gakkō désu.   No, it's a school.
13. Ginkō wa, dóko desu   Where is the bank?
    ka?
14. Asoko désu.   It's over there.
15. Dóno tatémono ga,   Which building is the movie
    eigákan desu ka?   theater?
16. Sono tatémono ga,   That building is the movie

	cigákan desu.	theater.
17.	Anáta wa, éiga ga, sukí desu ka?	Do you like movies?
18.	Amerika no éiga wa, dő desu ka?	How about American movies?
19.	Dáisuki desu.	They're swell. [I like them a lot.]
20.	Anáta wa, Nihon no éiga wa, kirai désu ka?	Do you dislike Japanese movies?
21.	Empitsu wa, dóko ni arimásu ka?	Where is the pencil?
22.	Tsukue no ue ni ari-másu.	It's on top of the desk.
23.	Tsukue wa, dóko ni arimásu ka?	Where's the desk?
24.	Heya no náka ni ari-másu.	It's in the room.
25.	Anáta wa, dóko ni imásu ka?	Where are you?
26.	Koko ni imásu.	I'm here.
27.	Heya no náka ni imásu ka?	Are you in the room?
28.	Iie, sóto ni imásu.	No, I'm outside.
29.	Tatémono no sóto ni imásu.	I'm outside the building.
30.	Niwa no náka ni imásu.	I'm in the garden.
31.	Anáta wa senséi desu ka, gakusei désu ka?	Are you a teacher or a student?

VOCABULARY ITEMS.

mannénhitsu	fountain-pen	shōnin	merchant
shimbun	newspaper	heitai	soldier
tēburu	table	súihei	naval man
mádo	window	sen-in	merchant sailor
to; dóa	door	senkyōshi	missionary
isu	chair	jitsugyōka	businessman
uchi (p. 428)	house, home	hito (p, 428)	person, people
ié	house	tomodachi	friend
éki; teishaba	railroad station	jimúsho	office
Beikoku;	America	hóteru	hotel
Amerika		yadoya	Japanese inn
Beikokújin;	an American	yūbínkyoku	post office
Amerikájin		daigákusei	college student
Nihón, Nippón	Japan	daigaku	college, university
Nihonjín	a Japanese	daigakúin	graduate school
gaikoku	foreign (lands)	daigakuínsei	graduate student
gai(kokú)jin	foreigner		

B. STRUCTURE NOTES.

2. 1. NOUNS. Words like **zasshi** 'magazine', **tēburu** 'table', **Nihonjín** 'a Japanese', **uchi** 'house', **kore** 'this one', **watakushi** 'I, me', **anáta** 'you', **náka** 'inside', **sóto** 'outside', **koko** 'here, this place' form a class called NOUNS. Nouns often precede a particle like **wa, ga, no, ni,** or occur before the word **désu** 'is [equals]'.

2. 2. PRENOUNS. The words **kono** 'this', **sono** 'that', **ano** 'that over there', **dóno** 'which' are part of a small class called PRENOUNS. These words precede a noun and modify its meaning, much as a noun is modified by a phrase consisting of a noun followed by the particle **no**: **kono gakkō** 'this school', **watakushi no gakkō** 'my school'.

2. 3. PLACE WORDS. Among the nouns there are some which may be called PLACE WORDS: **koko** 'this place,

here', **soko** 'that place, there', **asoko** 'over there', **náka** 'inside', **sóto** 'outside', **ue** (p. 428) 'topside, on top'. They are often used for situations we would express in English with prepositions like in, on, under, behind, above, between. Some more of these place words:

ushiro	'behind'	**máe**	'in front'
hidari	'left'	**migi**	'right'
shita (p. 428)	'below'	**sóba**	'beside, near'
chikáku	'near(by)'	**tonari**	'next door'

Here are some examples of the use of these words:

Éki wa ginkō no ushiro désu.	The station is behind the bank.
Watakushi no uchi wa asoko désu.	My house is over there.
Eigákan wa gakkō no sóba ni arimásu ka?	Is the movie theater beside the school?
Anáta no hón wa, ano shimbun no hidari ni arimásu.	Your books are on the left of those newspapers.
Tēburu wa, mádo no máe ni arimásu.	The table is in front of the window.
Isu wa tsukue no migi ni arimásu ka?	Is the chair to the right of the desk?
Shimbun wa isu no shitá ni arimásu.	The newspaper is underneath the chair.

2. 4. COPULAR NOUNS. The word **sukí** 'likable' is a special kind of noun called a COPULAR NOUN because it usually appears before some form of the copula

désu 'is [equals]'. Here are a few other copular nouns: **dáisuki** 'greatly liked', **kirai** 'dislikable, disliked', **dáikirai** 'hated, detested', **kírei** 'neat, pretty, clean'. Notice that the literal translation of **sukí desu** and **kirai désu** is '[something] is liked' and '[something] is disliked', but we freely translate them '[somebody] likes [something]' and '[somebody] dislikes [something]'.

2. 5. UNTRANSLATED ENGLISH WORDS. In English we seldom say just 'book'; we say 'a book, the book, some books, the books'. In Japanese, the situation is just the other way around. Since the Japanese have another way of implying that they've been talking about the noun, by making it the topic with the particle **wa**—**hón wa** 'the book, the books', they don't need a word to translate 'the'. And they usually leave it up to the situation to make it clear whether there are several things in question or just one, unless they want to focus your attention on the number itself, in which case the number word indicates just how many you are talking about. The Japanese, like everyone else, do not always bother to express things they think you already know. This doesn't mean they lack ways to say things we do, it just means they leave implied some of the things we are used to saying explicitly. Americans tend to use **watakushi** and **anáta** too much; omit pronouns when the reference is clear. **Watakushi** is often shortened to **watashi** (women also say **atashi**), and you may hear **ánta** for **anáta**. Men often say **boku** for 'I, me'; a rougher term is **ore** (much affected by students). **Kimi** is an intimate term for 'you'; a condescending form

is **omae** (sometimes used to small children), and an insolent term is **kisama**. But names and/or titles are often preferred for reference to 'you' and 'him'.

2. 6. PARTICLES. In English, we usually show the relations between words in the way we string them together. The sentences 'John loves Mary' and 'Mary loves John' both contain the same three words, but the order in which we put the words determines the meaning. In Japanese, relations between words are often shown by little words called PARTICLES. In this lesson you are introduced to several of these particles: wa, ga, ka, no, ni.

2. 7. PARTICLE **WA**. The particle wa sets off the TOPIC you are going to talk about. If you say **Watakushi wa jitsugyōka désu** 'I am a businessman', the particle shows you are talking about **watakushi** 'I'—what you have to say about the topic then follows. A pidgin-English way of translating this particle **wa** is 'as for': **Shimbun wa koko ni arimásu** 'As for the newspaper, it's here.' But it is better not to look for a direct translation for some of these particles—remember they just indicate the relationship between the preceding words and those that follow.

2. 8. PARTICLE **GA**. The particle ga shows the SUBJECT. In **Éiga ga sukí desu** 'I like movies' the particle **ga** shows that **éiga** 'movies' is the subject of **sukí desu** 'are liked.'

The difference between the particles wa and **ga** is one of emphasis. In English we make a difference in emphasis by using a louder voice somewhere in the sentence. We say 'I like MOVIES' or 'I LIKE movies', depending on which part of the sentence we want to bring out. In Japanese, the particle **ga** focuses our attention on the words preceding it, but the particle **wa** releases our attention to focus on some other part of the sentence. So, **éiga ga sukí desu** means 'I like MOVIES', but **éiga wa sukí desu** means 'I LIKE movies'. When there is a question word in the sentence (like **dáre** 'who', **dóre** 'which one', **dóno** 'which', **dóko** 'where'), the attention usually focuses on this part of the sentence, so the particle **wa** is not used: **Dóno tatémono ga éki desu ka?** 'Which building is the railroad station?' Since our attention is focused on 'WHICH building', the answer is **Ano tatémono ga éki desu** 'THAT building is the railroad station'. If the question is **Ano tatémono wa nán desu ka?** 'What is that building?', our attention which is released from **ano tatémono** 'that building' by the particle **wa** concentrates on 'WHAT', so the answer is **Ano tatémono wa éki desu** 'That building is a RAILROAD STATION,' or just **Éki desu** 'It's a railroad station.' Some sentences have both a topic—or several successive topics—and a subject:

Anáta wa, Nihon no éiga ga sukí desu ka?	'Do you like Japanese movies?'
Anáta wa, Nihon no éiga wa sukí desu ka?	'Do you LIKE Japanese movies?'

Because the difference in meaning between **wa** and **ga** is largely one of emphasis, you can often take a sentence and change the emphasis just by substituting **wa** for **ga**. The particle **wa** can be thought of us an ATTENTION-SHIFTER: the words preceding it set the stage for the sentence, and serve as scenery and background for what we're going to say. This can lead to ambiguity. The sentence **Tárō wa Hánako ga sukí desu** [literally 'Taro as topic, Hanako as emphatic subject, someone is liked'] can mean either 'Taro likes Hanako' [It's HANAKO that Taro likes'] or 'Hanako likes Taro [It's HANAKO that likes Taro]. The situation usually makes it clear which meaning is called for. If you have both **wa** and **ga** in a sentence, the phrase with **wa** usually comes first: the stage is set before the comment is made.

Sometimes two topics are put in contrast with each other: **Kore wa eigákan desu ga, sore wa ginkō désu** 'This is a movie-theater but that is a bank.' [The particle **ga** meaning 'but' is not the same particle as the one indicating the subject.] In this case, the emphasis is on the WAY in which the two topics contrast—in being a theater on the one hand, and a bank on the other.

2. 9. PARTICLE KA. The particle **ka** is placed at the end of a sentence to show that it is a QUESTION. It is as if we were pronouncing the question mark: **Ano ié desu** 'It's that house.' **Ano ié desu ka?** 'Is it that house?' A common way of asking a question in Japanese is to give two or more alternatives, one of which the answerer selects. **Anó hito wa heitai désu ka, súihei desu ka?** 'Is he a soldier or a sailor?' [Literally, 'Is he a soldier, is he a sailor?'] Alternative questions are further discussed in Note 7. 8.

2. 10. PARTICLE NO. The particle **no** shows that the preceding noun MODIFIES or LIMITS the noun following. **Watakushi no hón** 'my book', **heya no náka** 'the inside of the room', **ie no sóto** 'the place outside the house', **koko no gakkō** 'the schools of this place, the schools here', **Tōkyō no ginkō** 'banks in Tokyo', **Amerika no shimbun**

'American newspapers', Nihon no jitsugyōka 'businessmen
of Japan', watakushi no tomodachi 'my friend'. The expression noun + no is sometimes followed directly by the
copula désu 'is [equals]': Anáta no desu ka, watakushi
nó desu ka? 'Is it yours or is it mine?' The particle no
is often equivalent to the English translation 'of', but sometimes it is equivalent to 'in' or other words.

2. 11. PARTICLE NI.   The particle ni indicates a GEN-
ERAL SORT OF LOCATION in space or time, which
can be made more specific by putting a place or time word
in front of it. The phrase heyá ni means 'at the room,
in the room'; to say explicitly 'in[side] the room' you insert the specific place word náka 'inside': heya no náka ni.
Notice the difference between gakkō ni imásu 'he's at
school, he's in school' and gakkō no náka ni imásu 'he's
in[side] the school[house]'.

A phrase noun + ni is not used to modify another
noun, and it does not occur before désu 'is [equals]'; it
is usually followed by arimásu '[a thing] is [exists]' or
imásu '[a person] is [exists in a place]'. To say 'the people
in the room' you connect heya no náka 'the inside of the
room' with hito 'the people' by means of the particle no:
heya no náka no hito.

The particle ni is also used figuratively: Tomodachi
ni iimáshita 'He said TO his friend'. And it sometimes
shows PURPOSE: Sampo ni ikimáshita 'He went FOR
(or ON) a walk.' It is also used to indicate a CHANGE
OF STATE—Senséi ni narimáshita 'He became a teacher,
he turned into a teacher', Eigákan ni shimáshita 'They
made it into a theater'— and, after a copula noun, to

show MANNER—Kírei ni kakimáshita 'He wrote neatly.' Occasionally a particle like ni will be used in an expression which calls for an unexpected equivalent in the English translation: Dáre ni Nihongo o naraimáshita ka? 'Who did you learn Japanese FROM? (Who did you learn Japanese WITH?)' [The particle o is discussed in Note 3. 6. Do not memorize the verbs in the above examples; they will be taken up later.]

2. 12. WORDS MEANING 'IS'. In this lesson we find three different Japanese words translated 'is' in English: désu, arimásu, and imásu. The word désu is the COPULA and it means 'equals'. Whenever an English sentence containing the word 'is' makes sense if you substitute 'equals' for 'is', the Japanese equivalent is désu. 'He is my friend' [He = my friend] Anó hito wa watakushi no tomodachi désu. 'This is an office' [This = an office] Kore wa jimúsho desu. 'That's mine' [That = mine] Sore wa watakushi nó desu. Preceding the word désu, there is always a noun or a phrase consisting of noun + no or some other particle, but never wa, ga, o [discussed in 3. 6.], de [discussed in 3. 5], or ni.

When an English sentence containing the word 'is' makes sense if you re-word it '[something] exists', the Japanese equivalent is arimásu: Mannénhitsu ga arimásu ka? 'Do you have a fountain-pen? Is there a fountain-pen? [Does a pen exist?]' When the English sentence can be re-worded '[something] exists in a place' or '[something] is located', the usual Japanese equivalent is also arimásu: Mádo wa soko ni arimásu 'The window is there.' But often, especially if the topic is itself a place—a city, a building, a

street, a location—either **désu** or **(ni) arimásu** may be used:
Eigákan wa asoko désu ka? or **Eigákan wa asoko ni arimá-su ka?** 'Is the movie theater over there?' **Kanázawa wa dóko desu ka?** or **Kanázawa wa dóko ni arimásu ka?** 'Where is Kanazawa?'

When an English sentence containing the word 'is' makes sense re-worded as '[somebody] exists [in a place]' or '[somebody] stays [in a place]' or '[somebody] is located', the Japanese equivalent is **imásu** 'stays': **Anó hito wa dóko ni imásu ka?** 'Where is he?' **Sóto ni imásu** 'He's outside.'

There are other uses of these two verbs **arimásu** and **imásu** which we will examine later. It may help to think of tag meanings for these words as follows: **désu** 'equals', **arimásu** 'exists', **imásu** 'stays'. Note that 'exists' is the usual way of saying '[somebody] has [something]': **Empitsu ga arimásu ka?** or **Anáta wa, empitsu ga arimásu ka?** 'Do you have a pencil? (As for you,) does a pencil exist?'

2.13. INFLECTED WORDS. Words like **désu**, **arimá-su**, and **imásu** are called inflected words, because their shapes can be changed [inflected] to make other words of similar but slightly different meaning. In English, we change the shapes of inflected words to show a difference of subject—'I am, you are, he is; I exist, he exists', as well as a difference of time—'I am, I was; you are, you were'. In Japanese, the shape of an inflected word stays the same regardless of the subject: **Heitai désu** can mean 'I am a soldier, you are a soldier, he is a soldier, we are soldiers, you are soldiers, they are soldiers' depending on the situation. If you want to make it perfectly clear, you can put

in a topic: **Watakushi wa heitai désu, anáta wa heitai désu, anó hito wa heitai désu.**

2. 14. SENTENCE TYPES. In English, every normal sentence has a subject and a predicate. If there is no logical
subject, we stick one in anyway: 'IT rains' (what rains?),
'IT is John' (what is John—it?). Sentences which do not
contain a subject are limited to commands—'Keep off the
grass!' in which a sort of 'you' is understood, or to a special
style reserved for postcards and telegrams—'Arrived safely.
Wish you were here.' In Japanese, the normal sentence
type contains a predicate—**Arimásu** 'There is [some]', **To
désu** '[It] is a door'—and to this we may add a subject or
a topic, but it isn't necessary unless we wish to be explicit.
Since the topic of a sentence is usually obvious in real
conversation, the Japanese often doesn't mention it at all,
or occasionally throws it in as an afterthought.

A predicate may consist of a simple verb—**Arimásu,
Imásu**—or of a noun plus the copula—**Senkyóshi desu**
'It's [I'm] a missionary'—but it cannot consist of the copula alone. The Japanese can talk about the equation
$A = B$, that is A **wa** B **désu** as in **Kore wa shimbun désu**
'This is a newspaper', by dropping the topic (A) and just
saying $= B$, that is B **désu** as in **Shimbun désu** '[It] is a
newspaper'. But they never say just $=$ (**désu**) or give a
one-sided equation like $A = $ —— (A **wa** —— **désu**). Something has to fill the blank before the word **désu**, in all
cases.

2. 15. WORDS OF RELATED REFERENCE. Notice
the related shapes and meaning of the following classes
of words:

kore 'this one'	sore 'that one'	are 'that one there'	dóre 'which one'
kono '[of] this'	sono '[of]that'	ano '[of] that there'	dóno 'which'
konna 'this sorta'	sonna 'that sorta'	anna 'that-there sorta'	dónna 'what sorta'
koko 'here'	soko 'there'	asoko } 'over there' asuko }	dóko 'where'
kō 'in this way'	sō 'in that way'	ā 'in that way there'	dō 'in what way, how'
[watakushi 'I']	[anáta 'you']	[anó hito 'he, she']	dáre 'who'

The words in the column with watakushi are used to refer to something near the speaker. The words in the column with anáta refer to something near the person you are talking with, or to something you have just mentioned. The words in the column with anó hito refer to something at a distance from both you and the person you are talking with. For some situations, either those in the column with anáta or those in the column with anó hito may be heard, since the reference is a relative matter. Be sure to keep dáre 'who' and dóre 'which' distinct. Instead of konna, sonna, anna, dónna, we often hear the more colloquial kō iu, sō iu, ā iu, dō iu. (Note that iu 'says' is pronounced always pronounced as if spelled yū or you.)

Dónna hón desu ka?	What sort of book is it?
Sonna (or sō iu) éiga ga sukí desu ka?	Do you like that sort of movie?
Anna hito wa dáikirai desu.	I hate people of that [his] sort.
Dō desu ka?	How about it? Do you like (or want) it? How about some? How're ya?

Hón wa kono náka ni ari-   The book is in[side] this.
másu.

Sono ué ni shimbun ga   On top of [either above or
arimásu.   in addition to] that,
                      there is a newspaper.

2. 16. WORDS FOR RESTAURANT AND HOTEL.
There are a number of different words for various types
of restaurant in Japan. Perhaps the most universally useful word is **shokudō** 'dining hall' which may refer to the
dining-room in a Western-style house, or to the dining
hall of a hotel, or to any restaurant. Another handy word
for restaurant is **inshokúten.** You will sometimes hear
the word **résutoran** from the English word of French
origin. Other words: **kissa** or **kissáten** 'a kind of French-
type café', **meshíya** 'a one-meal working class restaurant'
[American Japanese often use this word to mean any
restaurant], **tempuraya** 'a restaurant specializing in tem-
pura** [seafood deep-fried in batter]', **udon-ya** 'a restaurant specializing in **udon** [a kind of noodles or spaghetti]',
sushíya a 'a restaurant specializing in **sushi** [pickled fish
and dishes spiced with vinegar]'. And a **sobáya** sells **osóba**
[noodle dishes]. Often the best translation for 'restaurant' is **tabéru tokoro** 'a place to eat'.

The word **ryōríya** nowadays refers to a large, palatial
establishment with geisha entertainment as well as food
and drink—a sort of 'night-club' or 'fancy restaurant'. Bars
are called either **bǎ** [from the English word], or **káfē,
kyáfue** [from 'café']. The dining-car on a train is called
shokudǒsha.

. A **kaikan** is a private club with various dining facilities
often open to the public.

The word **hóteru** usually refers to a Western-style hotel. Japanese-style hotels are called **yadoya**—literally
'night-stopping places'. In proper names, Japanese-style
hotels are referred to by the term **ryokan: Tanaka-ryókan**
'Tanaka's Inn', **Kanazawa-ryókan** 'The Kanazawa Inn'.
Americans often keep the distinction in English by saying
'hotel' and 'inn' respectively.

2. 17. WORDS FOR TOILET. As in English, there are
various oblique ways of talking about toilets in Japanese.
The plain everyday word is **benjó** [literally 'convenience-
place']; this is usually avoided by women, who may say
o-benjo [adding the honorific prefix **o-**], especially when
talking to children. A more common euphemism among
women, also occasionally used by men, is **gofujó** [some
make the last vowel short **gofujo**]. Another term, heard
more from women, is **habakari**. Probably the most
current polite term is **teárai** 'lavatory', usually said with
the honorific prefix **o-: o-teárai**. So when asking directions, you may say **O-teárai wa dóko ni arimasu ka?** But
note that **toirétto** or **tóire** are also now in vogue.

2. 18. THE WORD FOR 'WHAT'. The word meaning
'what' has two forms: **nán** before a word beginning with
t, d, or **n,** and **náni** before other words. *

Nán desu ka?	What is it?
Nán to nán no aida ni arimásu ka?	What two things is it be-tween? [It is in the space between what and what?]
Nán no náka ni arimásu ka?	What's it in?
Náni ga arimásu ka?	What is there? What do you have?

*But **nan-** 'how many' (p. 174) never has the shape **nani-**. And
compare **ná n(o)**, p. 141.

Náni o shite imásu ka?   **What are you doing?**

C. EXERCISES.

1. Fill in the blanks with the appropriate particles. Do it aloud; don't write the answers down.

1. Ano tatémono ——, nán desu —— ?	What is that building?
2. Watakushi —— isu désu ——, anáta —— isu désu —— ?	Is it my chair or your chair?
3. Rájio —— dóko —— arimásu —— ?	Where's the radio?
4. Dóno hón —— anáta —— désu —— ?	Which book is yours?
5. Ano hón —— watakushi —— désu.	That book is mine.
6. Tanaka-san —— Amerika —— shimbun —— sukí desu.	Mr. Tanaka likes American newspapers.
7. Watakushi —— Beikoku —— éiga —— dáisuki desu.	I like American movies very much.
8. Anáta —— empitsu —— dóre desu —— ?	Which one is your pencil?
9. Anó hito —— uchi —— imásu —— .	Is he at home?
10. Uchi —— náka —— imásu —— ?	Is he in the house?

2. Fill in the blanks with one of the words **désu, arimá-su,** or **imásu.**

1. Shimbun —— ka, zasshi —— ka?	Is it a newspaper or a magazine
2. Anáta wa jitsugyōka —— ka?	Are you a businessman?
3. Súihei wa dóko ni —— ka?	Where's the sailor?
4. Watakushi no uchi wa koko ——.	Here is my house.
5. Niwa wa uchi no ushiro ni ——.	The garden is in back of the house.
6. Senkyóshi no tomodachi wa jimúsho ni ——.	The missionary's friend is in the office.
7. Anáta no mannénhitsu wa kore ——ka?	Is your fountain-pen this one?

8. Anáta wa gakkō no náka ni —— ka?   Are you inside the schoolhouse?
9. Hóteru ga —— ka?   Is there a hotel?
10. Rájio ga —— ka?   Do you have a radio?

D. COMPREHENSION.

A. Brówn-san, konnichi wa. Ogénki desu ka?
B. Okage-sama de génki desu. Aoki-san wa?
A. Okage-sama de. Kore wa watakushi no tomodachi désu. Dōzo yoroshiku ['Please accept his acquaintance'].
T. Tanaka désu. Dōzo yoroshiku. ['I am T.; please accept my acquaintance'.]
B. Hajimemáshite ['How do you do']. Dōzo yoroshiku.
T. Brówn-san wa, Amerikájin desu ka?
B. Sō desu. Uchi wa Amerika désu.
T. Amerika no dōko desu ka? Nyūu-Yōku [New York] desu ka?
B. Iie, San-Furanshísuko [San Francisco] desu. Watakushi no uchi wa San-Furanshísuko no chikáku ni arimásu.
T. Sō desu ka? Brówn-san wa heitai désu ka?
B. Iie, súihei desu. Yokosuka ni imásu. Tanaka-san wa?
T. Watakushi désu ka? Watakushi wa gakkō no senséi desu.
B. Sensei no ['your'] gakkō wa Tōkyō ni arimásu ka?
T. Iie, kōgai desu. Watakushi no gakkō wa Aoki-san no uchi no chikáku ni arimásu.

B. Số desu ka? Aoki-san wa ginkō désu ně. ['You are at a bank, aren't you, Mr. Aoki.'] Dóno ginkō désu ka?

A. Mitsui-gínkō desu. Tōkyǒ-eki no sóba ni arimasu.

B. Éki no migi désu ka, hidari désu ka?

A. Hidari désu. Asoko désu. Ano tatémono no náka ni arimásu.

B. Số desu ka. ...Ja, shitsúrei shimásu. Sayonára.

A. Sayonára.

T. Sayonára.

NOTES: (1) When you don't know what to say in a polite situation, use sumimasén, a slightly less formal equivalent of osóre irimasu; it means 'please', 'thank you', 'I don't mind if I do have a second cup of coffee if it isn't too much trouble', and just about everything else. The appropriate reply is simply iie 'not at all'.

(2) Another handy expression is (Sore wa) ikemasén which can mean either '(That's) too bad; I'm sorry (to hear that)' or '(That's) no good; don't do it; we mustn't do it'. In the latter meaning, Damé desu is often used.

(3) When you want to ask directions, you can preface your question with either Chótto sumimasén kedo... or Chótto ukagaimásu ga...

(4) When you leave home you say Itte mairimásu! 'I'm going and will be back' and are sent off with Itte irasshái! 'Go and return'. When you come back you shout out Tadáima (kaerimáshita)! '(I've) just now (returned)' and are answered with Okaeri (nasái)! 'Welcome back'.

LESSON 3.

A. BASIC SENTENCES. 'Things To Do.'

1. Anáta wa íma, náni o shite imásu ka?

   What are you doing now?

2. Íma wa, Nihongo o hanáshite imasu.

   I'm talking Japanese now.

3. Anáta wa máinichi, náni o shimásu ka?

   What do you do every day?

4. Máinichi machí e itte, jimúsho de shigoto o shimásu.

   Every day I go to town and work in an office.

5. Só desu ka? Dóko ni súnde imasu ka?

   Oh? Where do you live?

6. Kógai ni súnde imasu.

   I'm living in the suburbs.

7. Kinō shigoto o shimáshita ka?

   Did you work yesterday?

8. Iie, kinó wa yasumí deshita.

   No, yesterday I had off.

9. Kōen e itte, sampo shimáshita.

   I went to a park and took a walk.

10. Sore kara, uchi e káette, hón o yomimáshita.

    After that, I returned home and read a book.

11. Kómban, góhan o tábete kara, éiga e ikimásu.

    This evening I'm going to the movie after dinner.

12. Anáta wa watakushi to issho ni ikimasén ka?

    Won't you come with me?

13. Nihon no éiga desu ka?

    Is it a Japanese film?

14. Iie, só ja arimasén. Amerika nó desu.

    No, it isn't. It's American.

15. Éiga o míte kara, súgu uchi e kaerimásu ka?	Are you going home right after (seeing) the movie?
16. Hái, súgu kaerimásu. Issho ni kité kudasai.	Yes, I'll go home right after. Please come along.
17. Arígatō gozaimásu. Kippu wa mō kaimáshita ka?	Thank you (I will). Have you bought your ticket yet?
18. Iie, eigákan de kaimashó.	No, we'll buy them at the theater.
19. Jidósha ni notte ikimashó ka, arúite ikimashó ka?	Shall we go by car or on foot?
20. Só desu ne.	Well, let me see. [Said while thinking.]
21. Eigákan wa ginkō to depáto no aida ni arimásu né.	The movie-house is between the bank and the department store, isn't it?
22. Arúite ikimashó.	Let's walk.
23. Kékkō desu.	O.K. (or—when offered something—No thank you.)
24. Jírō o tsurete kimashó ka?	Shall I bring [my younger brother] Jiro along?
25. Sono shōsetsu wa dō deshita ka?	How was that novel? Did you like it?
26. Ki ni irimáshita ka?*	Did you like it?

*irimáshita=hairimáshita, so 'did it enter your ki (spirit)?' Notice that you do not ordinarily translate 'liked' or 'disliked' by snkí deshita or kirai déshita as you would expect; these expressions are used only when the thing liked or the person who likes it is no longer around.

27. Kono dénsha wa Ginza   Does this streetcar go to
    e ikimásu ka?   the Ginza?
28. Watakushi wa kyónen,   I went from Kobe to Chi-
    Kóbe kara Chíba e   ba last year.
    ikimáshita.
29. Kóbe kara Tōkyō máde   I went by train from Kobe
    kishá de ikimáshita.   to Tokyo.
30. Sore kara, Chíba made   After that, I went on to
    jidósha de ikimáshita.   Chiba by car.

VOCABULARY ITEMS.

kékkō	fine, O.K.; plenty	nikú	meat
kōbá	factory	sakana	fish
hikōki	airplane	yasai	vegetables
fúne	ship	kōin, shokkō	factory hand
básu	bus	rōdōsha	worker
chiká,	subway	jimúin	office worker
chikatetsu		hyakushó	farmer
kánai	my wife	inaka	countryside
ókusan	your wife, his wife	Eigo	English (language)
shújin	my husband; the boss	byōki [désu]	[is] sick
goshújin	your husband	yoroshiku	regards, respects

B. STRUCTURE NOTES.

3. 1. TIME WORDS. In the preceding lesson we found
that place words like koko 'here', náka 'inside', hidari
'left', shita 'below' are a kind of noun in Japanese. Time
words are a similar sort of noun. Such words are íma
'now', kinó 'yesterday', kómban 'this evening', kyónen 'last
year', máinichi 'every day'. Here are some time words you
will find useful:

ototói; issakújitsu		kyónen	last year
	day before yesterday	kotoshi	this year
kyǒ	today	rainen	next year
ashitá; myǒnichi		sarainen	year after next
	tomorrow	tadáima	just now
asátte; myōgónichi		kinō no ása	yesterday morning
	day after tomorrow	késa	this morning
sakúban; yuube		myǒasa, myōchō; ashita no ása	
	last night		tomorrow morning
kómban	tonight	ítsu	when
myǒban; ashita no ban		súgu (ni)	}right away
	tomorrow night	jiki (ni)	

Here are some examples of these words in sentences:

Kyǒ wa dóko e ikimásu ka?	Where are you going today?
Tanaka-san wa kyō, kōbá de hataraite imásu.	Mr. Tanaka is working at the factory today.
Sakúban no shimbun wa dóko e ikimáshita ka?	Where did last night's newspaper go?
Anáta wa myǒban éiga e ikimásu ka?	Are you going to the movies tomorrow night?
Ashitá wa yasumí desu.	I'm off tomorrow.
Rainen Kamakurá e ikimásu.	I'm going to Kamakura next year.
Kotoshi wa, Níkkō e ikimáshita.	This year I went to Nikko.
Watakushi wa késa, machí e itte shigoto o shimásu.	This morning I go to the city and work.
Myǒasa wa, gakkō e itte, benkyō shimásu.	Tomorrow morning I go to school and study.
Ítsu Amerika e kaerimásu ka?	When are you going back to America?

3. 2. NOUNS WITH AND WITHOUT PARTICLES.

Most nouns usually occur followed by a particle of some sort, or by the copula—**kono hón wa...**, **góhan o...**, **byō-ki désu.** Some nouns occur either with or without a particle, with only a slight difference in meaning. The time words listed in note 3. 1. can be followed by the particle **wa**—**Máinichi wa shigoto o shimasén** 'I don't work EVERY day', or used alone without the particle—**Máinichi shigoto o shimásu** 'Every day I work'. When you use the particle **wa**, you are making the time word the topic of your sentence; often you are contrasting what happens at THAT time (...**wa**) with what happens at other times. When a noun is used without a particle it usually modifies either the whole sentence or the verb phrase at the end; this we can call the ADVERBIAL USE of a noun. There are some words which are nouns but are rarely followed by a particle. These we can call ADVERBS, but of course we don't mean they correspond to everything we call an adverb in English. Such a word is **mố** 'already, yet': **Mō shimbun o yomimáshita ka?** 'Have you read the newspaper yet?' **Mố yomimáshita** 'I've already read it'. This adverb **mō**, when unaccented, has another meaning 'again, further, still, some more': **Mō ichido itte kudasái** 'Please say it again', **Mo sukóshi yomimásu ka?** 'Are you going to read some more?' **Mō** is usually followed by some limiting adverb like **ichido** 'one time'; frequently the word is **sukóshi** which means 'a little bit' but can be left untranslated in **mō sukóshi.** If no limiting adverb is used, 'more' is usually **mótto.** An adverb with a somewhat similar meaning is **máda** 'still, yet, [not] yet'.

Shimbun wa mó yomimá-shita ka?	Have you read the news-paper yet?
Máda yomimasén.	I haven't read it yet.
Ano shimbun wa máda yo-mimásu ka?	Do you still read that news-paper?
Máda yomimásu.	I still read it.
Shimbun wa mótto (or mō sukóshi) yomimásu ka?	Are you going to read the newspaper some more?
Mō ichido yomimásu.	I'm going to read it once again.
Mó yomimasén.	⎰ I'm not going to read it any more. ⎱ I don't read it any more.
Mó sono éiga o mimáshita ka?	Have you seen that movie yet?
Máda desu.	Not yet. (It is still [to be].)

3.3. PARTICLES KARA, MÁDE, E.   After place words, the particle **kara** means 'from', the particle **e** means 'to' and the particle **máde** means 'to, as far as, up to'.   If you want to say 'from Kobe to Osaka' you can say either **Kóbe kara Ōsaka máde** or **Kŏbe kara Ōsaka e,** but there is a slight difference of meaning.   When you use the particle **e,** you are primarily interested in the two end-points; when you use **máde** you are also interested in the space, time or means-of-travel between the two points.   This differ-ence of meaning is so subtle, however, that you can just remember that either **máde** or **e** means 'to' when reference is to a place.

Many speakers in Eastern Japan often replace the

particle e with the particle ni. So you will also hear
Kóbe kara Ōsaka ni ikimáshita 'I went from Kobe to
Osaka'. You can say either Uchi e káette benkyō shimáshita or Uchi ni káette benkyō shimáshita 'I went [back]
home and studied'.

After kore 'this', sore 'that', or a time word, the particle kara has the meaning 'after, since': sore kara 'after
that', kore kara 'after this, from now on'—compare koko
kara 'from here'. In a similar way, the particle máde
means 'until': sore máde 'until that [happens]', kore máde
'until now [this]'—compare koko máde 'up to here, as far
as this place'.

[Kara with verbal expressions is discussed in notes 3. 10
and 4. 12. Máde with verbal expressions is discussed in
note 5. 18.]

Here are some more examples:

Góhan o tábete, sore kara éiga e ikimáshita.	I had dinner and after that went to a movie.
Kore kara máinichi benkyō shimásu.	After this I'm going to study every day.
Kore máde shimbun o yo-mimasén deshita.	Until now I haven't been reading the newspapers.
Kinó kara byōki désu.	He's been sick since yester-day.
Ashitá kara hatarakimásu.	I work from tomorrow (on). I start work tomorrow.
Myóban made sono shigoto o shite imásu.	We'll be doing that job until tomorrow night.

| Ítsu made Nihón ni imásu ka? | How long will he be in Japan? |
| Ítsu kara Nihón ni imásu ka? | How long has he been in Japan? |

3. 4. PARTICLE NÉ. The particle né [often shortened to just né] is frequently tacked on at the end of a sentence to soften its tone; it implies that the speaker wants the hearer to agree with him, or that he wants what he is saying to agree with what the hearer might think. It is often translated by a rhetorical question [one to which an answer really isn't expected] such as '...isn't it', '...doesn't he', '...wasn't it', or by something like '...you know', '...you see.'

Nakamura-san wa shokkō désu ne.	Mr Nakamura is a factory worker, isn't he?
Sakúban no shimbun ni arimáshita ne.	It was in yesterday's newspaper, you see.
Ano tatémono kara hidari e ikimásu ne.	From that building, you know, you just go left.
Má, kírei desu né.	My, isn't it pretty!
Ano jimúin wa Eigo o hanashimásu né.	That clerk speaks English, doesn't he?
Só desu ne.	Now let me see...
Inaka ni súnde imasu né.	They're living in the country, you know.

We all know people who can't say three words without inserting something like 'I mean', 'you know', or 'you see':

'Well, you see, it was Friday, you see, and, you know, that movie—you see, it was new—I mean, I hadn't seen it, so. .' In a similar fashion, some Japanese overwork the particle né, inserting it after every few words. This seems to be particularly true of the speech of women. For the foreign student, it is advisable to avoid using the particle except at the end of a sentence, as above.

3.5. PARTICLE DE. The particle de has two quite different meanings. One is 'by means of': Fúne de kimáshita ka, hikóki de kimáshita ka? 'Did you come by ship or by plane?' Another meaning is '[an action happens] at [a place]': Gakkō de benkyō shimásu 'I study at school.' You have already learned that the particle ni means 'at' in the sense of a location in space or time: Gakkō ni imásu 'I'm at school'. The difference of use between ni and de depends on whether you use a verb which means something inactive—'exists, lives, stays'—or something active— 'talks, works, studies, eats'. There are very few verbs of the inactive sort; you have had imásu 'stays, [a person] exists [in a place]', arimásu 'exists', and súnde imasu 'is living, residing'. With other verbs you will usually hear de for 'at', but occasionally a Japanese will use ni if his attention is focused on the person's existence rather than his action. In general, you will be doing best to remember that 'at' corresponds to ni with the verbs imásu, arimásu, and súnde imasu (also tomarimásu 'stops or stays at'); with other verbs—alone or in a phrase with imásu, like hataraite imásu—'at' corresponds to de. Further examples:

Hyakushǒ wa inaka de shi-goto o shimásu.	Farmers work in the country.
Gakkō de náni o shimásu ka?	What do you do at school?
Dóno eigákan de Amerika no éiga o mimásu ka?	What movie theater do you see American films at?
Máda inaka ni súnde imasu ka?	Are you still living in the country?
Dóko de sore o yomimá-shita ka?	Where did you read that?
Ano hóteru wa Ueno-kõen no sóba ni arimásu.	That hotel is near [along-side] Ueno Park.

3. 6. PARTICLE O. The particle o [written **wo** in some spelling systems, but pronounced o] shows that the preceding word is the object of the verb. **Náni o míte imasu ka?** 'What are you looking at?' **Hón o yomimáshita** 'I read a book'. The meaning of **o** is the opposite of that of **ga**, which is the particle indicating the subject of the verb, of the copula, or of the adjective [as we shall see later]. Notice the following sentences:

Koko de dáre ga náni o shimásu ka?	Who does what here?
Dáre ga dáre o mimáshita ka?	Who saw who?
Tárō ga Jírō o mimáshita.	Taro saw Jiro.
Jírō ga Tárō o mimáshita.	Jiro saw Taro.

Either **ga** or **o** can be replaced by the topic particle **wa**. That is, you can take either the subject or the object and make it the topic you are going to talk about. **Tárō wa Jírō o mimáshita** 'Taro saw Jiro', **Táro wa Jíro**

ga mimáshita 'It was Jiro that saw Taro', Jírō wa Tárō
o mimáshita 'Jiro saw Taro', Jírō wa Tárō ga mimáshita
'It was Taro that saw Jiro.' Notice the shift of emphasis
when one of the phrases is made the topic and released
from the focus of attention. The most common focus
of attention in both English and Japanese is on something
other than the subject. We say 'Taro saw Jiro' with a
slightly heavier stress on Jiro—that is the most colorless
way we can say it. In a similar way, the Japanese will say
Tárō wa Jírō o mimáshita. But in English we always
have to have a subject. A Japanese sentence is complete
without a subject—Góhan o tabemáshita 'I've eaten dinner'
[heaviest stress on 'dinner']. In this case, it is quite common to shift the emphasis over to just the verb itself, by
taking the object and turning it into a topic: Góhan wa
tabemáshita 'I've eaten dinner' [heaviest stress on 'eaten'].

The particle o is also used to show the place where a
verb of motion takes place: michi o arukimásu 'walks (in)
the street', sora o tobimásu 'flies (in) the sky', kōen o (or
de) sampo shimásu 'strolls (in) the park'. Notice also uchi
o demásu 'leaves the house'.

3. 7. PARTICLE TO MEANING 'WITH' AND 'AND'.
In ginkō to depáto no aida '[the place] between the bank
and the department store', the particle to means 'and'.
This is an exhaustive 'and' which means you have listed
everything in a series. There is also a selective 'and'
which means you have listed only some of the things in
a series; this is the particle ya. In an exhaustive listing
of two or more things, each noun is followed by the particle to except the last, which is followed by whatever particle is appropriate to link the phrase up with the rest of

the sentence.

Nikú to pán to sakana to yasai o tabemáshita.	We ate meat and bread and fish and vegetables [and that's all].
Nikú ya pán o tabemáshita.	We ate meat and bread [among other things].
Hyakushō to shokkō to ji-múin ga imáshita.	There were farmers and factory workers and office workers [and that's all].
Tōkyō to Ōsaka to Kyôto to Kôbe de shigoto o shi-te imáshita.	I was working in Tokyo, and Osaka, and Kyoto, and Kobe [and that's all].

In the phrase watakushi to issho ni 'together with me' the particle to means 'with'. You can say watakushi to kimáshita 'he came with me', but with verbs of motion it is more usual to add the phrase issho ni 'together': watakushi to issho ni kimáshita. Notice that just issho ni often corresponds to 'with me' or 'with you' or 'with us'.

Anáta wa dáre to hanáshite imáshita ka?	Who were you talking with?
Takayama-san to hataraite imásu ka?	Are you working with Mr. Takayama?
Watakushi to issho ni sam-po shimasén ka?	Won't you take a walk with me?
Issho ni kimásu ka?	Is he coming with us?

Occasionally the particle to is used in expressions which call for an unexpected equivalent in the English transla-tion: Watakushi wa anáta to chigaimásu 'I'm different

FROM you'. **Koko wa asoko to chigaimásu nĕ** 'It's different here FROM [what it is] there, isn't it?
3.8. EXPRESSIONS FOR ACCOMPANIMENT. **Ta-naka-san to issho ni ikimásu** means 'goes with Mr. Tanaka'; **Jírō o tsurete ikimásu** means 'brings Jiro along'. You use an expression of the latter type—or an expanded form, **Jírō o tsurete issho ni ikimásu**—when the person you are 'bringing along' is younger or socially inferior to you. [In the above sentence we assume it is elder-brother Taro talking.] If the person is your equal or superior then you say he 'comes along with' you. **Tárō wa [watakushi to] issho ni ikimásu** 'Taro is going along [with me].' The noun **issho** means something like 'a group [as contrasted with a single person]', so **issho ni** means 'in a group; with others'; **issho désu** means 'are together'.*
3.9. VERBS, POLITE MOODS. You have heard forms like **ikimásu** 'goes', **ikimáshita** 'went', **ikimashŏ** 'let's go; shall we go'. These are various moods of the same verb. Each verb, adjective, and the copula as well, can be changed in shape to correspond to different categories we call MOODS. [Compare the English forms 'go, went, gone, going'.]

In Japanese, each verb—and similarly each adjective and the copula—has two sets of forms, one polite, one plain. So far we have seen only the polite forms of verbs and the copula. In the next lesson we have some of the plain forms of these, and plain and polite forms of the adjectives. In normal polite conversation, it is customary to end a sentence with one of these polite forms. For a

---

*Issho refers to either people or things; (to) tómo ni is a less colloquial synonym.

further discussion on the use of polite and plain forms, see the next lesson.

In this lesson you find forms like shite 'doing', hanáshite 'talking', káette 'returned and', kité [kudasai] '[please] come', arúite [ikimásu] '[goes] on foot', tsurete [kimásu] 'brings along', tábete [kara] '[after] eating', [jidŏsha ni] notte [ikimásu] '[goes] riding [in a car]'. These forms are called GERUNDS. The use of gerunds is discussed below. You need not worry about how they are formed until the next lesson. Just learn them as they occur.

Below is a list of each verb you have heard, and the copula, with all the moods you have met so far. Examine the list, but do not memorize it.

MEANING	IMPERFECT	POLITE PERFECT	TENTATIVE	PLAIN GERUND
sees, looks	mimásu	mimáshita	mimashŏ	míte
stays, exists	imásu	imáshita	imashŏ	ite
eats	tabemásu	tabemáshita	tabemashŏ	tábete
comes	kimásu	kimáshita	kimashŏ	kité
does	shimásu	shimáshita	shimashŏ	shite
works	hatarakimásu	hatarakimáshita	hatarakimashŏ	hataraite
walks	arukimásu	arukimáshita	arukimashŏ	arúite
goes	ikimásu	ikimáshita	ikimashŏ	itte
talks	hanashimásu	hanashimáshita	hanashimashŏ	hanáshite
exists	arimásu	arimáshita	arimashŏ	átte
returns	kaerimásu	kaerimáshita	kaerimashŏ	káette
rides, gets on	norimásu	norimáshita	norimashŏ	notte
lives	sumimásu	sumimáshita	sumimashŏ	súnde
reads	yomimásu	yomimáshita	yomimashŏ	yónde
buys	kaimásu	kaimáshita	kaimashŏ	katte
equals, is	désu	déshita	deshŏ	dé

You will notice that the mood we call the Polite Imperfect ends in -másu for all the verbs [-su for the copula];

the Polite Perfect ends in -máshita for all the verbs [-shita for the copula]; and the Polite Tentative ends in -máshǒ for all the verbs [-shǒ for the copula]. The Plain Gerund ends in -te or -de [zero for the copula], and there are certain changes in the verb stem itself.

3. 10. USES OF THE GERUND. The gerund is used before kudasái 'please' to make a polite request. Mō ichido hanáshite kudasai 'Please say it again.' Mádo kara míte kudasai 'Please look out the window.'

The gerund is used with the particle kara to mean 'after [do]ing'. Sampo shité kara, uchi e kaerimáshita 'After taking a walk, I returned home.' Góhan o tábete kara, shimbun o yomimáshita 'After eating, I read my newspaper.'

The gerund is also used alone, at the end of a clause, to mean '[does] and' or '[did] and' or '[will do] and'. Machí e itte, jimúsho de shigoto o shimásu 'I go to town and work in an office'. Machí e itte, éiga o mimáshita 'I went to town and saw a movie'. Kōen e itte, sampo shimashǒ ka? 'Shall we go to the park and take a walk?'

The gerund is used in verb phrases with some form of the verb imásu to mean 'is [do]ing'. Náni o shite imásu ka? 'What are you doing?' Sakúban benkyō shite imáshita. 'Last night I was studying.' Nihon no dóko ni súnde imashǒ ka? 'Where will we be living in Japan?' These verb phrases show a kind of PROCESS or CONTINUING ACTION. They focus our interest on the fact that the action lasts for a while. The simple verb form, on the other hand, focuses our attention on the action itself—either a specific act [Náni o shimásu ka? 'What

do you do? What will you do?' **Sakúban benkyō shimá-**
shita 'Last night I studied'] or a series thought of as a set
of specific acts [**Máinichi hatarakimásu** 'Every day I work']
rather than as a set of continuing actions taking up a space
of time [**Máinichi hataraite imásu** 'Every day I'm working']. The exact difference between **shigoto o shimásu**
and **shigoto o shite imásu** is just as subtle as that between
'I work' and 'I'm working', and in many situations either
phrase would seem appropriate.

Sometimes the difference between the simple verb and
the gerund + **imásu** seems to lie in a slightly different focus of emphasis. In the sentence **Ichíji kara níji made**
hatarakimáshita 'I worked from 1 o'clock to 2 o'clock',
the principal emphasis is on the fact that I worked and
the time is incidental, additional information. But in the
sentence **Ichíji kara níji made hataraite imáshita** 'From
1 o'clock to 2 o'clock I was working', the emphasis—while
perhaps really focused on the DURATIVE nature of the
action; that is, on the word **imáshita**—seems to be more
on the time and what I was doing during the time   .

The gerund is also used in certain phrases with other
verbs. **Arúite ikimásu** 'He walks [he goes walking]', **Jidō-**
sha ni notte kimásu 'He comes by car [riding in a car]',
Jírō o tsurete kimashō ka? 'Shall I bring Jiro along [shall
I come bringing Jiro]?'

Notice that the gerund has no perfect, imperfect or
tentative meaning of its own, but takes on the mood of
the following (or final) verb.

ryokō shite imásu   I am traveling

ryokō shite imáshita	I was traveling
ryokō shite imashố	I will [probably] be traveling
Hibiya-kõen e itte sampo shimashố.	Let's go to Hibiya Park and take a walk.
Hibiya-kõen e itte sampo shimáshita.	I went to Hibiya Park and took a walk.
Hibiya-kõen e itte sampo shimasén ka?	Won't you go to Hibiya Park and take a walk?

3. 11. USE OF THE IMPERFECT, PERFECT, AND TENTATIVE MOODS.

The Imperfect mood [sometimes called the 'present tense'] indicates that an action has not been completed—it may or may not have begun, but it must be a definite, decided action. In the sentence Kinố kara byōki désu 'I've been sick since yesterday' we use the Imperfect because I'm still sick today. Dóko e ikimásu ka? 'Where are you going?'—Perhaps you haven't even started to go yet, but it's definite that you will go.

On the other hand, the Perfect mood [sometimes called the 'past tense'] shows that the action has been completed. Tanaka-san wa byōki déshita 'Mr. Tanaka was sick [but he's well now]'. Dóko e básu de ikimáshita ka? 'Where did you go by bus?'

The Tentative mood [sometimes called 'suggestive' or 'future' or 'probable future' or 'presumptive'] is used when an action isn't quite definite. You're not sure about it—maybe it will be, probably it will be, perhaps it has already been—or you're suggesting it for consideration.

Tanaka-san wa byōki deshó 'Mr. Tanaka must be sick—
I'm not sure, it isn't definite, but what do you think?'
Dóko e ikimashó ka? 'Where shall we go?—It hasn't been
definitely decided where we will go, but we will probably
go some place, so what shall we consider?' This sometimes
corresponds to English 'let us': **Arúite ikimashó** 'Let's
walk—it isn't definite that we will walk, but I'm suggesting it.' (cf. pp. 141, 388.)

3. 12. NEGATIVES. The polite Imperfect negative of
a verb is made by changing **-másu** to **-masén.** The polite
negative of the copula **désu** is the phrase **ja arimasén.*** Do
not confuse this with the word **arimasén** all by itself; this
is the negative of **arimásu** and means 'there isn't any'.
Notice the following sentences:

Pán ga arimásu. There is bread. **Kore wa pán desu.** This is bread.
Pán wa arimasén. There is no bread. **Kore wa pán ja** This isn't
                                           arimasén. bread.

Observe the change of particles in the examples. The
most common type of attention-focus for a negative sentence in Japanese is on the negation itself 'there ISN'T
any bread'. If you want to say 'There isn't any BREAD'
(that is, 'It's BREAD that we lack [rather than something
else]'), then you say **Pán ga arimasén.**

The polite Perfect negative is a phrase **-masén deshita**
[for the copula **ja arimasén deshita**], and similarly the
polite Tentative negative is **-masén deshó** [for the copula
ja arimasén deshō]. (cf. p. 141.)

---

*Or, often, **ja nái desu;** and **arimasén** is often **nái desu** (cf. pp.
83, 102, 147).

Pán ga arimáshita. There was bread.	**Sore wa pán deshita.** That was bread.
Pán wa arimasén deshita. There was no bread.	**Sore wa pán ja ari-masén deshita.** That was not bread.
Pán wa arimasén (or) nái deshō. There won't be any bread (I bet).	**Sore wa pán ja ari-masén (or nái) deshō.** That (probably) won't be bread.

3. 13. WORDS FOR 'WORK'. You have had two ways to say 'I work'. **Shigoto o shimásu** means 'I do my job', **hatarakimásu** means 'I work [often, but not necessarily, at something physical]'. These two words can frequently be used in each other's place, with no great change of meaning. There is another word meaning 'is employed' or 'works'—**tsutomemásu.** This has a somewhat more refined connotation. **Dóko ni tsutómete imásu ka?** 'Where are you employed?'

3. 14. VERBAL NOUNS. There are some nouns, like **sampo** 'a walk' and **benkyō** 'study', which can be followed directly by a form of the verb **shimásu** 'does'. These constitute a class of nouns we call VERBAL NOUNS. Other verbal nouns: **ryokō** 'trip, travel', **shutchō** 'business trip', **kekkon** 'marriage', **shōkai** 'introduction', **shitsúrei** 'rudeness', **shóbai** 'business, trading'. Here are some examples:

Kyónen Kánsai e ryokō shimáshita.	Last year I made a trip to Kansai [Western Japan].
Tomodachi ni shōkai shi-mashó.	Let me introduce you to a friend.

Sometimes the particle **o** is inserted with expressions of this type, especially if the noun has something modifying it: **Sono benkyō o shimáshita** 'I did that study'.

3. 15.   GOING IN VEHICLES. To say 'I went by train' you can say either **Kishá de ikimáshita** or **Kishá ni notte ikimáshita** [I went riding on a train]. The verb **norimásu** 'gets on board, rides'—like the verbs **imásu, arimásu,** and **súnde imasu**—takes the particle **ni,** here implying a change of position. **Dóko de fúne ni norimáshita ka?** 'Where did you board the ship?' Notice the difference between **Máinichi kishá ni norimásu** 'He rides the train every day', and **Máinichi kishá ni notte ikimásu** 'He goes [there] on the train every day'. To get off (or out of) a vehicle you use the verb **orimásu (órite): Jidósha o orimáshita** 'I got out of the car'. **(Básu o) dóko de orimashó ka?** 'Where shall we get off (the bus)?' **Orimásu!** 'Coming out! Getting off!'

3. 16. 'AS SOON AS'. A common way to say 'as soon as' is to use the gerund followed by **kara** 'after ...ing', and then begin the next clause with **súgu** 'right away, immediately'. **Góhan o tábete kara, súgu sampo ni ikimáshita** 'I went for a walk as soon as [right after] I ate dinner'. Sometimes the gerund is followed directly by the next clause without the particle **kara—Heyá ni háitte súgu senséi ni hanashimáshita** 'As soon as I entered the room I spoke to the teacher.'

C. EXERCISES.

1. Insert one of the particles **de** or **ni** in the appropriate blanks. Then translate the sentences. Do it all aloud.
    1. **Ano shokkō wa dóko —— hataraite imásu ka?**
    2. **Fúne —— kimáshita ka, hikóki —— kimáshita ka?**
    3. **Nán —— notte kimáshita ka?**

4. Nagata-san wa ano uchi —— súnde imasu nĕ.
5. Tōkyō-eki wa dóko —— arimásu ka?
6. Gakusei wa heya no náka —— imásu.
7. Soko —— benkyō shite imásu nĕ.
8. Támura-san wa watakushi o tsurete kishá —— norimáshita.
9. Machí e itte, tomodachi no uchi —— góhan o tabemáshita.
10. Ginkō —— tsutómete imasu.

2. Insert one of the particles ga or o in the appropriate blanks. Then translate the sentences.
   1. Watakushi wa Amerika no éiga —— sukí desu.
   2. Anáta wa mō góhan —— tabemáshita ka?
   3. Náni —— arimásu ka?
   4. Dáre —— heya no náka ni imásu ka?
   5. Dáre —— tsurete éiga e ikimáshita ka?
   6. Dóno benkyō —— shimashŏ ka?
   7. Téburu no ue no nikú wa, dáre —— tabemáshita ka?
   8. Senséi wa, dóno hón —— kaimáshita ka?
   9. Íma wa, dáre —— Nihongo —— benkyō shite imásu ka?
   10. Nihongo wa íma, dáre —— benkyō shite imásu ka?

3. The following sentences mean 'somebody does [or is] something'. Make them mean 'somebody doesn't [or isn't] something'.
   1. Watakushi wa sakana o tabemáshita.
   2. Watakushi wa kyō, benkyō shimásu.
   3. Ima wa, hataraite imásu nĕ.
   4. Rainen Yamanóshita e ikimásu.
   5. Sakúban sono hón o yónde imashita.
   6. Anó hito wa byōki deshŏ.

7. Sỏ desu ka?
8. Ano jitsugyōka wa Amerika e kaerimáshita.
9. Kono yadoya wa kirai désu.
10. Issho no dénsha de kimáshita ka?

D. COMPREHENSION.

[Watakushi wa Beikoku no senkyỏshi desu.
Yamada-san wa Nihon no jitsugyōka désu.
Watakushi to issho no dénsha ni notte imásu.]

Watakushi.   Móshi moshi, Yamada-san! Ohanashichū
             shitsúrei desu ga...
Yamada.   Anáta deshita ka? Komban wa, Báker-san.
             Ogénki desu ka?
Watakushi.   Génki desu. Anáta wa?
Yamada.   Kinỏ wa byōki déshita. Íma génki desu.
             Á, shitsúrei shimáshita.   Tomodachi no
             Suzuki-san o shōkai shimásu.   Báker-san désu.
Suzuki.   Dỏzo yoroshiku.   Báker-san wa Amerikájin
             deshỏ?
Yamada.   Sỏ desu. Senkyỏshi desu.
Suzuki.   Sỏ desu ka. Á, asoko wa watakushi no uchi
             désu. Osaki ni shitsúrei shimásu. Sayonára.
Yamada.   Sayonára.
Watakushi.   Anáta wa dóko de kono dénsha ni norimá-
             shita ka?
Yamada.   Shímbashi [a station in Tokyo] de norimáshi-
             ta. Késa machí e itte, jimúsho de shigoto o
             shimáshita. Sore kara, jidỏsha ni notte, kỏgai
             no kōbá e itte mimáshita. Kōbá o míte kara,
             súgu machí e káette Yoshida-san to góhan o

	tabemáshita. Anáta wa Yoshida-san no to-modachi désu né?

Watakushi. Sŏ desu ne... Sore wa Yoshida Kentárō-san desu ka?

Yamada. Iie. Yoshida Hideo-san désu.

Watakushi. Á sŏ desu ka? Watakushi no tomodachi wa sono Yoshida-san ja arimasén. Yoshida-san wa jitsugyōka désu ka?

Yamada. Sŏ desu. Kyónen, Yoshida-san wa Kánsai ni imáshita. Kŏbe de shigoto o shite imáshita. Kotoshi Kántō e káette, Yokohama de shi-goto o shite imásu. Anáta wa mŏ Kánsai e ikimáshita ka?

Watakushi. Máda desu. Rainen kánai o tsurete soko e ryokō shimásu.

Yamada. Sore wa kékkō desu ne. Watakushi no itoko [cousin] ga Amerika ni súnde imasu. Anó hito ni anáta o shōkai shimashŏ.

Watakushi. Arígatō gozaimásu. Myŏban watakushi no uchi e kite, góhan o tabemasén ka?

Yamada. Arígatō gozaimásu.

Watakushi. Dé wa, dŏzo. Omachi shite orimásu [I'll be expecting you]. Ja, shitsúrei itashimásu. Sayonára.

Yamada. Sayonára.

LESSON 4.

A. BASIC SENTENCES. 'The Weather.'

1. Kyǒ wa oténki ga íi desu ně.

It's nice weather today, isn't it.

2. Késa kumótte imashita ga, íma hárete hi ga déte imasu.

This morning it was cloudy, but now it is clear and the sun is out,

3. Ashitá wa dǒ deshō ka ně.

I wonder what it'll be like tomorrow.

4. Oténki ga íi to, máiasa sampo shimásu.

When the weather's nice, I take a walk every morning.

5. Shikáshi, áme ga fúru to, uchi ni ite, rájio o kikimásu.

However, when it rains, I stay at home and listen to the radio.

6. Amerika dé wa, háru ni náru to, áme ga yóku furimásu.

In America, when it gets to be spring, it rains a lot.

7. Fuyú wa samúi kara, ammari sampo shimasén.

In winter it's cold, so I don't take walks much.

8. Kaze ga fukimásu. Yukí mo furimásu.

The wind blows. It snows, too.

9. Natsú ni wa ryokō suru kotó ga sukí desu.

In the summer I like to travel.

10. Kyónen, úmi e itte,

Last year, I went to the

hamá de asobimáshita. | sea[shore] and had a good time at the beach.

11. Anáta wa oyogí ga dekimásu ka? | Can you swim?

12. Sukóshi dekimásu. Machí ni iru to, tokidoki Wai-emu-shíi-ē e itte oyógu koto ga arimásu. | I can a little. When I'm in town, I sometimes go to the YMCA and have a swim.

13. Anáta wa asoko e itta kotó ga arimásu ka? | Have you ever gone there?

14. Hái. Tomodachi to issho ni itta kotó ga arimásu. | Yes. I once went there with a friend.

15. Watakushi wa rainen mata, úmi e iku tsumori désu ga, anáta wa dǒ desu ka? | I intend to go to the sea[shore] again next year; what about you?

16. Watakushi no yasumí wa áki da kara, úmi e wa iku kotó ga dekimasén. | My vacation is in the Fall, so I can't go to the sea.

17. Yamá e itta kotó wa nái kara, Karúizawa e itte míru tsumori désu. | Since I've never been to the mountains, I plan to go to Karuizawa [and see it].

18. Kono éiga o mí ni ikimashǒ ka? | Shall we go see this movie?

19. Watakushi wa sakúban sore o míta kara, kómban wa sampo ni ikimashǒ. | I saw it last night, so let's go for a walk tonight.

20. Watakushi wa sukóshi tsukárete iru kara, góhan o tábete kara yasumimashó.

I'm a bit tired, so I think I'll go to bed [rest] right after dinner.

21. Máiban osokú made shigoto o suru to, byōki ni narimásu.

If you work till late every day, you'll get sick.

22. Amerika no éiga mo, Nihon no éiga mo, dáisuki desu.

I like both American movies and Japanese movies very much.

23. Furansu no éiga mo, sukí desu ka?

Do you like French movies too?

24. Furansu no éiga wa omoshirói keredomo, watakushi wa Furansugo ga wakarimasén kara...

French films are interesting, but I don't understand French, so...

25. Furansugo mo, Doitsugo mo wakarimasén.

I don't understand either French or German.

26. Watakushi mo só desu.

Me either. [Me too.]

27. Náni o motte kimáshita ka?

What did you bring?

28. Jibikí o motté kite imasu ka?

Have you brought your dictionary?

29. Sentakumono o tóri ni itté kara, náni o shimáshita ka?

What did you do after going to get your laundry?

30. Tegami o totte kimáshita.

I went and picked up my letters.

VOCABULARY ITEMS.

NOUNS		VERBS	
kodomo	child	neru	goes to bed, sleeps
onná, onna no hito	woman, girl	yasúmu	rests; retires; sleeps
		yobu	calls
onná-no-ko	girl	isógu	hurries
otokó-no-ko	boy	kawáku	gets dry, thirsty
otokó, otoko no hito	man, boy		
			ADJECTIVES
musumé, ojósan	girl, daughter	akai	is red
kaban	suitcase	aói	is blue
jígyō	business, enterprise	kurói	is black
sóra	sky	shirói	is white
sentakuya	laundry [place], laundryman	warúi	is bad
		ōkíi	is big
sentaku [o suru]	[does] the washing	chiisái	is little
damé [desu]	[is] no good, won't do	nagái	is long
		mijikái	is short
okáshi	pastry, cakes	hayái	is fast, is early
ame	(hard) candy	osoi	is slow, is late
nódo	throat		
terevíjon, térebi	television		
Kánsai	Western Japan		
Kántō	Eastern Japan		

B. STRUCTURE NOTES.

4. 1.   ADJECTIVES.   There are three classes of inflected forms in Japanese: verbs, adjectives, and copula.   You have observed the similar inflections of the verbs and the copula:

Náni o shimásu ka?	What do you do?	Nán desu ka?	What is it?
Náni o shimáshita ka?	What did you do?	Nán deshita ka?	What was it?
Náni o shimashō ka?	What shall we do?	Nán deshō ka?	What [do you think] it is [probably]?

...

The adjectives also have inflections for the same categories:

omoshirói desu   it's interesting
omoshírokatta desu   it was interesting
omoshirói deshō   it will [probably] be inter-
                            esting;
                            it must be interesting [I
                            think]

You will recall that the polite negative form of the copula **désu** 'equals, is' is a phrase—**ja arimasén** in the imperfect 'is not', and **ja arimasén deshita** in the perfect 'was not'. In a similar way, the polite forms of the adjectives—both affirmative and negative—consist of phrases. The phrases have two parts—a plain form of the adjective [discussed below] and a polite form of the copula. For the perfect, the plain perfect of the adjective (p. 94) is followed by the polite imperfect of the copula.*

The thing to remember about these phrases is that they are often parallel in use to a single verb form:

Kaimáshita. I bought.   **Omoshírokatta desu.** It was interesting.
Kaimashō I will probably   **Omoshirói deshō.** It will probably
buy; let's buy.   be interesting.

(For 'he will probably buy' see p. 141.)

Here are some more examples of adjectives:
Kinó wa oténki ga wáru-   Yesterday the weather was
katta desu.   bad.
Dóno éiga ga omoshirói   I wonder which movie will
deshō ka ně.   be [most] interesting?

---

*Sometimes you will hear forms like **omoshiṛói deshita** (=**omo-shírokatta desu**) but they are less common; see p. 142.

| Watakushi no jidṓsha wa kurói desu ga, anáta no wa aói desu. | My car is black, and yours is blue. |
| Amerika wa ōkíi deshō ně. | America must be pretty big [I think, isn't it?]. |

The negative of adjectives is a phrase consisting of the plain infinitive+arimasén (or nái desu) 'does not exist: wáruku arimasén 'is not bad', omoshíroku arimasén. This is further discussed in 5. 11.

4.2. PLAIN AND POLITE FORMS. For the same in-flectional category—like imperfect, perfect—a Japanese verb, adjective, or copula may have two forms: a plain form and a polite form. In familiar speech, only the plain forms occur. But in polite speech, of the sort Japanese will want to talk with you, the plain forms are limited in occurrence to some place other than at the end of the sentence. So, in the polite style of talking, you will say Áme ga furimá-shita 'It rained', but Áme ga fútta kara, ikimasén deshita 'Because it rained, I didn't go.' Occasionally you will hear a polite form used somewhere other than at the end of the sentence—for instance, someone may say Áme ga furi-máshita kara, ikimasén deshita. In fact, before the par-ticle ga meaning 'but, and', the polite form is the usual thing. And before the particle keredomo 'but, however', many people prefer to use the polite form.

The moods which occur at the end of a sentence are limited to the imperfect, perfect, and tentative. [For their uses, see 3. 11.] But within a sentence, there are a number of other moods, such as the gerund and the infinitive. The uses of the gerund were discussed in 3. 10; further uses

are found in 4. 17 and 4. 18. The uses of the infinitive
are covered in 4. 8. Here are some examples of the use
of plain and polite forms within sentences:

Ammari samúi to, byōki ni narimásu.	When it's too cold, I get sick.
Ammari oyóida kara, tsukaremáshita.	I got tired from swimming too much.
Késa tsukáreta kara, mō oyogimasén.	Since I got tired this morning, I won't swim any more [today].
Watakushi wa Amerika no heitai déshita ga, tomodachi wa Eikoku no súihei deshita.	I was an American soldier, but my friend was an English sailor.
Súihei datta keredomo, fúne ni notta kotó wa arimasén.	He was a sailor, but he has never ridden on a ship!

4. 3. SHAPES OF THE PLAIN FORMS. Any Japanese
inflected form may be broken up into a STEM and an
ENDING.   Japanese verbs fall into two main classes:
Consonant Verbs and Vowel Verbs.   The Consonant Verbs
are those with a stem which ends in a consonant; the
Vowel Verbs, those with a stem which ends in a vowel.
There are two classes of endings: those beginning with t-
[or, in some cases, d-] which have a rather constant shape;
and those which begin with other sounds and have an
alternating shape—one form after a Consonant stem, and
another form after a Vowel stem. The Vowel stems stay
the same, regardless of the ending; the Consonant stems

have an alternant form before the **t-** [or **d-**] endings. In other words, we have two kinds of stems, and two kinds of endings:

	STEMS		ENDINGS
1.	Vowel [constant]	A.	**t-, d-** [constant]
2.	Consonant [with an alternant before endings of type A]	B.	others [with alternants for the two types of stem]

Vowel stems end only in **-i** or **-e**: **mí-ru** 'sees', **tabé-ru** 'eats'. Consonant stems end in **-t[s]** as in **máts-u** 'waits', **-r** as in **nor-u** 'rides', **-[w]** as in **á-u** 'meets', **-s** as in **hanás-u** 'speaks', **-k** as in **kák-u** 'writes', **-g** as in **oyóg-u** 'swims', **-b** as in **yob-u** 'calls', **-m** as in **yóm-u** 'reads', and **-n** as in **shin-u** 'dies'. Verbs are usually mentioned by the plain imperfect form: **kau** 'buys'.

You will notice certain peculiarities in the above list of stem-final consonants. The verbs **áu** 'meets' and **kau** 'buys' are said to be Consonant stems, but the consonant with which they end—**w**—just doesn't occur in Japanese except before the sound **a** [as in **watakushi** 'I']. This means that for some of the endings, like the imperfect, these **w**-stem verbs don't display this stem-final consonant at all. That is why we put the **w** in brackets—to show that it disappears before every vowel except **a**. You will notice another sound in brackets—the [s] of the verb **mátsu** 'waits'. This verb stem basically ends in just **-t**, but the sound **t** does not occur before the sound **u** in Japanese, so that before an ending beginning with **u** the **t** is replaced by **ts**. In a similar way, since the combination **ti** does not normally occur in Japanese, before the infinitive ending -i the t becomes ch—mách-i 'waiting'. Since the sound si does not occur, the infinitive of hanás-u 'speaks' turns out to be hanásh-i 'speaking'.

There is only one verb with a stem ending in -n, shinu 'dies', and this is often replaced by a euphemism naku náru 'passes away'. The verb shinu is included in our list only for completeness.

Here are some models showing the formation of the plain forms:

	IMPERFECT	PERFECT	GERUND	INFINITIVE	ENGLISH
VOWEL	tabé-ru	tábe-ta	tábe-te	tábe[ZERO]	eats
STEMS	mí-ru	mí-ta	mí-te	mí [ZERO]	sees, looks
CONSONANT	máts-u	mát-ta	mát-te	mách-i	waits for
STEMS	nor-u	not-ta	not-te	nor-i	gets aboard
	á[w]-u	át-ta	át-te	á[w]-i	meets
	hanás-u	hanáshi-ta	hanáshi-te	hanásh-i	speaks
	kák-u	kái-ta	kái-te	kák-i	writes
	oyóg-u	oyói-da	oyói-de	oyóg-i	swims
	yob-u	yon-da	yon-de	yob-i	calls
	yóm-u	yón-da	yón-de	yóm-i	reads
	shin-u	shin-da	shin-de	shin-i	dies

The endings, then, are as follows:

IMPERFECT -ru after a Vowel stem, -u after a Consonant stem

INFINITIVE [-ZERO] after a Vowel stem, -i after a Consonant stem

PERFECT -da after -g, -b, and -d stems; -ta after all other stems

GERUND -de after -g, -b, and -d stems; -te after all other stems

The ZERO ending is an ending that has no shape at all. We know that there is SOMETHING there in the way of an ending only by comparing the use of the form—as in **Góhan o tábe ni ikimáshita** 'He went to eat'—with that of other forms which have a definite shape for the ending—as in **Tomodachi o yob-i ni ikimáshita** 'He went to call his friend.' Compare the English plural ending: three cats [cat-s], three sheep [sheep-ZERO].

The Consonant stems themselves change in the following ways before the endings beginning with **t-** or **d-**:

STEM IN IMPERFECT		STEM BEFORE T- OR D- ENDING	
-t[s]-	as in máts-u	-t-	as in mát-ta
-r-	as in nor-u	-t-	as in not-ta
-[w]-	as in á-u	-t-	as in át-ta
-s-	as in hanás-u	-shi-	as in hanáshi-ta
-k-	as in kák-u	-i-	as in kái-ta
-g-	as in oyóg-u	-i-	as in oyói-da
-b-	as in yob-u	-n-	as in yon-da
-m-	as in vóm-u	-n-	as in yón-da
-n-	as in shin-u	-n-	as in shin-da

Notice that both -k stems and -g stems change to -i-, yet we can still tell which stem it is because the ending starts with **d-** after the -i- which represents the -g stem, but with **t-** after -i- which represents the -k stem:

kák-u	writes	kái-ta	wrote
kag-u	smells [something]	kai-da	smelled [something]

However, we can not tell the difference between -b and -m stems (both of which change to -n-), because the ending begins with d- in both cases. The only way **yón-da** 'has read' [yóm-u 'reads'] can be distinguished from yon-da 'called' [yob-u 'calls'] is by the accent—or, of course, by the context in which each is used.

4. 4. LEARNING THE FORMS. Now, how should one go about learning these inflectional forms? You have read a description of how they are put together, and that may be of some help to you. But in order to be able to make up the forms for a new verb you hear, you will want to compare it with a verb you already know and make its forms by analogy, using the old verb for a model. You can take the verbs used in the lists here for your models. Learn their forms well, and then make forms for other verbs on their patterns.

When you come across a new verb, the first thing you want to know is: does it have a Consonant stem or a Vowel stem? Unless the verb ends in -eru or -iru in the imperfect, there is no doubt about it—it's a Consonant stem. But if the verb does end in -eru or -iru, you don't know whether it is a Consonant stem or a Vowel stem until you check one of the other forms, such as the infinitive or the perfect. Look at the following examples:

	'eats'	'returns'	'opens[something]'
Imperfect	tabéru : tabé-ru	káeru : ???	akeru : ???
Infinitive	tábe : tábe[zero]	káeri : káer-i	ake : ake[zero]
Perfect	tábeta : tábe-ta	káetta : káet-ta	aketa : ake-ta

From examining these forms, you know that akeru is a Vowel verb (ake-ru), because it behaves just like tabéru and always has a vowel before the ending. But káeru turns out to be a Consonant verb (káer-u), because it behaves like noru and has a consonant before every ending. In

this book we will show which of the -eru and -iru verbs
have Consonant stems by citing the imperfect form with
a hyphen before the ending [for the Consonant verbs only]:
káer-u 'returns'. Some other verbs ending in -eru and -iru:

CONSONANT STEMS		VOWEL STEMS	
ir-u	'is necessary'	iru	'stays, exists'
kír-u	'cuts'	kiru	'wears on body'
háir-u	'enters'	dekíru	'is possible'
hashír-u	'runs'	okíru	'gets up'
nigir-u	'grasps, takes hold'	oriru	'gets off'
		sugíru	'is in excess, does in excess'
shir-u	'knows'		
kér-u	'kicks'	déru	'goes out, leaves[a place]'
		haréru	'gets clear'
		ireru	'inserts, puts in'
		tsukaréru	'gets tired'

NOTE: Most verbs with the imperfect ending in -eru or
-iru are VOWEL VERBS.

Here are some examples of these verbs in sentences:

Senséi ni átte kara, súgu
heyá ni hairimáshita.

As soon as I met the
teacher [in the hall], I
entered the room.

Ano kodomo wa isóide ha-
shítte imáshita ga, súgu
ni tsukaremáshita.

The child was running in
a hurry, and he soon
got tired.

Yōfuku o kite imáshita.

He was wearing a suit.

Pán o kirimáshita.

He cut the bread.

Watakushi wa uchi e káet-
te kimashita keredomo
Jírō wa imasén deshita.

I returned home, but Jiro
wasn't [there].

4. 5. IRREGULAR VERBS. There are only a few common verbs which have slight irregularities of inflection. The verbs **kúru** [kimásu] 'comes' and **suru** [shimásu] 'does' are irregular in the plain imperfect itself. [We would expect something like *kí-ru and *shi-ru if the verbs were regular.] Nearly everywhere else these verbs behave the way you would expect a vowel verb ending in -iru to behave:

IMPERFECT [Irregular!]	PERFECT	GERUND	INFINITIVE
kú-ru	ki-tá	ki-té	kí[-zero]
su-ru	shi-ta	shi-te	shi[-zero]

The verb **ik-u** 'goes'—in Western Japan **yuk-u**—is irregular only in the way the stem changes the -k to -t instead of -i before the t-endings:

ík-u	it-ta	it-te	ik-i

[We might have expected a form like *i-ita instead of the actual **it-ta,** if the verb were regular.]

There is one other verb which is irregular in the imperfect only. This is the verb **i[w]-u** 'says, tells'. We write this form **iu,** but it is actually pronounced as if it were written **yuu** or **yū.**

i[w]-u=iu [yuu]	it-ta	it-te	i[w]-i=ii

Note that the perfect and gerund forms of **iu** 'says', **iku** 'goes' and **ir-u** 'is necessary' are the same: **itta, itte.** You can tell them apart only by the rest of the sentence. (But some people pronounce **yutta** and **yutte** for 'said' and 'saying'.) Here are some examples of irregular verbs in sentences:

Nágoya e kúru to, dóno shigoto o shimásu ka?	When you come to Nagoya, which job will you do?
Koko e kité kara, iroiro omoshirói koto o shite asobimásu.	Since coming here, I've been enjoying myself with all sorts of fun.
Só itte, uchi e kaerimáshita.	Saying that [thus], he returned home.
Asoko e itte, iroiro hanashimáshita.	He went there and talked about various things.
Sō ittá keredomo, asoko e itta kotó wa arimasén deshita.	He said so, but he had never been [gone] there.
Kore máde jidósha de itta kotó wa arimasén deshita.	Until this [time], I'd never gone by car.
Dó suru tsumori désu ka?	What do you intend to do?
Sō shite, eigákan e ikimáshita.	[We did that and] then we went to the movie theater.
Shigoto o shi ni ikimáshita ka?	Did he go to do the job?
Amerika e iku tokí wa, fúne de ikimásu ka?	When you go to America, do you go by ship?
Máda anó hito o shōkai shimasén deshita ka?	Haven't I introduced him already?
Kekkon shité kara, Kánsai e ryokō shimáshita.	After getting married, we made a trip to Western Japan.

4. 6. ADJECTIVES AND THE COPULA. Adjectives in Japanese end in -ai like akai 'is red', -oi like aói 'is blue', -ui like warúi 'is bad', and -ii like ōkíi 'is big'. They are inflected simply by adding certain endings to the vowel before the -i, which is the imperfect ending itself:

	IMPERFECT	PERFECT	GERUND	INFINITIVE
UNACCENTED	–i	-katta	-kute	–ku
ACCENTED	-i	--katta	--kute	--ku

The copula is somewhat irregularly inflected so the forms are best learned just as separate words, rather than being broken into stem and ending. The adjective íi 'is good' has an alternant form yói 'is good'; the other forms are all based only on the form yói.

MEANING	IMPERFECT	PERFECT	GERUND	INFINITIVE
'equals, is'	dá	dátta	dé	——
'is red'	aka-i	aká-katta	aká-kute	aka-ku
'is blue'	aó-i	áo-katta	áo-kute	áo-ku
'is bad'	warú-i	wáru-katta	wáru-kute	wáru-ku
'is big'	ōkí-i	óki-katta	óki-kute	óki-ku
'is good'	í-i, yó-i	yó-katta	yó-kute	yó-ku
'is non-existent'	ná-i	ná-katta	ná-kute	ná-ku

NOTE: The word dé can be either (1) the particle—as in Amerika dé wa Eigo o hanashimásu 'In America they talk English', (2) the gerund of the copula—as in Kore wa Eikoku no zasshi dé, sore wa Beikoku no zasshi désu 'This is an English magazine and that is an American one', (3) the infinitive of déru 'goes out, leaves'—as in Háiri mo, dé mo shimasén deshita 'He neither entered, nor did he leave.'

Here are some examples of inflected forms of adjectives

and the copula used in sentences:

Suzuki-san wa shokkō dátta kotó ga áru kara, kōba no shigoto ga yóku wakarimásu.

Mr. Suzuki was a factory-worker, so he knows factory work very well.

Watakushi wa Amerika no senkyŏshi de, íma kono machi no kyōkai de shigoto o shite imásu.

I'm an American missionary and I am now working at the local church.

Watakushi no heyá wa chiisái desu ga, anó hito no wa ŏkikute íi desu nĕ.

My room is small, but his is nice and big, isn't it.

Máiasa, háyaku okíru to, shigoto ga dekimásu nĕ.

If you get up early every morning, you can get the job done, you know.

Osoku kitá kara, dekimasén deshita.

Because I came late, I couldn't get it done.

Kishá wa osoku náru to, damé desu nĕ.

If the train is late, it's no good, you know.

Ano éiga wa watakushi ga kirai dátta kara, tomodachi mo mí ni ikimasén deshita.

Because I didn't like that picture, my friend didn't go see it either.

Omoshírokatta desu nĕ!

It was interesting, wasn't it!

Mŏ osoku náru kara, uchi e kaerimásu.

It's getting late now ('already') so I'm going home.

Kono kishá wa háyakute íi desu nĕ.

This train is nice and fast, isn't it.

4. 7. USES OF THE PLAIN IMPERFECT AND PER-
FECT. Both imperfect and perfect are used before the
particle kara with the meaning 'because': soko ni áru kara
'because it's there', soko ni átta kara 'because it was there'.
Notice the difference in meaning between gerund + kara
and perfect + kara: Tomodachi ga kité kara, issho ni góhan o tabemáshita 'After my friend came, we had dinner
together.' Tomodachi ga kitá kara, issho ni góhan o tabemáshita 'Because my friend came, I had dinner with him.'

Before keredomo 'however, but', both imperfect and
perfect occur: Watakushi wa gakkō e ittá keredomo benkyō shimasén deshita 'I went to school but I didn't study.'
Watakushi wa gakkō e ikú keredomo ammari benkyō
shimasén 'I go to school but I don't study very much.'

Before the particle to meaning 'when, if' only the imperfect occurs: Háru ni náru to, oténki ga yóku narimásu
'When it gets to be spring, the weather gets nice.' Kodomo wa senséi o míru to, súgu heya no náka e hairimáshita
'As soon as they spotted the teacher, the children would
go into the room.' Yukí ga fúru to, uchi ni ite asobimashó
'If it snows, let's stay home and enjoy ourselves [here].'
Notice that a sentence of the type ...[suru] to, súgu...
[shimásu] has about the same meaning as one of the type
...shité (kara), súgu ...[shimásu] 'as soon as...' [Com-
pare 3. 16.]

Before the phrases kotó ga sukí dcsu 'likcs to', kotó ga
dekimásu 'can', and tsumori désu 'intends to', only the
imperfect occurs:

Oyógu koto ga sukí desu.   I like to swim.

Oyogu koto ga sukí de-shita.	I used to like to swim [but now I am an invalid and can't].
Oyógu koto ga sukí deshō.	You must like to swim.
Sakana o tabéru koto ga dekimásu ka?	Can you eat fish?
Sakana o tabéru koto ga dekimáshita ka?	Could you eat fish? Were you able to eat fish?
Sakana o tabéru koto ga dekíru deshō. (p. 141)	We will probably be able to eat fish.
Yamá e iku tsumori désu.	I intend to go to the mountains.
Yamá e iku tsumori dé-shita.	I intended to go to the mountains.
Yamá e iku tsumori deshō.	You must be planning to go to the mountains.

Before the phrase kotó ga áru 'there exists the fact of', either imperfect or perfect is used, depending on the meaning. If you use the imperfect, the meaning is 'sometimes': Kōen e itte sampo suru kotó ga arimásu 'I sometimes go to the park and take a walk'. Áki ni mo samúi kotó ga arimásu 'It is sometimes cold in autumn too'. Another, more emphatic way to say 'sometimes' is to use the noun tokidoki 'from time to time' in an adverbial way: Toki-doki kōen e sampo ni ikimásu 'I sometimes go to the park to take a walk.' These two can be combined: Tokidoki kōen e sampo ni iku kotó ga arimásu 'Sometimes it hap-pens that I go to the park for a walk'.

If you use the perfect before kotó ga áru, the meaning is 'has ever done, once did': Hibiya-kōen e sámpo ni itta kotó ga arimásu ka? 'Have you ever been [gone] to Hibiya Park for a walk?' Soko e itta kotó wa arimasén 'I've never been there'. Kóbe e ryokō shita kotó ga arimásu 'I once took a trip to Kobe'. Mó soko e itta kotó ga arimáshita ga, máe no ryokō wa fuyú deshita 'I had already been there [once], but the trip before was [in] winter'.

4. 8. USES OF THE INFINITIVE. The infinitive is a noun-like form of verbs and adjectives. There is no copula infinitive, except in the Impersonal Style (de ári, see the Appendix on Other Styles, p. 418), where the copula is always a phrase. But the particle ni functions as the copula infinitive in such phrases as shízuka ni 'quietly' (compare háyaku 'swiftly') and byooki ni náru 'gets sick' (compare yóku náru 'gets well').

The verb and adjective infinitives are used before various particles just as nouns are. Kaban o tóri ni ikimáshita 'I went to pick up the suitcase'; compare Sampo ni ikimáshita 'I went for a walk.' Osokú made benkyō shimáshita 'I studied till late'; compare Ban máde benkyō shimáshita 'I studied till evening'. For emphatic contrast, a verb infinitive is sometimes followed by the particle wa and some form of the verb suru: Oyógi wa shimasén deshita ga, asobi wa, yóku shimáshita 'I DIDN'T do any swimming, but I DID do a lot of playing'. Similarly, an adjective infinitive is followed by wa and a form of the verb áru: Chíisaku wa arimáshita keredomo, wáruku wa arimasén deshita 'It WAS small all right, but it WASN'T bad.'

The adjective infinitive often modifies other verb and adjective forms without any particle—this is similar to the ADVERB use of nouns without particles:

Sámuku narimáshita.	It got cold.
Háyaku arúite kimáshita.	He came walking fast.
Zubón wa ammari mijíka-ku shimáshita.	He made the pants too short.
Nágaku hanásu to, nódo ga kawakimásu.	When I talk for a long time, I get thirsty [my throat gets dry].

The infinitive yóku—íi 'is good'—has three slightly different meanings: 'well; often; a lot.' These are illustrated below:

Yóku narimáshita.	He got well.
Áme ga yóku furimásu.	It rains a lot.
Mómoko-san wa yóku éiga e ikimásu.	Momoko goes to movies often.

The meanings 'often' and 'a lot' are similar to English 'a good deal' as in 'it rains a good deal' and 'she goes to the movies a good deal'.

The verb infinitive is used to make compound verbs. For example, you can add the verb tsuzukeru 'continues something' to any verb infinitive to make a compound verb with the meaning 'continues to do something':

hanashi-tsuzukeru	continues talking
nomi-tsuzukeru	goes on drinking
wasure-tsuzukeru	keeps on forgetting
mi-tsuzukeru	keeps on looking

Another way of saying the same sort of thing is to use the gerund of tsuzukeru followed by some form of the verb:

tsuzukete hanásu 'keeps on talking', **tsuzukete míru** 'keeps on looking'.

Another kind of compound verb is made with the verb **naósu** 'repairs, fixes, cures' added to the infinitive; this means 'does something again [correcting one's error]':

kaki-naosu	writes again, corrects
yomi-naosu	reads again [correctly this time]

Somewhat similar are compound verbs made by attaching **kaeru** 'changes something' (**kae-ru,** do not confuse with **káer-u** 'returns') to an infinitive:

ki-káeru	changes clothes [wear-changes]
nori-káeru	changes trains [ride-changes]

Still another kind of compound verb is made by adding either **hajimeru** 'begins something' or **dásu** 'puts something out; starts something' to an infinitive:

hanashi-dashimáshita	he started talking
áme ga furi-hajimemáshita	it began to rain

The polite forms of the verbs are actually the infinitive plus an auxiliary verb -**másu: aruki-másu, nori-másu, mi-másu, shi-másu, yomi-másu.** So it is easy to find the infinitive; just remove the -**másu.**

A special type of compound is made by adding **sugíru**

'is in excess' to a verb infinitive (or to just the stem of an adjective, or to a copular noun):

tabe-sugimásu	he eats too much
hanashi-sugimásu	he talks too much
hataraki-sugíru to	if you over-work
oso-sugíru to	if you are too late
ōki-sugíru kara	because it is overly large
chiisa-sugimásu	it is overly small
shizuka-sugíru deshǒ	maybe it is too quiet

Finally, the verb infinitive is the source of many derived nouns: yasumí 'vacation' from yasúmi 'resting', hanashí 'story' from hanáshi 'talking', hajime 'beginning' from hajime 'beginning somehting', oyogí 'swimming' from oyógi 'swimming', tōrí 'street' from tǒri 'passing by'. There are a few nouns derived from adjective infinitives like yoroshiku 'regards' from yoroshiku 'being nice'—yoroshii 'is nice', chikáku 'vicinity' from chikáku 'being near'.

A special kind of noun is derived by adding the noun káta 'manner' to the infinitive. The meaning of these nouns is 'way or manner of [do]ing':

hanashikáta	way of talking
yomikáta	way of reading
kakikáta	way of writing
shikata	way of doing, means

Here arc some examples of these in sentences:

Soko e iku tsumori dátta keredomo shikata ga arimasén.	I had planned to go there, but there's no way [to do it].

Ano Beikokújin no hana-shikáta wa omoshirói desu nế.	That American has an interesting (or amusing) way of talking, hasn't he.

4. 9. THE PLAIN NEGATIVE. The plain form of the verb **arimásu** 'exists' is **áru.** The negative form of this is not a verb at all, but the adjective **nái,** 'is non-existent [=does not exist]'. The adjective **nái,** then, is the plain adjective form corresponding to the polite verb form **arimasén.** The plain negative of other verbs are also adjectives derived from the verb stems by the addition of the suffix **-(á)nai**—this is discussed in 5. 11. Here are some examples of the adjective **nái:**

Jidŏsha ga nái kara, dén-sha ni notte ikimásu.	I don't have a car, so I go by streetcar.
Mannénhitsu wa naku nari-máshita.	My fountain-pen has disappeared [become non-existent].
Tanaka-san wa sakúban naku narimáshita.	Mr. Tanaka passed away [became non-existent] last night.
Watakushi wa hón o naku shimáshita.*	I lost a book [made it non-existent].
Jidŏsha ga nákute, ikima-sén.	Without a car, I'm not going [I have no car, and I'm not going.]
Empitsu ga nákatta kara, kakimasén deshita.	I didn't have a pencil, so I didn't write it.

*Naku-naru 'gets lost; dies' and **naku-suru** 'loses' have no accent. **Naku-suru** is also treated as **nakus-u,** a consonant verb.

4. 10.   THE PARTICLE MO.   The particle **mo** means
'even' or 'also'.   After numbers it is sometimes equivalent
to 'as little as' or 'as much as'.   When there are two
phrases in a row, each ending in **mo**, the translation is
'both... and...' if the predicate is affirmative, '[n]either...
[n]or...' if the predicate is negative.

Koko mo kírei desu.	It's nice here too.
Kodomo mo oyógu koto ga dekimásu.	Even a child can swim.
Watakushi mo kánai mo Beikokújin desu.	Both my wife and I are Americans.
Gyūnyū mo, kōhíi mo kirai désu.	I don't like either milk or coffee.
Yamada-san mo Yamamoto-san mo Eigo ga dekimasén.	Neither Mr. Yamada nor Mr. Yamamoto can speak English.
Yamada-san mo Yamamoto-san mo Furansugo ga dekimásu.	Both Mr. Yamada and Mr. Yamamoto can speak French.

4. 11.   PARTICLE TO MEANING 'WHEN'.   The particle **to** occurs after the plain imperfect with the meaning
'when, whenever, if'.   Another way to say 'when'—with
reference to some specific time—is to use either the imperfect (with present meaning) or the perfect (with past
meaning) and follow this with the noun **toki** [sometimes
tóki] 'time'.   If by 'when' you mean 'during the interval
of' you can use the word **aida** 'interval' preceded by either
the imperfect or the perfect (depending on the meaning).
Aida or toki can be followed by **wa**, **ni** or **ní wa**   Here

are some examples:

Ōsaka e iku to, dóko ni tomaru tsumori désu ka?

When you go to Osaka, where do you plan to stay?

Kyónen, Amerika ni ita tóki, oténki ga warúi to, uchi ni ite, terevíjon o mimáshita.

Last year, when I was in America, when(ever) the weather was bad, we stayed in and watched television.

Kánai ga yasúnde ita aida, kodomo wa asobimáshita.

While my wife was resting, the kids played.

Tōkyō ni iru aida wa, Marunouchi-hóteru de tomaru tsumori désu.

While in Tokyo, I plan to stay at the Marunouchi Hotel.

Tōkyō ni iru tóki ni wa, watakushi no uchi e asobi ni kimasén ka?

When you're in Tokyo, won't you come to visit (with) my family (or at my house)?

Inaka ni ita tóki, Eigo o hanashimasén deshita.

When I was in the country, I didn't talk (any) English.

Tokí ni, ítsu Kamakurá e iku tsumori désu ka?

By the way, when do you plan to go to Kamakura?

Chiisái toki kara, oyogí ga dekimásu.

I've known how to swim since I was little.

Natsu no aida ní wa, Shiba-kōen e sampo ni iku tóki mo arimásu.

During the summer, there are also times when I go to Shiba Park for a walk.

Hima dá to, tomodachi ni tegami o kakimásu .	When I have time, I write letters to my friends.

4. 12. PARTICLE **KARA** MEANING 'SINCE' AND 'BE-CAUSE'. The particle **kara** after a noun usually means 'from' in a physical sense: **Kóbe kara** 'from Kobe'. From this it is extended to mean 'from' or 'after' or 'since' in a temporal sense: **kinó kara** 'from yesterday, since yesterday', **sore kara** 'from that, after that', **Amerika e káeru toki kara** 'from the time I return to America', **Nihón e kitá toki kara** 'from the time I came to Japan, since I came to Japan'. After a GERUND also it has the meaning of 'after': **Góhan o tábete kara, rájio o kikimáshita** 'After eating, we listened to the radio.'

But after the plain IMPERFECT or PERFECT, this particle means 'since' in the causal sense of 'because': **Warúi sakana o tábeta kara, byōki ni narimáshita** 'Because I ate some bad fish, I got sick'. You will find it conven-ient to translate this **kara** as 'so', since the word 'so' fits into English syntax at about the same point that **kara** fits into Japanese syntax; the main difference is that we often pause BEFORE 'so', but the Japanese pause AFTER **kara**.

In English we say things like 'I HAVE BEEN ill since last night. I've BEEN in Japan since last year' using a past tense even though we are still ill or in Japan at the time we are talking. In Japanese, the imperfect is used for these situations: **Sakúban kara byōki desu. Kyónen kara Nihón ni imásu.** Here are some examples of the uses of **kara**:

Ano nikú o tábete kara,	As soon as I ate that meat

súgu byōki ni narimá-shita.	I got sick.
Mō góhan o tábeta kara, súgu eigákan e ikimashṓ.	We've already eaten, so let's go to the movie theater right away.
Mō osói kara, isóide ikimashō.	It's already late, so let's hurry.
Háyakatta kara, yukkúri arúite kimashita.	It was early, so I came on foot, leisurely.

4. 13. MULTIPLE PARTICLES. Sometimes a word is followed by more than one particle. In such cases the meaning of the last particle restricts the meaning of the entire phrase leading up to it. For example, in the phrase **Nihón de wa** the particle **wa** sets off **Nihón de** 'in Japan' as the topic; in **koko ní mo arimásu** 'there's some here too', the particle **mo** gives special 'also'-meaning to the phrase **koko ní** in this place'; in **Tōkyō kará no kishá** 'the train from Tokyo', the particle **no** makes the entire phrase modify **kishá** [what kind of a **kishá**? the sort about which you can say **Tōkyō kara**].

Particles which occur after other particles are usually only the topic particle **wa**, the subject particle **ga**, the object particle **o**, and the intensive particle **mo**; these particles have somewhat more general meanings than those of **to** 'with', **ni** 'at, to', **e** 'to', **de** 'at' **máde** 'till', **kara** 'from', etc. The particles **wa**, **ga**, **o**, and **mo** never occur in sequences with each other—their meanings are mutually exclusive.

Examples of multiple particles in sentences:

Dáre ga Kátō-san to haná-shite imáshita ka?

Who was talking with Mr. Kato?

Kátō-san to wa Kubota-san ga hanáshite imashita.

It was Mr. Kubota who was talking with Mr. Kato. [With the other people, somebody else was talking.]

Ano heyá ni wa isu ga ari-másu ka?

Are there any chairs in that room?

Kono heyá ni mo isu ga arimásu.

There are chairs in this room, too.

Dáre ga Amerika kara ki-máshita ka?

Who came from America?

Amerika kará wa, wata-kushi no senséi ga kimá-shita.

It's my teacher who came from America.

Karúizawa e no kishá wa hayái desu ga, Níkkō e no wa ammari háyaku wa arimasén.

The train to Karuizawa is fast, but the one to Nik-ko isn't too fast.

Ueno-kōen made wa, dén-sha ni notte ikimáshita. Soko kará wa, arúite iki-máshita.

We went as far as Ueno Park by streetcar. From there, we walked.

Tsukue no ué ni mo zasshi ga arimásu.

There are magazines on top of the desk too [as well as in other places].

Tsukue no ué ni wa zasshi mo arimásu.

On top of the desk there are also magazines [as well as other things].

Amerika dé wa, háru ni

In America, it rains a lot

mo, áki ni mo, áme ga   both in spring and in
yóku furimásu.   fall.

4. 14. **KOTÓ.** The word **kotó** means 'thing [that you
can't touch or see]'; there is another word **monó** which
usually means 'thing [that you can touch or see]'. **Monó**
is also a humble word for 'person' (=**hito**); a vulgar
synonym (in both meanings) is **yátsu.** [**Kono yátsu, sono
yátsu, ano yátsu, dóno yátsu** are usually abbreviated to
koitsu, soitsu, aitsu, dóitsu.] For another use of **monó,**
see p. 410.

Sometimes the word **kotó** means 'act' or 'fact'. In this
lesson there are two special expressions with kotó: [**iku**]
kotó ga arimásu 'there exists the fact of [my going]=[I]
sometimes [go]' and [**itta**] **kotó ga arimásu** 'there exists the
fact of my having [gone]=I have [gone], I once [went]'.
Note that the difference in meaning between these two
expressions is carried by the mood of the verb in front of
kotó—the perfect (**itta**) is used with the meaning 'once did,
ever did' [negative 'never did'], the imperfect (**iku**) is used
with the meaning 'sometimes does' [negative 'never does'].
If you want to put either expression entirely in the perfect, you change the mood of the verb **arimásu: iku kotó
ga arimáshita** 'there existed the fact of my going=I sometimes went', **itta kotó ga arimáshita** 'there existed the fact
of my having gone=I had once gone'.

The relationship between the plain forms of the verb
(**iku** and **itta**) and the word **kotó** is that of modifier to
modified, with the meaning 'which (does or is)'—that is,
a **kotó** WHICH iku or itta, a **kotó** ABOUT WHICH YOU
CAN SAY iku or itta. The plain inflected forms in Jap-

anese can modify a noun (like **kotó**) directly, without any particle. Nouns, on the other hand, have to be followed by the particle **no** (or a modifying form of the copula **na** or **no,** see 5. 3) to modify another noun. The modifier relationship is further discussed in 5. 1. Further examples of expressions with **kotó:**

Sono hón o yónda kotó ga arimásu ka?	Have you [ever] read that book?
Amerika no éiga o míta kotó wa arimasén.	I've never seen an American movie.
Wai-emu-shíi-ē e oyógi ni iku kotó ga arimasén ka?	Don't you sometimes [ever] go to the YMCA for a swim?
Taitei jimúsho e yukkúri arúite ikimásu ga, toki- doki isógu kotó mo ari- másu.	Usually I walk leisurely to the office, but sometimes I rush, too.
Kyónen made wa, Kama- kurá e itta kotó wa ari- masén deshita.	Until last year, I had never been to Kamakura.
Amerika dé wa, Nihon no éiga o míru kotó wa ari- masén.	In America we never see Japanese movies.
Amerika dé wa, Nihongo o hanásu kotó wa arima- sén deshita.	In America we never used to talk Japanese .
Amerika dé mo Nihongo o hanásu kotó ga arimásu.	Even in America, people sometimes talk Japanese.
Sakúban made wa, hikŏki	Until last night I had

ni notta kotó wa arima-sén deshita.	never ridden in an airplane.

Another use of the noun kotó is in the phrases kotó ga sukí desu 'likes to' and kotó ga kirai désu 'dislikes to'. The basic meaning of these phrases, preceded always by a plain imperfect form, is 'the fact [of doing something] is liked' and 'the fact [of doing something] is disliked'. Here are some additional examples of these phrases:

Kodomo wa okáshi o tabé-ru kotó ga sukí desu ně.	Children do like to eat pastry, don't they.
Hito o nágaku mátsu kotó wa kirai désu.	I dislike waiting for people [so] long.
Onná ni áu kotó wa sukí ja arimasén ka?	Don't you like to meet girls?

A further use of kotó is in the phrase kotó ga deki-másu 'can [do something], is able to'. The basic meaning of this expression is something like 'the fact [of doing something] is produced', but it is the usual way to say 'can'.* This is not the expression used to translate the English 'can' used for 'may' in the sense of permission—'Father says I can go'. That expression is translated by a special phrase discussed in note 8. 6.

Instead of plain imperfect+kotó ga dekimásu, sometimes you will hear a noun derived from the infinitive+

---

*If the verb is suru the whole phrase is often abbreviated to dekíru: benkyō (suru kotó ga) dekíru 'can study', yásuku (suru kotó ga) dekíru 'can make it cheaper'. Cf. benkyō (shi) ni iku 'goes to study' (p. 98).

ga dekimásu; the meaning then is something more specific like 'knows how to' rather than the general meaning 'is able to' (which includes the specific meaning):

Kyŏ wa byōki dá kara, oyógu kotó wa dekimasén.	I'm sick today, so I can't swim.
Kyónen wa oyogí ga dekimasén deshita ga, íma wa dekimásu.	Last year I couldn't [didn't know how to] swim, but now I can.
Arúite iku kotó ga dekimásu ka?	Can we go on foot?
Kono hón wa isóide yómu kotó ga dekimásu ka?	Can you read this book in a hurry?
Kono jí o káku kotó ga dekimásu ka?	Can you write this character?

4. 15. **TSUMORI.** Tsumori is a noun with the meaning 'intention'. Preceded by the plain imperfect (like suru 'does') and followed by some form of the copula (like désu 'is'), this noun makes a phrase with the meaning 'it is [someone's] intention to [do something]=someone plans to do something'. If you want to change the tense of the expression—'it WAS somebody's intention to do something=someone planned to do something'—you just change the mood of the copula: suru tsumori déshita.*

Tsukáreta toki wa, sukóshi yasúmu tsumori désu.	When I get ('have gotten') tired, I plan to rest a bit.
Kómban terevíjon o miru tsumori ja arimasén. Rá-	This evening I do not intend to watch televi-

---

*But sometimes you will hear shita tsumori desu 'it is my intention to have [done]' 'I have tried to': kírei ni káita tsumori desu 'I have tried to write neatly'.

jio o kiku tsumori désu.

sion; I plan to listen to the radio.

Sakúban uchi ni ite tegami o káku tsumori dátta keredomo, íi oténki datta kara, kánai o tsurete kōen e sampo ni ikimáshita.

Last night I had intended to stay home and write letters, but it was nice weather, so I took my wife to the park for a walk.

Dóno hóteru de tomaru tsumori désu ka?

What hotel do you plan to stay at?

Ítsu kodomo to asobu tsumori désu ka?

When do you intend to play with the children?

4. 16. MORE ADVERBS. Here are some more adverbs [nouns often used without particles to modify predicates or whole sentences, see 3. 2] you will want to know: **sukóshi** or **chótto** 'a little, some, a bit', **máiban** 'every evening', **máiasa** 'every morning', **saikin** 'lately', **takusán** 'lots', **shikáshi** 'however', **taitei** 'usually' **futsū** 'usually', **tokidoki** 'sometimes', **tabitabi** 'often', **dandan** 'gradually', **nakanaka** 'quite, rather, completely, at all', **zúibun** 'very (much)', **taihen** 'very' [literally 'awfully, terribly'—compare **Taihen désu** 'It's awful, it's terrible'], **totemo** 'completely, quite', **sōtō** 'rather, considerably', **daibu** 'mostly, for the most part'.

Taihen (or Zúibun) omoshirói desu ne.

It's very interesting, isn't it.

Fúmiko-san wa máiban Eigo o benkyō shimásu.

Fumiko studies English every night.

Tai̇tei yōfuku o kite imásu ga, tokidoki kimono o kiru kotó ga arimásu.

She usually wears Western clothes, but sometimes she puts on a kimono.

Máiasa háyaku ókite, isóide jimúsho e ikimásu.

Every morning she gets up early and hurries to the office.

Tabitabi éiga o mí ni ikimásu ga, éiga wa Amerika nó da to nakanaka wakarimasén.

I often go to the movies, but when the movie is an American one, I won't understand it at all.

Amerika no éiga wa futsū, totemo íi desu ne.

American movies are usually quite good, you know.

Shikáshi, warúi éiga mo arimásu ně.

But they (sometimes) have bad movies too, don't they.

Ano onná wa zúibun kírei desu ně.

That girl is quite attractive isn't she.

Watakushi wa nágaku byōki déshita ga, dandan yóku narimásu.

I was sick for a long time, but I'm gradually getting better.

Beikokújin wa dáibu jidōsha ni notte ryokō shimásu ně.

Americans for the most part travel by car, don't they.

Kono depáto wa sōtō ōkíi desu ně.

This department store's rather large, isn't it.

4. 17. MORE GERUND EXPRESSIONS.   ERRANDS.

The verbs mótsu 'holds, has, owns' and tóru 'picks up, takes' are used in several expressions meaning 'brings, takes, carries [things]'. **Motte iku** 'holds and goes = takes', totte iku 'picks up and goes, carries [off]'; **motte kúru** 'holds and comes = brings', totte kúru 'picks up and comes, carries [over]'. Remember, to take or bring PEOPLE requires the verb **tsureru**—hito o tsurete kúru 'brings someone [else]'—and is generally used only when the person being brought is socially inferior to the one bringing.

Here are some more examples:

Náni o mótte imasu ka?	What do you have (there)?
Ié o mótte imasu ka?	Do you own a house?
Jibikí o motté kite kudasai.	Please bring a dictionary.
Kono hón o motte ikimásu ka?	Are you taking this book (with you)?
Jíro o tsureté kite kudasai.	Please bring Jiro.
Kurói yōfuku o tótte kaban ni iremáshita.	He picked up a black suit and put it in his suitcase.
Éki e kaban o motte ikimáshita.	He went to the station carrying his suitcase.

In English, when someone goes on an errand and returns we mention his GOING and DOING THE ERRAND; we usually skip saying he came back: 'He went and got his laundry. He went and met Taro (and came back). I'm going to go fix the car. Let's go buy that book.' The Japanese usually skip the part about going, and mention DOING THE ERRAND and COMING back: **Sentakumono o totte kimáshita. Táro ni átte kimáshita. Jidōsha o naóshite kimásu. Ano hón o katte kimashō.**

4. 18. GERUND + IRU. In Lesson 2, we found that
the verb iru [imásu] means 'stays, [a living being] exist [in
a place]': Watakushi wa Nihón ni imásu 'I am in Japan',
Ono-san ga Kúre ni ita toki 'when Mr. Ono was in Kure',
Anáta wa íma dóko ni imásu ka? 'Where are you now?'
In Lesson 3, we found that a gerund [-te form] plus the
verb iru means '[somebody or something] is doing something'*:

Náni o shite imásu ka?	What are you doing?
Kōbá de hataraite imásu.	He's working at the factory.
Dóko ni súnde imásu ka?	Where are you living?
Anáta wa dóno hóteru ni tomátte imásu ka?	Which hotel are you stop- ping at?

With intransitive verbs—those which do not ordinarily
take a direct object, like 'goes, comes, gets tired, gets
cloudy, clears up, becomes'—there is another meaning for
the gerund + iru. With intransitive verbs denoting a
single, specific act—like 'gets to be something, becomes, goes,
comes, changes [into]'—the most usual meaning of this construction is the present RESULT of an action that has
ALREADY taken place. So tsukárete imasu usually doesn't
mean 'is getting tired'—but that meaning is possible in
certain situations—instead, it more often means just 'is
tired' [is in a state resulting from having become tired].
It's like the use of gerunds in series to show sequence of
action: Góhan o tábete, éiga o mí ni itte, káette kara, benkyō shite, tsukárete nemáshita 'I ate, went to see a movie,

---

*The first vowel of iru often drops: shite (i)másu, súnde (i)masu.
Accent note: shite ita = shité 'ta, shite iru = shité 'ru or shite 'ru.

and after returning, I studied, got tired, and went to bed'.
Tsukárete imáshita means 'I got tired and then stayed
(that way), I got tired and then (just) existed (that way) =
I was tired'; **tsukárete imásu** means 'I got tired and now
stay (that way), I got tired and now (just) exist (that
way) = I am tired'. The more usual meaning for **Jidŏsha
wa asoko de** (or **ni**) **tomatte imásu** is 'The cars are parked
over there'.

Remember that with the construction gerund + **iru**,
the subject can be either a living being or an inanimate
object; with **iru** all by itself, the subject is ordinarily limited to a living being. Here are more examples.

Sora ga haréru to, hi ga déte kimasu.	When the sky clears up, the sun comes out.
Sora ga hárete, hi ga déte kite imásu.	The sky is clear[ed] and the sun is [come] out.
Hayashi-san ga kité imasu.	Mr. Hayashi is here [has arrived].
Máda Hánako ga káette kite imasén ka?	Isn't Hanako back yet?
Máda gakkō e itte imasén ka?	Hasn't he gone to school yet?
Kodomo wa mŏ nete imásu.	The children are already asleep.
Kodomo ga nete ita aida (ni), watakushi wa kimo-no o kaban ni iremáshita.	While the children were sleeping, I put [our] clothes in the suitcases.

Kono jígyō wa mǒ ǒkiku nátte imasu ně.	This enterprise (business) has already gotten big, hasn't it.
Uchi no Tárō wa mō senséi ni nátte imasu.	Our Taro is [has] already become a teacher.
Góhan wa mǒ dékite imasu.	The meal's ready now. [dékite imasu = is produced or prepared and stays]

4. 19. **ASOBU.** The verb **asobu** means 'enjoys oneself'. It is used for English 'plays, has fun, goes on a pleasure trip, pays a (social) call, visits (for pleasure)' and other expressions. Here are some examples:

Kyónen Kamakurá e asobi ni ikimáshita.	Last year I went to Kamakura (on my vacation).
Kodomo wa uchi no sóba de asonde imásu.	The children are playing beside the house.
Kómban asobi ni kimasén ka?	Won't you come visit [us] this evening?
Machí e itte asobimashǒ.	Let's go to town and have some fun.

C. EXERCISES.

1. Insert the proper inflected forms in the blank spaces. Do it orally.

1. Náni o —— imásu ka?	What are you EATING?
2. Nihón no éiga o —— kotó ga arimásu ka?	Have you ever SEEN a Japanese film?
3. Soko de —— kotó ga arimasén ka?	Don't you ever SWIM there?

4. Éki de Yókota-san ni —— tsumori déshita.

I intended to MEET Miss Yokota at the station.

5. Kishá wa —— kara, sonó hito ni aimasén deshita.

The train WAS EARLY (fast), so I didn't meet her.

6. Kokuden ni —— kimáshita.

I came (RIDING) on the Government Electric.

7. Kánai wa kodomo o —— ni itte imásu.

My wife has gone to CALL the children.

8. Tárō wa hón o —— ni ikimáshita.

Taro went to BUY a book.

9. Ammari háyaku —— to, súgu tsukaremásu.

If you WALK too fast, you get tired right away.

10. Hima —— to,. úmi .e ——, hamá de —— kotó ga sukí desu.

When I AM at leisure, I like to GO to the sea(shore) and PLAY on the beach.

11. Amerika ni —— tóki mo, tokidoki Nihongo o —— kotó ga arimáshita.

Even when I LIVED in America, sometimes I TALKED Japanese.

12. Kyōto ni —— aida, dóko de —— tsumori désu ka?

Where do you intend to STAY (STOP) while you are in Kyoto?

13. Jidōsha wa dóko de —— imásu ka?

Where's the car PARKED?

14. Matsumoto-san wa máda —— imasén ka?

Hasn't Mr. Matsumoto COME yet?

15. Tegami o —— ni uchi e káette kite imasu.

I'm back home to WRITE a letter.

2. In each of these groups of expressions, one is a misfit. The others all have something grammatically in common. Can you pick the misfits?

1. (a) akai   (b) omoshirói   (c) isóide   (d) arúku
2. (a) déte imasu   (b) hanáshite   (c) tsukárete imasu   (d) kité imasu
3. (a) itta   (b) dátta   (c) yónda   (d) ákakute

4. (a) katte   (b) shírokute   (c) dé   (d) dátta
5. (a) désu   (b) dátta   (c) dé   (d) asobi
6. (a) chíisaku   (b) hataraki   (c) káku   (d) yómi
7. (a) aói   (b) tábeta   (c) míta   (d) nákatta
8. (a) ake   (b) mí   (c) dé   (d) kité
9. (a) kí   (b) nátta   (c) aketa   (d) déta
10. (a) háyaku   (b) iru   (c) arúku   (d) káku

3. Part of the following words can be translated by some form of the verb 'is'—'was, be, being, been'—in English. Pick these words out from the others.

(a) déte.   (b) dé   (c) dá   (d) ári
(e) i   (f) náru   (g) arúita   (h) déta
(i) désu   (j) ite   (k) imásu   (l) itte
(m) átte   (n) nátta   (o) demáshita (p) imáshita
(q) arimáshita   (r) deshŏ   (s) itta   (t) iru
(u) demashŏ   (v) déru   (w) ii   (x) átta
(y) áru   (z) irimásu

4. Here are some new verbs. Make up the forms to fill in the blanks for them by analogy with the verb whose forms are given on the right.

shiméru : ——— 'closes'   tabéru : tábeta 'eats'
níru : ——— 'resembles'   míru   : míta 'sees'
koshikakéru : ——— 'sits down'   déru   : dé 'goes out'
yamu : ——— 'stops, ceases'   yómu   : yónde 'reads'
tobu : ——— 'flies, jumps'   yobu   : yonda 'calls'
núgu : ——— 'takes off clothes'   oyógu   : oyóide 'swims'
haku : ——— 'puts on feet'   káku   : káita 'writes'
sóru : ——— 'shaves off'   noru   : notte 'rides'
kátsu : ——— 'wins'   mátsu   : máchi 'waits'
omóu : ——— 'thinks, feels'   áu   : átta 'meets'
dásu : ——— 'puts out, sends'   hanásu : hanáshi 'speaks'

D. COMPREHENSION.

[Watakushi wa Amerika kára no fúne de, Suzuki-san ni aimásu.]

Watakushi. Gomen nasái. Anáta wa Suzuki-san deshǒ?

Suzuki. Sǒ desu. Anáta wa Wílson-san desu ka? Dǒzo yoroshiku.

W. Dǒzo yoroshiku. Kyǒ wa oténki ga totemo íi desu ně.

S. Sǒ desu ně. Késa háyaku ókite, sukóshi sampo shite ita tokí wa, sóra ga máda kumótte ita keredomo, góhan o tábete kara míru to, mǒ dáibu hárete, hi ga déte kite imáshita. Anáta wa mǒ góhan o tabemáshita ka?

W. Máda desu. Watakushi to issho ni shokudō e itte, kōhíi o nomimasén ka?

S. Arígatō. Sono aida, iroiro hanásu kotó ga dekimásu ně. Tokí ni, anáta wa oyógu kotó ga sukí desu ka?

W. Dáisuki desu ně. Kono fúne de wa, oyógu kotó ga dekimásu ka ?

S. Dekimásu. Futsū, fúne de wa dekimasén ga, kono fúne wa sōtō ōkíi kara, dekimásu. Kōhíi o nónde kara, issho ni oyógi ni ikimasén ka?

W. Sore wa omoshirói deshō. San-Furanshísuko ni ita tóki, máinichi Wai-emu-shíi-ē e itte oyogimáshita. Anáta wa asoko e itta kotó ga arimásu ka?

S.   Arimasén. Nihón de wa tokidoki Kamakurá
          e itte, hamá de asobimásu. Soko no úmi de
          oyógu kotó mo arimásu. Anáta wa Nihon no
          dóko e iku tsumori désu ka?
W.   Tōkyō e iku tsumori désu. Shikáshi, wata-
          kushi wa jitsugyōka dá kara, tabitabi ryokō
          suru tsumori désu. Nágoya e mo, Ōsaka é
          mo ikimásu. Anáta wa Tōkyō ni súnde
          imasu ka?
S.   Iie. Yokohama désu. Tōkyō dé wa dóko
          de tomaru tsumori désu ka?
W.   Tōkyō dé wa, tomodachi ga súnde iru kara,
          sonó hito no uchi de tomaru tsumori désu
          ga, Ōsaka e itté kara wa hóteru deshō.
S.   Ōsaka ní wa hóteru ga takusán arimásu ga,
          Ōsaka-hóteru wa totemo íi desu. Ōkikute,
          kírei desu. Watakushi wa soko de tomatta
          kotó ga arimásu. Sore wa kyónen no natsu
          no kotó deshita. Kánai to kodomo o tsurete
          Ōsaka e yasumí ni ikimáshita. Taitei, úmi
          e ikimásu ga, kyónen wa Ōsaka soko e itte
          asobimáshita.
W.   Watakushi wa Ōsaka e itta kotó wa arimasén
          ga, sōtō omoshirói deshō. Ja, íma oyógi ni
          ikimashō ka?
S.   Hái, ikimashō.

LESSON 5.

A. BASIC SENTENCES. 'Business.'

1. Sakúban watakushi ga shimbun o yónde ita tokoró e Kitani-san ga asobi ni kitá n(o) desu.

   Last night when I had just been reading the paper, Mr. Kitani came to call.

2. Watakushi wa mádo kara Kitani-san ga kúru no o míta no de, tátte genkan e ittá n(o) desu.

   From the window I saw Mr. Kitani coming, so I stood up and went to the front door.

3. Sakúban asobi ni kitá Kitani-san wa Nîp-pon-Bōeki-Kabushiki-Gáisha no shachō ná n(o) desu.

   (The) Mr. Kitani who came to visit me last night is President of the Japan Trade Company, Inc.

4. Kitani-san no kaisha wa kaigai e iroiro na shinamono o yushutsu shite imásu.

   Mr. Kitani's company exports all sorts of goods overseas.

5. Kaigai kara yunyū suru monó wa takái no de, íma wa ammari yunyū shite imasén.

   Because the things they import from abroad are costly, they are not importing very much now.

6. Kitani-san to issho ni   The man who came with

kitá hito wa Ōsaka no kinuorimono-kŏba no shihái-nin no Ōtake-san déshita.

Mr. Kitani was Mr. Otake who is the manager of a silk-mill in Osaka.

7. Sono kōbá wa gaikoku no shihon o irete kaigai e yushutsu suru kinu-orímono o tsukúru n(o) desu.

His factory brings in foreign capital and makes silk fabrics to export overseas.

8. Kono kinu-orímono no kaisha no kabu o katta hitó wa Amerika ni súnde imasu.

The people who bought the stock of the silk-mill company live in America.

9. Ōtake-san wa gaikoku-káwase o shirábe ni Tōkyō e kitá n(o) desu.

Mr. Otake came to Tokyo to investigate the foreign-exchange (rates).

10. Sono kaisha no shasai wa Nihón de uranái de, Ōtake-san ga kaigai e itte uru kotó ni nátte imasu.

Instead of floating the company's bonds in Japan, Mr. Otake is to go abroad to sell them.

11. Asátte Tōkyō o tátsu kotó ni nátte iru kara, sakúban watakushi n(o) tokoró e asobi ni kitá n(o) desu.

He is to leave Tokyo day after tomorrow, so he came to visit me last night.

12. Ōtake-san wa tátsu mae ni, gaikoku-káwase no

I expect before Mr. Otake leaves (town) he will

keiken no áru hitó de, Kitani-san no kaisha ni tsutómete iru sháin to hanásu deshō.

talk to staff members employed by Mr. Kitani's company who have foreign-exchange experience.

13. Shihái-nin ga káeru made wa, dáre ga kawari ni kōbá o keiei surú deshō ka nế.

I wonder who'll run the mill in the manager's place while he is away.

14. Sensō no máe wa, watakushi mo sono kōbá ni tsutómete itá n(o) desu.

Before the war, I was also employed at that factory.

15. Sono kóro wa, rōdósha o sonna ni yatótte inakattá n(o) desu.

At that time they didn't hire so many workers.

16. Íma wa, sono kōbá de hataraite iru hitó wa óku narimáshita.

Now there are quite a few people working in that factory. [The people... have become numerous.]

17. Shikáshi (desu né), sono kōin wa chíngin ga yasúi n(o) de, yóku sutoráiki o shimásu.

But (you see), since the factory hands' wages are low, they strike a lot.

18. Watakushi wa íma n(o) tokoro, Asahi-shímbun no kishá na n(o) desu.

At present I'm a writer (reporter) on the newspaper Asahi.

19. Kéizai ya zaisei no kíji o káite imasu.

20. Seiji no kíji o káku no wa watakushi ja arimasén.

21. Kitani-san to Ōtake-san ga kúru máe ni kánai ga iroiro oishii tabémono o koshiraete mátte imáshita.

22. Watakushi wa asátte, issho ni hikōjō e itte Ōtake-san o mi-okuru tsumori ná n(o) desu.

23. Ma ni áu yō ni, Kitani-san no jidōsha ni notte iku kotó ni mátte imasu.

24. Sono kuruma wa chótto furúi no ni, yóku hashirimásu.

25. Ōtake-san wa Eigo ga yóku dekíru kara, Amerika de shasai o urú no ni komaránai deshō.

I write the articles on economics and finance.

I'm not the one who writes the articles on politics.

Before Mr. Kitani and Mr. Otake arrived, my wife had prepared various tasty foods and was waiting [with the foods for them].

I plan to go along to the airport day after tomorrow and see Mr. Otake off.

So as to* be on time, we are to go in Mr. Kitani's automobile.

In spite of the fact that his car is a bit old, it runs well.

Mr. Otake speaks English well, so I guess he won't have any trouble selling the bonds in America.

---

*For (suru) yó ni 'so as to (do)' see pp. 235-6.

26. **Eigo no dekínai hitó ni wa sō iu shigoto wa muzukashíi deshō né.**

That would be a difficult job for a person who didn't know English, wouldn't it.

27. **Watakushi wa Eigo no shimbun o yómu no ni, jibikí ga irimásu.**

I need a dictionary to read an English (language) newspaper.

28. **Wakaránai kotobá ga ói kara, háyaku yómu kotó wa dekínai n(o) desu.**

There are many words I don't understand, so I can't read rapidly.

VOCABULARY ITEMS

VERBS AND PHRASES

shirabéru	checks up on. investigates	**kariru**	borrows
		kasu	lends
yatóu	hires, employs	**[kishá ni]**	'meets the interval'
tsutoméru	gets (is) employed	**ma ni áu**	=is on time [for
tsukau	uses		the train]
tsukúru	makes, manufactures	**ir-u**	is needed, wanted
		uru	sells
hajimaru	it begins	**(ni) komáru**	is troubled (by),
hajimeru	begins it		has difficulties
owaru	it ends; ends it		(with)
yamu	it ceases	**yogoreru**	gets dirty, soiled
yaméru	ceases it, gives up (doing something)	**(hito ni) denwa o kakéru (or suru)**	
wasureru	forgets		makes a phone-call (to a person)

ADJECTIVES

sukunái	is little, are few	**kitanái**	is dirty
ói, [oói]	is much, are many	**isogashíi**	is busy, rushed

NOUNS

kaisha	company, firm, 'the office'	yunyú-hin	import goods
shádan	corporation	yushutsú-hin	export goods
dantai	group	hōkyū, sárarii	salary
kabu(shiki)	stock	kyūryō, chíngin	wages
kabushiki-gáisha	stock company, Inc. (="K.K.")	gekkyū	monthly salary
kabuya	stock-broker	sararíi-man, gekkyū-tori	salaried man, white-collar worker
Kabuto-chō	the Japanese "Wall Street"	kómon	adviser
ne(dan)	price	isha	doctor, physician
hajimé-ne	opening price	kusuri	medicine
taká-ne	the high (price)	keiken	experience
yasú-ne	the low (price)	taiken	an experience
owarí-ne	closing price	tokoro (p. 428)	place
shasai	(corporate) bonds	késhiki	scenery
sháin	staff, company employee	kamí	paper
		jishin	earthquake
shishá	branch office	káji, kásai	fire (accident)
hónsha	main office	hoken	insurance
shiten	branch store	takushii, háiyā	taxi, cab
honten	main store		
jígyō	enterprise	kuruma	car; taxi; cart
jitsugyō	business	shūsen	end of the war
misé	store, shop	(shū)séngo	after the war
sambutsu	products	shūscn (-chokugo)	(right after) the war

B. STRUCTURE NOTES

5.1. MODIFIERS. In English one noun can modify [restrict the meaning] of another noun just by standing next to it: 'Air-raid Precaution Instruction Manual; World War II Casualty Lists'. In Japanese, when one noun modifies another, the two are usually connected by the particle no. In the case of book titles, names of organizations and institutions, frequently several nouns may be combined to make a COMPOUND NOUN: **Hyōjun-**

Nihongo-Tokúhon 'Standard Japanese Language Readers', **Nippon-Bōeki-Kabushikí-Gáisha** 'The Japan Trade Co., Inc.' But these are special cases. Ordinarily, modifying nouns are followed by **no**:

Nihongo no jibikí	a Japanese (language) dictionary
Eikoku no jitsugyōka	an English businessman
sakúban no shimbun	last night's paper
watakushi no hón	my book
Ōsaka no kōbá	the Osaka factory; factories in Osaka

If you turned these phrases around and made them into full sentences they would read like this:

Kono jibikí wa Nihongo nó desu.	This dictionary is a Japanese one.
Sono jitsugyōka wa Eikoku nó desu.	That businessman is one of England's.
Sono shimbun wa sakúban no desu.	That newspaper is last night's.
Watakushi no hataraite iru kōbá wa Ōsaka nó desu.	The factory where I work is the Osaka one.

Now in English when a verb or verb phrase modifies a noun, it FOLLOWS the noun and is introduced by a word like WHICH, THAT, WHO, WHEN: 'The man WHO came yesterday, the book WHICH is on the table, the movie THAT I saw, the time WHEN we were in Osaka.' Notice that sometimes the introductory word may be omitted in English: 'the movie I saw, the time we went to Osaka'. Japanese verbs and verb phrases PRECEDE the noun they modify and HAVE NO INTRODUCTORY WORD OR LINKING PARTICLE:

kinō kitá hito	the man who came yesterday
tēburu no ue ni áru hón	the book which is on the table
míta éiga	the movie I saw
Ōsaka ni ita tóki	the time we were in Osaka

You have already had expressions like **iku tsumori** 'intention of going', **oyógu koto** 'the fact of swimming', **itta kotó** 'the fact of having gone'. These are examples of modifier expressions.

The modifying expression preceding a noun phrase may be very short or it may be quite long. It will always make a complete sentence by itself except that the predicate part is in the plain form, and you would want to change this to the polite form to use as a complete sentence. Notice that the MEANING of the juxtaposition between the modifying verb and the noun may be either that of SUBJECT or OBJECT relationship:

míta hito	the man who saw [it]
míta hito	the man whom [someone] saw

The relationship is usually made clear by the particles in the rest of the clause:

| sono éiga o míta hito | the man who saw that movie |
| watakushi ga míta hito | the man I saw |

The subject of a modifying clause is never followed by wa—that would make it the topic for the entire sentence, not just the modifying clause. It is marked either by **ga** (emphatic), or by **no** (non-emphatic). If you like, you may think of **no** as replacing the particle **wa** in modifying clauses:

Anó hito wa sono éiga o mimáshita.	He saw THAT MOVIE.
Anó hito no míta éiga...	THE MOVIE (that) he saw...
Anó hito ga sono éiga o mimáshita.	HE saw that movie.
Anó hito ga míta éiga...	The movie (that) HE saw..

In other words, only sentences have topics; clauses have subjects (or objects). The particle used for the non-emphatic subject of a clause is **no**, the particle used for the emphatic subject is **ga**. If the modifying clause is quite long and the subject is separated from the verb by a number of words, the emphatic subject particle **ga** is usually used.

Anáta no tábeta sakana wa yókatta desu ka?	Was the fish you ate all right?
Sakana o tábeta hito wa byōki ni narimáshita.	The people who ate fish got sick.
Ōtake-san o mátte iru hito	The person waiting for

wa Tárō desu.	Miss Otake is Taro.
Tárō no mátte iru tokoro wa ekimáe desu.	The place where Taro is waiting is the [square in] front of the station.
Tárō no mátte iru hito wa Ōtake-san désu.	The person Taro is waiting for is Miss Otake.
Tárō ga Ōtake-san o mátte iru tokoro wa ekimáe desu.	The place where Taro is waiting for Miss Otake is the station square.
Ekimáe de Ōtake-san o mátte iru Tárō wa watakushi no tomodachi désu.	Taro, who is waiting for Miss Otake at the station square, is my friend.
Kinō Tárō no uchi e asobi ni kúru tsumori dátta Ōtake-san wa késa no kishá de kitá no desu.	Miss Otake, who had planned to visit Taro's family yesterday, came by this morning's train.

When you hear long modifier clauses in actual conversation, you may be confused as to the breaking-point—where the modifier stops and the part modified begins. Listen for the PLAIN IMPERFECT and PERFECT forms—forms like **suru, shita; iku, itta; kúru, kita; tabéru, tábeta;** unless followed by a particle like **keredomo** or **kara,** they probably modify the word or phrase which follows. At the breaking point, stick in a 'which', and then make mental switch of the two parts around to the usual English order. This is just a first-aid measure, of course; after you get used to modifier clauses, you will be putting them in quite naturally like a Japanese, without worrying about the fact that in English you would reverse the order. Remember—everything up to the breaking point modifies the following noun expression. Notice the breaking points [indicated by a slant bar] in the following examples. But try to avoid pausing—the "breaking point" is in your head, not on your tongue.

Ano shimbun o katta/hito wa, Tárō deshō.

The person who bought that newspaper must be Taro.

Hón o yónde iru/ano musumé wa, kírei desu ně.

That girl who's reading the book is pretty, isn't she.

Ano hón o yónde iru/musumé wa, dáre deshō ka.

I wonder who the girl reading that book is.

Kinō, Aoki-san ni átta / toki, áme ga futté imashita.

Yesterday when I met Mr. Aoki, it was raining.

Oyógi ni itta / tokoro wa, dóko desu ka?

Where did they go to swim?

Háyaku ókita/hito wa, mǒ dekakemáshita.

The people who got up early have already left.

Nihongo o benkyō shite iru / aida wa, Eigo o hanashimasén.

When we're studying Japanese, we don't talk English.

5. 2. ADJECTIVE MODIFIER CLAUSES. In English, adjectives work much like nouns. Just as nouns stand in a row modifying each other, an adjective can modify a noun just by standing next to it: 'a good book, nice weather.' In Japanese, you will recall, nouns can not modify by simple juxtaposition. Japanese adjectives, however, work like Japanese verbs—they modify just by standing next to a noun phrase: **ii hón** 'a book WHICH

IS good = a good book', íi oténki 'weather WHICH IS good = nice weather'. Notice that the full meaning of real adjectives in Japanese is not just 'good, bad, white, red' and the like but 'IS good, IS bad, IS white, IS red' etc.: íi kara 'because it's good', wárukatta keredomo 'it was bad, but', shírokute íi kara 'it's nice and white, so...' Some Japanese words which TRANSLATE as English adjectives—because two languages never dovetail their word classes together completely—are NOUNS in Japanese and when they are modifiers they behave as nouns: byōki 'sick [state]', byōki no hito 'a sick person'; futsū 'usual(ly)', futsū no hitó 'the usual person'; ippai 'full', ippai no hako 'a full box'.*

Just as verbs can have a subject in Japanese, so can adjectives. And in modifier clauses, the particle which follows the subject is either ga (emphatic) or no (non-emphatic):

oténki ga warúi tokoro   a place where the WEATH-
                          ER's bad
oténki no warúi tokoro   a place where the weather's
                          BAD

Here are some additional examples of adjectives in sentences:

Okane no nái hito wa tabéru kotó ga dekimasén.	A man who hasn't any money can't eat.
Okane no nákatta hito wa	The man who didn't have

---

*Compare the adverb yukkúri 'leisurely, slow' (yukkúri shita hanashikáta 'a leisurely manner of speaking') and the copular nouns on p. 136.

tabéru kotó ga dekima-
sén deshita.

Toshókan wa hón no ói
tokoro desu né.

Hito no sukunái tokoro ga
sukí desu.

Késhiki no íi tokoro wa
sukúnaku arimasén né.

Ataráshikute íi jidósha wa
taihen takái desu né.

Kodomo no asobu kōen wa
sōtō ōkíi tokoro deshō.

Dandan sukúnaku nátta
okane wa mó hotóndo
naku narimáshita.

Chíisakatta kodomo wa mó
ōkiku narimáshita né.

Tabemóno no oishii tokoro
de tabemashó.

Kao no kitanái kodomo
désu.

any money couldn't eat.

A library is a place where
there are lots of books
[the books are many],
isn't it.

I like a place where there
aren't many people
[people are few].

There are quite a few
places where the scen-
ery is nice, aren't there.
[places are not few]

A good new car [a car
which is new and good]
is very expensive, isn't it.

The park where the child-
ren play must be rather
large.

My money, which has grad-
ually gotten less, is now
almost gone.

The little child [the child
who was little] had al-
ready gotten big, you see.

Let's eat some place where
the food is good [tasty].

He's the child with the
dirty face.

5. 3. COPULA MODIFIER CLAUSES. Something special happens when a copula clause—like **senkyōshi desu** 'it's a missionary', **byōki désu** 'he's sick', **kírei desu** 'it's pretty'—is used as a modifier clause. From the following analogies—

hito ga tabéru : tabéru hito   oténki ga íi : íi oténki

we would expect something like—

Brown-san ga senkyŏshi da : senkyŏshi da Brówn-san

Instead, what actually occurs is **senkyŏshi NO Brówn-san** 'Mr. Brown WHO IS a missionary'. Now this **no** is not the particle which shows that one noun modifies another—it isn't 'Mr. Brown's missionary', it is 'Mr. Brown WHO IS the missionary'. Instead, this **no** is a special form of the copula, an alternant of the word **dá** which occurs whenever a copular clause is put in the modifier position before a noun phrase. You can see the difference between the particle **no** and the copula-alternant **no** [= **dá**] here:

jitsugyōka no tomodachi   the businessman's friend
jitsugyōka no tomodachi   the friend WHO IS a businessman

Since the two expressions sound just alike, you have to tell from context or situation which **no** it is you are hearing. Most of the time, there is little doubt.

5. 4. COPULAR NOUNS IN MODIFIER CLAUSES. But **no** is not the only alternant of **dá**—there is also an alternant **ná** which occurs after COPULAR NOUNS. These are a special sort of noun which do not often occur before particles like **wa, ga, o**—but occur before some form of the copula [**désu, dá, ná**] or before the particle **ni**. When these copular-noun clauses—like **kírei desu** 'is pretty'—occur in modifier position, the expected form **dá** occurs in the alternant shape **ná–kírei na onná** 'girls WHO ARE pretty' or 'pretty girls'. In citing nouns it is convenient to note the ones which are copular nouns by adding in parentheses (**na**). Here are some common ones:

báka (na)	fool, foolish	**jōbu (na)**	strong, rough
kírei (na)	pretty, neat, clean	**shitsúrei (na)**	rude
sukí (na)	liked, likable	**téinei (na)**	polite
dáisuki (na)	greatly liked	**taihen (na)**	terrific, terrible,
kirai (na)	disliked, dislikable		quite a
dáikirai (na)	greatly disliked	**suteki (na)**	excellent, swell
rakú (na)	comfortable	**rippa (na)**	splendid, elegant
shízuka (na)	quiet	**kékkō (na)**	excellent, satisfactory
génki (na)	healthy, good-spirited	**jōzú (na)**	skilful, good at
bénri (na)	convenient	**hetá (na)**	unskilful, poor at
fúben (na)	inconvenient	**yūmei (na)**	famous, well-known
iyá (na)	unpleasant	**nigíyaka (na)**	lively, bustling, gay
hén (na)	queer, odd	**daijóbu (na)**	safe, OK

Most nouns belong to the ordinary class that have **no** for the copula alternant [**byōki no hito, shokkō no Tanaka-san**]. Some nouns belong to either class—ordinary or copular. An example is **iroiro**: you can say either **iroiro no** or **iroiro na** (commonly pronounced **iron-na**) to mean 'various, of various sorts'; it is also used as an adverb (instead of **iroiro ni,** which does not occur). There are a few copular nouns which do not occur except before **ná** in a modifier clause; they are replaced in a sentence-final clause by a derived adjective:

chíisa na heyá a small room   óki na fúne   a big ship
heyá wa chiisái the room is small fúne wa ōkíi desu the ship is big
desu

In these cases you can use the derived adjective for the modifier clause too: chiisái heyá or chíisa na heyá 'a small room', ōkíi fúne or óki na fúne 'a big ship'. There's virtually no difference in meaning; it's like the difference between English 'little' and 'small', 'big' and 'large'.*

When you have two copular nouns modifying the same noun phrase, the first takes the gerund of the copula dé 'is and': shízuka de kírei na tokoro 'a place that is quiet and (is) pretty'.

Here are some examples of copular nouns in sentences:

Taihen na kotó o shimáshita.	He did something terrible.
Kirai de fúben na tokoro desu.	It's an inconvenient place and I dislike it.
Báka na kotó o itte imásu.	He's saying stupid things.
Taihen shitsúrei na hito desu né.	He's a very rude person, isn't he.
Nigíyaka de taihen na tokoro désu.	It's a terribly bustling place.
Senséi wa génki na hito desu né.	The teacher is good-spirited, isn't he.
Kore wa bénri de kírei na heyá desu.	This is a convenient, clean room.
Iroiro na tokoro e asobi ni iku kotó ga sukí desu ka?	Do you like to go visiting various sorts of places?

Before the verb náru 'becomes', the particle ni occurs

*Ōki ni occurs in Kyoto speech with the meaning dó mo '(thank you) ever so much.'

after a copular noun, just as after any other noun: **byōki ni narimáshita** 'he got sick', **génki ni narimáshita** 'he got his health back'. With other verbs, the particle **ni** makes the meaning of the copular noun 'in such a manner':

Shízuka ni shite kudasái.	Please be quiet [behave in a quiet way].
Máinichi génki ni shite imásu ně.	He's in good spirits every day [behaves in a good-spirited manner].
Ano onná wa Eigo o jōzú. ni hanashimásu.	That girl talks English well.

5. 5. THE NOUN **NO**. You have had two kinds of no—the particle and the copula-alternant. There is yet a third kind of **no** which is a noun. This noun has two somewhat different meanings 'one WHO' and 'fact THAT'. In some expressions this word is used much like **hito** 'person': **Sakana o tábete irú no wa anáta no tomodachi désu ka?** [or ...tábete iru hito wa...] 'Is the one [the person] who is eating fish your friend?' **Kono jidōsha o mótte irú no wa dáre desu ka?** 'Who's the one who owns this car?' In some expressions, the noun **no** is used like **kotó** 'fact': **Amerika no éiga o míru no ga sukí desu** [or ...míru kotó ga...] 'I like to see American movies'. In other expressions it has certain special uses. Here are some additional examples:

Ano kírei na onná to haná-shite irú no wa kinō wa-takushi no uchi e asobi ni kitá Yamáguchi Jírō desu.	The one talking to that pretty girl is Jiro Yama-guchi who came to visit my family yesterday.

Shimbun o kai ni ittá no wa dáre desu ka?	Who is the one who has gone for the paper?
Oyógi ni ittá no wa dáre desu ka?	Who is the one who went for a swim?
Eigo no shimbun o yómu no wa muzukashíi deshō.	It must be hard to read an English newspaper.
Kírei na onná o míru no wa íi desu.	It's nice to look at pretty girls.
Nihongo o hanásu no wa yasashíi keredomo káku no wa muzukashíi desu.	Talking Japanese is easy; however, writing it is hard.

5. 6. NO DESU. The noun **no** followed by the copula makes a special expression meaning 'it is a fact that...' This is a very common formula in Japanese—it may be tacked on at the end of any sentence [with the verb or adjective or copula in either plain imperfect or plain perfect] just as an additional refinement, which somewhat softens the directness of the statement.* The expression **yasúnde irú no desu** '[it's a fact that] he's resting' means about the same thing as **yasúnde imasu** 'he's resting', but it makes the expression somewhat more formal.

| Dóko e ikú no desu ka?= Dóko e ikimásu ka? | Where is he going? |
| Dóno éiga o míta no desu ka?=Dóno éiga o mimáshita ka? | What movie did you see? |

---

*As a result, **n(o) desu** is somewnat more common wnen the sentence is not completed but left dangling with a particle like **kedo... (ga...)** 'but...' or **kara...** 'so...'

Kono hón o yónde irú no desu. = Kono hón o yónde imasu.	I'm reading this book.
Kono jidósha wa atarashíi no desu. = Kono jidósha wa atarashíi desu.	This car is new.
Kinō no éiga wa totemo o-moshírokatta no desu. = ... totemo omoshírokatta desu.	The movie yesterday was quite interesting.

For many of the **no desu** expressions, there is possible ambiguity—they could mean either 'it is the one who...' or 'it is a fact that...': **Kono hón o yónde irú no desu ka?** can mean either 'Is it the one who is reading this book?' or 'Is it a fact that [someone] is reading this book? = Is [someone] reading this book?' In such cases, the context usually clears up the doubt. Sometimes there is no good paraphrase of the type 'it is a fact that' for the **no desu** expression:

Oteárai ni ittá no deshō.	He must have gone to the restroom.
Mó káette kitá no deshita ka?	Had he already returned?

Notice the use of the copula forms **dátta** and **ná[= dá]**; before the noun **no** the plain imperfect copula appears in the form **ná** regardless of whether preceded by an ordinary noun or a copula noun:

Súihei dátta no desu. = Súihei deshita.	He was in the Navy.

Heitai ja nákatta no desu. = Heitai ja arimasén deshita.	He wasn't a soldier.
Íma kōin ná no desu.= Íma kōin désu.	He's a factory worker now.
Kírei na no desu ně. = Kírei desu ně.	It's pretty, isn't it. It's a pretty one, isn't it.

In rapid speech, the word **no** is often shortened just to **n:**

Éiga o mí ni ikú n desu ka?	Are you going to the movies?
Anáta wa Nihongo ga totemo jōzú na n desu ně.	You're quite good at Japanese, aren't you.
Máda hetá na n desu.	I'm still [rather] poor [at it].

Notice that the combination **ná n** [from **ná no**] is NOT the same as the word **nán** [alternant of **náni** before words beginning with **t, d, n**] 'what'. Cf. p. 53.

5. 7. VERB + DESHŌ. Many people go a step farther and drop the **no** completely from the expressions discussed above: **Dóko e ikú desu ka?** 'Where's he going?', **Oteárai ni ittá desu** 'He went to the men's room'. As a general thing, this usage is frowned upon by speakers of Standard Japanese and should perhaps be avoided by the student. However, certain forms which have become a part of Standard Japanese originated in this dropping of the **no**: the polite forms of the adjective—**atarashii desu, íi desu**—came from the forms **atarashíi no desu, íi**

no desu. Some older Japanese still consider it poor style to say **atarashii desu, ii desu**—preferring at least **atarashíi n desu, íi n desu**—but the younger people use the forms without even the **n** constantly, so that they are now a part of Standard Japanese. This helps explain the existence of two polite forms for the perfect adjective: **íi deskita** and **yókatta desu.** They come from the expressions **íi no deshita** 'it was a fact that it is good' and **yókatta no desu** 'it is a fact that it was good'. The latter type phrase—**yókatta desu**—is much more current than the former, which many people do not seem to use at all.

In a similar way, expressions consisting of imperfect or perfect adjectives plus **no deshō** 'will probably be the fact that...; must be...' created the now Standard forms **íi deshō** 'it must be good' [compare **Tanaka-san deshő** 'It must be Mr. Tanaka'], **yókatta deshō** 'it must have been good' [compare **Tanaka-san dátta no deshō** 'it must have been Mr. Tanaka']. (see also note on p. 432.)

There already existed a polite tentative for verbs: **ikimashő, hanashimashő, asobimashő.** These polite tentatives once had the meaning 'will probably do' just as the polite copula **deshő** still has the meaning 'will probably be'. Sometimes the tentatives of verbs are still used with the 'probably' meaning,* but most of the time now they mean either 'I think I'll..., I guess I'll...' or

---

*For example, in modern writings you will see **arő** (=**áru darō**), **narő** (=**náru darō**), **dekiyő** (—**dekíru darō**), **ieyő** (=**ierú darō** 'probably can say'); also tentative adjectives in -**karő** (=-**i darō**) such as **yokarő** (=**íi darō**) and **nakarő** (=**nái darō**). In radio weather reports you may hear **Áme ga furimashő** (=**fúru deshō**) 'It will probably rain' and **Kumorimashő** (=**Kumóru deshō**) 'It will probably get cloudy.' Note also **(de) gozaimashő** in Lesson 9.

'Let's. . .': **Tanaka-san to hanashimashǒ** 'I think I'll talk to Mr. Tanaka'; **Arúite ikimashǒ** 'Let's walk'. For the meaning 'probably', a plain form of the verb is used—either imperfect or perfect, depending on the meaning—followed by the tentative copula **deshǒ** [from **no deshǒ** it's probably a fact that' with the **no** dropped]. This is quite Standard usage and often has the flavor of English 'must [be], I bet that. . ., I'll bet. . .,' Sometimes **kitto** or **tábun** 'no doubt, probably' is added, often at the very beginning of the sentence, just to emphasize the probability. Here are some additional examples:

Íma hi ga déte irú deshō.	The sun must be out by now.
Tábun sǒ deshō.	Likely it is.
Kamakurá e ikú no wa omoshirói deshō.	It would be fun to go to Kamakura.
Okane ga nákatta deshō.	I bet he didn't have any money.
Dǒ shita deshō ka?	How come? How did it [probably] happen that way?
Kodomo o tsurete asobi ni ikimashǒ.	Let's take the children and go visiting [or playing].
Kodomo o tsurete asobi ni ikú deshō.	She'll probably take the children and go visiting.
Kodomo o tsurete asobi ni ittá deshō.	She's probably taken the children visiting.
Tábun, okane ga nái kara, tabéru kotó ga dekínai deshō.	I suppose, since he hasn't any money, he won't be able to eat.

5. 8. KA NÉ. The final particles **ka né** mean something like 'I wonder' or 'is it, do you think'. They are often preceded by a tentative expression:

Dóko e ikimashó ka né.	I wonder where I should go.
Sono tegami o dáre ga káita deshō ka né.	I wonder who wrote that letter.
Só (deshō) ka né.	I wonder if that's right. [I think it probably isn't right.]
Só ja nái (deshō) ka né.	I wonder if that's not right. [I think it probably is right.]

5. 9. NO DE. The expression verb [or adjective or copula] + **no de** 'it being a fact that; it is a fact that... and' has a special meaning: 'because 'or 'since'. This is similar to the meaning of **kara**. In most places **no de** and **kara** seem interchangeable, but there is a slight difference of meaning—**no de** emphasizes the REASON, **kara** emphasizes the RESULT:

Kyónen yamá e ittá kara, oyógu kotó ga dekimasén deshita.	Last year I went to the mountains, SO I COULDN'T SWIM.
Kyónen yamá e ittá no de, oyógu kotó ga dekimasén deshita.	Last year I couldn't swim BECAUSE I WENT TO THE MOUNTAINS.

Here are some additional examples:

Máda shimbun o yomá-	I hadn't read the news-

nakatta kara, sore o motte ikimáshita.

paper yet, so I took it with me.

Máda shimbun o yománakatta no de, sore o motte ikimáshita.

I took the newpaper with me because I hadn't read it yet.

Okane ga nákatta no de, tabéru kotó ga dekínakatta deshō.

He probably couldn't eat because he hadn't any money.

Máinichi benkyō shite irú no de, dandan jōzú ni narimásu ně.

You're getting gradually better because you study every day, you see.

Éiga ga dáisuki datta no de, máinichi mí ni ittá no desu.

He went to see the movies every day because he liked movies very much.

5. 10. **NO NI.** After a verb in the imperfect mood, the expression **no ni** 'to the fact that, at the fact that' has two different meanings: 'in the process of doing, for the purpose of doing, in order to do' and 'in spite of the fact that...' The two meanings are distinguished by context; often the particle **wa** follows **no ni** in the first meaning, and the whole expression is frequently followed by a phrase indicating something is necessary ['in the process of doing something']. Only the second meaning occurs when **no ni** follows adjectives or the copula in imperfect or perfect moods, and when it follows verbs in the perfect mood. Here are some examples of the first meaning 'in the process of':

Ryokō surú no ni wa, okane ga irimásu ne.

You have to have money to travel, you know [in

the process of traveling, money is necessary].

Tegami o káku no ni kamí ga irimásu.
To write letters, you need paper.

Benkyō surú no ni, hón ga irimásu.
In studying you need books.

Here are some examples of the second meaning 'in spite of the fact that':

Máinichi benkyō surú no ni, jōzú ni narimasén.
In spite of the fact that I study every day I still don't get good.

Áme ga futté ita no ni, sampo ni ikimáshita.
He went for a walk in spite of the fact it was raining.

Jidōsha de ikanai to, ma ni awánai no ni, arúite ikimáshita.
In spite of the fact you don't get there on time unless you go by car, he walked.

Samúi no ni, natsu no kimono o kite imáshita.
It was cold, but he was wearing his summer clothes [anyway] .

The first meaning of **no ni** 'in the process of' should be kept distinct from the meaning 'for the purpose of, with the aim of'; this meaning is usually expressed by the noun **tamé** 'sake', which is often followed by **ni** and sometimes by **wa** or **ni wa**. The expression **tamé (ni) (wa)** may be preceded by a plain imperfect verb form or by a noun + **no**:

Benkyō suru tamé ni gakkō e ikimáshita.	He went to school in order to study.
Benkyō no tamé ni gakkō e ikimáshita.	He went to school for study.
Nán no tamé ni Nihón e kimáshita ka?	For what purpose did you come to Japan?
Atarashíi zasshi o yómu tame ni, toshókan e ikimashǒ.	I guess I'll go to the library to read the new maga- zines.
Tomodachi o mi-okuru ta- mé ni Tōkyǒ-eki e ikimásu.	I'm going to Tokyo Station to see a friend off.

The word **tamé** is also used after a modifying phrase by many speakers as a virtual equivalent of **kara** 'because:

Háyaku ókita tame, ma ni aimáshita.	I got up early, so I was on time.
Eigo ga dekínai tame, ko- marimásu.	I have difficulties because I can't talk English.

5. 11. PLAIN NEGATIVE. The polite negative ends in **-masén** for verbs—**hanashimasén, ikimasén,** and consists of a special construction for the copula **ja arimasén,** and for adjectives—infinitive [-ku]+**arimasén.**

The plain negative of 'exists' is a completely different word, the adjective **nái** 'is non-existent' (p. 102). The plain negative of the copula is **ja nái,** of adjectives **-ku nái.** And, in colloquial usage, (**ja**) **nái desu** is often used for (**ja**) **arimasén, -ku nái desu** for **-ku arimasén.** Cf. p. 83.

The plain negative of every other verb is an adjective made by adding the ending -(a)na-i to the stem of the verb. The ending is -ánai added to the stem of an accented CONSONANT verb, -anai to the stem of an unaccented consonant verb; and '-nai added to the stem of an accented VOWEL verb, -nai to the stem of an unaccented vowel verb.

	ACCENTED			UNACCENTED	
		VOWEL VERBS			
'eats'	tabé-ru	tabé-nai	'sleeps'	ne-ru	ne-nai
'rises'	okí-ru	okí-nai	'stays'	i-ru	i-nai
		CONSONANT VERBS			
'becomes'	nár-u	nar-ánai	'rides'	nor-u	nor-anai
'meets'	á[w]-u	aw-ánai	'buys'	ka[w]-u	kaw-anai
'talks'	hanás-u	hanas-ánai	'lends'	kas-u	kas-anai
'writes'	kák-u	kak-ánai	'hears'	kik-u	kik-anai
'swims'	oyóg-u	oyog-ánai	'smells'	kag-u	kag-anai
'chooses'	eráb-u	erab-ánai	'calls'	yob-u	yob-anai
'reads'	yóm-u	yom-ánai	'stops'	yam-ṳ	yam-anai
'waits'	mát[s]-u	mat-ánai	'dies'	shin-u	shin-anai

Notice how the 'disappearing' w appears in forms like awánai and kawanai (compare áu, kau). Also notice the disappearance of the s in stems like mát[s]-u.

The verb ìku 'goes' forms its negative regularly: ik-anai. The verbs kúru 'comes' and suru 'does' both have irregular stems: kó-nai 'does not come', shi-nai 'does not do'.

Each of the negative adjectives is conjugated like any other adjective—for example the adjective nái 'is nonexistent' or akai 'is red':

IMPERFECT	ná-i	tabé-na-i	aka-i	kaw-ana-i
PERFECT	ná-katta	tabé-na-katta	aká-katta	kaw-aná-katta
GERUND	ná-kute	tabé-na-kute	aká-kute	kaw-aná-kute

5. 12. NEGATIVE INFINITIVE. In addition to the regular negative infinitive (as in **tabénaku náru** 'gets so he doesn't eat', **mienaku náru** 'becomes invisible'), there is a DERIVED COPULAR NOUN with similar meaning but different uses. This form has the ending '-azu after an accented CONSONANT stem, -azu after an unaccented consonant stem; ⌐ -zu after an accented VOWEL stem, -zu after an unaccented vowel stem.

A list of the special negative infinitives for all the types of verbs given earlier: **ne-zu, óki-zu, i-zu, mát-azu, nár-azu, nor-azu, áw-azu, kaw-azu, hanás-azu, kas-azu, kak-azu, kik-azu, oyóg-azu, kag-azu, eráb-azu, yob-azu, yóm-azu, yam-azu, shin-azu.** The irregular verbs are **kó-zu** 'not coming' and **se-zu** 'not doing'. Notice that **kó-zu** is similar in its irregular vowel to **kó-nai**, but **se-zu** is different from **shi-nai**. The appropriate form for **nái** is **árazu**, but it is not used in speech. The -(a)zu form is usually limited to a set expression with the particle **ni** meaning either 'without doing' or 'instead of doing', depending on the context. Here are some examples:

Éiga e ikazu ni, kōen e itte sampo shimashŏ.	Instead of going to the movies, let's go to the park and take a walk.
Góhan o tábezu ni, isóide jimúsho e ikimáshita.	I rushed off to the office without eating.
Tsuchiya-san ni áwazu ni	I can't go back without

wa, káeru kotó wa deki-masén.	meeting Mr. Tsuchiya.
Tomodachi o mátazu ni, súgu ni úmi e hairimá-shita.	He went into the sea right away, without waiting for his friend.
Kono hón o kawazu ni, toshókan de yomimashŏ.	I guess I'll read this book at the library instead of buying it.
Isógazu ni, yukkúri aruki-mashŏ.	Let's walk slowly, without hurrying.
Uchi ni ite benkyō sezu ni, éiga o mí ni ittá deshō.	I bet he went to the movies instead of staying home and studying.

Another way to say 'instead' is to use two full sentences, with the second beginning sono kawari (ni) 'instead of that':

Hón wa kawánakatta desu. Sono kawari ni zasshi o kaimáshita.	He didn't buy books; instead, he bought magazines.

5. 13. IMPERFECT NEGATIVE+DE. Instead of using -(a)zu ni to say 'without doing' or 'instead of doing' you can use the plain imperfect negative -(a)nai+the copula gerund dé 'being'. This construction is also sometimes used with kudasái in direct negative requests: Am-mari hanasánai de kudasái 'Please don't talk too much'.

Uchi e benkyō ni kaétte kónai de, machí e éiga o	Instead of coming home to study, I'll bet he went to

mí ni ittá deshō.

Shimamura-san ni tegami o kakánai de, denwa o káketa deshō.

Baba-san wa okane o karinái de, sono jidósha o kaimáshita.

Kono zasshi o kawanái de kudasái.

town to see a movie.

He must have phoned Mr. Shimamura instead of writing him.

Mr. Baba bought his car without borrowing any money.

Please don't buy this magazine.

5.14. **HAZU.** Hazu is a noun meaning something like 'normal expectation'; preceded by a modifier clause [which ends with the plain imperfect mood] and followed by some form of the copula it means 'is (supposed) to, is expected to.'

(But not 'supposed to' in the sense of obligation 'ought to'; see pp. 291, 293.)

Kúru hazu no hitó ga kónai to komarimásu.

Kónai hazu no hitó ga kúru to komarimásu.

Kúru hazu no (or Kúru hazu dátta) hitó ga kónakatta kara komarimáshita.

Senséi wa Nihongo de hanásu hazu desu.

When people who are expected don't come, it is upsetting.

When people expected not to come show up, it is upsetting.

We were put out that the people who were expected didn't show up.

I expect the teacher will talk in Japanese.

Note the difference between this word hazu—what is

generally expected, and tsumori—what the subject expects or intends to do (p. 111). Hazu usually refers to what I expect of OTHER people; it is sometimes close to ...ni chigai nái 'there is no doubt that' (p. 392) as in Mŏ Tanaka-san ni átta hazu desu 'I feel sure that he has already met Mr. Tanaka'. What I expect of myself is usually (suru) tsumori dá 'I intend to (do)' or (suru) kotó ni nátte iru 'it is arranged [for me] (to do)' (p. 388).

To make the negative you usually say hazu wa nái (rather than hazu ja nái); or, you can make the preceding verb negative: Ténki ga warúi kara Tanaka-san ga kúru hazu wa arimasén or...kónai hazu desu 'Mr. Tanaka surely won't come (=kitto kónai darō) in such bad weather'.

5.15. **TOKORO.** The noun tokoro 'place' has several special uses. (Cf. p. 428.) When you speak of going to a person, doing something at a person's, coming from a person, in Japanese you usually say 'to, from, or at the PLACE of that person':*

Isha no tokoró kara shújin no tokoro e ikimáshita.	From the doctor's, I went to my boss.
Watakushi no tokoró e kité kudasai.	Please come to me.

Tokoro can also refer to time as well as place. It then means 'the time or occasion when something is [was] happening', and it is followed by the copula or by a particle. Here are some of the expressions that result:

---

*In fact tokoro is used when you are going to anything that is not itself a place: mádo no tokoró e iku 'goes to the window'.

yómu tokoró desu	he is [just] about to read
yómu tokoró deshita	he was [just] about to read
yónda tokoró desu	he has just [now] read
yónda tokoró deshita	he had just [then] read
yónde iru tokoró desu	he is just [now] reading
yónde ita tokoró deshita	he was just [then] reading
yónde ita tokoró desu	he has just been reading
yónde ita tokoró deshita	he had just been reading

Instead of the copula, you can have the particle **e** followed by some clause which INTERRUPTS the action of the clause preceding **tokoro**:

Shimbun o yónde iru tokoró e kimáshita.	He came just when I was reading the newspaper.
Kánai ga dekaketa tokoró e tomodachi ga kimáshita.	Just when my wife had gone out, some friends came.
Eigákan e háitte iru tokoro o mimáshita.	I saw them enter the theater.
Sénsei ga hanáshite iru tokoro o chótto kiite, sore kara kaerimáshita.	I listened to the teacher talking for a bit and then went home.

Ordinarily, only the imperfect mood precedes **tokoro** in a construction with a verb of perception. It is very much like the use of **kotó** or **no** 'fact': **Eigákan e háitte iru tokoró o mimáshita=Eigákan e háiru no o mimáshita** 'I saw them enter the theater [saw the fact of their entering]'; **Sénséi ga hanáshite iru tokoró o chótto kiite, sore kara kaerimáshita** 'I listened to the teacher talking for a bit and then went home'.

There are occasional opportunities for ambiguity. Jidŏsha o tsukútte iru tokoró o mimáshita could mean either 'I saw them making cars' or 'I saw the place where they make cars'; Jidŏsha o tsukútte iru tokoró e kimáshita could mean 'I came while they were making cars' or 'I came to the place where they make cars'.

5. 16. VERBS FOR LEAVING. The usual verb for 'leave' is déru. There is a compound verb dekakeru consisting of the infinitive of déru [dé] + -kakeru 'begins to, starts to' [= -hajimeru]. This is often used when a person leaves on an errand, with the implication that he gets started on his way. If a person leaves town on a trip you use a special verb tátsu, which usually has the meaning 'stands up'. Tátsu also has the meaning '[an airplane] takes off, but tobi-tátsu is more explicit, and you can use déru 'leaves' instead. The place you leave is followed by the object particle o. The verb for 'arrives' is tsukú; the particle for the place is e 'to'.

Anáta no kishá wa sakúban Nágoya o demáshita ka?	Did your train leave Nagoya last night?
Anáta wa ítsu Nágoya o tachimásu ka?	When are you leaving Nagoya?
Éki o déte (kara), massúgu arúite kudasai.	When you leave the station, please walk straight ahead.
Íma dekakemásu.	I'm going out now.
Kómban Tōkyō o tátte, ashita no ása Kyŏto e tsukimásu.	I'll leave Tokyo tonight and get into Kyoto tomorrow morning.

Hiroshima o tátte kara, dóko e iku hazu désu ka? Mainen Kinki-chíhō e shut-chō shimásu.

After they leave Hiroshima, where are they to go? Every year I make a [business] trip to the Kinki [Kyoto-Osaka] area.

5. 17 MAE NI AND ÁTO DE. To say 'before something happens' or 'before something happened' you use the IMPERFECT mood followed by máe ni 'in front of..., in advance of...': **Anáta ga kúru máe ni, shújin wa mō dekakemáshita** 'My husband went out before you came.' **Góhan o tabéru máe ni, shimbun o yomimashó.** 'Before I eat, I guess I'll read the newspaper.'

To say 'after something happens' or 'after something happened' you use the PERFECT mood followed by áto de 'being after...': **Anáta to hanáshita áto de, sono tegami o káita no desu** 'I wrote that letter after I had talked with you', **Senséi ni denwa o káketa áto de, watakushi no tokoró e kité kudasai** 'Come to me after you phone the teacher.'

Notice that you always use the same mood in front of these two expressions—IMPERFECT + máe ni, PERFECT + áto de—regardless of the English translation. The differences of tense in English are mostly conditioned by the tense of the verb in the final clause, and this is all indicated by the mood of the final verb in the Japanese sentence.

Now you have had two ways to say 'after doing some-

thing': gerund [-te] + kara and perfect [-ta] + áto de. The
principal difference of use is that the -te kara construction refers to actions IN SEQUENCE [either time sequence or logical sequence], whereas -ta áto de is used for
actions not necessarily in immediate sequence, just separated in time. Góhan o tábete kara, éiga o mí ni ikimáshita 'I went to see a movie after eating' implies that
there is a direct sequence, with nothing else of importance happening between the time I ate and the time I
saw the movie: I saw the show right after dinner. Góhan
o tábeta áto de, éiga o mí ni ikimáshita 'I went to see a
movie after I had eaten' does not imply this sequence;
perhaps I did the dishes, studied for a while, and then
went for a walk before taking in a late show. Additional
examples:

Kishá ga déru máe ni, shimbun o kaimáshita.	I bought a newspaper be- fore the train left.
Kishá ga Yokohamá-eki o déte kara, shimbun o yomi-hajimemáshita.	When the train left Yoko- hama Station I started to read the paper.
Nágoya o déta áto de, sho- kudósha e itte góhan o tabemáshita.	I went to the diner and had dinner after we [had] left Nagoya.
Shokudósha e iku máe ni, Ōsaka e shutchō suru Amerika no jitsugyōka to iroiro hanashimáshita.	Before I went to the diner, I had an interesting chat with an American busi- nessman who was on a trip to Osaka.
Sore kara, kodomo o yonde,	After that, I called the

kánai to kodomo o tsurete shokudósha e ittá no desu.	children and took my wife and the children to the diner.
Sensō ga hajimaru máe ni, Fukúoka ni súnde imáshita.	Before the war began, I was living in Fukuoka.
Sensō ga owatta áto de, iroiro na tokoro ni súnde imasu.	Since the war ended, I have been living in various places.

There are two other things to notice about **máe** and **áto**. **Máe** refers either to space or to time—'before' or 'in front of'. **Áto** usually refers only to time 'after'—for space you ordinarily use **ushiro** 'behind'. The second thing is that **máe** and **áto** are nouns and may be modified by prenouns [**kono, sono, ano,** etc.] or by a noun + the particle **no**. For example: **kono máe** 'before this', **sono áto** 'after that', **sensō no máe** 'before the war', **góhan no áto** 'after the meal'. Instead of **áto de**, sometimes the synonymous expression **nochí ni** is used.

Kono máe ni dóko ni imáshita ka?	Where were you before?
Sukóshi áto de íi desu ka?	Is it all right [if I do it] a little later?
Áto de shite kudasái.	Do it later (on).
Íma desu ka, áto desu ka?	Is it to be now or later [that you want it, will do it, etc.]?
Máe ni mo, ushiro ní mo arimásu.	We have some both in front and behind.

5. 18. MÁDE AND UCHI. The particle **máde** after a noun means 'as far as, up to'; after the IMPERFECT mood of a verb or the INFINITIVE [-ku] of some adjectives, it means 'until something happens or is':

Kishá ga déru máde, éki de machimashŏ.	Let's wait at the station till the train leaves.
Kishá ga déru máde, mátte imásu.	I'm waiting till the train leaves.
Kishá ga déru máde, éki de mátte imáshita.	We waited at the station till the train left.
Máinichi osokú máde benkyō suru kotó ga kirai désu.	I don't like to study till late every day.

The noun **uchi** means 'interval, inside' [the derived meaning 'house' is a specialized example of this]. Following a verb or an adjective—imperfect or perfect—it means 'while something does or is something; was or did something'. **Uchi** may be followed by **ni** or **wa** or **ni wa**:

Kodomo ga nete iru uchi ni, zasshi o yomimashŏ.	While the children are asleep, I guess I'll read a magazine.
Kodomo ga nete ita uchi ni, iroiro hanashimáshita.	We talked about various things while the children were asleep.

In many cases **uchi** and **aida** seem interchangeable, both meaning '[during] the interval.'

After a negative, **uchi** means 'while something [still] doesn't happen; as long as something [still] isn't so' and this is a common Japanese way to say 'before something happens, before something is so':

Senséi ga kónai uchi ni, asobimashǒ.	Let's play before the teacher gets here.
Okane ga naku naránai uchi ni, éiga o mí ni ikimashǒ.	Let's go to the movies before we run out of money.
Wasurenai uchi ni, kusuri o nomimashǒ.	I guess I'll take [drink] my medicine before I forget.
Níkkō o mínai uchi wa, kékkō to iwanái de kudasai.	Until you've seen Nikko, don't say **kékkō** ['splendid'].

[**To** is the quoting particle, discussed in Lesson 6. This proverb is usually quoted in the Plain Style with **iú na** instead of **iwanái de kudasai**. For the Plain Style, see p. 420.]

5. 19. VERBS MEANING 'KNOWS'. There are two verbs often translated 'knows': **shir-u** and **wakáru**. **Shir-u** takes a direct object—**Kono kotó o shitte imásu ka?** 'Do you know this [fact]?'—and in the affirmative it is most often used together with **iru**. In the negative, it occurs without the **iru**: **Shirimasén** 'I don't know'. This verb is used for knowing specific facts and people:

Tézuka-san o shitte imásu ka? Shirimasén.	Do you know Mr. Tezuka? No, I don't.

Anáta ga kinō watakushi no tokoró e asobi ni kita kotó wa shirimasén de-shita.	I didn't know you came to visit me yesterday.
Fúne de ikú no o shitte imáshita ka?	Did you know we were to go by boat?

From the infinitive of this verb [shiri] + the infinitive of áu 'meets' [ái] is derived the noun shiriai 'acquaintance'. Shiriai to hanáshite imashita 'I was talking with an acquaintance.'

When by 'know' we mean 'understand, know what someone said, catch on' then the verb is wakáru 'is distinguished, is understood'; this verb does not take a direct object—the word corresponding to the English object is the subject [just like éiga ga sukí desu 'I like movies']:

Kono kotobá ga wakari-másu ka?	Do you understand this word?
Wakarimasén nĕ.	I don't get it.
Kono séntensu ga wakáru to, súgu tsugí mo wakari-máshita.	When I got this sentence, I immediately under-stood the next.
Nihongo ga wakarimásu ka?	Do you know [understand] Japanese?
Eigo ga (or wa) wakaránai deshō.	They probably don't know English.
Sukóshi wa wakáru deshō.	They surely know it a little.
Shikáshi, wakaránai koto-	Still, there would be many

bá ga ói deshō.   words   they   wouldn't
                                       know.

5. 20. TALKING A LANGUAGE. To say 'he speaks
English' you usually say in Japanese 'he can [speak] English; as for him, English is produced'—**Anó hito wa Eigo
ga dekimásu.** So when people ask you **Nihongo ga dekimásu ka?** you'll probably want to answer **Sukóshi dekimásu** or **Chótto dekimásu** 'I speak [it] a little.' To say
'he's talking in Japanese' you use the particle de: **Nihongo
de hanáshite imasu.** To say 'he talks Japanese' you can
say **Nihongo o hanashimásu.**

Nihongo de itte kudasái.	Please say it in Japanese.
Kono kotobá wa Eigo de itte kudasái.	Please say this word in English.
Kono búnshō wa mō ichi-do Nihongo de yónde kudasai.	Please read this sentence again in Japanese.
Sore wa mō ichido Nihon-go de itte kudasái.	Please say that (sentence) again in Japanese.
Nihongo no dekíru Bei-kokújin wa sukunái de-shō.	There must be few Amer-icans who speak Japa-nese.

C. EXERCISES.

1. Some of the forms given below are negative—they
    mean someone does NOT do something, or is NOT
    something. Pick out the negative forms.

(a) **mátazu**	(b) **nákute**	(c) **sukunái**
(d) **akaku nái**	(e) **hazu**	(f) **sukúnaku naku**
(g) **awánakatta**	(h) **kakánai**	(i) **sukúnakatta**

(j) káerazu	(k) kitanái	(l) ja nákute
(m) náku	(n) kitánaku	(o) yókatta
(p) kizu	(q) kózu	(r) kírazu
(s) sezu	(t) naránakatta	(u) yonda
(v) ikimasén	(w) nái deshō	(x) kírei na n desu
(y) omoshíroku nái n desu	(z) arimasén deshita	

2. Each of the following sentences means something like 'that [something] does or is [something]'. Change each one so that it means 'it or he is the [something] that does or is [something]'. For instance, change the first one to: **Kinuoríkōba de hataraku shokkō désu** 'He's the worker who works at the silk-mill.'

1. Ano shokkō wa kinuoríkōba de hatarakimásu.
2. Ano tomodachi wa kinō asobi ni kimáshita.
3. Ano eigákan wa Ueno-kŏen no sóba ni arimásu.
4. Ano Tanaka-san wa jimúsho de tsutómete imasu.
5. Ano kodomo wa oyógu kotó wa dekimasén.
6. Ano kishá wa ashita háyaku Kyŏto e tsukimásu.
7. Ano heyá wa kitanái desu.
8. Ano musumé wa éiga o mí ni ikimasén deshita.
9. Ano jimúin wa byōki désu.
10. Ano kōen wa shízuka de kírei desu.
11. Anó hito wa sakúban okane ga arimasén deshita.
12. Ano Tanaka-san wa kono kōbá de hataraku shokkō désu.

3. Each of the following sentences means something like 'somebody does something'; change each one to mean 'this is the something somebody does.' For instance, change the first one to: **Kore wa néko no**

tábeta sakana désu 'This is the fish the cat ate.'

1. Néko wa sakana o tabemáshita.
2. Watakushi wa tomodachi ni tegami o kakimáshita.
3. Byōki no hito wa kusuri o nomimáshita.
4. Anó hito wa kodomo o yobimáshita.
5. Watakushi wa éiga o mimáshita.
6. Anáta wa shigoto o shimáshita.
7. Watakushi wa isha o yóku shitte imásu.
8. Watakushi wa késa zasshi o yónde imáshita.
9. Senséi wa kotobá o mō ichido iimáshita.
10. Shiháinin wa kōbá o ōkiku shimáshita.

4. Each of the following sentences means something like 'somebody does something to [or with, or for, or at, or from] something or somebody or somewhere'; change each one to mean 'that is the thing or person or place somebody did something'. For instance, change the first one to **Anó hito wa shiháinin no hanáshite ita shokkō désu** 'That is the worker the manager was talking to.'

1. Shiháinin wa shokkō to hanáshite imashita.
2. Watakushi mo gakkō de Eigo o benkyō shimáshita.
3. Mainen yasumí ni yama no tokoro e ikimásu.
4. Máinichi shokudō de góhan o tabemásu.
5. Watakushi wa machí kara kimáshita.
6. Tomodachi wa inaka no tokoro ni súnde imasu.
7. Shiháinin wa ginkō máde isóide arúite ikimáshita.
8. Musumé wa kimono o misé de kaimáshita.
9. Senséi wa mádo kara sóto o míte imashita.
10. Watakushi wa fúne de ikimáshita.

5. In each of the items below, there are two sentences. Combine these into one sentence meaning 'Instead of doing [something], [someone] did [something else]'. Do each one first with forms that end -(a)zu ni; then do it with the plain negative imperfect+the copula gerund—-(a)nái de. After that, translate the sentenee. For instance, the first one will be Éiga o mí ni ikazu ni, uchi ni ite benkyō shimáshita and Éiga o mí ni ikanái de, uchi ni ite benkyō shimáshita 'Instead of going to see the movie, I stayed home and studied.'

1. Éiga o mí ni ikimasén deshita. Uchi ni ite ben-kyō shimáshita.

2. Shimbun o yomimasén. Sampo shimashó.

3. Koko e asobi ni kimasén deshita. Eigákan e ittá deshó.

4. Inoue-san wa yamá e ikanái deshō. Umi e ikú deshō.

5. Kuríhara-san wa máinichi góhan o tabemasén. Kusuri o nomimásu.

6. Jidósha ni noránakatta desu. Arúite ittá n desu.

7. Uchi e kaerimasén deshita. Kōen e itte osokú made sampo shite imáshita.

8. Shiháinin ni tegami o kakimasén deshita. Denwa o kakemáshita.

9. Machi no shokudō de tabemasén. Uchi e kaeri-mashó.

10. Watakushi wa kómban shigoto o shimasén. Ko-domo to asobimashó.

6. Supply the appropriate verb forms. Do it orally.

1. Éiga o —— ni —— máe sukóshi benkyō shimáshita.	Before going to see the movie, I studied a little.
2. Sensō ga —— kara, shokkō ni narimáshita.	After the war ended, I became a factory worker.
3. Góhan o —— kara, dekakemashó.	Let's go out right after eating.
4. Mō sono éiga o —— kara, uchi ni ite tegami o kakimashó.	I've already seen that movie, so I guess I'll stay home and write a letter.
5. Watakushi ga —— tokoro e Yamada-san ga kimáshita.	Mr. Yamada came just as I was about to go out.
6. Kōen no sóba ni —— —— no ni, soko e sampo ni —— kotó wa arimasén.	Altho he is living near the park, he's never gone there for a walk.
7. Tegami o —— no ni pén ga irimásu.	You need a pen to write a letter.
8. Kishá ga —— made machimashó ka?	Shall we wait till the train leaves?
9. Kusuri o —— uchi ni wa, góhan o tabemasén.	You don't eat before [until] you take your medicine.
10. Sonna hón o —— tsumori ja nái deshō.	You surely don't intend to buy such a book.

7. Change each of the following sentences to mean 'it

is a fact that [something] happens or is]'; say each one first with **no desu**, then with just **n desu**. Remember you use a PLAIN form before the **no**. For instance, the first one will be **Nakamura-san ga machí o tátsu tokoro o míta no desu** and **Nakamura-san ga machí o tátsu tokoro o míta n desu.**

1.	**Nakamura-san ga machí o tátsu tokoro o mimáshita.**	I saw Mr. Nakamura leave town.
2.	**Góhan o tábete kara, uchi e kaerimáshita.**	After eating, we returned home.
3.	**Éki de watakushi no kōbá de hataraite iru shokkō ni aimáshita.**	At the station, we ran into a worker who works at my factory.
4.	**Yukí ga fúru to, yamá ga shíroku narimasu.**	When it snows, the mountains get white.
5.	**Okane ga sukúnakatta no ni, iroiro asobí-máshita.**	In spite of the fact we hadn't much money, we had a lot of fun.
6.	**Wakaránai kotobá ga ōi no de, jibikí ga irimásu.**	I need a dictionary because there are lots of words I don't understand.
7.	**Shimbun o yómu no ni mo jibikí ga irimásu ka?**	Do you need a dictionary to read newspapers too?
8.	**Úmi de oyóida kotó ga arimásu ka?**	Have you ever swum in the sea?
9.	**Íma dekakemásu ka?**	Are we leaving now?

10. Kyónen Kanázawa e   Last year, I took a trip
    shutchō shimáshita.   to Kanazawa.

D. COMPREHENSION.

Tanaka.   Konnichi wa, Aoki-san. Ogénki desu ka?
Aoki.   Arígatō gozaimásu. Dóko e ikimásu ka?
T.   Watakushi wa ashita Kóbe e shutchō surú
           kara, íma éki e kippu o kai ni iku tokoró
           desu.
A.   A, só desu ka. Watakushi wa góhan o tá-
           beta tokoro ná no de, sukóshi sampo ni
           dekaketá n desu. Éki made issho ni arúite
           ikimashó.
T.   É...Are ga anáta no jimúsho desu ka?
A.   Iie, ano ókikute shirói tatémono no náka
           ni arimásu. Nippon-Bōeki-Kabushiki-Gáisha
           no hónsha na n desu. Íma ammari isogá-
           shiku arimasén. Sore wa yunyū suru monó
           wa sōtō takái kara desu. Iroiro Nihón de
           tsukútta shinamono o yushutsu suru kotó
           mo áru no ni, gaikoku-gáwase ga muzukashíi
           kara, kaigai de kau kaisha wa sukunái desu.
T.   Watakushi no tokoró mo só desu. Kinuorí-
           mono o tsukúru no ni, gaikoku no shihon ga
           irimásu. Shacho no Takada-san wa Amerika
           e shasai o uri ni iku tsumori ná n desu.
           Takada-san o shitte imásu ka?
A.   Shirimasén. Amerika de shasai o uri ni iku
           hitó da kara Eigo ga yóku dekíru deshō né.

T. Só desu. Takada-san wa sensō no máe ni Amerika no óki na kaisha ni tsutómete ima-shita. Sensō no aida, Nihón e káette Nippon-Sambutsu-Kabushiki-Gáisha no shá-in ni nátte, shūsengo shachō ni nátta no desu.

A. Dó shite kabu mo Nihón de urazu ni, gai-koku de urimasén ka?

T. Sore wa watakushi wa yóku wakarimasén kedo, chótto muzukashíi deshō.

A. Anáta no kishá wa ása háyaku déru n desu ka?

T. Só desu...Shutchō shité kara súgu kaeránai de, Kóbe o tátte Miyanóshita e yasumí ni iku tsumori désu.

A. Só desu ka? Watakushi wa kotoshi wa oka-ne ga nái no de, kánai no uchi e yasumí ni ikú deshō. Shízuka de késhiki no íi inaka dá kara, tábun omoshirói deshō.

T. Watakushi wa inaka ga dáisuki desu. Kyó-nen chíisakute shízuka na tokoro e asobi ni ittá n desu.

A. Ja, éki wa asoko dá kara, watakushi wa koko de shitsúrei shite jimúsho e kaerimásu.

T. Sayonára.

LESSON 6.

A. BASIC SENTENCES. 'Shopping.'

1. Kinŏ wa futarí no tomodachi to issho ni kai-
   mono ni ikimáshita.

   Yesterday I went shop-
   ping with two of my
   friends.

2. Ginza máde dénsha ni
   notte ittá no de, jíp-
   pun mo kakarimasén
   deshita.

   Since we went on a streetcar, it didn't take even
   10 minutes to (get to)
   the Ginza.

3. Arúite iku to, ichijíkan
   mo kakarimásu.

   When you walk, it takes
   all of an hour.

4. Chōdo kúji ni Ginza e
   tsukimáshita.

   We got to the Ginza just
   at 9 o'clock.

5. Kaimono wa háyaku shi-
   nai to, misé ga kómu
   kara komarimásu né.

   If you don't do your shopping early, the stores
   get crowded so it's an-
   noying, you know.

6. Mázu, hón-ya e itte, jibikí o sansatsu kattá
   no desu.

   We went to a bookshop
   first and bought three
   dictionaries.

7. Wa-éi-jisho o issatsu, sore
   kara Ei-wá-jisho o ni-
   satsu kattá no desu.

   We bought one Japanese-
   English Dictionary and
   two English-Japanese
   Dictionaries.

8. Sono aida ni, hitóri no
   tomodachi wa tonari
   no misé e itte kutsú-

   Meanwhile, one of my
   friends went to the store
   next door and bought

shita o nisoku kattá
no desu.

9. Sore kara issho ni tokeiya e háitte, tokei o
hanjikan gúrai míte
imashita.

10. Sukí na tokei ga futatsu
átta keredomo, am-
mari nedan ga táka-
katta kara kawazu ni
déte kitá no desu.

11. Hitótsu wa kín no tokei
dé, mō hitótsu wa gín
no tokei déshita.

12. Gín no wa nimán-en de,
kín no wa yommán-
en deshita.

13. Tokeiya o déte kara, depáto e iku tochū de,
míkan o utte iru hitó |
o míta no desu.

14. Watakushi no dáisuki na
míkan ga kono-goro
yásuku nátta kara,
soko de ichidásu kai-
máshita.

15. Depáto de wa tomodachi
wa mannénhitsu o ní-

two pairs of socks.

After that we went into a
watch-seller's together
and looked at watches
for about half an hour.

Although there were two
watches we liked, the
prices were too high so
we came out without
buying them.

One was a gold watch and
the other one was a
silver watch.

The silver one was ￥ 20,-
000, and the gold one
was ￥ 40,000.

After leaving the watch-
seller's, on our way to
the department store we
saw a man selling tan-
gerines.

Lately   tangerines,   of
which I'm very fond,
have become cheap, so
I bought a dozen there.

At the department store
(one of) my friends

hon kaimáshita.

bought two fountain pens.

16. Ōkíi no to chiisái no o kaimáshita.

He bought a big one and a little one.

17. Dṓ shite níhon kattá n deshō ka?

I wonder how come [why] he bought two?

18. Tábun íppon wa ókusan no tamé ni kattá deshō.

I suppose he probably bought one for his wife.

19. Watakushi wa senshū kása o naku-shitá no de, amagása ka kōmorigasa o íppon kau tsumori déshita ga, depắto ni ita toki, kaú no o wasuremáshita.

I lost my umbrella last week, so I had intended to buy a [Japanese-style] paper umbrella or a [Western-style] cloth umbrella, but when I was in the department store, I forgot to buy it.

20. Depắto o déta toki wa, mṓ jūichíji ni nátte itá no desu.

When we left the department store, it had already gotten to be 11 o'clock.

21. Uchi e káeru made ni, máda ichijikan gúrai átta no de, sono aida gimbura o shimáshita.

Since we had about an hour before going back home, during that time we took ourselves a 'gimbura' [a stroll on the Ginza].

22. Ginza-dṓri ni wa iroiro no omoshirói misé ga arimásu.

On Ginza Avenue there are all sorts of interesting shops.

23. Hodō dé mo monó o utte iru hitó ga irú kara, totemo nigíyaka na n desu.

There are people selling things on the sidewalks too, so it is quite lively.

24. Kuri o hitofúkuro katte, sore o michi de tabemáshita.

We bought a bag of chestnuts and ate them on the street. [NOTE: Japanese do not ordinarily eat things while walking on the street.]

25. Sore kara, kodomo no tamé ni okáshi o hitóhako kattá no desu.

Then I bought a box of candy for my children.

26. Késa no kaimono wa nijíkan shika kakarimasén deshita.

This morning's shopping took only two hours.

27. Sore wa kínjo no misé de shokuryóhin dake kattá kara na no desu.

That's because I only bought groceries at the neighborhood stores.

28. Nikúya e itte gyūniku o sambyaku-gúramu to butaniku o gohyakugúramu kattá no desu.

I went to the butcher's and bought 300 grams of beef and 500 grams of pork.

29. Sore kara, yaoya e itte, jagaimo ya ninjin ya ona ya hōrénsō ya endō o kaimáshita.

After that, I went to the vegetable-store and bought potatoes and carrots and salad-greens and spinach and peas (and other things).

30. Yaoya dé wa futsū
kudámono o utte
imasén kara, yasai o
katté kara kudamo-
noya e itte mimáshita
ga, ringo ya momo ya
budō ya nashí ya ichi-
go wa minna takái
kara, kaki dake kai-
máshita.

At vegetable-stores they
do not usually sell
fruits, so I went to a
fruit-seller's and looked,
and the apples and
peaches and grapes and
pears and strawberries
(and other things) were
all expensive, so I just
bought (some) persim-
mons.

VOCABULARY ITEMS.

NOUNS

senshū	last week	yōniku	lamb
konshū	this week	hámu	ham
raishū	next week	shió, oshio	salt
séngetsu	last month	koshó	pepper
kongetsu	this month	chá, ocha	[Japanese green]
raigetsu	next month		tea
Nichiyō, Nichiyóbi	Sunday	kōcha	black tea
Getsuyō, Getsuyóbi	Monday	shōyú, oshōyu	soy-sauce
Kayō, Kayóbi	Tuesday	abura	oil
Suiyō, Suiyóbi	Wednesday	mamé	beans
Mokuyō, Mokuyóbi	Thursday	daizu	soybeans
Kin-yō, Kin-yóbi	Friday	íngen	kidney-beans
Doyó, Doyóbi	Saturday	suika	watermelon
tanjóbi	birthday	komé, okome	rice [uncooked]
kinémbi	anniversary	góhan	boiled rice;
kekkon no	wedding		food, meal
kinémbi	anniversary	tamanégi	[common] onion
kisen	steamship, liner	négi	scallion,
tori, kotori	bird		green onion
niwatori	chicken	nira	leek
toriniku, chikín	chicken (meat)	ninniku	garlic

daikon	turnip-like	sakanaya	fish-market,
	Japanese		fish-seller
	white radish	hirú	midday
kabu	turnip	hirú kara	afternoon
kyúri	cucumber	shokuji	meal

ADJECTIVES

sugói	"swell", wonderful	takái	is high,
hoshíi	is desirable,		is expensive
	is wanted	yasúi	is cheap, is easy

VERB

[jikan ga]	takes (time);	[okane ga]	costs, takes
kakáru	time is taken	kakáru	(money)
	or required		

B. STRUCTURE NOTES.

6. 1. NUMERALS AND NUMBERS. In Japanese there are two classes of words corresponding to English number words: NUMERALS and NUMBERS. A number is a compound word consisting of a numeral (like ichí 'one') plus a COUNTER (like -mai, the counter for flat thin objects).* You use simple numerals when you are talking about figures in the abstract, as in an arithmetic problem, where you are not counting anything in particular; you use numbers when your figures apply to something more definite, like a certain number of books, pencils or people, or a certain quantity of water, distance, time, or money.

---

*The basic accent patterns for numbers are complicated; here the details are skipped. The most complete description is that in Meikai Nihongo Akusento Jiten (Sanseidō, Tokyo 1957). To ask 'how many...' you attach either iku- or (more often) nan- (cf. p. 53) to the counter.

6.2. OTHER QUANTITY WORDS. In addition to numbers there are some other words which indicate quantity in a more general way. These words are nouns, often used as adverbs, just like the numbers. Here are some you will find useful:

takusán	lots, much, many
sukóshi	a little, a few, a bit
minná	all, everything, everybody
iroiro	various (cf. p. 136)

The word **minná** has only the meaning 'everybody' when used as a noun with some particle: **Minná ga kimáshita** 'Everybody came' or **Minna kimáshita** '[They] all came'. When used as an adverb it means 'all' or 'every' and can refer to people or things: **Hito o minna mimáshita** 'I saw all the people', **Jidósha o minna mimáshita** 'I saw all the cars'.

Here are some examples of these words in sentences:

Jidósha ga takusan soko ni tomatte imásu.	There are lots of cars parked there.
Takusán no hitó ni aimáshita.	I met many people.
Okane ga sukóshi arimásu.	I have a little money.
Kono sukóshi no nikú o tábete kudasai.	Please eat this little bit of meat.
Iroiro no tokoró kara kimáshita.	They came from various places.
Hón ga iroiro arimásu ně.	You have all sorts of books, haven't you.

6.3. USE OF NUMBERS AND QUANTITY WORDS.
These words occur as ordinary nouns, connected by **no** to the nouns they modify; they occur also as adverbs, without any particle following, and in this case they usually follow the noun+particle expression to which they refer—though sometimes they are put at the very beginning, as if modifying the whole sentence.*

If the particle after the noun is any particle other than **wa, ga,** or **o,** the number or quantity word must precede as a regular modifying noun: **futarí no hitó kara** from two people, **takusán no tokoró made** to many places.

But if the particle after the noun is **wa, ga,** or **o,** the number or quantity word can either precede with **no,** or follow as an adverb with no particle at all. There is a slight difference of meaning; if the quantity word or number is used as an adverb the noun is referred to in an INDEFINITE fashion: **empitsu ga níhon** 'two pencils (some or any two pencils)', **ocha ga sukóshi** 'a little bit of tea'. If the quantity word or number is used as a modifying noun, the reference is more DEFINITE: **ní-hon no empitsu ga** 'THE two pencils', **kono sukóshi no ocha ga** 'this little bit of tea'.

This is about the only place where Japanese maintains the English distinction between 'A man' (**hito wa hitóri**) and 'THE man' (**hitóri no hitó wa**), and it is possible only when the particle involved is **wa, ga,** or **o.**

When a number or quantity word is used as an ad-

---

*And sometimes you hear them in other positions (in spite of the following rule): **Machí de gakusei sannín ni** (or **gakusei ni san-nin**) **aimáshita** 'I ran into three of the students in town'.

verb with no particle following, it's as if the meaning were
'to the extent of...': **tegami o nítsū kakimáshita** 'I wrote
letters to the extent of two=I wrote two letters', **tegami
o takusan kakimáshita** 'I wrote letters to the extent of
a lot=I wrote a lot of letters'.*

Here are more examples:

Kono futarí no Amerikájin wa watakushi no tomodachi désu.	These two Americans are my friends. (cf. **Kono Amerikájin wa futarí to mo watakushi no tomodachi désu** 'Both of these Americans are my friends'.)
Sakúban senséi ga futari asobi ni kimáshita.	Last night two teachers came to call on me.
Futarí no senséi wa Nihongo ga dekimásu ka?	Do the two teachers know Japanese?
Nihongo ga sukóshi dekimásu.	They know a little Japanese.
Mannénhitsu o námbon kaimáshita ka?	How many fountain pens did you buy?
Sámbon kaimáshita.	I bought three.

6. 4. PRIMARY AND SECONDARY NUMERALS.
The numeral system of Japanese includes a PRIMARY
set—most of which was borrowed from the Chinese—and a
SECONDARY set, consisting of early native Japanese
elements. The secondary system is used only for counting certain things, and is virtually limited to the first ten

---

*Number and quantity words with a final accent (including
words like **takusán**) lose the accent when used as adverbs—that is,
without a following particle or copula.

digits. After ten, even those things counted with the secondary set take the primary numerals, and some people use primary numerals for still lower figures. A given numeral or number often has variant forms; when these are listed below, the more common variant is given first. In certain combinations, only one of the given variants may occur, but in general they are used interchangeably.

6. 5. PRIMARY NUMERALS. From one to ten, the digits are simple words. From ten to twenty they are. compound words consisting of **jū** 'ten' plus one of the other digits. The even tens (twenty, thirty, forty, etc.) are compound words consisting of one of the digits plus **jū** 'ten'. In other words, the Japanese reads 13 as 'ten-three' and 30 as 'three-ten': if the first element is larger than the second, the compound is like an addition problem $(10 + 3)$; if the first element is smaller than the second, then the compound is like a multiplication problem (3×10).

The hundreds and thousands work like the tens; 300 is 3×100 (**sám-byaku**), 3000 is 3×1000 (**san-zén**). You will notice some changes in the pronunciation of the individual elements when they occur in certain compounds. These are summarized below in note 6. 8.

Other numerals (like 21, 103, 1007, 2326) consist of a phrase of several words: **sanzén sámbyaku sánjū san** '3333'.

Here is a list of the primary numerals:

0	réi; zéro; maru	2	ní	5	gó
½	hán	3	san	6	rokú
1	ichí	4	yón; shí	7	ráná; shichí

8	hachí	24	níjū yón;	77	nanajū nána;	
9	kyû; kú		níjū shí		shichijū shichí	
10	jû	25	níjū gó	80	hachijû	
11	jûichí	26	níjū rokú	88	hachijū hachí	
12	jûní	27	níjū nána;	90	kyûjū; kujû	
13	jûsan		níjū shichí	99	kyûjū kyû;	
14	jûyón;	28	níjū hachí		kujū ku	
	jûshí	29	níjū kyû;	100	hyakú;	
15	jûgo		níjū kú		ippyakú	
16	jûrokú	30	sánjū	200	nihyakú	
17	jûnána;	40	yónjū; shijû	300	sámbyaku	
	jûshichí	44	yónjū yón;	400	yónhyaku;	
18	jûhachí		shijû shí		shihyakú	
19	jûkyû;	50	gojû	500	gohyakú	
	jûku	55	gojū gó	600	roppyakú	
20	níjū	60	rokujû	700	nanáhyaku;	
21	níjū ichí	66	rokujū rokú		shichihyakú	
22	níjū ní	70	nanájū;	800	happyakú	
23	níjū san		shichijû	900	kyûhyaku	

1,000	sén; issén	10,000	mán; ichimán
2,000	nisén	20,000	nimán
3,000	sanzén	30,000	sammán
4,000	yonsén; shisén	80,000	hachimán
5,000	gosén	100,000	jûmán
6,000	rokúsén	500,000	gojûmán
7,000	nanasén; shichisén	1,000,000	hyakumán
8,000	hassén	100,000,000	óku; ichíoku
9,000	kyûsén; kusén	100,000,000,000	chö; itchö

6. 6. ARITHMETIC. To ask 'how much is [so and so]' you can say íkura desu ka? or íkura ni narimásu ka? But unless you're talking about prices it is more common to say íkutsu desu ka? 'how many is it' or íkutsu ni narimásu ka? 'how many does it become'. In talking about prices you can also say íkura shimásu ka? 'how much does it

cost [do they make it]'.

Common arithmetic problems are said as follows:

Ní ni san o tasu to, íkutsu ni narimásu ka?	How much is 2 + 3? [When you add 3 to 2, how many does it become?]
Kyǔ kara yón o hiku to, gó ni narimásu.	9 − 4 is 5. [When you extract 4 from 9, it becomes 5.]
Hachí ni nána o kakéru to, íkutsu ni narimásu ka?	How much is 8 × 7? [When you multiply 7 by 8, how much does it become?]
Sánjū rokú o san de waru to, jūní ni narimásu.	36 ÷ 3 is 12. [When you divide 36 by 3, it becomes 12.]

6. 7. COUNTERS. There are two kinds of counters: UNIT COUNTERS (like 3 pounds, 2 hours, 4 years) and CLASS COUNTERS (like 400 head of cattle, a loaf of bread, 2 sheets of paper). The first kind refer to a quantity of something divisible like water, time, money, distance; the second kind to general classes of things that aren't ordinarily divisible, like animals, people, pencils, books.

Here is a list of some common unit counters:

‐en, ‐en	Yen [Japanese currency unit]	–jíkan	hours
		‐ji	o'clock
–sén	Sen [former currency unit]	‐fun	minutes
		‐byǒ	seconds
‐doru	dollars	–shúkan	weeks

-chŏ	Cho [Japanese unit of length, about 119 yards], 'blocks' [away]	-kágetsu	months
		-gatsú	month names
		-nen	years
		-sai	years of age
		-do	times
-gúramu	grams	-kái	times*
-kirogúramu, -kiro	kilograms	-kai	floor, storey*
-métoru	meters	-péiji	pages; page number
-kirométoru, -kiro	kilometers	-ri	Ri [Japanese mile, 2.44 miles]
-senchimétoru, -sénchi	centimeters	-shakú	Shaku [Japanese foot, about 1 foot]
-miri	millimeters		
-máiru	miles [English]		
-ínchi	inches [English]	-sún	Sun [Japanese inch, 1.2 inches]
-póndo	pounds [English— weight or money]	-nimmae	portion [of food], serving

Here is a list of some common class counters:

-dai	vehicles, mounted machines
-hai	containerfulls
-hon	slender objects (pencils, bridges, tubes, sticks, cigarets, bottles, flowers)
-mai	flat, thin objects (sheets, newspapers, handkerchiefs, dishes)
-satsu, -satsú	[bound] volumes (books, magazines)
-ken	buildings
-seki	warships
-sō	ships
-tsū, -tsū	documents, letters, communications
-tō	large domesticated animals (horses, cows)
-hikí	animals, fishes, insects

*cf. san-kái '3 times', san-gai '3rd floor'.

6. 8. SOUND CHANGES. There are a few irregularities when certain numerals are combined with counters. These are summarized below.

1. The last syllable of **ichí** and **hachí** is usually replaced by p before p, t before t or ch, s before s or sh, k before k:

ip-péiji	1 page	hap-péiji	8 pages
it-tō	1 animal	hat-tō	8 animals
it-tsū	1 letter	hat-tsū	8 letters
ít-chō	1 cho	hát-chō	8 cho
is-sén	1 Sen	has-sén	8 Sen
is-shakú	1 foot	has-shakú	8 feet
ík-ken	1 building	hák-ken	8 buildings

2. The numeral **jŭ** is usually replaced by **jip-** before p, **jit-** before t or ch, **jis-** before s or sh, **jik-** before k. Some speakers outside Tokyo use **jup-**, **jut-**, **jus-**, and **juk-** instead of the forms with the vowel **i**.

jip-péiji	10 pages
jit-tō	10 animals
jit-tsū	10 letters
jít-chō	10 Cho
jis-sén	10 Sen
jis-shakú	10 feet
jík-ken	10 buildings

3. The numerals **sán** and **yón** and the element **nan-** 'which, how many' are written **sam-**, **yom-**, **nam-** before b, p, or m.

sam-péiji	3 pages	yom-péiji	4 pages	nam-péiji	how many pages
sám-byō	3 seconds	yóm-byō	4 seconds	nám-byō	how many seconds
sám-mai	3 sheets	yóm-mai	4 sheets	nám-mai	how many sheets

This change to **m** in the spelling works for any **n** before **b, p,** or **m** within a word, so **sén** '1,000' becomes **sem-, mán** '10,000' becomes **mam-.**

4. Before some counters beginning with a voiced sound, the counter **yón** '4' appears in the form **yo-: yó-en** '4 Yen', **yó-nen** '4 years', **yó-ji** '4 o'clock', **yo-jíkan** '4 hours', **yo-jǒ** '4 mats'. Compare **yóm-byō** '4 seconds', **yón-jū** '40', **yom-mán** '40,000'. For some words, where both forms are heard, the longer is to be preferred: **yó(m)-ban** 'number 4', **yo(m)-bai** '4 times (as much)', **yó(n)-retsu** '4 rows', **yó(n)-do** '4 times'.

5. Counters beginning with **h** or **f** (including the numeral **hyaku** 'hundred' when the second element in a compound numeral), replace this by **p** after **ichi-** (**ip-**), **hachi-** (**hap-**), **jú** (**jip-**). After **san-** (**sam-**), **nan-** (**nam-**), counters change initial **h** to **b**, initial **f** to **p**. After **yon-** (**yom-**), some speakers change initial **h** or **f** to **p**, but other speakers—probably a majority—keep the initial **h** intact.

ip-pyakú	íp-pon	íp-pai	ip-pikí	íp-pun
hap-pyakú	háp-pon	háp-pai	hap-pikí	háp-pun
——	jíp-pon	jíp-pai	jíp-pikí	jíp-pun
sám-byaku	sám-bon	sám-bai	sám-biki	sám-pun
nám-byaku	nám-bon	nám-bai	nám-biki	nám-pun
——	sém-bon	sém-bai	sém-biki	(sém-pun)
——	mám-bon	mám-bai	mám-biki	(mám-pun)
yón-hyaku	yón-hon	yón-hai	yón-hiki	yón-fun
(yóm-pyaku)	(yóm-pon)	(yóm-pai)	(yóm-piki)	(yóm-pun)

6. The numerals **roku-** and **hyaku-** become **rop-** and **hyap-** before counters beginning with **h-** or **f-**; the counters replace **h-** or **f-** by **p-**. Some speakers use **rop-** and

hyap- before counters beginning with a basic **p-** also. Some speakers maintain the basic forms **roku-h-** and **roku-f-**, **hyaku-h-** and **hyaku-f-**, insetad of **rop-p-** and **hyap-p-**.

róp-pon, rokú-hon	hyáp-pon, hyakú-hon
róp-pai, rokú-hai	hyáp-pai, hyakú-hai
rop-piki, roku-hiki	hyap-piki, hyaku-hiki
róp-pun, rokú-fun	hyáp-pun, hyakú-fun
roku-péiji, rop-péiji	hyaku-péiji, hyap-péiji

7. The numerals **roku-** and **hyaku-** become **rok-** and **hyak-** before counters beginning with **k-**: **rók-ken** '6 buildings', **hyák-ken** '100 buildings'.

8. After **san-** '3', **sen-** '1,000', **man-** '10,000', **nan-** 'how many', the elements **–sén** meaning 'thousand' (but NOT **–sén** meaning 'Sen'), **–shakú** 'feet', **–sún** 'inches', **⸚seki** 'warships', **⸚sō** 'ships', **-kai** 'floor', and **⸚ken** 'buildings' are respectively **–zén**, **–jakú**, **–zún**, **⸚zeki**, **⸚zō**, **–gai**, and **⸚gen**.

san-zén '3,000'	——	——	nán-zen 'how many thousand'
san-jakú '3 ft'	——	——	nán-jaku 'how many feet'
san-zún '3 inches'	——	——	nán-zun 'how many inches'
sán-zeki '3 warships'	sén-zeki '1,000 warships'	mán-zeki '10,000 warships'	nán-zeki 'how many warships'
sán-zō '3 ships'	sén-zō '1,000 ships'	mán-zō '10,000 ships'	nán-zō 'how many ships'
sán-gen '3 bldgs.'	sén-gen '1,000 bldgs.'	mán-gen '10,000 bldgs.'	nán-gen 'how many bldgs.'

9. With most counters, either **ku** or **kyú** may be used for '9', either **shichí** or **nána** for '7', either **shí** or **yón** (**yo-**) for '4'. For some counters only one of the forms occurs: **Shigatsú** 'April', **Shichigatsú** 'July', **Kugatsú** 'September'; **yóji** '4 o'clock', **kúji** '9 o'clock'.

6. 9. SECONDARY NUMERALS. The secondary set of numerals run from 1 to 10, and for each digit there are two forms—a long form, used when the numeral is a word by itself, and a short form, used when the numeral is combined with a counter. In addition, there are a few special short forms, used on enumerative occasions, like 'counting off' in drill practice.

AS A WORD		IN A NUMBER	COUNTING OFF
1.	hitótsu	hitó-	hí, híi, hito
2.	futatsú	futá-	fú, fǔ, futa
3.	mittsú	mí-	mí, míi
4.	yottsú	yó-	yó, yǒ
5.	itsútsu	itsú	í, íi, ítsu
6.	muttsú	mú-	mú, mú
7.	nanátsu	naná-	ná, nǎ, nána
8.	yattsú	yá-	yá, yǎ
9.	kokónotsu	kokóno-	kóko
10.	tǒ	tó-, tǒ-	tó, tǒ
How many?	íkutsu	íku-	———

The secondary numerals are used with certain counters. They are also used by themselves to count words which do not take any special counter: **kaban ga hitótsu** 'one suitcase', **futatsú no mádo wa** 'the two windows', **mittsú no tsukue** '3 desks'. For counting above 10, the primary numerals are used: **kaban ga jŭgo** '15 suitcases', **níjū no mádo wa** 'the 20 windows', **juichí no tsukue** '11 desks'.

The secondary numerals are also commonly used to give ages: **Ano kodomo wa itsútsu deshō** 'That child must be five [years old].' **Watakushi wa kotoshi sánjū desu** 'I'm 30 this year.' **Anáta wa íkutsu desu ka?** 'How old are you?' There is a special word for '20 years old', **hátachi**. A somewhat more formal way of stating ages is with the primary numerals+the counter **-sai** 'years of age': **Anáta wa nánsai desu ka? Nijíssai desu.** 'How old are you?? I'm 20.'

6. 10. SECONDARY COUNTERS. Here are some counters often used with the secondary numerals. Some speakers use the secondary numerals only for the first few numbers, then switch to the other set; other speakers do not switch to the primary set of numerals until eleven.

-ashi	steps, paces	-ma	rooms
-ban	nights	-sara	platefuls
-fúkuro	bagfuls	-saji	spoonfuls
-hako	boxfuls	-sóroe, -sóroi	sets, suits
-heya	rooms	-taba	bunches
-kire	slices, cuts, pieces	-tsuki	months[=-kágetsu
-kumi	groups, sets (of matched objects)		used with primary numerals]

6. 11. COUNTING PEOPLE. There are some irregularities in the set of numbers used to count people. Most of the numbers are made up of primary numbers + the counter **-nin**, but there are different forms for 1, 2, and 4. [The expected forms *ichinin, *ninin do occur in some compounds: **ichinin-nori** 'a 1-rider ricksha', **ninin-nori** 'a 2-rider ricksha'.]

hitóri	1 person	hachínin	8 people
futarí	2 people	kyŭnin,	
sannín	3 people	kunín	9 people
yonín,		jŭnin	10 people
yottarí	4 people	jūichínin	11 people
gonín	5 people	nánnin	how many
rokúnin	6 people		people?
nanánin,		níhyaku	
shichínin	7 people	níjū nínin	222 people

6. 12. COUNTING BIRDS. The usual counter for birds is ⌐wa, which has the forms ⌐pa and ⌐ba after certain numerals:

1. ichí-wa
2. ní-wa
3. sám-ba
4. yó-wa, yón-wa, yóm-ba, shí-wa
5. gó-wa
6. róp-pa, rokú-wa
7. naná-wa, shichí-wa
8. háp-pa, hachí-wa
9. kyŭ-wa, kyŭ-ha, kú-wa
10. jíp-pa
        nám-ba   'how many birds?'

6. 13. COUNTING DAYS. There are a number of irregularities in counting days. The numbers mean either 'so-and-so many days' or 'the so-and-so-many-th day of the month', except that these two meanings are distinguished for the first number—ichinichi '1 day', tsuitachi or ichíjitsu '1st day'. An exclamation point has been

placed before each number in the list with irregularities deserving special attention:

1st day	l	tsuitachi, ichíjitsu
1 day		ichinichi
2 days, 2nd day	l	futsuka
3 days, 3rd day		mikka
4 days, 4th day		yokka
5 days, 5th day		itsuka
6 days, 6th day	l	muika
7 days, 7th day	l	nanoka, nanuka
8 days, 8th day	l	yōka
9 days, 9th day		kokonoka
10...		tōka
11...		jūichinichi
12...		jūninichi
13...		jūsannichi
14...	l	jūyokka
15...		jūgonichi
16...		jūrokunichi
17...		jūshichinichi
18...		jūhachinichi
19...		jūkunichi
20...	l	hatsuka
21...		níjū ichinichi
22...		níjū ninichi
23...		níjū sannichi
24...	l	níjū yokka
25...		níjū gonichi
26...		níjū rokunichi

27...	níjū shichinichi
28...	níjū hachinichi
29...	níjū kunichi
30...	sanjūnichi
31...	sánjū ichinichi

how many days,
which day of month?   **nánnichi**

Most of the numbers are made up of primary numerals + the counter -nichi (in rapid speech sometimes pronounced -nchi), but the numbers from 2 thru 10, 14, 20, and 24 contain elements from the set of secondary numerals + the counter -ka.

Corresponding to the noun **tsuitachi** (or **ichíjitsu**) 'first of the month' there is a word **misoka** meaning 'last of the month', and also a word **ōmísoka** meaning 'last day of the year'.

6.14. NAMES OF THE MONTHS. The names of the months are made by adding the counter -gatsú to the primary numerals:

January	**Ichigatsú**	July	**Shichigatsú**
February	**Nigatsú**	August	**Hachigatsú**
March	**Sángatsu**	September	**Kúgatsu**
April	**Shigatsú**	October	**Jūgatsú**
May	**Gógatsu**	November	**Jūichigatsú**
June	**Rokugatsú**	December	**Jūnigatsú**

Notice that the older variants for 4, 7, and 9 (**shi-, shichi-, ku-**) are always used in the month names instead of the more common forms **yon-, nana-, kyū.** There is also another word for January, **Shōgatsú.**

Be sure to differentiate **Nigatsú** '(the second month =) February' from **nikágetsu** 'two months'. To ask 'which month' you say **nángatsu, to** ask 'how many months' you say **nankágetsu.**

6.15. GIVING DATES. To say which year it is, you attach the counter **-nen** to the appropriate numerals: **sén kyúhyaku gojū nínen '1952'.** If you add the month, it follows this, and then comes the day of the month—and, if you like, the day of the week and the time of day: **Sén kyūhyaku gojŭ ichínen rokugatsú níjū sannichi getsu-yóbi gógo sánji '3 p.m., Monday, 23 June 1951.'** This whole expression then works like a noun (or an adverb).

6. 16. TELLING TIME. To say it is such-and-such o'clock, you use a primary numeral + the counter **-ji: yóji desu** 'it's 4 o'clock'. If you want to say 'it's five minutes past five (5:05)' you say **góji gófun desu** or **góji gófun sugí desu**—the word **sugí** means 'exceeding, more than'. To say 'it's five minutes before five (4:55)' you say **góji gófun máe desu—máe** of course means 'before, in front of'.* Or you can say **yóji gojūgófun** just as you can say 'four fifty-five' in English. To say 'at' a certain time, you use the particle **ni: góji ni kimáshita** 'he came at five'.

If you want to add 'a.m.' and 'p.m.', you put the words **gózen** 'before-noon' and **gógo** 'after-noon' in front of the time expression. So 'from 9 a.m. to 9 p.m.' is **gózen kúji kara gógo kúji made.**

---

*The accent of the word preceding **sugí** or **máe** (as well as **gúrai** and **góro** in 6.17, **zútsu** in 6.28, **góto ni** and **óki ni** in 6.29) is usually lost in these combinations.

To say 'half-past ten' or the like, you just add -hán 'and a half' at the end of the time expression: gógo rokuji-hán 'half past six in the evening'.

Notice the difference between sánji '(the third hour=) 3 o'clock and sanjíkan '3 hours'; to ask 'what time (=which hour, what o'clock)' you say nánji, to ask 'how much time, how long (=how many hours)' you say nanjíkan.

6. 17. **GÚRAI AND GÓRO.** The particle gúrai means 'approximate quantity, about so much'; the particle góro means 'approximate point in time, about then'. So yoji-kan gúrai means 'about 4 hours', yoji góro (ni) '(at) about 4 o'clock.' Sén kyūhyaku nijŭnen gúrai means 'about 1920 years', but sén kyŭhyaku nijūnen góro means 'about the year 1920'. The idiom kono-goro (or konó-goro) means 'recently' (=chikágoro). Compare the related noun kóro 'time, era, period' as in sono kóro wa 'at that time (period)'. Gúrai is often written (and sometimes pronounced) kúrai; there is a related noun kurai which means 'position, rank'. Notice also the idioms kono-kurai (or kono-gurai) and kore-kurai (=kore gúrai) 'this much, to this extent'.

6. 18. **PARTICLE YA.** The particle ya is used to make an incomplete enumeration. When you list several things, but have not exhausted all the items on your list, you use ya—if you do exhaust the list, giving all the items, then you connect the items with the particle to. Notice that the particles to and ya usually occur after every item in the list EXCEPT THE LAST—after it, you use whatever particle is appropriate to show the relationship between the whole phrase and the rest of the sentence.

Hón-ya de wa hón to zasshi
    to shimbun o utte imásu.

At the bookshop they sell
    books, magazines, and
    newspapers [and that's
    all].

Hón-ya de wa hón ya zasshi
    ya shimbun o utte imásu.

At the bookshop they sell
    books, magazines, and
    newspapers [and other
    things—stationery, etc.].

Tēburu no ue ní wa em-
    pitsu to mannénhitsu ga
    arimásu.

On the table there's a
    pencil and a fountain
    pen.

Tsukue no ue ní wa kamí
    ya hón ya takusán no te-
    gami ga arimáshita.

On the desk there was pa-
    per, books, and lots of
    letters [and other things].

6. 19.   NÁDO, NÁNKA. The particle nádo is used after a
noun, with or without other particles (including ga, o, and
wa) following.   The English equivalent is often 'and the
like, et cetera, and so on, or something of the sort'.   The
force of the particle is to make the limits of the preceding phrase somewhat more vague.   It often occurs after
a group of nouns which are usually connected to each
other by the particle ya, but sometimes the particle is
omitted.

Gyūniku ya butaniku nádo
    o kaimáshita.

I bought beef and pork and
    the like.

Yaoya wa yasai nádo o utte
    imásu.

The grocer sells vegetables
    and so forth.

Asa nado wa yóku sampo   Of a morning, I often go
ni ikimásu.   for a walk.

Occasionally the particle **nádo** occurs after a verb or
adjective in the plain imperfect or perfect:

Amerika e shutchō suru   He's talking of making a
nádo to itte imásu (or   business trip to America
...suru tó ka itte...).   (and the like). (cf. p.
                              213.)

The particle **nánka** means 'the likes of' with negative
or deprecatory implications: **Watakushi nánka sonna
kotó wa dekimasén** 'A person like me wouldn't be able
to do such a thing'. **Eigo nánka shirimasén** 'I don't know
any ENGLISH (it's too hard for me)!'

6. 20. PARTICLE **KA** MEANING 'OR'. You have
learned the particle **ka** as a sort of audible question-mark.
It also occurs after a noun with the meaning '(either...)
or...'. Here are some examples:

Hón ka zasshi o katte yo-   I guess I'll buy a book or
mimashǒ.   magazine to read.
Ashitá ka asátte ikú deshō. I expect he'll go either to-
                               morrow or the next day.

Daikon o hitótaba ka fu-   I guess I'll buy 1 or 2
tátaba kaimashǒ.   bunches of Japanese
                               white-radishes.

Aoki-san (tó) ka Suzuki-san Aoki or Suzuki (or some-
ga kimásu.   one) will come.

Notice the difference in meaning between these two sentences:

Ocha ka kōhíi ga (or wa) sukí desu ka?	Do you like tea or coffee (either one)?
Ocha ga sukí desu ka, kōhíi ga sukí desu ka?	Do you like tea or coffee (which one)?

6. 21.   PARTICLES WA AND O WITH IKÁGA DESU KA? If you offer a person some tea you usually say Ocha wa ikága desu ka? 'How about some tea?' In this expression, the particle used is wa. [You may sometimes hear Ocha o ikága desu ka?] If you use a quantity word, however, the particle may be o. Ocha o ippai ikága desu ka? 'How about a cup of tea?' Ocha o mō sukóshi ikága desu ka? 'How about a little more tea?' The use of o is probably conditioned by the implication of 'drinking', which would take a direct object: Ocha o nónde wa ikága desu ka? 'As for drinking tea, how about it?'

6. 22.   HITÓTSU. Sometimes the word hitótsu is used, not to mean 'one' of something, but to mean 'just' or 'a little' or 'some' or 'once':

Okáshi o hitótsu ikága desu ka?	How about some pastry?
Shimbun o hitótsu yónde mimashō.	Guess I'll read the paper.
Zasshi o hitótsu mimashō.	Guess I'll just have a look at the magazine.

6. 23. 'ONLY'–DAKÉ AND SHIKA. There are two common ways to say 'only' in Japanese: **daké** and **shika**.

Daké is a particle which means something like 'to the extent of', 'to the limit of'. When following a noun which would ordinarily take the particle **ga** or **o**, usually only **daké** occurs; but if the noun is followed by some particle other than **ga** or **o**, then both **daké** and the particle occur—usually in that order. Here are some examples of **daké**:

Sakúban watakushi daké éiga o mí ni ittá no desu.	Last night I was the only one who went to see the movie.
Kono zasshi daké yomimasén deshita.	This is the only magazine I didn't read.
Kore wa senséi dake ni itte kudasai.	Please tell this only to the teacher.
Tēburu no ué ni wa pán dake áru n desu.	There's nothing but bread on the table.

The colloquial particle **(k)kirí** can replace **daké** in a few of its uses: **sore (k)kirí desu** 'that's all'; **(k)kirí** is never followed by another particle. (See also p. 256.)

Daké sometimes occurs after a verb or adjective with the meaning 'as much as': **hoshíi dake** 'as much as you desire [as is desired]', **dekiru dake** 'as much as possible'.* Examples:

Dekiru dake háyaku kakimáshita.	I wrote as fast as I could.
Átta dake tabemáshita.	I ate everything there was.

---

*The verb **dekíru** loses its accent in this phrase, but other tonic words usually retain their accents.

The other common way to say 'only' is to use the particle shika 'but only'. This particle is ALWAYS FOLLOWED BY THE NEGATIVE; shika + the negative has about the same meaning as daké + the affirmative: **Kudámono dake kaimáshita** = **Kudámono shika kaimasén deshita** 'I only bought fruit; I bought nothing but fruit'. The basic meaning of shika is something like '[nothing] but, except for'. So **Tanaka-san shika kimasén deshita** means something like 'except for Mr. Tanaka [somebody] didn't come', that is 'ONLY Mr Tanaka came'.

The particle shika, like the particle daké, usually does not occur together with the particles **ga** or **o**. If it occurs with other particles, the others PRECEDE shiká. With daké it is more common for the other particles to FOLLOW:

Senséi dake ni iimáshita.	I told only the teacher.
Senséi ni shika iimasén deshita.	I told only the teacher.

If you want to use 'only' + a negative in English ('Only the teacher I didn't tell'), you have to use daké in Japanese, since shika + the negative would give just the opposite meaning:

Senséi dake ni iimasén deshita.	Only the teacher I didn't tell.

Both shika + the negative (but with an affimative meaning in the English translation) and daké with either the negative (with negative meaning in English) or the affirmative are used to translate English 'only' after an ordinary noun. After a number or quantity word, just shika + the negative is used to mean 'only'—daké means 'just, neither more nor less than':

Jūjíkan kakarimáshita.	It took ten hours.
Jūjíkan dake kakarimáshita.	It took just ten hours. [Which seems neither long nor short.]
Jūjíkan shika kakarimasén deshita.	It took only ten hours. [Which seems short.]

Notice also the following sentences:

Jūjíkan mo kakarimáshita.	It took all of ten hours. It took even ten hours. [Which seems long.]
Jūjíkan mo kakarimasén deshita.	It didn't take even ten hours.

6.24. APPROXIMATE NUMBERS. Two consecutive numbers can often be combined to mean 'about 2 or 3, about 3 or 4', etc. These are then added to a single counter. Not all possible combinations occur; for instance, none occur with the counter -ji 'o'clock'. For those which do not occur, you can use two full words connected by the particle ka 'or': sánji ka yóji ni kúru deshō 'He'll come around 3 or 4 o'clock', Shigatsú ka Gogatsú deshō 'It will be April or May'. Here are some examples of approximate numbers:

ichinijíkan	1 or 2 hours
nisan-en	2 or 3 Yen
sán-yokka	3 or 4 days

shigomai	4 or 5 sheets
goroppon	5 or 6 pencils
rokushichinen	6 or 7 years
shichihachiinchi	7 or 8 inches
hakkukágetsu	8 or 9 months
nisannin	2 or 3 people
san-yonin	3 or 4 people

Note that the combination of 9 + 10 does not occur with the meaning '9 or 10'; kujíssai would mean '90 years old' rather than '9 or 10 years old'—to say the latter, you say kyûsai ka jíssai.

The higher numerals also combine in similar fashion:

san-yon-hyakugúramu	300 or 400 grams
jūgorokunen	15 or 16 years
nanájū shigoen	74 or 75 Yen
nanájū rokushichien	76 or 77 Yen

The secondary numerals usually do not combine in the same way. Instead, the two consecutive numbers are connected by ka: hitótaba ka futátaba 'one or two bunches'.

6. 25. FRACTIONS. To express ordinary fractions, like $3/4$ or $2/3$ or $5/8$, the Japanese say something like 'three of four parts, two of three parts, five of eight parts' using the counter -bun 'part'. For 'one-half' there is the special word hambún, and for 'so-many and a half' the regular number takes the suffix -hán 'and a half': jūichiji-hán '11:30', sanshūkan-hán '$3^1/_2$ weeks', yonen-hán '$4^1/_2$ years', sampun-hán '$3^1/_2$ minutes'.

To translate '21 is one-third of 63' you say Níjū ichí wa, rokujū san no sambun no ichí desu. To translate

'This is half of that', you replace the expected expression sore no by sono and say **Kore wa, sono hambún desu.**

6. 26. PERCENTAGE. Percentage is shown in Japanese by three different counters: **-rin** '.001 [one-tenth of one percent]', **-bu** '.01 [one percent]', and **-wari** '.10 [ten percent]'. In-between percentages are given by combining these numbers: **níwari sámbu ichírin** '.231 [23.1 percent]'. To say '200 is 25 percent of 800' you say **Nihyakú wa, happyakú no níwari góbu desu;** to say '25 percent of 800 is 200' you say **Happyakú no níwari góbu wa, nihyakú desu.** To say 'That is 33 percent of this' you say **Soré wa kono sánwari sámbu desu.** The element **-bu** also means 'part' in some words; and **ichíbu** can mean 'a part, one part' as well as 1 percent. **Bú** and **bún** both occur as words with the meaning 'part', but more commonly they are combined in the word **búbun** 'part, parts'.

6. 27. MULTIPLES. To express 'two times (as much or as big, etc., as something else), three times, four times' and so forth, you use the counter **-bai** 'multiple'. To say '60 is 3 times 20' you say **Rokujū wa níjū no sambai désu.** To say 'This is 2 times (as much as) that' you say **Kore wa sono nibai désu.** '4 times' is usually **yo(m)bai;** '7 times' **nanabai** or **shichibai;** '9 times' **kubai** or **kyūbai.** Compare these multiples with the stating of simple multiplication problems: **Níjū ni sán o kakéru to rokujú ni narimásu** '20 × 3 = 60'.

6. 28. ZÚTSU. The particle **zútsu** is placed immediately after a number [numeral + counter] to mean something like 'distributively'. In the English translation you will find its equivalent as 'each, every, at a time, apiece'. The

exact reference of the phrase number+**zútsu** is sometimes in doubt. The sentence **Hitotaba zútsu kaimáshita** could mean (1) Everybody bought one bunch, (2) We bought one bunch of each [vegetable], (3) We bought one bunch at a time. The total information actually supplied us by the sentence is: somebody bought, one bunch was the extent, and there was a distributive relationship between the buying and the one bunch. The NATURE of the relationship 'each of us; of each [vegetable]; at a time' has to be inferred from the context or the situation. Often a few additional words in the sentence will help indicate which of the three distributive relationships is referred to:

(1)	**Minná ga hitotaba zútsu kaimáshita.**	Everybody bought one bunch apiece.
(2)	**Négi to ninjin o hitotaba zútsu kaimáshita.**	We bought one bunch each of onions and carrots.
(3)	**Máiasa hitotaba zútsu kaimáshita.**	We bought one bunch (at a time) every morning.

These sentences, too, could be construed with the other meanings, but the additional contexts make the given meanings more probable. There is a similar ambiguity with the English word 'each'.

Here are some additional examples:

Sakúban rokúnin no tomo-dachi ni tegami o ittsū zútsu kakimáshita.	Last night I wrote each of my six friends a letter.
Kono ame o hitotsu zútsu tábete kudasai.	Please eat this candy a piece at a time.

Góhan o tábete kara, kusuri to oyu o ippai zútsu nónde kudasai.	After eating, drink one glass each of medicine and hot water.
Niwatori o ichiwa zútsu kaimashő.	Let's buy one chicken apiece. OR Let's buy one

chicken at a time. OR Let's buy one chicken of each kind.

6. 29. GÓTO NI, ÓKI NI. The expression **góto ni** is added to a noun or noun phrase to give the meaning 'every so many, each and every': **nijikan góto ni** 'every two hours', **sannen góto ni** 'every three years'.* The same expression after a verb is equivalent to ...**ta(m)bí ni** 'every time that': **kúru goto ni＝kúru ta(m)bi ni** 'every time he comes'. (The expression is not used after the copula or adjectives, including negatives in **-nai** and desideratives in **-tai**.)

The expression **óki ni** (from the infinitive of **oku** 'puts aside') means 'regularly skipping': **ichinichi óki ni** 'every other day', **sangen óki ni** 'every fourth house'.

C. EXERCISES.

1. See how fast you can count from 1 to 100. Use the most common primary numerals. [Most Japanese counting fast will use **shí** for 4, **shichí** for 7, and **ku** for 9.] Now count from 1 to 100 by twos; next, try it by threes. Count from 100 to 1000 for-

---

*For **toshi góto ni** 'every year', **tsuki góto ni** 'every month', **shūkan góto ni** 'every week', and **hi goto ni** [accent irregular!] 'every day', the more common expressions are **maitoshi (mainen), maitsuki (maigetsu), maishū,** and **máinichi**. There is also a suffix **-goto** 'including even': **ringo o kawa-goto tabéru** 'eats the apple, skin and all'.

wards and then backwards, by hundreds.

2. Count out 31 days. Count out 15 people.

3. Read the following numbers in Japanese. Remember that numbers above 10,000 are read in units of 10,000:

(a) 34, (b) 77, (c) 106, (d) 370, (e) 9, (f) 610, (g) 213, (h) 12,000, (i) 1,000,000, (j) 16,400,000, (k) 7,356,200, (l) 103,238,416, (m) 19.

4. Read the following sums of money. The symbol ￥ means Yen.

(a) ￥500, (b) ￥3,500, (c) ￥12,050, (d) ￥25,000, (e) ￥300,000, (f) ￥25.50, (g) ￥2,150,425.75, (h) $ 595, (i) $ 2,500.

5. Give the following dates in Japanese:

(a) 12 October 1492, (b) 7 December 1941, (c) 10 September 1945, (d) 12 January 1946, (e) 30 July 1950, (f) 24 November 1948, (g) 14 February 1952, (h) 6 April 1953, (i) 4 March 1947, (j) 8 May 1954, (k) 10 August 1960, (l) 1 June 1951.

6. Here is a group of sentences based on **Getsuyôbi** 'Monday'; change this to each day of the week, with appropriate changes in the other sentences.

Kyô wa Getsuyôbi desu. Kinô wa Nichiyôbi deshita. Ototói wa Doyôbi deshita. Ashitá wa Kayôbi desu. Asátte wa Suiyôbi desu.

7. Below are some sentences with blanks for numbers.

Pick out the appropriate numbers from the list on the right. Then translate the sentences.

1. Ocha o —— nónda no desu.
2. Mannénhitsu ga —— arimásu.
3. Kisen ['steamship'] o —— mimá-shita.
4. Sono —— no tegami wa dáre ga káita deshō ka?
5. —— no tatémono kara hito ga takusán déte kimáshita.
6. Jidósha o —— shika kawanákatta n desu.
7. Kamí ga —— irimásu.
8. Anó hito no káita —— no hón o yomimáshita ka?
9. Inú ga —— shika inákatta n desu.
10. —— no senséi wa eigo ga deki-másu.
11. Kumamoto máde ikú no ni, —— kakáru deshō.
12. Kotori ga —— kí no ue ni to-matte imáshita.
13. Musumé wa sakana o —— shika tabemasén deshita.

(a) futsuka
(b) nisanzō
(c) ichídai
(d) nisambai
(e) sámba
(f) nitsū
(g) jíppon
(h) nisatsu
(i) ichinimmae
(j) ippikí
(k) shigomai
(l) sángen
(m) futarí

8. Do the following arithmetic problems in Japanese. Don't write anything down; do them in your head.

(a) $24 + 36 = ?$ (b) $48 \div 4 = ?$
(c) $7 - 2 = ?$ (d) $6 \times 7 = ?$

(e) $7 + 8 = ?$ (f) $154 - 93 = ?$

(g) $530 + 220 = ?$ (h) $990 \div 3 = ?$

(i) $6 - 6 = ?$

9. Read the following numbers in Japanese; remember to make the appropriate sound changes.

(a) 10-tō, (b) 8-tsū, (c) 50-sén, (d) 1⌐ken, (e) 8-shakú, (f) 10⌐chō, (g) 3⌐mai, (h) ?⌐peiji, (i) 4-en, (j) 3⌐hon, (k) 3⌐fun, (l) 3-hiki, (m) 3-bai, (n) 3⌐hai, (o) 1-hai, (p) 10⌐fun, (q) 4⌐fun, (r) 4-nen, (s) 3⌐ken, (t) 3-sún, (u) 3-sén [Sen], (v) 3,000, (w) ?-shakú, (x) 4-jíkan, (y) 4⌐byō, (z) 100⌐ken, (aa) 3-seki, (bb) 31–sai, (cc) 104-en, (dd) 144-nen.

10. **Nánji desu ka?** —— **désu.** Fill in the blank with each of the following times:

(a) 10:00 (b) 12:30 (c) 3 p.m. (d) 8:30 a.m. (e) 9:15 (f) 5:27 (g) 6:10 (h) about 4 p.m. (i) 9:45 (j) 12.50 p.m. (k) about 1.30

D. COMPREHENSION

[Íma Némoto-san no ókusan wa Fukúi-san no ókusan to hanáshite iru tokoro désu.]

N. Kinŏ wa Ginza e kaimono ni ikimáshita ga, kono-goro wa iroiro na monó ga tákaku nátte irú no de, ammari kaimono ga deki-masén deshita.

F. Sŏ desu ka? Ŏki na depǎto de mo, takái desu ka?

N. Totemo takái desu nĕ. Watakushi wa atarashíi kása ga irú keredomo, depắto e itte míru to, amagása wa happyakuen dé, kōmorigása wa sén gohyakúen mo surú kara, kawazu ni déte kitá n desu.

F. Shokuryŏhin no nedan mo kono-goro tákaku narimáshita nĕ. Késa yaoya e itte hōrénsō o sambyakugúramu, ninjin o futátaba, daizu o gohyakugúramu shika kawanákatta no ni, nihyakú gojū rokúen gojissén ni narimáshita.

N. Nikú mo sŏ desu nĕ. Toriniku daké wa yasúi deshō. Késa kuji-han góro ni nikúya e itte míru to, gyūniku ya yōniku wa nákatta n desu ga, butaniku no nedan wa hyakugúramu hyaku gojŭen deshita.

F. Uchi dé wa senshū sakana shika tabénakatta n desu. Kínjo no sakanaya ní wa totemo íi sakana ga átte, nedan mo sōtō yásukatta n desu.

N. Watakushi wa sakana ga dáisuki desu ga, shújin wa kirai dé, kodomo mo ammari sukí ja nái no de, kono-goro wa ammari tabemasén.

F. Íma nánji desu ka?

N. Chōdo jūichíji jūgófun ni narimásu.

F. Isha no tokoró e kodomo o tsurete ikimásu kara, shitsúrei itashimásu. Sayonára.

N. Sayonára.

LESSON 7.

A. BASIC SENTENCES. 'Life in Japan.'

1. Nihón to iu kuni wa Amerika to chigau tokoró ga ói desu.

The country of Japan has many points where it differs from America.

2. Dónna tokoró ga chigaú ka to iu to, tsugí no yó na tokoró desu.

When you ask what sort of points are different, it's as follows.

3. Mázu, Nihon no ié wa Amerika no yóri mo chiisái yō desu.

First, Japanese houses seem to be smaller than American ones.

4. Uchi no náka e háiru toki ni wa, génkan de kutsú ya geta o nugimásu.

When you enter a house, you take off your shoes and clogs in the entrance-hall.

5. Sore kara, (kutsú ka geta o núide kara,) agarimásu.

Then, after you've taken off your shoes or clogs, you enter [go up].

6. Saikin, kábā o haite, kutsú o haita mama agaru kotó mo arimásu.

Lately, sometimes people also put on [cloth] 'covershoes' and go right in with their shoes on.

7. Heya no náka ni wa, tatami ga shiite átte, yuka wa miemasén.

Inside the room, mats are spread and you can't see the floor.

8. Shōji ya fusuma ya itádo o tsukatte, ōkíi

A big house is divided up into separate little

uchí o betsubetsu no chiisái heyá ni shite arimásu.

rooms by using shōji [translucent sliding paper doors], fusuma [opaque sliding paper doors], and itádo [wooden sliding doors].

9. Taitei shōji wa zashikí to engawa no aida ni átte, fusuma wa cha-nomá to nakanóma no aida ni átte, itádo wa katteguchi ni ari-másu.

Usually the translucent paper doors are between the drawing-room and the veranda, the opaque paper doors are be-tween the tea-room and the central room, and the wooden doors are at the kitchen entrance.

10. Yóru ni náru to, amádo to iu monó o engawa no mawari ni shime-másu.

When it becomes night, they close the [things called] amádo around the veranda.

11. Sore wa dorobō ga hai-ránai yō ni, sore kara mata áme ya kaze ga uchi no náka e hairá-nai yō ni suru tamé desu.

That is in order to keep thieves from entering, and further to keep rain and wind from coming into the house.

12. Seiyōma no iriguchi ya benjo no iriguchi ní wa, dóa mo arimásu.

At the entrance to the Western-style room and and at the entrance to the toilet, there are

[Western-style wooden]
doors too.

13. Zashikí ni wa, tokonoma ga átte, tokonoma ní wa kakémono ga kákete arimásu.

In the drawing-room there is a **tokonoma** [raised alcove or recess used for ornamental purposes and as a sort of family shrine], and in the **tokonoma** is hung a scroll.

14. Daidokoro wa katte tó mo iimásu.

The kitchen is also called katte.

15. Chanomá to imá de wa, dóchira ga ōkíi desu ka?

Of the tea-room and the living room, which is the larger?

16. Futsū wa ima no hǒ ga ōkíi desu.

Usually the living room is larger.

17. Furobá ya semmenjo wa benjó to onaji tokoro ni arimásu ka?

Is the bathroom and the lavatory in the same place as the toilet?

18. Iie, chigaimásu. Furobá to iu tokoro wa betsu ná n desu.

No, it isn't. The [place called the] bathroom is separate.

19. Dóko de góhan o tabéru ka shitte imásu ka?

Do you know where they eat?

20. Daidokoro kara shokuji o chanomá ka imá e motté kite, soko de suwatte tabemásu.

They bring the food [meal] from the kitchen into the tea-room or living room. and eat it sitting there.

21. Sore kara, yóru ni nátte neru toki, dǒ shimásu ka?

Well then, when it gets to be night and they sleep, what do they do?

22. Oshiire kara yágu ya futon o dáshite, tatami no ué ni shikimásu.

They take padded over-quilts [yágu] and padded under-quilts [futon] out of the closets and spread them on the mats.

23. Kore wa "toko" to itte, Nihonjín wa yóru neru kotó o "toko ni háiru" to ka "toko ni tsukú" to ka iimásu.

This is called a toko, and Japanese call going to bed at night "toko ni háiru" [goes into the bed] or "toko ni tsukú" [contacts the bed].*

24. Naruhodo sǒ desu ka. Amerikájin wa shindai ni nemásu ně.

Oh, I see. Americans 'go to bed', you know. [OR sleep in a bed]

25. Nihon no uchi wa sonna ni chigau to iu kotó o shirimasén deshita.

I didn't know Japanese houses were so different.

26. Chikágoro made wa Nihón de wa, Jūnigatsu sánjū ichinichi ni umareta kodomo wa, tsugí no hi ni futatsú ni náru to iu kotó o shitte imáshita ka?

Did you know that until recently in Japan a child born on 31 December would become 2 years old the next day?

*But nowadays the latter expression means 'takes to one's bed with illness'.

27. Sore wa kazoé-doshi to itte, Nihon no shūkan dé wa Amerika no hitó ga ichiban odoroku kotó darō to omoimásu.

That is called Japanese-count age, and I think it must be the most surprising of Japanese customs to an American.

28. Umareta bákari no akambō wa mō íssai de, sore kara toshí o tóru no wa tanjóbi ja nákute, Shínnen na n desu kara né.

It's because a baby just born is treated as one year old already and then the adding on [taking up] of a [new] year is not [on] one's birthday, but [at] New Year's, you see.

28a. Kéredomo, sono shūkan wa sensōgo kawari-máshita.

But that custom changed after the war.

29. Anáta wa Amerikájin ni shité wa, Nihon no shūkan ni daibu nárete imasu né.

For an American you're rather well used to [accustomed to, versed in] Japanese customs, aren't you.

30. Watakushi wa Nihonjín ni kiite mitái kotó ga ói keredomo, anáta hodo Nihongo ga dekínai kara, komari-másu.

There are lots of things I'd like to find out from the Japanese, but my Japanese isn't as good as yours, so I really have a hard time.

VOCABULARY ITEMS.

NOUNS

kuchi	mouth, opening	shikii	runners [for sliding doors]
-guchi	opening, entrance, exit, recess	suríppa	house slippers
iriguchi	entrance	ōsetsuma	parlor [= seiyōma]
deguchi	exit	óngaku	music
jochū	maid	mōfu	blanket
hi (p. 428)	day	zabúton	[seat] cushions
yotei	plan, expectation, schedule	chawan	bowl, rice-bowl
		toshí	year, age
júnsa, omáwari-san	policeman	shinchūgun	Occupation (Forces)
mizuúmi	lake	chūryūgun	Security Forces
kóe	voice	totsuzen	suddenly
inú	dog	zutto	by far; all the time, straight through
umá [mmá]	horse		
mura	village		
kí	tree, wood	tsugí (no)	following, next
itá	wood, board	hontō (no)	real, true, really

VERBS

chiga[w]u	is different	tsukú	contacts, touches, arrives, adheres, sticks, hits
kawaru	is changed, changes		
agaru	goes up, enters [Japanese house]	kazoéru	counts, enumerates
shiku	spreads something out	umareru [mmareru]	gets born, is born
kakéru	hangs something up	naréru	gets accustomed, gets used to
hiku	draws out, takes out, pulls out, extracts	nárete iru	is accustomed to, is versed in
		naku	cries, weeps
dásu	puts out; mails	(e) yoru	drops in (at)
okuru	sends, sends off	tsukúru	makes, builds

suwaru	sits	oshieru	teaches, instructs,
koshikakéru	sits [Western-	nará[w]u	learns
	style only]	ara[w]u	washes

ADJECTIVES			
nemui	is sleepy	tsuyói	is strong
mazúi	is tasteless,	wakái	is young
	inconvenient	yasashii	is easy; is gentle

NOTE: **Furúi** 'is old' is the opposite of **atarashíi** 'is new'—it does not refer to age. The opposite of **wakái** 'is young' is **toshiyorí desu** 'is [an] old [person].' To say a person is 'older' you can say either **toshí ga ue desu** or **toshiue désu**. To say a person is 'younger' you can say either **toshí ga shita desu** or **toshishita désu**.

B. STRUCTURE NOTES.

7. 1. QUOTATIONS. When you want to quote what somebody says, asks, thinks, believes, writes, etc, you either do it directly by quoting his exact words, or indirectly by giving the gist of what he says. So you can say either 'Taro says "I'm going to see a movie" ' or 'Taro says he's going to see a movie.' In Japanese, both these sentences are treated the same way: **Tárō wa éiga o mí ni iku to iimásu.** The particle **to** shows that the preceding words are a quotation, either direct or indirect. Japanese usually quote by giving the gist of a statement or question, rather than its exact words, when these would differ. For instance, to say 'Taro asked (me) "Are you going to the movies?" ', you could say **Tárō wa (watakushi ni) anáta ga éiga o mí ni ikú ka to kikimáshita**, but it would be more common to say **Tárō wa watakushi ga éiga o mí ni**

ikú ka (to) kikimáshita 'Taro asked if I was going to the movies'. Notice how the tense of English verbs sometimes changes when we shift a direct quotation to an indirect—'Taro asked "Are you going" ' but 'Taro asked if I was going'. Japanese verbs keep the same mood they would have in direct quotation, even when you're summarizing rather than giving the exact words. Note the particles in kómban kúru TO KA itte imáshita 'was saying SOMETHING ABOUT coming tonight'. (Cf. pp. 193, 375.)

It is more common always to use a PLAIN form before the quoting particle to, but sometimes you will hear the POLITE form, especially if the speaker is trying to quote the exact words:...ikimásu ka to kikimáshita.

Sometimes you can't tell how much of the sentence is to be included in the quotation, except by context. The sentence Watakushi wa senkyŏshi da to iimáshita can mean either 'I said that [somebody] is a missionary' or '[somebody] said that I am a missionary'; unless the situation indicated otherwise, the topic watakushi wa would probably be taken to refer both to the subject of the quotation and to the person who said it: 'I said that I was a missionary.'

The quoting particle to—not to be confused with the particle meaning 'with' or 'and', or with the particle meaning 'whenever, if'—is often pronounced with a special high pitch and an abruptly clipped vowel. You will sometimes hear this special high pitch used with other words; it shows that the speaker is injecting an added liveliness, a special color, to his words. Japanese often make a slight pause before—and sometimes after—the quoting particle.

In quoting a question you use the verb **kiku** 'asks' or the phrase **kiite míru** 'tries asking, asks to see, finds out'. Sometimes the particle **to** is omitted in questions, particularly in the tentative mood: **ikú ka kiite mimashŏ** 'let's ask if he's going'. The verb **kiku** also means 'listens, hears': **Júnsa kara kikimáshita** 'I heard it from the policeman', **Hára Chíeko-san o kikimáshita** 'I heard Chieko Hara [the pianist]', **Júnsa ni kikimáshita** 'I asked the policeman', **Hára-san ni kikimáshita** 'I asked Miss Hara'.

The plain copula **dá** is usually omitted before **ka**. If you are quoting a question like **shiháinin desu ka** 'is it the manager' which includes the polite copula, instead of replacing **désu** with the plain form **dá**, you usually omit the copula altogether: **Shiháinin ka to kikimáshita** 'He asked if it was the manager.' If an adjective is used, of course, you just put it in the plain form:

Heyá wa ōkíi desu.	The room is big.
Heyá wa ōkíi to iimáshita.	He said the room was big.
Heyá wa ōkíi desu ka?	Is the room big?
Heyá wa ōkíi ka to kiki-máshita.	He asked if the room was big.

The meaning of the quotation particle **to** is something like 'close quotes' or 'end of quotation', but it gets translated various ways in English: he said THAT he'd come, she asked IF there was any, I thought [ZERO] I'd go.

Here are some more examples of quotations:

Watakushi wa dóno taté-mono ga yūbínkyoku ka	I inquired which building was the postoffice.

to kiite mimáshita.

Hanjíkan oyógu to, tsuka-réru to iú n desu.

He says he gets tired when he swims for a half-hour.

Shújin wa dekakeru toki ni, súgu káeru to ittá no desu.

My husband said he'd be right back when he went out.

Jírō ga kitá toki, kippu o mó kattá ka to kiki-mashó.

When Jiro arrives, I'll ask him if he has already bought the tickets.

Tanaka-san ni Níkkō e asobi ni itta kotó ga áru ka kiite mimashó.

I'll find out whether Mr. Tanaka has even been to Nikko [for pleasure].

Shachō wa Kánno-san ga Ōsaka e shutchō suru hazu dá to ittá n desu.

The president of the company said that Mr. Kanno is supposed to go to Osaka on a business-trip.

Yasai no hóshiku nái to itta hitó wa nikú dake kattá n desu ka?

Did the person who said he didn't want any vegetables buy only meat?

Tanaka-san wa okane ga sukóshi shika nái kara, yasumí ni nátta kere-domo, asobi ni iku kotó ga dekínai to itte imá-shita.

Mr. Tanaka was saying he had only a little money, so although he has a vacation, he can't go anywhere.

Dáre ga gaikoku-káwase no shigoto no keiken ga áru ka to shachō wa kiite mimáshita.

The president of the company inquired who had experience in foreign-exchange work.

Uchi e káette yasúmu tsu-

I said I was going home

mori dá to ittá n desu ga,   to bed but I met a
tomodachi ni átta kara,   friend so we went to see
issho ni éiga o mí ni ittá   a movie together.
n desu.

7. 2. **TO IU.** When a phrase ending in **to iu** [**to yuu**] modifies a noun, there are several possible meanings:

If the noun refers to a message or the like, the part preceding **to iu** may be a quotation or paraphrase of the content: **Tanaka-san ga ashita kúru tsumori dá to iu tegami ga kimáshita** 'A letter came which said that Mr. Tanaka intends to come tomorrow.' Compare **Kono tegami wa Tanaka-san ga ashita kúru tsumori dá to iimásu** 'This letter says that Mr. Tanaka intends to come tomorrow.'

If the part preceding **to iu** is a name, the expression means 'which is called, which is named': **Máru-biru to iu tatémono** 'the building called the Marunouchi Building', **Nippon-Yūsen-Káisha to iu kaisha** 'the company called the NYK [Japan Mail Line]', **Tanaka Tárō to iu shokkō** 'a factory-worker called Taro Tanaka', **Kanazawa-ya to iu inshokúten** 'a restaurant named the Kanazawa-ya', **Kaigan-ryókan to iu yadoya** 'a Japanese inn called the K. [Seaside Inn]', **Ōsaka-Máinichi to iu shimbun** 'the newspaper called Osaka Mainichi [Osaka Daily]'.

If the noun modified is **kotobá** 'word', **séntensu** or **búnshō** 'sentence', **jí** 'written character', the expression **to iu** means something like 'which is said, which is read'—that is, it refers directly to the word, sentence, or character: **kabushiki-gáisha to iu kotobá** 'the word **kabushiki-gáisha**', chotto mátte kudasai to iu búnshō 'the sentence [which reads] "please wait a minute" ', hón to iu jí 'the character [which is read] hón.' To say 'how do you say this word in Japanese' you say **Kono kotobá wa Nihongo de nán to iimásu ka?** To say 'how do you say this sentence in Japanese' you usually just say **Kore wa Nihongo de dŏ iimásu ka?** To say 'how do you write this sentence in Japanese' you say **Kono búnshō wa (or Kore wa) Nihongo de dŏ kakimásu ka?**

If the expression is followed by **kotó** or **nó** 'fact', the meaning is something like 'the fact that'. This sort of expression is often used with verbs of knowing or informing. **Ashita kúru tsumori dá to iu kotó o shitte imáshita ka?** 'Did you know he was planning to come tomorrow?' **Ashita kúru tsumori dá to ittá no wa kikoemasén deshita** 'I hadn't heard that he had said he was planning to come tomorrow'. **Kyŏ kónai to iu kotó o kakimáshita** 'He wrote that he wouldn't come today.'

The expression **nán to iu** before a noun sometimes has the flavor 'just what, just which'. It's a somewhat less specific way to inquire **dóno**. **Nán to iu hón desu ka?** 'Just what book is it?', **Dóno hón desu ka?** 'Which book is it?' If you have a certain, limited number of possibilities in mind when you ask 'which' or 'what' you will probably say **dóno**, but if the field is wide open for an answer, you are more likely to say **nán to iu**. This expression is sometimes used as a sort of exclamation 'What a...!': **Nán to iu íi oténki deshō nĕ** 'My what a nice day (it seems to be)!'

Here are some more examples of **to iu**:

Soko e ikitaku nái to iu kotó wa Eigo de dó iimásu ka?	How do you say [I don't want to go there] in English?
Sháin to iu kotobá wa Eigo de nán to iimásu ka?	What do you call sháin [staff-member] in English?
Aói to iu jí o káku kotó ga dekimásu ka?	Can you write the character for 'blue'?
Asahi-shímbun to iu jí o yomimáshita.	I read the characters [which said] Asahi-shimbun.
Ohara Hídeo-sensei to iu yūmei na isha ni denwa o kakemáshita.	I phoned a famous doctor called Dr. Hideo Ohara.
Haná to Heitai to iu hón o yónda kotó ga arimásu ka?	Have you ever read the book [called] Flowers and Soldiers?
Anáta ga mó kitá to iu kotó wa shirimasén deshita.	I didn't know you had [already] arrived.
Kore o Nihongo de sō iu tó wa shirimasén deshita.	I didn't know this sentence was said that way in Japanese.
Kore to iu yotei ga arimasén.	I haven't any definite plans [any plans you could put your finger on, any you could say 'it's this' about].
Nán to iu éiga o míta n desu ka?	What movie did you see?

Okane ga nái kara asobi ni   I guess I'll write a letter
iku kotó ga dekínai to iu   saying I haven't any mon-
tegami o kakimashǒ.   ey, so I can't go on a
          vacation trip.
Cf. p. 378.

7. 3. THE PLAIN TENTATIVE. When you quote a
sentence like ikú deshō 'he'll probably go' or ittá deshō
'he probably went', you usually change the polite tentative
copula deshǒ into the corresponding plain form darǒ:
ikú darō to omoimásu 'I think he'll probably go', ittá
darō to omoimásu 'I think he must have gone'. The
word preceding darǒ may be a verb form, as above, or
it may be a noun or an adjective. For instance, to quote
the sentence Jitsugyōka deshǒ 'He must be a businessman'
you say something like Jitsugyōka darǒ to omoimásu 'I
think he must be a businessman'. To quote the sentence
kodomo wa nemúi deshō 'The child is probably sleepy'
you say something like Kodomo wa nemúi darō to omoimásu 'I think the child is sleepy'. And to quote the sentence Kodomo wa némukatta deshō 'The child must have
been sleepy', you say something like Kodomo wa némukatta darō to omoimásu 'I think the child must have been
sleepy'. In rapid speech the form -katta darō is usually
contracted to -kattarō, so you will hear Kodomo wa né-
mukattarō to omoimásu.

⌒ Just as there is a form darǒ corresponding to deshǒ,
there is a plain tentative form corresponding to the polite
tentative form of each verb. The polite tentative forms,
you will recall, end in -mashǒ. The plain tentative forms
end in -yǒ [accented verbs] and -yō [unaccented] for VOW-

EL stems, and in -ǒ [accented] and -ō [unaccented] for CONSONANT stems. The plain tentative forms for kúru and suru are irregularly koyǒ and shiyǒ. Here are some examples:

VOWEL VERBS

MEANING	IMPERFECT -ru	TENTATIVE -yō	POLITE TEN-TATIVE -mashǒ
sleeps	ne-ru	ne-yō	ne-mashǒ
eats	tabé-ru	tabe-yǒ	tabe-mashǒ
puts in	ire-ru	ire-yō	ire-mashǒ
looks at	mí-ru	mi-yǒ	mi-mashǒ
stays	i-ru	i-yō	i-mashǒ

CONSONANT VERBS

MEANING	IMPERFECT -u	TENTATIVE -ō	POLITE TEN-TATIVE -i-mashǒ
is needed	ir-u	ir-ō	ir-i-mashǒ
returns	káer-u	kaer-ō	kaer-i-mashǒ
waits	mát[s]-u	mat-ǒ	mach-i-mashǒ
talks	hanás-u	hanas-ǒ	hanash-i-mashǒ
meets	á[w]-u	a-ǒ	a-i-mashǒ
writes	kák-u	kak-ǒ	kak-i-mashǒ
swims	oyóg-u	oyog-ǒ	oyog-i-mashǒ
calls	yob-u	yob-ō	yob-i-mashǒ
reads	yóm-u	yom-ǒ	yom-i-mashǒ

These plain tentative verbs are used when you want to quote a sentence which would—if not quoted—end in the polite tentative with the meaning 'let's do so-and-so' or 'I think I'll do so-and-so'.* For example, if a friend says to you Kōen e sampo ni ikimashǒ 'Let's go to the park for a walk', you could report his suggestion this way: Tárō wa kōen e sampo ni ikō to iimáshita 'Taro suggested

---

*See also p. 142 (note).

we go to the park for walk.' If you want to quote yourself as thinking Góhan o tábete kara súgu benkyō shima-
shố 'I'll study right after eating', you will probably say
Góhan o tábete kara, súgu benkyō shiyō to omoimásu
'I'll think I'll study right after eating'. Of course, if
you're really talking to yourself, you won't use polite
forms at all—you'll use plain style instead. [This style
is discussed briefly in the Appendix.] Here are some
further examples of the plain tentative:

Goji-han góro ni uchi e kaerố to omótte imáshita ga, shigoto ga takusan átta kara, káeru kotó wa dekimasén deshita.	I was thinking I would return home around half past five, but I had too much work, so I couldn't make it.
Kánai wa kyō hirú kara kōcn e itte kodomo to asobō to itte imáshita.	My wife was suggesting we go to the park this afternoon and play with the children.
Sono éiga o mí ni ikána-kattarố to omoimásu.	I don't think he would have gone to see a movie of that sort.
Kono yōfuku wa hitótsu no kaban ni ireru kotó ga dekínai darō to omoi-másu.	I doubt we'll be able to pack [all] these clothes in one suitcase.
Sensei no tomodachi wa, kotoshi okane ga nái no de asobi ni ikánai darō to omou to kakimáshita.	My friend who is a teacher wrote that he thinks he won't go on a holiday this year because he

kimáshita .

Asoko ni súnde iru Ameri-
ka no hitó wa senkyóshi
ka to kiite miyó to omoi-
másu.

hasn't much money.

I think I'll just ask if that
American living over
there is a missionary.

Shújin wa ashita Nomura-
san no tokoró e asobi ni
ikō to iimáshita.

My husband suggested we
go visit Mr. Nomura to-
morrow.

7. 4. TENTATIVE + TO SURU. The plain tentative
sometimes occurs followed by the particle to and
some form of the verb suru 'does'. This sort of expression has two different meanings. One meaning is 'is
about to do something'; this expression is usually in a
non-final clause, followed by a clause which tells of something which held up the action. For example, Dekakeyō
to shita tokí ni, tomodachi ga asobi ni kitá n desu 'When
I was about to go out, a friend dropped in for a visit'.
This usage may be combined with the use of tokoro to
mean 'just': Dekakeyō to suru tokoró e tomodachi ga a-
sobi ni kitá n desu 'Just as I was about to go out, a friend
dropped in for a visit', Yasumó to suru tokoró o míta
kara, nágaku hanásazu ni káetta n desu 'I saw that he
was about to go to bed, so I came back without talking
very long'. Shimbun o yomó to shite iru tokoró desu 'I'm
just on the point of reading the paper'. Shimbun o
yomó to shite iru tokoró deshita 'I was just on the point
of reading the paper'.

The other meaning of the tentative+**to suru** is 'tries to do' with the usual implication that the attempt was unsuccessful. **Yōfuku o minna hitótsu no kaban ni ireyō to shimáshita ga, ireru kotó ga dekimasén deshita** 'I tried to get all the clothes into one suitcase, but couldn't.' [Compare 7. 6.]

7. 5. NOUN+TO (NI) SHITE. When a noun is followed by **to shite** or **to shité wa** the English equivalent is 'as', 'for', or 'considered as' in expressions like 'for a serviceman', 'as a missionary'. The particle **ni** usually substitutes for **to** when the characteristic is more permanent: 'for an American', 'as a woman', 'being a child', etc.

Amerika no hitó ni shité wa, Nihongo ga jōzú desu ně.	His Japanese is quite good for an American isn't it.
Senkyōshi to shite Nihón e kitá n desu.	He came to Japan as a missionary.
Jitsugyōka to shité wa, sonna kotó o yóku shitte ímásu.	For a businessman, he knows [about] such things well.
Kono shokudō no tabé-mono to shité wa, mázuku arimasén.	For food at this restaurant, it doesn't taste bad.

7. 6. GERUND+MÍRU. An expression consisting of the gerund of a verb+some form of the verb **míru** 'sees' has two slightly different meanings: 'does something **to**

see (how it will turn out), does something and finds out'
or 'tries to do something (to see how it will turn out)'.
Compare this with the meaning of the tentative + **to suru**
'tries to do (but doesn't succeed), starts to do'.

Ano shokudō de góhan o tábete mimashǒ ka?	Shall we try eating at that restaurant?
Nihongo no shimbun o yónde mitái desu.	I'd like to try reading a newspaper in Japanese.
Júnsa ni kiite míru kara, chotto mátte kudasai.	I'll just find out from the policeman so wait here a minute.
Senséi ni kiite míta kotobá wa kore déshita.	The word I asked the teacher [about] was this one.
Kono zasshi o míte mimasén ka?	Won't you try looking at this magazine (and see how you like it)?
Kamí o hyakúmai sono hón-ya de katte míta n desu.	I bought 100 sheets of paper at that bookstore (to see how they'd do).
Dóno eigákan e itte mimashǒ ka?	Which movie-theater shall we try [going to] tonight?

7. 7. DESIDERATIVES: To say 'I want to do something' you use a special kind of adjective which is derived from verb infinitives. The infinitive, you will recall, is the verb form which ends in ZERO for vowel verbs
(**tábe, ne, mí**) and in **-i** for consonant verbs (**káeri, hana-
shi, oyógi, káki**). To this infinitive form you add the

ending -tái [if the verb has an accent in the imperfect, -tai if it has no accent]. The resulting form is called a DESIDERATIVE or DESIDERATIVE ADJECTIVE, because it means something is desired to be done.

The final -i of the ending -tai is itself, of course, the regular adjective ending for the plain imperfect. A desiderative adjective is inflected just like any other adjective:

Imperfect	ikitai	wants to go	yomitái	wants to read
Infinitive	ikitaku	wanting to go	yomítaku	wanting to read
Gerund	ikitákute	wants to go and	yomítakute	wants to read and
Perfect	ikitákatta	wanted to go	yomítakatta	wanted to read

In the form **ikitaku** you have first the desiderative adjective **ikita-** + the adjective infinitive ending **-ku**; then within the form **ikita-** you find the verb infinitive **iki-** + the desiderative element **-ta-**; finally, within the form **iki** you have stem **ik-** + the verb infinitive ending **-i**.

Here are some examples of the formation of desideratives:

VOWEL VERBS

STEM	IMPERFECT -ru	INFINITIVE -ZERO	DESIDERATIVE -tai	MEANING
ne-	neru	ne	netai	wants to sleep
tabé-	tabéru	tábe	tabetái	wants to eat
ire-	ireru	ire	iretai	wants to insert
mí-	míru	mí	mitái	want to see
ki-	kiru	ki	kitai	wants to wear
kí-	kúru	kí	kitái	wants to come
	[Irreg.]]			
shi-	suru	shi	shitai	wants to do
	[Irreg.]]			

CONSONANT VERBS

STEM	IMPERFECT -u	INFINITIVE -i	DESIDERATIVE -i-tai	MEANING
kír-	kíru	kíri	kiritái	wants to cut
káer-	káeru	káeri	kaeritái	wants to return
mát-	mátsu	máchi	machitái	wants to wait
hanás-	hanásu	hanáshi	hanashitái	wants to talk
áw-	áu	ái	aitái	wants to meet
kák-	káku	káki	kakitái	wants to write
oyóg-	oyógu	oyógi	oyogitái	wants to swim
yob-	yobu	yobi	yobitai	wants to call
yóm-	yómu	yómi	yomitái	wants to read
ik-	iku	iki	ikitai	wants to go

There are two usages with respect to the particle indicating WHAT you want to do. The older and more widely accepted usage favors the particle ga: Sakana ga tabetái desu '(I) want to eat the fish'. This treats the basic meaning of tabetái as 'is desired to be eaten'; compare sakana ga sukí desu '(I) like fish' which has the basic meaning 'fish are liked'. A common colloquial usage today favors the particle o: Sakana o tabetái desu. This is treating the basic meaning of tabetái as really 'wants to eat'.

Of course, here as elsewhere, either ga or o may be replaced by wa when the emphasis is shifted away from the noun they follow. Sakana wa tabetái desu 'I want to EAT the fish (but LEAVE the other things).'

The person doing the desiring will be either the topic with the particle wa or the emphasized subject with the particle ga, depending on the specific emphasis. This sometimes leads to ambiguity. Tanaka-san wa Nakamura-

san ga yobitái desu can mean either 'Mr. Tanaka wants to call MR. NAKAMURA' or 'MR. NAKAMURA wants to call Mr. Tanaka', since all it tells us literally is 'With Mr. Tanaka for the topic and the emphasis on Mr. Nakamura, somebody wants to call somebody.' This ambiguity parallels that of **Tárō wa Hánako ga sukí desu** ['With Taro for the subject and the emphasis on Hanako, somebody is liked by somebody'] which can mean either 'Taro likes HANAKO' or 'HANAKO likes Taro'.

Such ambiguities are straightened out, of course, by the situation and the context.

English 'like' (as in 'I like coffee') usually corresponds to Japanese **sukí desu**, but in the expression 'I'd like to', which means 'I want to', it corresponds to **-tái desu**. 'I think I'd like to go' is **ikitái to omoimásu**. Here are some sentences illustrating the use of desideratives:

Nisanjíkan netai to omoimásu.	I think I'd like to sleep for 2 or 3 hours.
Kore o hitótsu no kaban ni irctákatta n desu ga, hairánakatta kara, futatsú ni iretá n desu.	I wanted to put these things into one suitcase, but I couldn't so I put them in two.
Sonna kotó wa iitakú wa arimasén.	I don't want to say things like that.
Kírei na kimono o kitai to itte imásu. .	She says she wants to wear a clean [or pretty] dress.
Pán no kirítakatta hitó wa dáre deshita ka?	Who was the person who wanted to cut the bread?
Nára e itte mitái to omoi-	I think I'd like to go take

másu.

Háyaku kaeritái kara, dénsha ni notte ikimashǒ.

Anáta to hanashitái to iu hitó ga kité imasu.

Sfeatsei ni aítaku wa arimasén yo.

Anáta wa kono ittsū no tegami o kakítaku arimasén ka?

Kánai wa kodomo o yobitai to itte sóto e demáshita.

Watakushi no yomitái hón ga takusan áru kara, yóku toshókan e itte mimásu.

Mizuúmi de oyogitái kara, yasumí ni wa úmi e ikanái de, yamá e ikō to omótte imasu.

in Nara.

Let's go on a streetcar—I want to be back early.

A man has come who says he wants to talk with you.

I DON'T want to run into the teacher.

Don't you want to write this one letter?

My wife said she wanted to call the children and went outside.

There are a lot of books I want to read so I go to the library often (to see about them).

I think I'd like to swim in a lake, so I'm wondering if I should(n't) go to the mountains instead of the sea(shore) for my vacation.

7. 8. ALTERNATIVE QUESTIONS. An alternative question is one in which you give the listener two or more choices for an answer: **Jidǒsha de ikimáshita ka, básu de ikimáshita ka, kishá de ikimáshita ka, hikǒki de ikimáshita ka?** 'Did you go by car, or by bus, or by train, or by plane?' In answer to such a question, the listener picks out the appropriate alternative and replies, perhaps, **Kishá de ikimáshita** 'I went by train'. If the inquirer has omitted the correct alternative in his question, the person answering may say something like **Chigaimásu— fúne de ikimáshita** 'It's different (from all those)—I went by ship.' **Chigau** is a verb meaning 'is different'; the expression **chigaimásu** is often used with about the same meaning as **só ja arimasén**, to inform a person he is mistaken in his assumptions. Do not confuse this verb with the related verb **machigau** 'makes a mistake'. **Chigaimáshita** means 'it was different (than someone assumed)'; **machigaimáshita** means 'I (or he) made a mistake.'

In quoting alternative questions, you usually replace polite verb forms with plain forms, and then follow the entire expression with some verb meaning 'knows, informs, asks, forgets, remembers' or the like; ordinarily the quoting particle **TO** is omitted. Some examples:

ALTERNATIVE QUESTION	QUOTED ALTERNATIVE QUESTION
Ōsaka désu ka, Kóbe desu ka?	Ōsaka ka, Kóbe ka wasuremáshita.
Is it Osaka or Kobe?	I've forgotten whether it's Osaka or Kobe.
Fúne de ikimáshita ka, hikóki de ikimáshita ka?	Fúne de ittá ka, hikóki de ittá ka, obóete imasu ka?
Did he go by ship or plane?	Do you remember whether he went by ship or by plane?

Senkyŏshi deshita ka, shin-
chŭgun no hitó deshita
ka?

Was he a missionary or a
member of the Occupa-
tion?

Sono jidŏsha wa aói desu
ka, kurói desu ka?

Is his car blue or black?

Gohyakúen desu ka, sen-
en desu ka?

Is it ¥500 or ¥1,000?

Hibiya-kŏen desu ka, Ueno-
kŏen desu ka?

Is it (at) Hibiya Park or
Ueno Park?

Kanda ni súnde imashita
ka, Koishikawa ni súnde
imashita ka?

Was he living in Kanda or
in Koishikawa?

Chiyodá-ku de tsutómete
imásu ka, Chūŏ-ku de tsu-
tómete imásu ka?

Senkyŏshi datta ka, shin-
chŭgun no hitó datta ka,
shirimasén.

I don't know whether he
was a missionary or a
member of the Occupa-
tion.

Sono jidŏsha wa aói ka,
kurói ka, kiite mimashŏ.

Let's find out if his car is
is blue or black.

Gohyakúen ka, sen-en ka,
oshiete kudasai.

Please tell [instruct] me
whether it's ¥ 500 or
¥1,000.

Hibiya-kŏen ka Ueno-kŏen
ka, wakarimasén.

I'm not sure whether it's
(at) Hibiya Park or Ue-
no Park.

Kanda ni súnde itá ka,
Koishikawa ni súnde itá
ka, shitte imásu ka?

Do you know whether he
was living in Kanda or
in Koishikawa?

Chiyodá-ku de tsutómete
irú ka, Chūŏ-ku de tsu-
tómete irú ka, kiite mi-
mashŏ.

| Is he employed in Chiyoda (ku) or in Chuo (ku)? | I'll find out whether he's employed in Chiyoda (ku) or in Chuo (ku). |

Sometimes Japanese add the expression **sore tó mo** '[also with that =] or else' like an adverb before the last alternative suggested in an alternative question: **Shíba de hataraite imásu ka, sore tó mo Shinagawa de hataraite imásu ka?** 'Is he working in Shiba or (else) is he working in Shinagawa?' The expression **sore tó mo** only emphasizes the fact that you are presenting alternatives—the sentence would mean just about the same without the expression.

Often the last alternative is generalized to just **dó ka** '[or how is it =] or what?' which seems to correspond to the English translation 'whether... or not'. **Jidósha de ittá ka, dó ka wakarimasén dcshita** 'I wasn't sure whether he had gone by car or not.' In this case, **dó ka** might represent **fúne de ittá ka** 'or went by boat', **uchi ni itá ka** 'or stayed at home', or any number of other expressions. When you don't have any particular contrasting alternative to present, in order to say 'whether something happened [or not]' you still use **dó ka**. To say, 'I don't know whether he's arrived yet', you have to say something like **Mó kitá ka dó ka wakarimasén,** that is 'I don't know whether he's arrived or not.' In English we feel free to drop the 'or not' without changing the meaning, but Japanese always put in the **dó ka** to get the meaning 'whether'.

In everyday English we often use 'if' with about the

same meaning as 'whether'—'I don't know IF he's come yet'. This IF of course does not mean the same thing as the IF in 'if it rains, I won't go'. We know the two IF's don't mean the same thing, because in the former case we can substitute WHETHER and get the same meaning, but in the latter we cannot.

Here are some more examples of alternative questions with **dố ka:**

SIMPLE QUESTION	QUOTED ALTERNATIVE QUESTION
Akásaka desu ka?	**Akásaka ka dố ka wasure- máshita.**
Is it Akasaka?	I've forgotten whether it's Akasaka (or not).
Kisen de ikimáshita ka?	**Kisen de ittá ka dố ka, obóete imasu ka?**
Did he go by steamship?	Do you remember whether he went by steamship?
Senkyốshi deshita ka?	**Senkyốshi datta ka, dố ka, shirimasén.**
Was he a missionary?	I don't know whether he was a missionary.
Jidốsha wa aói desu ka?	**Jidốsha wa aói ka dố ka kiite mimashố.**
Is the car blue?	Let's ask if the car is blue.
Gohyakúen desu ka?	**Gohyakúen ka dố ka oshi- ete kudasái.**
Is it ￥500?	Please tell me whether it's ￥500 (or not).

Sometimes, after giving several alternatives, the ques-

tion will be summed up by a general question, which
could have been used by itself instead of suggesting some
possible answers:

Jidŏsha ni notte ikimásu
  ka, kishá ni notte iki-
  másu ka, nán ni notte
  ikimásu ka?

Are you going by car, on
  the train, or how?

Kudámono o kai ni ikimásu
  ka, yasai o kai ni ikimásu
  ka, náni o kai ni iki-
  másu ka?

Are you going to buy fruit
  or vegetables or what?

Occasionally the summarizing general question is introduced by the lively adverb **ittai** 'in general; basically':

Tegami o káite imásu ka,
  rájio o kiite imásu ka,
  terevíjon o míte imásu
  ka, ittai náni o shite
  imásu ka?

Is he writing letters, or
  listening to the radio, or
  looking at television, or
  what the devil IS he doing?

Dáisuki to ittá ka, dáikirai
  to ittá ka, ittai nán to
  ittá ka, oshiete kudasái.

Please tell me, did they say
  they liked it, or hated it,
  or what in the world did
  they say?

Ashita kúru ka asátte kúru
  ka, ittai ítsu kúru ka wakarimasén nĕ.

I don't know whether
  they'll come tomorrow
  or the next day or just
  when, you see.

7.9. YŎ. The copular noun **yŏ**, which is always followed by some form of the copula (**dá, ná, désu,** etc.) or

by the particle ni, has the meaning 'appearance, state, shape, way.'* There are several uses of this word and these are summarized here:

(1) A noun phrase+no+yǒ+the copula means something is LIKE the noun phrase—it IS (or HAS) the APPEARANCE of the noun phrase:

Koko wa Amerika no yǒ desu. (. . .A. mítai desu.)	This place is like America (or seems to be America).
Sono éiga no hanashí wa chōdo (or maru-de) watakushi no keiken no yǒ deshita.	The story of that movie was just like my experiences.
Shízuka de kírei na yǒ na (kírei mitai na) tokoró desu.	It's a place that seems to be quiet and nice.

(2) A noun phrase+no+yǒ+ni means IN A WAY LIKE the noun phrase, IN A MANNER LIKE the noun phrase.

Nihonjín no yǒ ni (or N. mítai ni) hanashimásu.	He talks like a Japanese.
Watakushi no yǒ ni shite kudasái.	Do it the way I do.
Ginkō no yǒ ni miemáshita.	It looked like a bank.
Kodomo no yǒ ni naki-dashimáshita.	He burst into tears like a child.

(3) A modifying phrase+yǒ+the copula means it APPEARS or SEEMS that the phrase is so. When this

---

*A colloquial synonym of. . . (no) yǒ (na) in the meanings 'like' and 'seeming to be' is . . .mítai (na). Do not confuse with mítai 'wants to see'.

entire expression is followed by some noun or noun phrase
(the copula then appearing in the form ná, of course) the
meaning is something like '[the noun] which seems to be
of a sort that [the phrase] is so'.

Musumé wa naite iru yǒ desu.	The girl seems to be crying.
Atarashíi yō na jidǒsha ni notte itá n desu.	He was riding in a car that seemed to be new.
Ashita kúru yǒ (or kúru mitai) desu ga...	He seems to be coming tomorrow, but...

(4) A modifying phrase + yǒ ni has one of three
meanings:

(a) in a way AS IF the modifying phrase is so
(b) in a way SO THAT the modifying phrase
     will be so
(c) in a way which AGREES WITH or COR-
     RESPONDS TO the modifying phrase

Examples of each of these:

(a) Sono éiga ga (or o,) ki ni itta yǒ ni míte imashita.	He was watching the movie as if he really liked it.
Okane ga sukúnaku nátta yǒ ni miemáshita.	It looked as if the money was mostly gone [had gotten small in quantity].
Yamá 'e yasumí ni ikitai yǒ ni hanáshite	He was talking as though he would like to go to

imashita.

(b) Ashita kúru yǒ ni nátte imasu.

the mountains for a vacation.

It has been arranged [it is in a state as a result of having become] so that they will come tomorrow.

Kono heyá wa bénri na yǒ ni shimáshita né.

They made this room [so that it would be] convenient, didn't they.

Kotobá o wasurenai yǒ ni máinichi benkyō shimásu.

He studies every day so he won't forget the words.

(c) Wakái hito no yǒ ni asobimásu.

He plays like a young person.

Senséi ga iu yǒ ni watakushi wa búnshō o kiité kara, sore o iimásu.

I say the sentence after hearing it [read], as the teacher tells [us].

Shújin ga shitai yǒ ni shimáshita.

I did as my husband wished.

Wasurenai yǒ ni hón-ya e yotte, Nigatsú no Sékai o katte kudasai.

Don't forget to stop in at the bookshop and buy (a copy of) the February Sékai [World — a magazine].

The last example shows the usual way to translate the English 'don't forget to (do something)'—wasurenai yǒ ni (shite kudasái), that is 'do it in a way that corresponds to your not forgetting.' Other examples of this usage:

Wasurenai yǒ ni Kúdō-san no uchí e asobi ni iki-mashǒ.	Let's not forget to go visit Mr. Kudo.
Wasurenai yǒ ni máiban kánai ni tegami o káita n desu.	I remembered to write my wife every night.
Wasurenai yǒ ni kore o kaban ni irete kudasái.	Don't forget to pack these (things) in the suitcase.

Notice that **Kotobá wa wasurenai yǒ ni benkyō shimásu** can mean either 'He studies in order not to [so that he won't] forget the words' or 'He doesn't forget to study the words'. If the sentence is said **Kotobá o wasurenai yǒ ni benkyō shimásu,** the former meaning ('so that') is more likely; if it is said **Wasurenai yǒ ni kotobá o benkyō shimásu,** the latter meaning is more likely.*

7. 10. QUOTING REQUESTS. The usual way to make a request is to use the gerund + **kudasái** 'please do (something for me)'. To quote such a request in the exact words, you say something like **Yukkúri hanáshite kudasai to iimáshita** 'He said, "Please talk slow."' Ordinarily, however, you just give the gist of the request and say **Yukkúri hanásu yó ni (to) iimáshita** 'He told me to talk slow.' This is a special use of the expression consisting of a modifying phrase (with a plain imperfect verb) + **yǒ ni** in the meaning 'so that'. It may be thought of as a sort of shortening of **yǒ ni shite (kudasai)** '(please) behave in a way so that' or **yǒ ni suru** '(to) behave in a way so that'. In other words **Yukkúri hanásu yǒ ni to iimáshita**

---

*In some of its uses **yǒ (ni)** can be replaced by **tǒri (ni)** 'way:' **Sono tǒri desu**=**Sono yǒ desu** 'It's that way (=like that)', **senséi ga itta tǒri ni** (or **yǒ ni**) 'as the teacher told us'.

is a sort of shortening of **Yukkúri hanásu yǒ ni suru to
iimáshita** 'He told me to behave in a way so that I talked
slow.'

Shújin wa kómban made ni sono tegami o káku yǒ ni to iimáshita.	The boss told me to write that letter by this evening.
Senséi ni mō sukóshi hakkíri hanásu yǒ ni to iitai to omoimásu ga...	I feel I'd like to ask the teacher to talk a bit clearer, but...
Jírō ni Tárō ni áu yǒ ni to itte kudasái.	Please tell Jiro to meet Taro.

Notice that when you have several possible occurrences
of phrases ending with **ni** in a sentence, the one immediately preceding a verbal expression usually modifies that
particular expression, and any preceding phrases with **ni**
modify larger units of the sentence, or the sentence as
a whole, or the final verb:

**Tárō ni Jírō ni Tanaka-san ni áu yǒ ni to iu yǒ ni to
kakimáshita.**
I wrote Taro to tell Jiro to meet Mr. Tanaka.

The modifying expressions in this sentence work as follows:

Tárō ni ....**kakimáshita.**
.........**Jírō ni**................**iu yǒ ni to**.........
.............**Tanaka-san ni áu yǒ ni to**..............
      [**Tanaka-san ni áu yǒ ni + to**]
      [**Tanaka-san ni áu yǒ + ni**]
      [**Tanaka-san ni áu + yǒ**]

[Tanaka-san ni + áu]
[Tanaka-san + ni]

The verb 'asks' in English has two different meanings:
INQUIRES and REQUESTS. When the meaning is
INQUIRES you usually say 'asks if, asks whether'; when
the meaning is REQUESTS you usually say 'asks for, asks
someone to'. In the meaning INQUIRES, the Japanese
equivalent is ...ka (to) kiku; in the meaning REQUESTS,
the Japanese equivalent is ...yǒ ni (to) iu.

7. 11. PARTICLE YO. The particle yo at the end of
a sentence gives an INSISTIVE emphasis to what you're
saying. It is often used in warnings. The English translation sometimes gives the flavor best by just using an
exclamation mark.

Nedan ga tákaku wa ari-masén. Yasúi desu yo.	The price isn't high, it's cheap!
Samúi desu yo.	It's sure cold!
Mǒ dekaketá n desu yo.	I tell you they've already gone out!
Warúi nikú o tabérn to, byōki ni narimásu yo.	When you eat bad meat, you get sick.
Damé desu yo.	It's no good [= don't do it; I won't do it].
Daijǒbu desu yo.	It'll be ok!
Hontō désu ka? Hontō désu yo.	Are you sure? Sure I'm sure.

The meaning of yo is in some ways the opposite of
that of né. Yo means you insist on your statement, what-

ever the other person may say or think; **né** asks the other person to agree with you, suggests that you think he already knows what you're saying, and implies you might be willing to modify what you've said if you were mistaken about his agreement.

7. 12. MIÉRU AND KIKOERU. The verb **míru** means 'sees'; the related verb **miéru** means either 'is seen, appears' or 'can see'. The verb **kiku** means 'hears' or 'listens' (**kiku** meaning 'asks' is a homonym); the related verb **kikoeru** means 'is heard, is audible' or 'can hear'. The verbs **míru** and **kiku** may be preceded by an object marked by the particle **o**: **éiga o mimáshita** 'I saw a movie', **rájio o kikimáshita** 'I listened to the radio'. The verbs **miéru** and **kikoeru** are never preceded by the particle **o**—instead you use the particles **wa** and **ga**, depending on the emphasis. If the meaning is 'can see, can hear', the person who can see or hear usually takes the particle **wa**, and the thing seen or heard takes the particle **ga**.

Kono tatémono no ué kara, Fúji-san ga miemásu.	Fuji is visible from the top of this building.
Anáta wa watakushi ga miemásu ka?	Can you see me?
Anáta wa watakushi ga kikoemásu ka?	Can you hear me?
Watakushi ga miénai tokoro kara déte kimáshita.	I came out from a place where I couldn't be seen. OR He came out from a place I couldn't see.
Senséi no iu kotó ga yóku	Let's go to a place where

kikoeru tokoró e ikimashố.	we can hear the teacher better.*
Yama no ué ni wa umá ga nisantō miemáshita.	On top of the mountain two or three horses appeared.
Totsuzen óki na kóe ga kikoetá n desu.	Suddenly a loud [great] voice was heard.

7. 13. PRENOUNS+NI. The prenouns **konna** 'this sort of', **sonna** 'that sort of', **anna** 'that-there sort of', **dón-na** 'which sort of' occur before nouns and also before the particle **ni**. In this latter use they have about the same meaning as **kono yố ni, sono yố ni, ano yố ni, dóno yố ni** (or **kō, sō, ā, dố**) 'like this, like that, like that-there, like what' with the emphasis on extent rather than manner.

Dónna ni shimashố ka?	What way shall I do it? How shall we make it?
Máinichi sonna ni hataraku to, byōki ni narimásu yo.	If you work like that everyday, you'll get sick!
Konna ni takusan irimasén nế.	You see, I don't need (want) this much.
Anna ni shízuka na tokoro wa sukunái deshō.	Such quiet places must be rare.

7. 14. GERUND + ARU. The gerund + the verb **iru** 'stays, exists' means somebody or something is DOING SOMETHING: **hataraite imásu** 'he's working'. If the verb is INTRANSITIVE the meaning may be something is in a state as a result of doing or becoming something—

*Cf. **Senséi ga yóku kikoeru tokoró e ikimashố** Let's go to a place where the teacher can hear us better'. (In Japanese, unlike English, you do not "hear" PEOPLE, you hear WHAT THEY SAY.)

hárete imásu 'it's cleared up', tsukárete imásu 'I'm tired'. The gerund of a TRANSITIVE verb is used before forms of the verb áru 'exists' to mean something is in a state resulting from someone's action on it, in a condition affected by someone's action: **Tegami wa káite arimásu** 'The letter is written.' It may help to think of the literal meaning of such a sentence as something like 'as for the letter, somebody writes and—it exists [in the resulting state]' or 'as for the letter, it exists—how?—in a manner such that somebody has written'. Here are some examples of transitive verbs used in simple sentences and then in this special use of gerund + **áru**:

Monó o kaban ni iremáshita.	I packed the things in the suitcase.
Monó wa kaban ni irete arimásu.	The things are packed in the suitcase.
Sakana o mó tabemáshita.	I already ate the fish.
Sakana wa mó tábete arimasu.	The fish is already eaten.
Sono shigoto o shimáshita.	I did that job.
Sono shigoto wa shite arimásu.	That job is done.
Kitte to kakimáshita.	He wrote 'stamps'.
Kitte to káita mádo e ittá n dcsu.	I went to a window (with a sign) on which was written 'stamps'.

When there exists an intransitive verb parallel in meaning to a transitive one—like **kikoeru** 'is heard', **kiku** 'heard'; **miéru** 'is seen', **míru** 'sees'; **aku** 'is open', **akeru** 'opens'—

the expression transitive gerund+áru is less often used:*

Takái yamá ga miemásu.	Tall mountains are seen.
Ongaku ga kikoemáshita.	Music was heard.
To ga aite imásu ka?	Is the door open?

The negative form of a gerund + áru is, of course, the gerund + nái:

Kutsú wa kaban ni irete arimasén.	The shoes haven't been put in the suitcase.
Máda káite nái tegami ga takusán arimásu.	There are lots of letters still unwritten.

7.15. THE NOUN HǑ. The word hǒ has the basic meaning 'alternative, choice of one as opposed to another'; it also has the meaning 'direction, side, place'. Both of these meanings seem to be present in expressions like migi no hǒ ni 'on the right (as opposed to the left)', higashi no hǒ ni 'in the East (as opposed to other sections of the country, or as opposed to other directions)'. Watakushi no hǒ may mean either 'me (as opposed to somebody else)' or 'my direction, my section'. The noun hǒ can be preceded by any noun + the particle no. In addition it may be preceded—just as may any other noun—by a modifying expression: a verb or adjective or copula clause, with the inflected word in a plain form (perfect or imperfect). Ōkíi hǒ means 'the big one—as opposed to the little one; the big alternative; the choice of the big one'; kōbá de hataraku hǒ means 'the choice of working in a factory; working in a factory as opposed to working other places, or to taking a vacation, or doing something

---

*I have been unable to elicit -te áru examples for míru, kiku, mátsu, and uru (but kau is all right), or for the several verbs meaning 'bring' and 'wear' (p. 257). But causatives (p. 395) from ALL verbs seem to produce examples of -te áru readily.

else'. For a special use of hǒ, in addition to those described in this lesson, see Note 8. 13.

7. 16. COMPARISONS. The adjective íi just means 'something is good'; the adjective takái means 'something is expensive'. To say 'something is BETTER, something is MORE expensive' you also use íi and takái but you often add something somewhere in the sentence to bring out the fact that you are making a comparison. Either you're comparing one thing with another with respect to some quality—'this is better (than that), that is more expensive (than this)', or you are comparing two qualities with respect to one thing: 'this is better (than it used to be), that is more expensive (than it is useful)'.

If you only mention the one thing, or the one quality, and leave the other item of comparison implied, you usually add hǒ after the word referring to the stated item of comparison:

Éiga no hǒ ga sukí desu.	I prefer movies. (I like the alternative of movies, as opposed to something else.)
Dénsha de iku hǒ ga íi desu.	It's better to go by streetcar. (The alternative of going by streetcar is good—as opposed to going another way.)
Chiisái hǒ o kattá n desu.	I bought the smaller one. (I bought the little alternative—as opposed to the

| | big one.) |
| Kutsú o núida hǒ ga íi desu. | It's better with your shoes off. |

Notice the difference of meaning between **hǒ** 'alternative, choice' and **nó** 'one, thing': **chiisái no o kattá n desu** 'I bought a small one', **dénsha de ikú no ga íi desu** 'it's good to go by streetcar'.

If you mention both items of comparison, the particle **yóri** '(more) than'* is used to set off the standard of comparison:

1. **Inú wa umá yóri chiisái desu.**   Dogs are smaller than horses. (Dogs, more than horses, are small.)

In such a sentence, you do not ordinarily need the noun **hǒ** 'alternative'. But if you want to emphasize the subject of the comparison, you usually do it by adding not just the emphatic subject particle **ga**, but **(no) hǒ**:

2. **Inu no hǒ ga, umá yóri chiisái desu.**   DOGS are smaller than horses.

You can then change the word order around to give a slightly different emphasis:

3. **Uma yori, inu no hǒ ga chiisái desu.**   It's DOGS that are smaller than horses.

And you can set off the first expression **umá yori** '(more) than horses' as the topic with the attention-releasing particle **wa**, in order to concentrate the emphasis still more on the subject of the comparison:

---

*Sometimes 'other than' or 'rather than'.

4. Umá yori wa, inu no hǒ   (What are) smaller than
   ga chiisái desu.   horses are dogs.

Actually, all four of these sentences are probably best translated the same way in English 'Horses are smaller than dogs', since the differences of emphasis in Japanese are more subtle than those in English. But bear in mind that the differences do exist.

Often the particle yóri is followed by mo with only a slight change of emphasis: **Inú wa umá yori mo chiisái desu** 'Dogs are smaller (yet) than horses.'

If, for the items of comparison, instead of nouns you have two adjectives or verbs or copulas (or their phrases), you can follow the patterns of sentences 2, 3, and 4 above, placing hǒ and yóri directly after the plain imperfect form. Type 4 is more common for copula phrases.

2. **Hataraku hǒ ga, yasú-   (I think) it would be bet-
   mu yori íi deshō.   ter to work than to rest.
   Osoi hǒ ga, hayái yóri   I think it's better slow
   íi to omoimásu.   than fast.
   [Bénri na hǒ ga, shízuka   [I prefer it convenient
   na yóri sukí desu.]   rather than quiet.]**
3. **Yasúmu yori, hataraku
   hǒ ga íi deshō.
   Hayái yori, osoi hǒ ga
   íi to omoimásu.
   [Shízuka na yóri, bénri
   na hǒ ga sukí desu.]**
4. **Yasúmu yori wa, hataraku hǒ ga íi deshō.**

Hayái yori wa, osoi hǒ
ga íi to omoimásu.
Shízuka na yóri wa, bén-
ri na hǒ ga sukí desu.*

*It is surprising to find na
before a particle, but...na yori
is to be explained as an abbreviation of...na no yori.

But the pattern of sentence 1 above cannot be directly
applied, since the particle **wa** does not ordinarily follow
the plain imperfect of verb, adjectives, or the copula.
Instead you can use the plain imperfect + **no wa**:

1. Hataraků no wa, yasúmu (no) yori íi deshō.
   Osói no wa, hayái (no) yori íi to omoimásu.
   Bénri na no wa, shízuka na (no) yori sukí desu.

In comparing two actions, which involve the same verb
with two different objects, you can be very explicit and
repeat the verb:

1. Nihongo o yómu no wa, Eigo o yómu (no) yori
   muzukashíi desu.
2. Nihongo o yómu hǒ ga, Eigo o yómu yori muzukashíi desu.
3. Eigo o yómu yori, Nihongo o yómu hǒ ga muzukashíi desu.
4. Eigo o yómu yori wa, Nihongo o yómu hǒ ga muzukashíi desu.

'It's more difficult to read Japanese than to read English.'

Or you can drop the repetition of the verb:

1. Nihongo o yómu no wa, Eigo yóri muzukashíi desu.
2. Nihongo o yómu hǒ ga, Eigo yóri muzukashíi desu.
3. Eigo yóri, Nihongo o yómu hǒ ga muzukashíi desu.

4. Eigo yóri wa, Nihongo o yómu hố ga muzukashíi
    desu.

And there are occasional variants for the last two:

3a. Eigo o yómu yori, Nihongo no hố ga muzukashíi
     desu.
4a. Eigo yómu yori wa, Nihongo no hố ga muzuka-
     shíi desu.

Now notice the different ways you can say 'I am younger
than you':

1. Watakushi wa anáta yori wakái desu.
2. Watakushi no hố ga anáta yori wakái desu.
3. Anáta yori, watakushi no hố ga wakái desu.
4. Anáta yori wa, watakushi no hố ga wakái desu.

In addition, there are other less common possibilities:

5. Watakushi ga anáta yori wakái desu.
6. Watakushi ga anáta no hố yori wakái desu.
7. Watakushi no hố ga anáta no hố yori wakái desu.
8. Watakushi wa anáta no hố yori wakái desu.
9. Anáta yori watakushi ga wakái desu.
10. Anáta no hố yori watakushi ga wakái desu.
11. Anáta no hố yori watakushi no hố ga wakái desu.

And the number of possibilities may be increased still
more by inserting the particle mo after each occurrence
of yóri (except when yóri is already followed by wa).

When you are comparing two things without naming
them directly, just referring to them by distinguishing

characteristics (as 'the red one and the blue one') all 11 possibilities are common:

1. Akái no wa aói no yori takái desu.
2. Akai hǒ ga aói no yori takái desu.
3. Aói no yori, akai hǒ ga takái desu.
4. Aói no yori wa, akai hǒ ga takái desu.
5. Akái no ga, aói no yori takái desu.
6. Akái no ga aói hǒ yori takái desu.
7. Akái hǒ ga aói hǒ yori takái desu.
8. Akái no wa aói hǒ yori takái desu.
9. Aói no yori akái no ga takái desu.
10. Aói hǒ yori akái no ga takái desu.
11. Aói hǒ yori akai hǒ ga takái desu.

The most common of these are probably 3, 5, and 11.

If we put together these possibilities into a couple of tables, illustrating all the ways to say 'A is more something than B', they look like this:

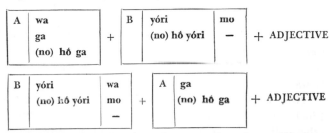

Sometimes the adjective of comparison is modified by the adverbs **zutto** 'by far' or **chótto (sukóshi)** 'a bit': **Amerika no hǒ ga zutto ōkíi desu** 'America is lots larger.'

Another way to say 'more' when you mean 'more than

before' or 'more than now' or the like, is to use the adverb **mótto: Mótto hakkíri hanáshite kudasái** 'please talk more clearly', **Mótto yukkúri arúite kudasái** 'please walk more slowly'. (But **mō sukóshi...** is often better.)

7. 17. QUESTIONS WITH COMPARISONS. Sometimes you want to ask a question about WHICH of two or more things is MORE or MOST something—'Which is bigger, the bank or the theater?', 'Which is the most expensive, beef, pork, or lamb?' For such questions, in Japanese you first set up the list of things you are going to ask about. This may be done in several ways:

1.	**A to B to C to (wa)**	(as for) A and B and C
2.	**A to B to C no uchí (wa)**	(as for) among A and B and C
3.	**A to B to C dé (wa)**	(as for) being A and B and C
4.	**A to B to C no uchí de (wa)**	(as for) being among A and B and C

Note that each of these expressions may or may not be followed by the topic particle **wa**. Ordinarily, the last **to** of the first expression will drop before **wa: A to B to C wa.**

Now after you've listed the possible items, you ask which one is selected as the more (or most) something-or-other. If there are just two items you ask the question with the word **dóchira** (often pronounced **dótchi**) 'which one' or **dóchira no hŏ** (**dótchi no hŏ**) 'which alternative':

Ginkō to eigákan de wa,   Which is bigger—the bank

dóchira (no hǒ) ga ōkíi   or the theater?
desu ka?
Hatoyama-san to Ichiba-   I wonder which would be
san dé wa, dóchira ga íi   better—Mr. Hatoyama or
deshō ka ně.   Mr. Ichiba?

If you ask about three or more things, the question word is dóre 'which (of several)', and if it is three or more people, dáre 'who'. In addition you add the word ichiban 'number one; most of all' before the adjective.

Gyūniku to butaniku to   Which is the most expen-
yōniku no uchí de wa,   sive—beef or pork or
dóre ga ichiban takái   lamb?
desu ka?
Hatoyama-san to Ichiba-   I wonder who would be
san to Kánaya-san no   best—Mr. H. or Mr. I. or
uchi, dáre ga ichiban íi   Mr. K.?
deshō ka ně.

7. 18. **ICHIBAN.** The counter -ban refers to numbers: ichí-ban means 'number one'. Shedding the accent, ichiban is used as an adverb to mean 'most of all':

Nihón de ichiban takái   The tallest mountain in
yamá wa Fúji-san desu.   Japan is Mt. Fuji.
Anáta no ichiban sukí na   What's your favorite fish?
sakana wa nán desu ka?
Ichiban ōkíi ringo o tábe-   He ate the biggest apple.
ta n desu.
Ichiban hayái kishá wa   I wonder which is the
dóre deshō ka?   fastest train?

7. 19. ORDINAL NUMBERS. To say 'first, second, third', etc., you can add the suffix -me to any number: **issatsu-me, nisatsu-me, sansatsu-me** 'the 1st book, the 2d book, the 3d book'; **ippom-me, nihom-me, sambom-me** 'the 1st pencil, the 2d pencil, the 3d pencil' [note the automatic change in the Hepburn Romanization of **n** to **m** before **m**]; **ichinichi-me, futsuka-me, mikka-me** 'the 1st day, 2d day, 3d day'. If you mention the noun, this follows the ordinal and is connected to it by the particle **no:** **sambom-me no empitsu** 'the 3d pencil', **nisatsu-me no hón** 'the 2d book', **yonim-me no hito** 'the 4th person'. Instead of using a specific ordinal number, you can add -me to the numbers made with the counter -ban, and use these with any noun: **ichibam-me no empitsu** 'the 1st pencil', **nibam-me no hón** 'the 2d book', **sambam-me no hito** 'the 3d person'.

Another way to make words meaning '1st, 2d, 3d', etc., is to prefix **dai-** to any primary numeral: **daiichi, daini, daisan, daiyon,** etc. These words are less commonly used than the ones given above with **-me,** but you will often hear **daiichi** in proper names: **Daiichi-Hóteru, Daiichi-Bírujingu.**

7. 20. PARTICLE HODO AND NEGATIVE COMPARISONS. The particle **hodo** means 'extent, to the extent of, as much as'. It is used in negative comparisons. To say 'You are not so young as he' a Japanese says **Anáta wa anó hito hodo wákaku arimasén** 'as for you, you're not young, as much as he.'

This particle is sometimes used also in questions about 'as much as', when you rather expect a negative answer:

'Is pork as expensive as beef?' **Butaniku wa gyūniku hodo takái desu ka?** The expected answer is **Iie, butaniku wa gyūniku hodo tákaku arimasén** 'No, pork is not so expensive as beef.' If you are expecting an affimative answer to a question about 'as much as', then you use either **no yǒ ni** 'in the manner of', **to onaji yǒ ni** 'in the same manner as', or **gúrai** 'about (as much as)':

Gyūniku wa yōniku no yǒ ni takái desu ka?	Is beef expensive like lamb?
Gyūniku wa yōniku to o-naji yǒ ni takái desu ka?	Is beef as expensive as lamb?
Gyūniku wa yōniku gúrai takái desu ka?	Is beef as expensive as lamb?

In each case you expect the answer **Hái, sǒ desu.**

The particles **hodo, gúrai** and **bákari** are all three used after numbers and quantity words to mean 'about so much':

Ichijíkan gúrai kakarimásu.	
Ichijíkan bákari kakarimásu.	It takes about 1 hour.
Ichijíkan hodo kakarimásu.	
Sukoshi gúrai tabemáshita.	
Sukoshi bákari tabemáshita.	I ate just a little.
Sukóshi hodo tabemáshita.	

After a noun or verb or adjective, the particle **hodo** means 'extent':

Yamá hodo hón o kaimá-shita.	He bought a mountain of books (books to the extent of a mountain).

Anáta hodo Nihongo ga jōzú ni naritái desu.	I want to get to be as good in Japanese as you are (to the extent you are).
Shigoto ga dekínai hodo tsukárete imasu.	I'm too tired to work (to the extent that I can't work).
Senséi ni náru kotó ga dekíru hodo benkyō shimáshita.	He studied enough to be able to be a teacher (to the extent of being able to become a teacher).

[For another special use of **hodo** see 8. 16.]

7. 21. NARUHODO. From the expression **náru hodo** 'to the extent of becoming or getting to be' comes the adverb **naruhodo** 'just so, quite right, truly, indeed, ever so much, really'. This is often used where we would say 'Oh, I see'. Japanese will frequently punctuate another person's discourse with **Naruhodo.... naruhodo.... naruhodo sǒ desu ně....naruhodo...** just as we show a running appreciation for information received and presumably assimilated by saying 'Oh I see... yes... yes... uh-huh... mmm... that's right... quite... just so...,' etc.

7. 22. BÁKARI. The particle **bákari** means 'just, nothing but'. It is used after the plain forms of the imperfect, perfect and gerund, and also after nouns. When used after nouns, it may be followed by another particle— **yūbínkyoku bákari e** 'only to the postoffice'—but the particles **o, ga,** and **mo** are usually omitted. Heie aie some examples after nouns:

Okáshi bákari tabéru to, byōki ni narimásu yo.	If you eat nothing but pastry, you'll get sick.
Jidósha ni wa watakushi bákari notte imáshita.	I was the only one in the car.
Eigákan bákari e itte, benkyō shimasén.	He just goes to the movies and doesn't study.
Asoko ni súnde irú no wa Amerikájin bákari desu ka?	Are the people who live there just (or all) Americans? Do only Americans live there?

Here are some examples after gerunds:

| Júnsa ni kiite bákari imashita. | I was just asking the policeman. |
| Máiban osokú made bíiru o nónde bákari imásu. | They just drink beer every night till late. |

After imperfects and perfects, the bákari is followed by some form of the copula. There are two possible meanings for the expression perfect + bákari + copula: (1) 'has only done, has done nothing but,' (2) 'has just done, has barely finished doing'. The latter meaning is more common.

Tegami wa káita bákari desu.	I've just written the letter.
Anó hito wa denwa o kakéru bákari de, sukóshi mo tegami o kakimasén.	He only telephones; he never writes letters at all.
Toshiyori wa máinichi kōen e itte sampo suru bá-	The old man just goes to the park and takes walks

kari de, sukóshi mo ha-
tarakimasén.
every day, and doesn't
work at all.

Uchi o déta bákari déshita.
We had just left the house.

7. 23. MAMÁ. The noun **mamá** occurs at the end of
a phrase, either with no particle following (adverb usage)
or with the particle **ni** showing manner, or with some
form of the copula. It means 'as, as it is, just as is, intact, just, leaving it as it is'. Here are some examples:

Tegami o káita mamá deshita.	I had written a letter and left it there.
Kutsú o haita mamá, uchi e agattá n desu ka?	Did he go right in the house with his shoes on?
Sono mamá de kimáshita.	He came as he was.
Góhan o tábeta mamá, chawan o araimasén de-shita.	They had eaten and left the bowls without wash-ing them.
Hón o kárita mamá, kae-shimasén deshita.	He borrowed the book and didn't return it.
Nihón e itta mamá, tegami mo dashimasén deshita.	He went to Japan and didn't even send a letter (from there).

A colloquial equivalent is **(k)kirí (de): Hón o oitá
(k)kiri demáshita** 'He went out leaving the book where
it was', **Ittá (k)kiri (de) kaerimasén deshita** 'He (left and)
has never come back'. For another use of **(k)kirí**
(=**daké**) see p. 195.

7. 24. ONAJI. The word **onaji** 'the same' works both
as a noun and as a pre-noun. It functions as a noun when
followed by the copula: **onaji désu** 'it's the same'. It

functions as a pre-noun when followed by a noun: **onaji hito** 'the same man', **onaji kotó desu** 'it's the same thing'. To say 'this is the same as that' you say **Kore wa sore to onaji désu**; to say 'this is not the same as that' you say **Kore wa sore to onaji ja arimasén**; to say 'this is different from that' you say **Kore wa sore to chigaimásu**. Notice that in each of these identifications, the particle used is **to** 'with'.

Many Japanese prefer the expression **onaji gakkō e ikimásu** to **issho no gakkō e ikimásu** 'we go to the same school' .Theoretically, there is a slight difference of meaning—the former could mean 'he goes to the same school he used to' or 'the same school as the one mentioned in the newspapers' or the like, whereas the latter could only mean 'he goes to the same school as somebody else does.'

7.25. CLOTHING. Japanese have several different verbs meaning 'puts on (to some part of the body), wears'. To say someone IS WEARING something or WEARS something you usually use the gerund form of one of these verbs followed by **imásu**: **Kimono o kite imásu** 'She's wearing a kimono.' Here are the verbs and some of the items of clothing that go with them:

haku	'puts on legs or feet'	kutsú	shoes
		geta	wooden clogs
		zōri	straw sandals
		hakimono	hose; also footgear in general
		kutsúshita	socks
		tabi	Japanese split-toe socks

		zubón	trousers
		mompei	women's bloomer slacks
		zubónshita	undershorts
		momohiki	"long-Johns"
		hakama	Japanese men's trousers
kiru	'puts on trunk of body'	kimono	Japanese kimono, or clothes in general
		yōfuku	Western style clothes; suit, dress
		shitagi	underwear; undershirt, slip
		sebiro	business suit
		waishatsu	shirt
		haori	Japanese outer garment
		gaitō	overcoat
		chokki	vest
kabúru	'puts on head'	bōshi	hat
hameru	'puts on fingers'	tebúkuro	gloves
		yubiwa	ring
		udedokei	wristwatch
		udewa	bracelet
		udekázari	bracelet
kakéru	'sets on, hangs on'	mégane	glasses, spectacles
		kubiwa	necklace
		kubikázari	necklace
tsukéru	'attaches'	kazarimono	ornaments
shiméru	'fastens' }	obi	Japanese woman's sash
musubu	'ties' }		
		kawaobi	leather belt
		nékutai	necktie
musubu	'ties'	kutsuhimo	shoelaces

The general verb for removing garments of all sorts

is **núgu** 'takes off, gets out of'.   But for **mégane** 'spectacles' and **yubiwa** 'ring' you use either **hazúsu** 'removes' or **tóru** 'takes (away)'.

C. EXERCISES.

1. Here are some sentences. Put each of the declarative sentences into the frame 'Taro said...' [**Tárō wa** .... **to iimáshita**], put each of the interrogative sentences into the frame 'Taro asked...' [**Tárō wa**... **ka (to) kikimáshita**], and put each of the imperative sentences into the frams 'Taro told Jiro to...' [**Tárō wa Jírō ni** .... **yŏ ni (to) iimáshita**].   Remember to change the quotation-final verbs, adjective and copula into the appropriate plain forms.

1. **Mŏ sono éiga o mimá-shita.**   I've already seen that movie.

2. **Yūbínkyoku wa dóko desu ka?**   Where's the postoffice?

3. **Tegami o kírei ni káite kudasai.**   Please write the letter neatly.

4. **Kómban hachiji góro ni kité kudasai.**   Please come around 8 this evening.

5. **Anáta ni iitai kotó ga arimásu.**   There's something I want to tell you.

6. **Senkyŏshi wa dáre desu ka?**   Which one's the missionary?

7. **Kyŏto wa Tōkyō to chigau tokoró ga ŏi desu.** There are many points where Kyoto differs from Tokyo.

8. Fusuma wa ichímai no   Fusuma are made of a
kamí de tsukurimásu.   single sheet of paper.
9. Nihonjín wa geta ka   The   Japanese   enter
kutsú o núide uchi e   houses with their shoes
agarimásu.   off.
10. Shízuka ni shite kudasai.   Please be quiet.

2. Here are some lists of words. In each list there are
one or two words which do not belong. Pick out
the misfits, and tell what the other words have in
common that the misfit lacks.

1. kutsú	2. shōji	3. zashikí	4. benjó	5. shitagi
kábā	fusuma	engawa	habakari	waishatsu
hakimono	itádo	zabúton	gofujō	tebúkuro
kutsúshita	amádo	chanomá	oteárai	sebiro
zubón	dóa	imá	obenjo	yōfuku
bōshi	ichido	seiyōma	furobá	gaitō
zubónshita	to	benjó	semmenjo	yubiwa

3. Supply the appropriate PLAIN TENTATIVE form
for each of the words in brackets in the sentences
below. Then translate the sentences.

1. Sono éiga o mí ni [iku] to omoimásu.
2. Kógai ni súnde iru [dá] to omoimásu.
3. Yóji ni náru to, tomodachi wa sukóshi [yasúmu]
to iimásu.
4. Watakushi ga [dekakeru] to shita tóki ni, shújin
ga denwa o kákete kitá n desu.
5. Késa koko e asobi ni [kúru] to suru tokoró e,
Inoue-san ga uchi e asobi ni kimáshita.
6. Benkyō [suru] to shite iru tokoró deshita.

7. Kómban kánai ni tegami o [káku] to omótte imasu.
8. Tanaka-san ni [áu] to omótte imasu.
9. Jírō wa tsukáreta kara uchi e [káeru] to ittá n desu.
10. Osoku naránai uchi ni, kodomo o [yobu] to omoimásu.
11. Watakushi wa shokudō de góhan o [tabéru] to iimáshita.
12. Júnsa ni kiite [míru] to shita tokoró e anáta ga kimáshita.

4. Give the proper DESIDERATIVE ADJECTIVE from the bracketed verb in each of the following sentences. For example, the first one will be **Yomítakatta** 'which [someone] wanted to read'.

1. [Yómu] hón o wasure-máshita.

   I forgot the book I wanted to read.

2. Kore wa anáta no kaban no náka ni [ireru] to omótte imasu ga... ga...

   I'd like to put these things in your suitcase...[if I may].

3. Éiga o míte kara, súgu uchi e [káeru].

   I want to go home right after the movie.

4. Sonna monó wa watakushi wa [tabéru] arimasén yo.

   I certainly don't want to eat such things.

5. Ínaba-san wa ókusan ni tegami o [káku] to iimásu.

   Mr Inaba says he wants to write a letter to his wife.

6. Éki de Kimura-senséi ni [áu] to omoimásu.

   I think I'd like to meet Dr Kimura at the station.

7 Dáre ga okáshi o [kíru]   Who wants to cut the
   ka?   cake?
8. Dónna kimono ga [kiru]   What sort of kimono do
   ka?   you want to wear?
9. Nisanjíkan [neru] to o-   I think I'd like to sleep
   moimásu.   for a couple of hours.
10. [Iu] kotó wa ói desu.   There's lots I'd like to
                             say.
11. Kodomo wa kōen de [a-   The children are saying
    sobu] to itte imásu.   they'd like to play in
                             the park.
12. Watakushi mo kōen e   I'd like to go to the park
    sampo ni [iku].   for a walk too.

5. Each of the following sentences consists of some alternative questions. Make each one mean: (a) I
   don't know whether... [...shirimasén], (b) I've for-
   gotten whether... [...wasuremáshita], (c) let's ask
   whether... [...kiite mimashŏ], (d) do you know...
   [...shitte imásu ka?]. For example, the first one
   will be: (a) Tanaka-san ka, Nakamura-san ka, shirimasén. (b) Tanaka-san ka, Nakamura-san ka,
   wasuremáshita. (c) Tanaka-san ka, Nakamura-san ka,
   kiite mimashŏ. (d) Tanaka-san ka, Nakamura-san ka,
   shitte imásu ka?

   1. Tanaka-san désu ka, Nakamura-san désu ka?
   2. Nágoya deshita ka, Shizúoka deshita ka?
   3. Ano tatémono wa, ōkíi désu ka, chiisái désu ka?
   4. Hóngō ni súnde imashita ka, sore tó mo Asákusa
      ni súnde imashita ka?

5. Íma hataraite imásu ka, hataraite imasén ka?
6. Ashita kimásu ka, asátte kimásu ka?

The following sentences are simple questions. Make them alternative questions in your quotation by adding dŏ ka 'whether or not'. For instance, the first one will be (a) Fúne datta ka, dŏ ka, shirimasén. (b) Fúne datta ka, dŏ ka, wasuremáshita. (c) Fúne datta ka, dŏ ka, kiite mimashŏ. (d) Fúne datta ka, dŏ ka, shitte imásu ka?

7. Fúne deshita ka?
8. Éiga o mí ni ikimáshita ka?
9. Monó o minna hitótsu no kaban ni iremáshita ka?
10. Heyá wa kírei desu ka?
11. Íma hataraite imásu ka?
12. Ashita kimásu ka?

6. Each of these sentences means 'something is or does something'. Make each of them mean 'something seems like it is or does something'. For instance, the first one will be Kodomo wa naite iru yŏ desu 'The child seems to be crying.'

1. Kodomo wa naite imásu.	The child is crying.
2. Néko ga sakana o tabemáshita.	The cat ate the fish.
3. Kono mizuúmi wa ōkíi desu.	This lake is large.
4. Kono misé wa depắto desu.	This shop is a department store.
5. Asoko wa hóteru deshita	That place was a hotel,

nĕ.	wasn't it.
6. Ano rōdósha wa íma hataraite imásu.	That worker is working now.
7. Tanaka-san no tomodachi wa inaka ni súnde imasu.	Mr Tanaka's friend lives in the country.
8. Osoku narimáshita nĕ.	It has gotten late, hasn't it.
9. Dénsha wa kónde imasu.	The streetcar is crowded.
10. Kono nikú wa totemo íi desu.	This meat is just fine.

7. Each of the following sentences 'somebody did something'; change them to mean 'something is done, something is in a state resulting from getting done'. For instance, the first one will be **Pán wa (or ga) kítte arimasu** 'The bread is cut'.

1. **Pán o kirimáshita.**
2. **Kono tegami o kakimáshita.**
3. **Watakushi no hón mo kaban ni iremáshita.**
4. **"Sakanaya" to iu jí o kakimáshita.**
5. **Kusuri o nomimáshita.**
6. **Gyūniku o mŏ minna tabemáshita.**

8. Translate each of the following sentences into Japanese. [Where several translations are possible, only one is listed in the key.]

1. The bank is larger than the watch-shop.
2. Are apples as expensive as tangerines?
3. This is the biggest department-store in Japan.

4. You're not as young as he is, are you.
5. Of apples, tangerines, and persimmons, which do you like best?
6. He said that the black ones are cheaper than the blue ones.
7. I think I'd like to buy the bigger one.
8. I think I'd like to buy the biggest one.
9. I think I'd like to buy the big one.
10. It's easier to speak Japanese than to write it.
11. Which is more expensive—the book or the magazine?
12. This meat seems better than that.

D. COMPREHENSION.

[Futarí no Gaikokújin wa Nihongo de hanáshite imasu.]

Brown. Ross-san, anáta wa nisannen gúrai shika Nihón ni súnde inai no ni, mō daibu nárete iru yó desu ně.

Ross. Máda Amerika ni ita tóki, Nihón e kitái to omótte, Nihongo o gorokkagetsu gúrai benkyō shimáshita. Nihón e tsúite, kisen o oríru to, súgu wakáru yó ni narimáshita. Sore kara, óki na machí e ikazu ni, inaka e itte, totemo chíisa na murá ni súnde, ninen hodo Nihongo bákari hanáshite imáshita. Sono aida ni Nihonjin no shūkan ni nárete kitá n desu.

Brown. Só desu ka. Watakushi wa shūsen-chokugo shinchūgun no heitai to shite sankágetsu

bákari Tōkyō ni imáshita ga, soko wa Eigo
no yóku dekíru Nihonjín ga ói kara, ammari
Nihongo o tsukaimasén deshita. Sore kara,
Amerika e káette benkyō shinákatta kara,
íma Nihón de Nihongo o benkyō shite imásu.
Shūsengo Nihón ni kité watakushi ga ichiban
odoroitá no wa kutsú o núide uchi e háiru
kotó deshita.

Ross. Sō desu ně. Watakushi no tomodachi wa
íma machí de kábā o haite kutsú o haita
mama agaru kotó mo áru to itte imásu ga,
sono hō ga bénri deshō ně.

Brown. Máda Nihon no ié no kotó wa ammari wakarimasén. Amerika to chigatte, heyá ga sukunái yō desu ně.

Ross. Sukóshi chigaimásu. Shōji ya fusuma ya itádo o tsukatte, ōkíi uchí o iroiro chíisa na
heyá ni shite imásu kedo ně.

Brown. Shōji to fusuma to itado no uchi dé wa, dóre
ga ichiban tsuyói desu ka?

Ross. Ichiban tsuyói no wa itádo désu. Sore kara,
itádo yóri mo, amádo no hō ga tsuyói desu.
Shōji ya fusuma wa kamí de tsukurimásu ga,
itádo ya amádo wa itá de tsukúru n desu.

Brown. Dóa wa arimasén ka?

Ross. Áru kotó mo arimásu. Seiyōma ya benjó ni
arimásu.

Brown. Tokonoma to iú no wa ittai nán desu ka?

Ross. Tokonoma to iú no wa zashikí ni áru, yuka
yóri tákakute chíisa na tokoro dé, soko ní wa
kakémono ga kákete aru n desu.

Brown.   Nihon no uchí ni wa shíndai ga nái yō desu
           ga, netai to omóu to dǒ surú n desu ka?
Ross.   Netaku náru to, oshiire kara futon ya mǒfu
           o dáshite, tatami no ué ni shikú n desu. Sore
           wa toko to iimásu.
Brown.   Zabúton wa futon to onaji gúrai no ǒkisa
           ('size') desu ka?
Ross.   Chigaimásu. Futon no hǒ ga zutto ōkíi
           desu.
Brown.   Góhan ga tabetái toki, dǒ surú n desu ka?
Ross.   Sore wa kō desu. Tatami ka zabúton ni
           suwatta mamá de tabéru n desu.
Brown.   Naruhodo sǒ desu ka. Iroiro gomendō désu
           ga,* máda kiite mitái kotó ga hitótsu ari-
           másu keredomo...
Ross.   Dǒzo, goenryo náku.
Brown.   Soṛe wa ně. Dǒ shite Jūnigatsu sánjū ichi-
           nichi ni umareta kodomo wa, tsugí no hi ni
           futatsú ni nátta to iimásu ka?
Ross.   Sore wa kazoédoshi to iimásu ně. Umareta
           bákari no akambō wa mō íssai dá to iú n
           desu. Sore kara, toshí o tóru hi wa tanjǒbi
           ja arimasén. Shōgatsu ná n desu. Kono
           shūkan wa tábun watakushi ga ichiban odo-
           roita kotó datta to omoimásu. Kéredomo,
           kazoédoshi to iu shūkan wa nisannen máe
           ni kawarimáshita.

*It's very bothersome but...'

LESSON 8.

A. BASIC SENTENCES. 'Telephone Calls.'

1. Chotto jimúsho no dáre ka ni denwa o kaketái n desu ga...

   I want to call someone at the office...

2. Anáta no uchi no denwa o tsukatté mo íi desu ka?

   May I use your phone?

3. Anáta ga kinō watakushi ni denwa o káketa toki wa, machi no dóko ka kara káketa n deshō né.

   When you phoned me yesterday, you must have called from somewhere in town.

4. Só desu. Kōshūdénwa datta kara, okane o irenákereba narimasén deshita.

   That's right. It was a public phone, so I had to put money in it.

5. Chōkyóri o kakéru toki ni, okane o sukóshi shika motte inákattara komáru deshō né.

   When you call long distance, if you [found you] had only a little money, you'd have a hard time wouldn't you.

6. Jidōdénwa wa bénri desu ga, dáiyaru (or bán) o mawasu tokí, yóku bangō o machigaemásu.

   Dial [automatic] telephones are convenient but I often dial the wrong number when I dial.

7. Kono denwa wa furúi denwa dé, bán ga nái kara, juwáki o hazusu to kōkánshu no kóe ga kikoemásu.

This telephone is an old one and hasn't a dial, so when you pick up the receiver you hear the operator's voice.

8. Nihon no kōkánshu wa watakushi ga náni mo wakaránai hodo téinei na kotobá o tsukatte hanashimásu.

Japanese operators use such polite language, I don't understand a thing.

9. Sono téinei na kotobá o hitótsu ka futatsu naraitái kara, dŏzo oshiete kudasái.

I want to learn one or two of those polite words, so please teach me.

10. Tatóeba, kōkánshū ga 'námban o oyobi désu ka' to ittára, sore wa dŏ iu ími desu ka?

For example, if the operator should say 'Námban o oyobi désu ka, what does that mean?

11. Sore wa 'námban o yobimásu ka' to iu ími de, 'námban e okake ni náru n desu ka' tó mo iimásu.

That means 'What number are you calling?' and is also said Námban e okake ni náru n desu ka [=Námban e kakemásu ka?].

12. Sō shitára, watakushi wa dŏ ittára íi deshō ka?

Then what should I say after that?

13. 'Marunóuchi no yón réi nána réi' to iu yŏ ni ittára íi deshō.*

You should say something like 'Marunouchi [exchange] 4070.'

*Or Ní yón ichí no... '241-4070.' And 'two' is sometimes said futá.

mǒ denwa o kákete hanáshite itára, kō-kánshu ga 'ohanashi-chū de gozaimásu' to iimásu.

other end [over there] is (busy) talking on the phone, the operator will say 'The line is busy'.

15. Sono tokí wa, juwáki o kákete shibáraku mát-te kara mō ichido den-wa o kákete mítara íi n desu.

Then, you should hang up the receiver and wait two or three minutes and then try calling again.

16. Amerika dé wa dóko no uchí ni mo, denwa ga áru yō desu ně.

In America they seem to have telephones in houses everywhere.

17. Dáre ka to hanashitái toki wa, itsu dé mo dekimásu ně.

When you want to talk to someone, you can do it any time.

18. Dáre to mo hanashítaku nákereba, denwa ga nákute mo íi desu.

If you don't want to talk to anybody, you don't have to have a phone.

19. Áru hito wa denwa wa átte mo nákute mo kamawánai to iimásu ga, watakushi wa mái-nichi kakéru kara, nákattara komarimá-su.

Some people say it makes no difference to them whether they have a phone or not, but I make calls every day, so if I didn't have one, I'd be in a fix.

20. Móshi, denwa ga nákat-tara ittai dǒ suru de-shō ka ně.

I wonder just what I would do if I didn't have a phone.

21. Kánai wa jochū ni am-

My wife has to tell the

mari nágaku denwa
de hanáshite wa ike-
nai to iwanákereba
narimasén.

22. Sore kara, máinichi mái-
    nichi tomodachi ni
    denwa o shite kínjo
    no uwasa nádo bakari
    shite wa damé da to
    mo iimásu.

23. Áru toki ni wa, denwa o
    kakéru yori, dempō o
    útsu hō ga íi kotó mo
    arimásu.

24. Kómban Kóbe e chōkyo-
    ridénwa o kakéru tsu-
    mori déshita ga, tega-
    mi o káita hō ga íi
    deshō ka né.

25. Watakushi wa kinō, ji-
    músho de tegami o
    gorokutsū káita shi,
    dempō o nisantsū útta
    shi, denwa o nando
    mo kakemáshita.

26. Isogáshikereba, isoga-
    shíi hodo shigoto ga
    omoshirói desu.

27. Denwa wa tsukaéba, tsu-
    kau hodo bénri da to

maid not to talk too
long on the phone.

Then, she also tells her
it's no good to call
friends up day after day
just to talk [make]
neighborhood gossip
and the like.

Sometimes it happens that
it's better to send a te-
legram than to phone.

I had intended to make
a long distance call to
Kobe this evening, but
I wonder if I'd better
write (instead).

Yesterday at the office I
wrote 5 or 6 letters, sent
2 or 3 telegrams, and
many any number of
phone calls [made calls
any number of times].

The busier we are, the
more interesting the job
is.

The more I use the
phone, the more I real-

íu kotó ga wakarimá-su.

ize how convenient it is.

28. Jimúsho ni wa, denwa no kázu wa ókereba, ói hodo íi desu.

The more phones an office has the better.

29. Myóban issho ni éiga o mí ni iku kotó ga de-kínakattara anáta ni goji góro made ni denwa o suréba íi desu ka?

If I can't go with you to the movies tomorrow night, is it OK to phone you by around 5?

30. Íma denwa ga hanashi-chū dá kara, chotto matánakereba nari-masén.

The line is busy right now, so I'll have to wait a bit.

VOCABULARY ITEMS.

NOUNS AND PHRASES

denwa, denwáki	a telephone	naisen	inside line,
(hito ni) denwa	(makes) a phone		extension
(o kakéru, suru)	call (to a person)	denwáshitsu	phone booth
kōshū	the public	denwa-chō	phone book
kōshūdénwa	a public phone	denwáryō	call charge, toll
chōkyóri	long distance	kínjo	neighborhood
chōkyoridénwa	long-distance	uwasa (o suru)	(talks) gossip
	phone call	ensoku	picnic
jidō-	automatic	toshókan	library
jidōdénwa	dial telephone	fūtō	envelope
bán, dáiyaru	the dial	ími	meaning
bán, bangō,		mukō (no)	the one opposite,
denwabángō	telephone number		the one across
kázu	number (of)		the way, the
gaisen	outside line		other fellow

aité	the other party; partner; adversary	sono uchi (ni)	in the near future, by and by
ichinichi-jū	all day long	nakanaka	for a long time
shibáraku	a while; a little while; quite a while	[+ negative]	[doesn't]; with difficulty [does]
		-chū	in the midst of, busy with

PRENOUN

higashi	east	áru	a certain [probably derived from the verb áru 'who (which) exists']
nishi	west		
minami	south		
kita	north		

VERBS AND PHRASES

mawasu	turns around, revolves, rotates something	(kōkánshu ga hito ni denwa o) tsunágu	(the operator) connects (the phone to someone), puts thru (the call to someone)
bán o mawasu	dials, turns the dial; dials the number		
bangō o mawasu	dials a number	denwa o kariru	borrows the use of someone's phone
denwa o kíru	[cuts the phone-call=] hangs up, ends the call	denwa ga naru	the phone rings
juwáki o hazusu	removes the receiver, takes the receiver from the hook	(náni ka o nani ka to) machigaeru	mistakes (something for something), misses
		machigau	makes a mistake, is mistaken
juwáki o oku	puts the receiver down	tatoéru	compares, talks figuratively, uses examples
denwa o oku	hangs up		
juwáki o mimí ni ateru	puts the receiver to one's ear	tatóeba	[if one uses examples=] for example
denwa o hiku	installs [puts thru] a phone	útsu	strikes, hits
dempō o útsu	sends a telegram	kóe ga déru	a voice comes out, is heard [on phone]
(hito ni) miséru	shows (people)		
mora[w]u	receives		

denwa ni déru	answers the phone	(o-)kotozuke,	a message
kotozukéru,	takes (gives) a	(o-)tsutae	
tsutaeru	message	ma-mó-naku	before long, soon

B. STRUCTURE NOTES.

8. 1. INTERROGATIVES + KA AND MO.

An interrogative is a word which asks a question—a regular noun like dáre 'who', dóre 'which', náni 'what'; an adverb noun like dó 'how', íkura 'how much', íkutsu 'how many, what number', ítsu 'when, what time'; or a pre-noun like dóno 'which one', dónna 'what sort of'.

These interrogatives occur also followed by the particles ka and mo with special meanings. When followed by mo, the meaning of the phrase is GENERALIZED—something like 'every, all' if the predicate is affirmative, 'no, none, not at all, not any' if the predicate is negative. For example Itsu mo kimásu 'He comes all the time', Itsu mo kimasén 'He never comes'. When the pre-nouns occur, the particle mo follows the noun modified: Dóno éiga mo mí ni ikimásu 'He goes to see every movie', Dóno éiga mo mí ni ikimasén 'He doesn't go to see any movies'. The phrases consisting of interrogative + mo occur more often with the negative than with the affirmative; in the affirmative, phrases of the type interrogative + dé [copula gerund] + mo are often used instead. [These are discussed in 8. 3]

All of the interrogatives except the pre-nouns—dóno 'which', dónna 'what sort of'—occur followed by ka, and the resulting phrases have an INDEFINITE meaning, something like 'some, any'; **Dáre ka kimáshita** 'Someone came', **Náni ka arimásu ka?** 'Is there anything there?' [Compare **Náni ga arimásu ka?** 'What is there?'], **Ítsu ka oasobi ni kité kudasai** 'Please come to visit us sometime'.

The expressions with **ka** and **mo** are often used also with additional particles, but the particles **wa**, **ga**, and **o** usually do not occur. The meaning of the **wa**, **ga**, or **o** you might expect is carried by the juxtaposition of the phrase with the rest of the sentence and the general context. For the expressions ending in **ka**, any additional particles usually come AFTER the particle **ka**; for the expressions with **mo**, the additional particles usually come BEFORE the particle **mo**. Thus we find **Dóko ka e ikimáshita** 'He went some place', but **Dóko e mo ikimasén deshita** 'He didn't go anyplace.' An exception is the way you say 'in some way' **dó ni ka**—this follows the pattern of **dó ni mo** 'in (not) any way, in no way; in every way.' The simple expressions **dó ka** and **dó mo** are not used with these meanings, perhaps because of the existence of the special expressions **dó ka** 'please' [an old-fashioned form of **dózo**] and **dó mo** 'ever so much, very' as in **Dó mo arígató gozaimásu** 'Thank you very much.'

Here is a list of the expressions with **ka** and **mo**:

INTERROGATIVE	...+KA	...+MO	
		+AFFIRMATIVE*	+NEGATIVE
dáre 'who'	**dáre ka** 'somebody, anybody'	**dáre mo** 'everybody'	'[not] anybody, nobody'
dóchira 'which'	**dóchira ka** 'either one'	**dóchira mo** 'both'	'[not] either one, neither one'

*But these are often replaced by INTERROGATIVE+**DE MO** (8.3). Note that **dóchira de mo** means 'either one' but **dóchira mo** means 'both.'

dóre 'which'	**dóre ka** 'any one'	**dóre mo** 'all, any'	'[not] any one, no one'
dóko 'where'	**dóko ka** 'somewhere, anywhere'	**dóko (de) mo** 'everywhere'	'[not] anywhere, nowhere'
dó 'how'	**dó ni ka** 'anyhow, somehow'	**dó ni (de) mo** 'in every way'	'[not] in any way, in no way'
íkura 'how much'	**íkura ka** 'some amount'	**íkura (de) mo** 'ever so much, a large amount'	'[not] much, no great amount'
íkutsu 'how many'	**íkutsu ka** 'some number, several'	**íkutsu mo** 'ever so many, a large number'	'[not] many, no great number'
ítsu 'when'	**ítsu ka** 'sometime, anytime'	**ítsu mo** 'always'	'[not] any time, never'
náni 'what'	**náni ka** 'something, anything'	**náni mo**=**nán de mo** 'everything'	'[not] anything, nothing'
nán-C. 'how many C.' [C.=any counter]	——	**nán-C. mo** 'any number of C.'	'[not] many C.'
dóno N. 'what N.' [N.=any noun]	——	**dóno N. mo** 'every N'	'[not] any N., no N.'
dónna N. what sort of N.'	——	**dónna N. mo** 'all sorts of, any kind of N.'	'[not] anything, no N., no sort of N.'

Notice that the English translations 'any, anyone, anybody, any time' etc. correspond to the phrases with **ka** IF THE ENGLISH CONTAINS AN AFFIRMATIVE VERB ('Did you see anyone?'—**Dáre ka mimáshita ka?**), but to the phrases with **mo** IF THE ENGLISH CONTAINS A

NEGATIVE VERB ('I didn't see anyone'—**Dáre mo mi-masén deshita**).

There is a special use of the INDEFINITE EXPRESSIONS in apposition to some noun phrase. An expression like **dáre ka** 'somebody' can be followed immediately by a phrase telling who the somebody is (in general terms)—**dáre ka gaikoku-káwase no shigoto no keiken ga áru hito** 'somebody who has experience in foreign-exchange work'. An expression like **dóko ka** 'some place' can be followed immediately by a phrase specifying the sort of place—**dóko ka oyógu kotó no dekíru tokoro** 'some place we can swim'. An expression like **ítsu ka** 'some time' can be followed immediately by a phrase delimiting the time—**ítsu ka Tōkyō ni iru toki** 'some time when you're in Tokyo'. And an expression like **náni ka** 'something' can be immediately followed by a phrase limiting the thing—**Náni ka heya no náka ni áru monó desu ka?** 'Is it something in the room?' The expressions **íkura ka**, and **nán-C. ka** are also used this way: **Íkura ka okane ga irimásu** 'I need some [amount of] money'; **Íkutsu ka kaban ga arimáshita** 'There were a number of suitcases'; **nán-satsu ka hón o kaimáshita** 'I bought a number of books'. But in each of these cases, the expressions with **ka**—like numbers and quantity words in general—can follow the expression noun + particle: **Okane ga íkura ka irimásu. Kaban ga íkutsu ka arimáshita. Hón o nánsatsu ka kaimáshita.** In fact, the latter usage is more common.

The word **kesshite** 'definitely [not]' is a more emphatic way to say 'never' than **ítsu mo**: **Íi senséi wa kesshite Eigo o hanashimasén yo.** 'A good teacher never talks English.'

Here are some examples of indefinite and generalized interrogative expressions used in sentences.

Dáre ka mimáshita ka?	Did you see someone?
Dáre ka sensei no yó na hitó o mimáshita.	I saw someone like the teacher.
Dáre mo ikitái darō to omoimásu.	I think everyone will want to go.
Dáre mo kimasén ka?	Isn't anyone coming?
Kono zasshi no uchí de, dóre ka totte yomimashṓ.	I think I'll take one of these magazines and read it.
Dóre ka atarashíi no ga hoshíi desu ka?	Do you want one of the new ones?
Dóre mo omoshirói desu ka?	Are they all interesting?
Dóre mo yomítaku arimasén.	I don't want to read any of them.
Kodomo wa dóko ka de asonde irú deshō.	The children must be playing somewhere.
Kodomo wa dóko ka kōen no náka de asonde irú deshō.	The children must be playing somewhere in the park.
Yamá wa dóko ni mo arimásu ně.	Mountains are everywhere aren't they.
Watakushi wa dóko e mo ryokō shita kotó wa arimasén.	I've never taken a trip anywhere.
Kono nítsū no tegami no uchí, dóchira ka yónde	Please read either one of these two letters.

kudasai.

Kono nítsū no tegami (o or wa) dóchira mo yónde kudasai.

Please read both of these letters.

Dóchira mo yomimasén ka?

Aren't you going to read both of them?

Dǒ ni ka shite Nihón e kaeritái to omótte imáshita.

I was thinking I wanted to come back to Japan somehow or other.

Dǒ ni de mo shite Nihongo o benkyō shitái desu.

I want to study Japanese in every way (possible).

Dǒ ni mo ryōríya to iu kotobá o iu kotó ga dekimasén deshita.

He wasn't able to say the word "ryōríya" at all [in any way].

Nihón ni wa, yamá ga íkura mo arimásu ně.

In Japan there are ever so many mountains, aren't there.

Okane wa íkura mo arimasén kara ně.

You see, I haven't any great amount of money, so...

Kodomo wa ame o íkutsu ka tabetái to itte imásu.

The child is saying he'd like to eat some [pieces of] candy.

Ame o sonna ni íkutsu mo tabéru to, byōki ni narimásu yo.

If you eat such a great amount of [a great many pieces of] candy, you will get sick!

Íkutsu mo tabemasén deshita.

I didn't eat a great many.

Ítsu ka issho ni éiga ka náni ka mí ni ikimasén ka?

Won't you go with me some time to see a movie or something?

Ítsu ka oténki no íi hi ni inaka e ensoku ni ikimashŏ.

Ítsu mo Eigo shika hanasánai hito wa nakanaka Nihongo ga jōzú ni narimasén yo.

Ítsu mo Eigo o hanásazu ni, máinichi benkyō suréba, súgu ni Nihonjin no yŏ ni Nihongo ga dekíru deshō.

Hako no náka ni wa náni ka háitte iru yō desu.

Náni ka chíisa na isu no yŏ na monó ga háitte imasu.

Watakushi no hako no náka o míru to, náni mo háitte imasén deshita.

Anáta wa nán de mo dekimásu ně.

Kono toshókan ni wa, hón ga nambyakusatsu mo arimásu.

Watakushi no tokoró made

Sometime when it's a nice day, let's go to the country for a picnic.

A person who is always talking just English doesn't get good in Japanese for a long time [finds it hard to get good in Japanese].

I bet if you never talk English and study every day, you'll soon know Japanese like a Japanese.

There seems to be something [entered] in the box.

There seems to be something like a small chair inside.

When I looked in my box, there was nothing in it [at all].

You're able to do (just about) everything, aren't you.

There are ever so many hundreds of books in this library.

It takes no time at all to

nánjikan mo kakarima-
sén.

Koko ni áru zasshi wa,
dóno zasshi mo Amerika
kara kimáshita.

Dóno zasshi mo Nihón kara
kónakatta n desu.

Watakushi wa dónna éiga
de mo sukí desu.

Shújin wa ítsu mo dónna
éiga de mo mí ni ikitaku
nái to itte imásu.

Dáre ka ni tegami o kaki-
mashṓ.

Dáre ni mo tegami o mise-
masén deshita.

Dáre ni mo tegami o misé-
nai de kudasái.

Dóko ka kara kitá deshō.

Dóko kara mo kónakatta n
desu yo.

Náni ka komátta kotó ga
áttara watakushi ni itte
kudasái.

Iu kotó wa nán de mo Ni-
hongo de itte kudasái.

Nán to mo iimasén deshita.

get to my place.

Of the magazines here,
every magazine came
from America.

None of the magazines
came from Japan.

I like all sorts of movies;
I like all movies.

My husband is always say-
ing he doesn't want to
go see any [sort of] mov-
ies at all.

I think I'll write a letter
to someone.

I didn't show the letter to
anyone.

Please don't show the letter
to anybody.

It must have come from
some place.

[I tell you] it didn't come
from anywhere at all.

If you run into any trouble.
let me know.

Everything you say, say it
in Japanese.

He said nothing.

8. 2. GERUND + MO. The literal meaning of a gerund [the -te form] + mo is something like 'even doing, even being so'. It can often be freely translated 'even if [or though] somebody does something, even if something is so'.

Umi e itté mo, oyógu kotó ga dekínai kara, omoshíroku nái deshō.	Even if I went to the beach, I can't swim so it probably wouldn't be any fun.
Sono éiga o mí ni ikitákute mo okane wa arimasén.	Even if I want to see that movie, I haven't any money.
Kono heyá e wa, shachō dé mo hairimasén yo.	Even the president of the company doesn't go into this room. [Even being president, one doesn't..]
Nihón de wa, kodomo dé mo Nihongo ga dekimásu né.	In Japan, even the children speak Japanese, you know.

The last two examples show a use of the copula gerund **dé.**

Dé mo often starts a sentence 'But..., Yet...', as do **Shikáshi, Kéredomo (Kéredo, Kédo),** and **Tokoró ga** 'But...'

Sometimes you have two phrases gerund+**mo** with the meaning 'whether someone does one thing or does something else, whether one thing is so or the other is so'. The two gerunds can be either two different verbs, or the same verb in affirmative and negative forms, or the same verb with different objects or modifiers.

Oténki ga yókute mo, wá-
rukute mo, máinicki sam-
po ni ikimásu.

I go for a walk every day,
whether the weather is
good or not.

Tanaka-san ga issho ni kité mo, kónakute mo wa-
takushi wa ikimásu yo.

I'm going whether Mr. Ta-
naka comes along or not.

Kyóto e itté mo, Ōsaka e
itté mo, yóku asobimásu
né.

You'll have a good time,
whether you go to Kyoto
or to Osaka, you see.

Often, the concluding clause consists of the word **kamaimasén** 'it doesn't matter; it makes no difference'. This is
a special meaning of the negative form of the consonant
verb **kama[w]-u** 'is concerned about, pays attention to, goes
to trouble for, takes care of, entertains'. Here are examples:

Eiga o mí ni itté mo, sampo ni itté mo, kamaima-
sén.

I don't care whether we go
to a movie or go for a
walk.

Heyá wa ókikute mo, chíi-
sakute mo, kamaimasén
ka?

Does it make no difference
whether the room is
large or small?

More examples of **-te mo** constructions.

Bénri de mo, fúben de mo,
kamaimasén.

I don't care whether it's
convenient or inconven-
ient.

Jírō ga ikitákute mo, ikitaku nákute mo, wataku-
shi wa ikitái desu yo.

I sure want to go, whether
Jiro goes or not.

Tákakute mo, yásukute mo, kono hón ga (or o) kaitái n desu.

I want to buy this book, whether it's expensive or not.

Tanaka-san wa watakushi dé mo anáta de mo dáre de mo íi to iimáshita.

Mr. Tanaka said anyone would be OK, either [whether it be] you or me or anyone (else).

Tsukárete ité mo, sampo ni ikimáshita.

Even though I was tired, I went for a walk.

The last sentence could also be said **Tsukárete irú no ni sampo ni ikimáshita** 'In spite of the fact that I was tired, I went for a walk.' Or **Tsukárete itá keredomo sampo ni ikimáshita** 'I was tired, but I went for a walk anyway.' Further uses of **-te mo** constructions are taken up below.

8. 3.   INTERROGATIVE + GERUND + MO.   In an affirmative sentence an interrogative + **mo** has a GENERALIZED or INCLUSIVE meaning—'everybody, everywhere, everyone'.   Usually, however, this expression is expanded to interrogative + GERUND + **mo**.   If there isn't a modifying verb, then the gerund is that of the copula **dé** 'being'.   Here are some examples of the phrases.

INTERROGATIVE + -te + mo		INTERROGATIVE + dé + mo	
dáre ga kité mo	whoever comes	dáre de mo	anybody at all (whoever it may be)
dóchira ni shité mo	whichever I decide on	dóchira de mo	either one (whichever it may be)
dóre ga hóshikute mo	whatever I want	dóre de mo	any one at all (whichever one it may be)

dóko e itté mo	wherever you go	**dóko de mo**	any place at all (wherever it may be)
dó (ni) shité mo	however I may do it	**dó (ni) de mo**	anyway at all (however it may be)
íkura shité mo	however much it costs	**íkura de mo**	any amount at all (whatever amount it may be)
íkutsu átte mo	however many may exist	**íkutsu de mo**	any number at all (however many it may be)
ítsu tsúite mo	whenever it arrives	**ítsu de mo**	any time at all (whenever it may be)
náni o míte mo	whatever I look at	**nán de mo**	anything at all (whatever it may be)
nán-C. naku-shité mo	however many C. I lose	**nán-C. de mo**	any number of C. at all (whatever number of C. it may be)
dóno N. ga mítakute mo	whichever N. I want to see	**dóno N. de mo**	any N. at all (whatever N. it may be)
dónna N. ga itté mo	whatever sort of N. I need [ir-u]	**dónna N. de mo**	any sort of N. at all (whatever sort of N. it may be)

Here are examples in sentences.

Dónna shigoto o shité mo, dekiru dake yóku shi-másu.
Whatever job he does, he does it the best he can.

Amerika ni súnde iru hito wa, dáre de mo jidósha o mótte iru yō desu nḗ.

It seems as if everyone living in America owns a car, doesn't it.

Sukí na monó wa, dóre de mo katte kudasái.

Please buy any one you like.

Dóchira de mo íi deshō.

Either one at all will be OK.

Okane wa íkura de mo arimásu kara. . .

I have plenty of money (so don't worry).

Kaban o íkutsu de mo motte hikóki ni noru kotó wa dekimasén.

You can't go on a plane with an unlimited number of suitcases.

Ítsu de mo okáshi o tábete imasu.

They're always eating pastry.

Nán de mo dekimásu nḗ.

He can do anything at all, can't he.

Denwa o nándo de mo kákete kudasai.

Please telephone any number of times.

Dóno misé de mo, téinei na kotobá o tsukatte monó o utte imásu.

At every shop they sell their things using (speaking with) polite words.

Kono yakusha sáe háitte iréba, dónna éiga de mo sukí desu nḗ.

You see, I like any movie at all, provided this actor is in it.

Dóno júnsa ni kiité mo, súgu wakarimásu yo.

You'll find out regardless which policeman you ask. You'll find out from any policeman.

Dáre no uchi e asobi ni

I take my children along.

itté mo, kodomo o tsure-
te ikimásu ně.

Íkura benkyō shité mo, na-
ráu koto ga dekínai yō
desu.

Dó shite mo ichido Ameri-
ka e asobi ni itte mitái
to omoimásu.

Kodomo wa ame o íkura
tábete mo máda hoshíi
yō desu ně.

Ítsu ensoku ni ikitái to o-
mótte mo, áme ga furi-
dásu yō desu ně.

Ítsu de mo só desu ně.

Hako no náka ni náni ga
háitte ité mo, kamaima-
sén.

Kutsú wa dóno kaban ni
ireté mo, kamaimasén.

Tegami o nántsū káite mo,
máda kakánai tegami ga
yamá hodo áru yō desu.

Dóno misé de katté mo,
nedan ga takái desu ně.

whomever I visit.

However much I study it,
I can't seem to learn it.

I'd like to go to America
for a visit very much (in
every possible way).

However much candy
children may eat, they
still want more, don't
they.

It seems to burst out raining every time I want to
go on a picnic.

It's always that way, isn't it.

It doesn't matter what may
be in the box.

It makes no difference
which suitcase you put
the shoes in.

Regardless how many let-
ters I write, there seem
to be lots still unwritten.

The prices are high at all
the shops, aren't they.
[Whatever shop you buy
at...]

8. 4. THE PROVISIONAL MOOD. The provisional mood has meanings something like 'if something happens [now or in the future]; provided something happens'. It is made by adding the following endings to the stems of verbs and adjectives ['tonic' means the verb has an accent in the imperfect, 'atonic' means it has no accent in the imperfect]:

	VERBS		ADJECTIVES
	CONSONANT STEMS	VOWEL STEMS	
TONIC	´-eba	´-reba	´ –kereba
ATONIC	–éba	–réba	´-kereba

The provisional of the copula dá is irregular: nára 'if it is, provided it equals'. The provisionals of kúru and suru are kúreba and suréba.

Here are some examples of provisional forms; the meaning of each one is 'if (provided) something happens' or 'if (provided) something is so'.

VOWEL VERBS

MEANING	IMPERFECT -ru	PROVISIONAL -reba
'sleeps'	ne-ru	ne-réba
'eats'	tabé-ru	tabé-reba
'puts in'	ire-ru	ire-réba
'looks at'	mí-ru	mí-reba
'stays, exists'	i-ru	i-réba

CONSONANT VERBS

MEANING	IMPERFECT -u	PROVISIONAL -eba
'is needed'	ir-u	ir-éba

'returns'	káer-u	káer-eba
'waits'	mát[s]-u	mát-eba
'meets'	á[w]-u	á-eba
'writes'	kák-u	kák-eba
'swims'	oyóg-u	oyóg-eba
'calls'	yob-u	yob-éba
'dies'	shin-u	shin-éba

ADJECTIVES

MEANING	IMPERFECT -i	PROVISIONAL -kereba
'is blue'	aó-i	áo-kereba
'is red'	aka-i	aká-kereba
'is good'	í-i, yó-i	yó-kereba
'wants to meet'	aitá-i	aíta-kereba
'wants to go'	ikita-i	ikitá-kereba
'does not ride'	norana-i	noraná-kereba
'does not see'	mína-i	mína-kereba
'does not read'	yomána-i	yomána-kereba

COPULA

MEANING	IMPERFECT	PROVISIONAL
'equals'	dá [ná, no]	nára

The word **nára** sometimes appears after other inflected forms: **surú nara** (=surú no nara) 'if it is a matter of doing', **shitá nara** (=shitá no nara) 'if it is a case of having done'.

The provisional of negative adjectives—**shinákereba** 'if I don't do'—is usually equivalent to English 'unless' + the affirmative:

Tanaka-san ga issho ni kó-nakereba, omoshíroku nái deshō.	It won't be any fun unless Tanaka comes along.
Sono éiga wa mínakereba, íi ka warúi ka wakaránai deshō.	We won't know whether the movie's good or bad unless we see it.

Here are some examples of the provisional used in sentences.

Áme ga fúreba, sampo ni ikimasén.	If it rains, I'm not going for a walk.
Íma okáshi o tabéreba, góhan wa tabétaku nái deshō.	If you eat the pastry now, you won't want to eat your dinner.
Nihongo de hanáseba, súgu wakarimásu.	If you speak in Japanese, they'll understand right away.
Eigo de iéba, wakaránai deshō.	If you tell them in English, they probably won't understand.
Kono kusuri o nómeba, génki ni náru deshō.	I think you'll get all right, if you take this medicine.
Watakushi nára, sonna éiga o mí ni ikimasén.	As for me, I'm not going to see such a movie. [If it's me...]
Inaka nára, shízuka na tokoro ga ói deshō.	If it's the country [you're talking about or going to], there are probably lots of quiet places.
Sonna ni fúben nara, soko	If it's so inconvenient, I

ni sumítaku wa arima-   certainly don't want to
sén yo.   live there.

8. 5. OBLIGATION.   For   the   expression 'someone
MUST or HAS TO do something' Japanese has several
equivalents.   One of the most common is the use of the
provisional form of the negative adjectives derived from
the verbs [**yom-ánakereba** 'if I do not read'] + the negative
of the verb **náru** [**narimasén** 'it does not become = it won't
do']． So to say 'I must read this book' you say **Kono hón
o yománakereba narimasén** 'If I do not read this book,
it won't do.'

Instead of **narimasén,** you can use **damé desu** 'it's no
good' or **ikemasén** 'it can't go = it's no good, it won't do'.
Yománakereba narimasén and **yománakereba damé desu**
and **yománakereba ikemasén** all mean about the same
thing 'I have to read.'

Instead of the provisional of the negative adjective
-(a)nakereba, you can use the gerund of the negative adjective **-(a)nakute**+the particle **wa,** with a meaning something
like '[as for] not doing...[as the topic]'. In these expressions
of obligation, **yománakereba** 'if I do not read' and **yománakute wa** 'as for not reading' are equivalent. So you
can say 'I have to read this book' in any of the following
ways:

1. **Kono hón o yománakereba narimasén.**
2. **Kono hón o yománakereba damé desu.**
3. **Kono hón o yománakereba ikemasén.**
4. **Kono hón o yománakute wa narimasén.**
5. **Kono hón o yománakute wa damé desu.**

6. **Kono hón o yománakute wa ikemasén.**

The first and last patterns (1 and 6) are more commonly heard than the others.*

8. 6. PERMISSION. To say 'someone MAY do something'—and in colloquial American speech we often use the word CAN in this same sense, rather than in the sense of 'ability'—the Japanese use the gerund -te + the particle **mo** 'even' + some form of the adjective **íi** 'it is good, it is OK'. The expression -te mo íi desu means something like 'even doing something is OK.' To say 'You may read this book' you say **Anáta wa kono hón o yónde mo íi desu.** To ask 'May I visit Mr Tanaka?' you say **Watakushi wa Tanaka-san no uchi ni asobi ni itté mo íi desu ka?** Instead of **íi desu, kamaimasén** can be used to mean 'OK'.

8. 7. DENIAL OF PERMISSION = PROHIBITION. To say 'someone MAY NOT do something' Japanese usually use a statement of PROHIBITION 'someone MUST NOT do something'. This consists of the plain gerund of the affirmative verb -te+the particle **wa+ikemasén** or **narimasén** or **damé desu.**

The expression -te wa ikemasén means something like 'as for doing something, it's no good', that is 'don't do it'. You have already had one way to say 'Don't read this book'—**Kono hón o yománai de kudasai.** The use of the plain negative+the copula gerund+**kudasái** is a rather direct way of ORDERING someone not to do something. Except when talking to inferiors, Japanese

---

*Forms ending -(a)nakute wa are often pronounced -(a)nakucha; they can end a sentence with the same meaning as if followed by **ikemasén: Kaeránakucha** 'I'll have to go home'.

usually prefer a more subtle prohibition. Even the type discussed here is rather strong when talking to an equal or superior; it is better to SUGGEST someone not do something rather than PROHIBIT them from doing it.

Each of the following sentences means 'Don't read this book', but they would ordinarily be said only to children, maids or social inferiors, or in making some sort of generalized impersonal statement (like 'Keep off the grass!').

1. Kono hón o yónde wa ikemasén.
2. Kono hón o yónde wa narimasén.
3. Kono hón o yónde wa damé desu.

If you want to make the injunction a bit stronger, you can add the insistive particle yo at the end: **Kono hón o yónde wa ikemasén yo!**

Notice the use of the prohibitive as a denial of a request for permission:

Éiga o mí ni itté mo íi desu ka?	May I go see the movie?
Itté wa ikemasén.	No, you may not.

And note that -te wa is often shortened to **-cha, -de wa** to **-ja** (p. 423).

8.8. DENIAL OF OBLIGATION. To deny obligation 'someone NEED NOT or DOES NOT HAVE TO do something' you use the gerund of the negative adjective **-(a)nakute + mo + íi.** The meaning of the expression **-(a)nakute mo íi** is something like 'even not doing it [even if someone doesn't do it], it's OK'. So, to say 'you don't have to read this book' you say **Kono hón o yománakute mo íi desu**. If you want to ask 'Do I have to take the medicine?' you can say either **Kusuri o nománakereba narimasén ka?** if you're just wondering, or, if you're hoping for permission not to take it, you can ask **Kusuri o nománakute mo íi desu ka?** 'Is it all right even if I don't take the medicine? May I go without the medicine?'

8. 9. OBLIGATION, PROHIBITION, PERMISSION: SUMMARY. Here is a summary of the forms discussed in the preceding sections.

OBLIGATION 'must, has to'

DENIAL OF OBLIGATION
'need not, doesn't have to'

-(a)nakereba $\left\{ \begin{array}{l} \textbf{narimasén} \\ \textbf{ikemasén} \\ \textbf{damé desu} \end{array} \right.$

['if does not do, is no good']

-(a)nakute wa $\left\{ \begin{array}{l} \textbf{ikemasén} \\ \textbf{narimasén} \\ \textbf{damé desu} \end{array} \right.$

['not doing is no good']

-(a)nakute mo íi

['even not doing is OK']

PERMISSION 'may, can'

-te mo íi

['even doing is good']

DENIAL OF PERMISSION=
PROHIBITION
'may not, must not'

-te wa $\left\{ \begin{array}{l} \textbf{narimasén} \\ \textbf{damé desu} \\ \textbf{ikemasén} \end{array} \right.$ (yo)

['doing is no good']

A confusing point about these expressions is that what looks like the negative equivalent of permission—the form **-(a)nakute mo íi**—is not the denial of permission, but the denial of obligation. On the other hand, what looks the affirmative equivalent of the obligation expression—the

form -te wa ikemasén—is the denial of permission=prohibi-
tion. This is just a case of misleading formal similarities.

Some students find it easier to remember these expressions as single units: -(a)nakereba-narimasén 'must',
-(a)nakute-wa-ikemasén 'must', -(a)nakute-mo-íi 'need not',
-te-mo-íi 'may', -te-wa-ikemasén 'must not'. However you
learn them, remember the following points:

(1) Japanese often pause within the expression, before the last word: -(a)nakereba, narimasén; -(a)nakute wa,
ikemasén; -(a)nakute mo, íi desu; -te mo, íi desu.

(2) You will also want to learn the less common
variants -(a)nakereba ikemasén, -(a)nakute wa damé desu;
-(a)nakute wa narimasén, -(a)nakute wa damé desu.*

(3) The final word may be inflected in various ways
to fit the whole expression into the sentence properly,
as in some of the following examples.
Examples.

Kómban benkyō shináke-reba naránai node, myó-ban issho ni éiga o mí ni ikimashó ka?	If you have to study to-night, shall we go see the movie tomorrow night?
Kōbá de hatarakanákereba naránai no wa iyá desu yo.	I sure hate to have to work at the factory.
Kore wa kómban kakána-kereba naránai tegami désu kara...	This is a letter that I have to write tonight (so)...
Yománakute mo íi hón o yónde mo íi desu ka?	May we read the books we don't have to read?

*You may also hear -(a)nai to damé desu.

Isha wa myōgónichi kara kusuri o nománakute mo íi to iimáshita.

The doctor said I didn't have to take the medicine (starting) from day after tomorrow.

Doyŏbi wa machí e ikaná-kute mo yókereba, inaka e ensoku ni ikimashŏ ka?

Provided we don't have to go to town, shall we go to the country for a picnic?

Kodomo ga míte mo íi éiga desu ka?

Is it a movie children can see?

Jírō o tsurete itté mo yóke-reba, anáta to issho ni ikimashŏ.

If I may bring Jiro with me, I'll go with you.

Itté wa ikenai kotobá o ii-máshita.

He said a word he wasn't supposed to [he shouldn't have].

Nihongo o benkyō shite iru aida Eigo o hanáshi-te wa ikemasén yo.

While you're studying Japanese you mustn't talk English.

Eigo o hanáshite wa ike-nákereba, Nihongo de nán de mo iu kotó ga dekíru yō ni narimásu nĕ.

If you aren't allowed to talk English, then you get so you can say everything in Japanese, you see.

Rainen Amerika e kaerá-nakereba ikemasén.

I have to go back to the States next year.

Jírō ga kómban kónakere-ba damé desu yo.

Jiro's got to come tonight.

Kyónen Nihongo o yóku benkyō shinákute wa na-

Last year I had to study Japanese hard [a lot].

rimasén deshita.

Amerika e iku hito wa Eigo ga dekínakute wa damé desu né.	A person going to America has to know English, doesn't he.
Kodomo ni sonna ni naité wa damé da to itte kudasái.	Tell the child it mustn't cry like that.
Osoku kité wa ikenái deshō.	We mustn't arrive late.

8. 10. THE CONDITIONAL MOOD: FORMS. The conditional mood has several meanings: 'if something had happened; supposing something happens; when something happened, when something has happened' and the like. The forms are made by adding the endings **-tara** and **-dara** and **-kattara** to the stems of verbs, adjectives and the copula in the same way as the perfect endings **-ta** and **-da** and **-katta** are added.

	ENDING FOR TONIC WORDS	ENDING FOR ATONIC WORDS
VOWEL VERB STEMS		
-e-	} **⌐-tara**	**-tára**
-i-		
CONSONANT VERB STEMS		
-t- / -t-		
-r- / -t-		
-w- / -t-	} **⌐-tara**	**-tára**
-s- / -shi-		
-k- / -i-		

```
-g- / -i-
-b- / -n-       }  ⌐ -dara            -dára
-m- / -n-
-n- / -n-
```

ADJECTIVE STEMS
⌐-kattara   ⌐kattara

COPULA
dát-tara

Here are some model conditional forms, alongside the corresponding perfect forms. You can give the conditional forms a tag translation 'if or when....'.

VOWEL VERBS

MEANING	IMPERFECT -ru	PERFECT -ta	CONDITIONAL
eats	tabé-ru	tábe-ta	tábe-tara
looks at	mí-ru	mí-ta	mí-tara
comes	kú-ru [Irreg.!]	ki-tá	ki-tára
does	su-ru [Irreg.!]	shi-ta	shi-tára
stays	i-ru	i-ta	i-tára

CONSONANT VERBS

MEANING	IMPERFECT -u	PERFECT -ta	CONDITIONAL -tara / -dara
is needed	ir-u	it-ta	it-tára
goes	ik-u	it-ta [Irreg.!]	it-tára [Irreg.!]
says	i[w]-u [Irreg! =yuu]	it-ta [or yut-ta]	it-tára [or yut-tara]
waits for	mát[s]-u	mát-ta	mát-tara
rides	nor-u	not-ta	not-tára
meets	á[w]-u	át-ta	át-tara

speaks	hanás-u	hanáshi-ta	hanáshi-tara
writes	kák-u	kái-ta	kái-tara
swims	oyóg-u	oyói-da	oyói-dara
calls	yob-u	yon-da	yon-dára
reads	yóm-u	yón-da	yón-dara
dies	shin-u	shin-da	shin-dára

ADJECTIVES

MEANING	IMPERFECT -i	PERFECT -katta	CONDITIONAL -kattara
is red	aka-i	aká-katta	aká-kattara
is blue	aó-i	áo-katta	áo-kattara
is bad	warú-i	wáru-katta	wáru-kattara
is big	ōkí-i	ŏki-katta	ŏki-kattara
is good	í-i, yó-i	yó-katta	yó-kattara
is non-existent	ná-i	ná-katta	ná-kattara
wants to go	ikita-i	ikitá-katta	ikitá-kattara
doesn't hurry	isogána-i	isogána-katta	isogána-kattara

COPULA

MEANING	IMPERFECT	PERFECT	CONDITIONAL
equals, is	dá [ná, no]	dát-ta	dát-tara

8. 11. THE CONDITIONAL MOOD: USES. In the meaning 'supposing something happens [now or in the future], supposing something is so' the conditional is very similar to the provisional with its meaning 'provided something happens, provided something is so'. For a hypothetical condition in the PAST, you use only the conditional. In the meaning 'when' we find the conditional, or the plain imperfect + the particle to 'whenever' or 'right when', or the plain imperfect or perfect + toki

(ni) '(at) the time that'—but not the provisional. For the meaning 'if' there are three possibilities: conditional 'supposing that', provisional 'provided that', and plain imperfect + particle to 'if = whenever'.

The difference between the conditional and the provisional is often one of explicit doubt; if you use the conditional -tara form, you show some doubt as to whether something will happen or not 'if it should happen (but I doubt it will)', but if you use the provisional form you are making a hypothesis without saying anything about the likelihood of its being true: 'if it happens'.

Here are some sentences showing the differences between the conditional and the provisional with the meaning 'if' under a present or future hypothesis. There are also sentences illustrating the particle to with the meaning of a repeated or habitual 'if = whenever'.

Sono kotó o Nihongo de ittára, súgu wakáru deshō.	If you were to say that in Japanese, they'd understand right off.
Sono kotó o Nihongo de iéba, súgu wakáru deshō.	If you say that in Japanese, they'll understand right off.
Sono kotó o Nihongo de iu to, súgu wakarimásu.	If (whenever) you say that in Japanese, they understand you right off.
Sore o tábetara, byōki ni narimásu.	If you were to eat that, you'd get sick.
Sore o tabéreba, byōki ni narimasú.	If you eat that, you'll get sick.

Sore o tabéru to, byōki ni narimásu.	If (whenever) I eat that, I get sick.
Oténki ga yókattara, ikimásu. ⎫ **Oténki ga yókereba, ikimásu.** ⎬	If the weather is nice, I'll go.
Oténki ga íi to, sampo ni ikimásu.	If (whenever) the weather's good, I go for a walk.
Nihon no éiga dattara, ikimasén.	If it should be a Japanese movie, I won't go.
Nihon no éiga nara, ikimasén.	If it is a Japanese movie, I won't go.
Nihon no éiga da to, ikimasén.	If (whenever) it is a Japanese movie, I don't go.

Here are some sentences with the hypothetical condition in the past; only the conditional is used, and the following clause often ends with an expression consisting of a plain perfect followed by the tentative of the copula— -**ta deshō**—sometimes with **ga** or **keredomo** [or abbreviated forms **keredo, kedo**] added at the end to show that the condition was unfulfilled.

Sono kotó o Nihongo de ittára, wakátta deshō.	If you'd said that in Japanese, they'd have understood.
Sono hón-ya wa Ei-wá-jisho o utte itára, issatsu kattá deshō ga...	If that bookshop had sold [been selling] English-Japanese dictionaries, I'd have bought one, but (they weren't so I didn't).

| Oténki ga yókattara ittárō to omoimásu. [ittárō = ittá darō] | If the weather had been good, I think I'd have gone. |
| Amerika no éiga dattara, ittá deshō kedo... | If it had been an American film, I'd have gone, but (it wasn't so I didn't). |

In all of the sentences where the conditional forms mean 'if', it is possible to add the word **móshi** 'supposing, if, say' at the beginning of the sentence. Although the word **móshi** is thus in the same position as the English word 'if', the meaning of the latter is carried by the conditional form at the end of the clause, and the function of the **móshi** is just to reinforce that meaning and to act as a signal telling the listener to expect a conditional form. So you're more apt to put **móshi** at the beginning if the clause is very long. You do NOT use **móshi** with the provisional. Here are some examples with **móshi**:

Móshi, kyónen, watakushi ga Kyóto e itta toki, anáta mo ittára sono onná ni átta deshō ga...	If you too had gone to Kyoto when I did last year, you'd have met that girl, but (you didn't).
Móshi anó hito ga Amerika kara kitá bakari no senkyóshi dattara, dó shite sonna ni yóku Nihongo ga dekíru deshō ka?	If he were a missionary who had just come from America, how come he knows Japanese so well?
Móshi, uchi no náka e háitte mite, heyá ga ammari chíisakattara dó shimásu ka?	What will you do if, say, you go in the house [to see], and the rooms turn out to be [are] too small?

Móshi, watakushi ga jíssai dattara, sonna kotó ga dekínai darō to omoimásu.	If I were ten years old, I don't think I could do such a thing

Here are some sentences illustrating the difference between the conditional meaning 'when'—with emphasis on what happened at the time; plain imperfect or perfect + **toki (ni)** meaning 'when, at the time that'—with emphasis on the time that something happened; and plain imperfect + **to** 'whenever'—a general condition, with a repeated or habitual conclusion.

Watakushi ga ittára, Jírō wa nakú deshō.	When (or if) I go, Jiro will probably cry.
Watakushi ga iku tokí ni, Jírō wa nakú deshō.	Jiro will probably cry when I go.
Watakushi ga ittára, Jírō wa nakimáshita.	When I went, Jiro cried.
Watakushi ga itta tokí ni, Jírō wa nakimáshita.	Jiro cried when I went.
Watakushi ga iku to, Jírō wa nakimásu.	When(ever) I go, Jiro cries.

The sentence **Watakushi ga ittára, Jírō wa nakimáshita** would be in answer to a possible question **Anáta ga ittára, Jírō wa dó shimáshita ka?** 'What did Jiro do when you left?' The sentence **Watakushi ga itta tokí ni, Jírō wa nakimáshita** would be in answer to a possible question **Jírō wa ítsu nakimáshita ka?** 'When did Jiro cry?'

Notice the use of the perfect before **tokí ni** sometimes even when the tense of the whole sentence is future: **Kondō-san ga kitá toki ni, góhan o tabemashō** 'Let's eat when [that is, after] Mr Kondo gets here'. **Watakushi ga déta tokí ni, Jírō wa nakú deshō** would mean 'Jiro will probably cry when I have left.'

Here are some more examples of conditional forms with the meaning 'when':

Eigákan e itte mítara, mŏ míta kotó no áru éiga deshita.
When I went to the theater and looked, it was a film I had already seen.

Nisanjikan benkyō shitára, sampo ni ikimashō.
When we've studied for 2 or 3 hours, let's go for a walk.

Kono zasshi o yóndara, machí e kaimono ni ikimashō.
When I've read this magazine, I guess I'll go to town to shop.

Júnsa ga kitára, kiite mimashō.
When the policeman comes, we'll find out.

Hitó o mítara, dorobō to omoimásu.
When I see a stranger [another person], I think "a thief". [This is a proverb usually quoted in the plain imperative: ...**to omoe** 'When you see a stranger, think "a thief"!' = 'Don't trust strangers.']

Sometimes the difference of meaning between conditional **-tara** and imperfect + **to** is not one of specific versus habitual ['when' versus 'whenever'] but of ordinary sequence = conditional, versus IMMEDIATE or SUDDEN sequence = imperfect + **to**.

Tanaka-san o mítara, kon- nichi wa to iimáshita.	When I saw Mr T. I said hello.
Tanaka-san o míru to, minna wakarimáshita.	One look at Mr T. and everything was clear [I understood everything].

Some speakers prefer the conditional for both meanings. 8. 12. ADVICE. To ask for advice—'What should I do? Should I do this?'—you ordinarily use an expression like one of the following:

Náni o shitára íi deshō ka?	[If I were to do what, would it be good.]
Náni o suréba íi deshō ka?	[If I do what, will it be good.]
Dŏ shitára íi deshō ka?	[If I were to do how, would it be good.]
Dŏ suréba íi deshō ka?	[If I do how, will it be good.]
Kō shitára íi deshō ka?	[If I were to do like this, would it be good?]
Kō suréba íi deshō ka?	[If I do like this, will it be good?]
Kō shitára dŏ deshō ka?	[If I were to do like this, how would it be?]
Kō suréba dŏ deshō ka?	[If I do like this, how will it be?]

Each expression consists of two parts—a proposed hypothesis [if-clause] with either the conditional or the provisional, since the proposal refers to the future, and a conclusion [then-clause] which asks either how the hypothesis is or whether the hypothesis is all right. The interrogative word may be either in the hypothesis (dǒ shitara...) or in the conclusion (...dǒ deshō ka), but you do not find interrogatives in both the if-clause and the then-clause.

This is the usual polite way of asking and giving directions in Japanese. Notice the difference between the Japanese and English equivalents in this exchange:

Koko kara Sannomiyá-eki wa dǒ ittára íi deshō ka?	How do you get to Sannomiya station from here?
Sanchō kita no hǒ e ittára íi deshō.	Go 3 blocks to the north.
Sore kara, Kita-nagasa-dǒri ni kitára, massúgu saki ni ittára, íi deshō.	Then, when you come to Kita-nagasa Avenue, go straight ahead.

Here are some more examples of sentences containing advice. The English equivalents contain words like 'should, ought'.

Dóno dénsha ni nottára íi deshō ka?	What streetcar should I take?
Nánji no kishá de ittára íi deshō ka?	Which train should I go on?
Kore o mō sukóshi benkyō suréba íi to omoimásu.	I think you ought to study this a little more.

Kodomo o tsurete kitára dō deshō ka?	Should I bring the children?
Nihongo de káitara, dǒ deshō ka?	Should I write it in Japanese?
Rōmaji de kákeba íi deshō.	You ought to write it in Roman letters.
Hitótsu itte mitára íi deshō ka?	Should I just go see?
Andō-san ga kitára, náni o shitára íi deshō ka?	When Mr Ando comes, what should we do?
Senséi ga kónakattara, dǒ suréba íi deshō ka ně.	I wonder what we should do if the teacher doesn't come.
Mō sukóshi máttara íi deshō.	I think you should wait a little longer.

Sometimes an English equivalent might include the expression 'better' or 'had better', but this is often closer to the Japanese expression discussed in the next section.
8.13. 'HAD BETTER'. One way of giving advice in English is to say things like 'You'd better do like this', 'I better be there before the teacher arrives'. In such sentences, there is usually the slight implication that a comparison is being made—it would be better to do something than not to do it. The nearest Japanese equivalent is the plain perfect + hǒ 'alternative' + some form of the adjective íi 'is good':

| Nihongo de káita hǒ ga íi deshō. | I think you'd better write it in Japanese. |
| Senséi ga kúru mae ni soko e itta hǒ ga íi to omoi- | I think I better get there before the teacher comes. |

másu.

Súihei ni nátta hố ga yókatta deshō ga né.	It would have been better to become a Navy man, but (I didn't, you see).
Ókusan mo kúru yō ni to itta hố ga íi desu.	You'd better tell your wife to come too.

Notice that for this meaning 'had better' the form in front of **hố** is always perfect, regardless of the mood of the final expression. If you use the imperfect mood, the meaning is 'it is better to', which has a slightly different flavor:

Morau yóri yaru hố ga íi desu.	It is better to give than to receive.
Watakushi ga iku hố ga íi deshō.	It would be better for me to go [than for you to, or than for me to stay].
Senséi ni náru hō ga íi desu.	It is better [for someone] to become a teacher.
Sore o iu hố ga íi desu.	It is better to say that.

8. 14. THE PARTICLE SÁE. The particle **sáe** 'even, only, just' is more strongly emphatic than **mo** 'even; also'. It singles out a word or phrase for a particularly acute focus of attention. Like **mo**, **sáe** follows nouns, nouns + the copula gerund (**dé**), and infinitives. Other particles may occur after the noun before **sáe** or **dé sae**, but **ga**, **o** and of course the focus-shifting **wa** do not ordinarily occur. Here are examples of **mo** and **sáe** after nouns,

nouns + dé, and infinitives. After nouns the translation is often 'just'; after infinitives 'only'.

Toshiyorí mo asonde imásu.	The old man is playing too.
Toshiyorí sae asonde imásu.	Even the old man is playing.
Amerika kará mo yunyū shita monó o utte imásu.	They sell things (which have been) imported even from America.
Amerika kará sae yunyū shita monó o utte imásu.	They sell things (which have been) imported all the way from America.
Sammán-en mo áreba, jū-bún desu.	If we have all of ¥30,000 it will be enough.
Sammán-en sae áreba, jū-bún desu.	If we just have ¥30,000 it will be enough.
Yukkúri hanásu to, watakushi mo wakarimásu.	When they talk slow I too understand.
Yukkúri hanásu to, watakushi dé sae wakarimásu.	When they talk slow, even [being] I understand.
Amerika kara dé mo kité iru hito ga imásu ka?	Are there people here even from America (too)?
Amerika kara dé sae kité iru hito ga imásu ka?	Are there people here all the way from America?
Yasúmi mo suréba, hataraki mo shimásu.	He not only rests—he works too [if he even rests, he also works].
Yasúmi sae suréba, yóku narimásu.	If you just [if you'll only] rest, you'll get better.

Ichinichi-jū né mo shináke-reba, góhan o tábe mo shimasén deshita.	All day long he neither slept nor ate.
Sonna ni shitsúrei na tega-mi o káki sae shinákatta-ra, asobi ni ittá deshō.	If only he hadn't written such a rude letter, I'd have gone to see him.
Omoshíroku mo nái deshō.	It wouldn't be interesting at all.
Omoshíroku sae nákereba, kippu o uru kotó ga de-kimásu ně.	You can only buy tickets if it isn't interesing, you know.
Osokú sae áttara, ma ni átta deshō.	If it had just been late, we would have made it (in time).
Osokú sae áreba, ma ni áu deshō.	If it is only late [=only if it's late] we'll make it.

Notice the patterns verb-infinitive + **sáe...** **suréba** and adjective-infinitive + **sáe...** **áreba.** These are the usual ways to put a clause with the meaning 'if something will ONLY do something or be something'—the actual verb or adjective meaning is carried by the infinitive, and **suréba** and **áreba** function as a sort of dummy or auxil-iary to carry the provisional ending -(r)eba and the mean-ning 'if'. The concluding, main clause of the sentence gives the result to expected, granted 'ONLY' that the provision be so.

If both the provisional clause and the resulting con-clusion are considered as completed ('if someone had done... then something would have happened'), the conditional is usually used instead of the provisional—shitára for suréba, áttara for áreba. And you will sometimes hear the conditional even though the provisional clause and the resulting conclusion are not completed.

8. 15. THE EXPLICIT USE OF NI. Some expressions which require a verb + a direct object in English are equivalent to Japanese expressions with a subject + a verb or copula phrase:

Sakana ga sukí desu.	Fish are liked = I like fish.
Búnshō ga wakarimásu.	Sentence is clear = I understand the sentence.
Oyógu kotó ga dekimásu.	Fact of swimming is possible = I can swim.
Tokei ga {**hoshíi desu.** / **irimásu.**	A watch is wanted = I want a watch.

You will recall that if the person doing the liking, understanding, wanting or being able is mentioned in the sentence, it is usually as the topic: **Watakushi wa sakana ga sukí desu. Tanaka-san wa oyógu koto ga dekimásu. Anáta wa búnshō ga wakarimásu. Musumé wa tokei ga hoshíi desu.** However, if there is a shift of emphasis to the person, there is a switch of particles and positions for the person and the equivalent of the English object: **Tokei wa musumé ga hoshíi desu** 'The GIRL wants the watch.'

This shift of emphasis and switch of particles occasionally leads to ambiguity: **Táró wa Hánako ga sukí desu** 'Taro likes Hanako' or '(It's) HANAKO (who) likes Taro.' One way to avoid this ambiguity explicily is to use the particle **ni** after the person corresponding to the subject of the English equivalent: **Tárō ni wa Hánako ga sukí desu.** Even this is not always completely unambiguous. For simple sentences this explicit use of **ni** is infrequent in conversation, but in longer phrases, particlarly if there are particles other than **wa** (for instance, **mo or sáe**), the particle **ni** is sometimes used even where no ambiguity would result from its omission.

Nihón de wa kodomo ní sae Nihongo ga wakarimásu né.	In Japan, even the children can understand Japanese you see.
Yukkúri hanásu to, watakushi ní sae wakarimásu.	When you talk slow, even I understand.
Sonna kírei na tokei wa, watakushi ní mo hoshíi desu.	I too would like such a pretty watch.

Sometimes this very use of **ni** causes ambiguity:

Jochū ní sae káku kotó no dekíru yō na tegami déshita.	It was the sort of letter that even a maid could write. OR It was the sort of letter that someone could write even to a maid.

Notice that the sentence **Watakushi ga miénai tokoro kara demáshita** can be construed in either of these ways:

Watakushi ga / miénai tokoro kara demáshita.	I came out of a place which [someone] could not see.

| Watakushi ga miénai toko-ro kara / demáshita. | [Someone] came out of a place which I could not see. |

And, since the '[someone]' could be 'I', either version would have a possible interpretation 'I came out of a place I couldn't see'.

With the use of the explicit **ni**, the sentence can be made somewhat more specific:

| Watakushi ni miénai toko-ro kara / demáshita. | [Somebody] came out of a place which I could not see. |

8. 16. THE MORE...THE MORE... Sentences like 'the sooner, the better', 'the more, the merrier', 'the more I look at the girl, the prettier I think she is', 'the more I eat fish, the less I like it', 'the less I see of him the better' are the equivalent of a Japanese construction involving one verb or adjective given first in the provisional, then repeated in the plain imperfect + **hodo** 'extent, to the extent that', followed by the other verb or adjective in a concluding form:

Háyakereba, hayái hodo íi desu.	The sooner the better. [If it is early, to the extent that it's early, it is good.]
Ókereba, ói hodo nigíyaka na n desu.	The more the merrier.
Sono onná o míreba, míru hodo kírei da to omoimásu.	The more I look at that girl the prettier I think she is.

Sakana wa tabéreba, tabé-
ru hodo kirai ni nari-
másu.

The more I eat fish the less
I like it [to the extent
that I eat, I get to dis-
like it].

Anó hito ni awánakereba,
awánai hodo íi desu.

The less I see of him the
better. [If I don't meet
him, to the extent that
I don't meet him, it's
good.]

Daidokoro wa ókikereba,
ōkíi hodo bénri na n
desu.

The bigger a kitchen is,
the more convenient.

Éiga o mí ni ikéba, iku
hodo omoshíroku náku
náru to omoimásu.

The more I go to movies,
the worse they get.

8. 17.   THE PARTICLE SHI.   The particle **shi** (perhaps
derived from the infinitive of **suru** which is **shi** 'doing')
connects clauses with the meaning 'and also'.   The verb,
adjective, or copula at the end of the clause preceding
shi is either plain imperfect or perfect. You have already had one way to connect clauses with the meaning
'and'—by using the gerund which means 'does and' or
'is and'. The difference between the use of the gerund
and the use of the plain imperfect or perfect + the particle **shi** lies in the tightness of the connection between
the two clauses. If there is some sort of sequence in
time or logic between the clauses, in the order in which
they are given, then you use the gerund. But if you are
just presenting a series of two or more clauses without

any particular sequence in their arrangement, you use the expression with shi. Here are a couple of sentences of exaggerated length which show the difference.

Kinŏ wa shimbun o hanjikan gúrai yónde itá shi, machí e kaimono ni ittá shi, kodomo o tsurete isha no tokoro e ittá shi, Amerika ni súnde iru tomodachi ni tegami o káita shi, góhan o ryōri shitá shi, asobi ni kitá senkyŏshi to hanáshite itá shi, shújin to issho ni éiga o míta kara, háyaku kara osokú made isogáshikatta deʒu.

Yesterday I read the papers for a half hour or so, and I also went to town shopping, and I took the children to the doctor's, and I also wrote a letter to a friend who is living in America, and I fixed dinner, and I talked with a missionary who came on a visit, and I also saw a movie with my husband, so I was busy from early till late.

Kinŏ wa shimbun o hanjikan gúrai yónde, machí e kaimono ni itte, kodomo o tsurete isha no tokoro e itte, Amerika ni súnde iru tomodachi ni tegami o káite, góhan o ryōri shite, asobi ni kitá senkyŏshi to hanáshite ite, sore kara shújin to issho ni éiga o míta kara, háyaku kara osokú made

Yesterday I read the papers for a half hour or so, and then I went to town shopping, and then I took the children to the doctor's and then I wrote a letter to a friend living in America, and then I fixed dinner, and then I talked with a missionary who came to visit, and then I saw a

isogáshikatta desu.	movie with my husband, so I was busy from early till late.

In the second sentence, all of the actions are understood to be in sequence. In the first sentence, they are understood to be mentioned at random. They might, of course, be in sequence, but you do not know this from the sentence itself.

Here are some more examples of shi.

Ano tatémono wa takái shi ōkíi kara, jimúsho ga ōi desu.	That building is tall and also big, so it has a lot of offices.
Koko wa shízuka da shi, bénri da kara, sumitái to omoimásu.	This place is quiet and also convenient so I think I'd like to live (here).
Kimura-san wa jidósha ga hoshíi shi, okane mo áru kara, kaú deshō.	Mr K. wants a car, and he even has the money so he'll probably buy one.
Kyónen wa, natsú wa suzúshikatta shi, fuyú wa atatákakute taihen hén na n deshita ně.	Last year the summer was cool and the winter was warm; it was quite odd, wasn't it.
Kodomo wa naite itá shi, éiga wa ammari omoshíroku nákatta shi, máda uchi de shinákereba naránai kotó ga takusan átta kara, eigákan o déte háyaku káette kitá n desu.	The children were crying and it wasn't a very good movie, and I had lots of thing still to do at home, so I left the theater and came back early.

8. 18. CORRELATIVE COMPOUNDS. There are a few nouns made up from interrogatives and other correlative words to give a meaning of a non-specific nature:

dáredare	so-and-so, somebody or other
náninani	such-and-such, something or other, what-you-may-call-it, what all
dókodoko	somewhere or other
dókosoko	someplace or other
korékore	such-and-such a one
arékore	this or that, one thing or another
kárekore	about, approximately
achirakóchira atchíkotchi, achíkochi	here and there, hither and thither, fore and aft

The word **sorézore,** however, has a distributive rather than a non-specific meaning: 'severally, respectively.' Here are a few examples of the use of these words.

Dáredare-san ga byōki dá to iimáshita.	He said someone or other was sick.
Háko no náka ni wa náninani ga háitte imáshita ka?	What all was inside the box?
Korékore ga háitte imáshita.	There was this and that inside.
Kánai wa dókosoko no uchí de wa, kodomo ga umareta to itte imáshita.	My wife was saying a baby had been born in some home or other.

Arékore to isogashíi desu.	I'm busy with this and that, with various things.
Shújin no háha wa arékore to sewa o yakimásu.	My mother-in-law sticks her nose into everything [various things]. [**Yaku** = 'bakes, cooks'.]
Kodomo wa achíkochi de asonde iru yó desu.	The children seem to be playing here and there [all about].
Tegami wa sorézore no fū-tō ni háitte imasu.	The letters are in their respective envelopes. Each letter is in its envelope.
Kárekore níji desu.	It's around 2 o'clock.

C. EXERCISES.

1. Under each item below there are two sentences. Change the verb, adjective, or copula of the first sentence into the appropriate PROVISIONAL form, and combine the two clauses into one sentence with the meaning 'if..., then...'; translate the completed sentences.

   1. Watakushi wa nijikan gúrai shika nemasén. Mō sukóshi benkyō suru kotó ga dekimásu.
   2. Kodomo wa ammari okáshi o tabemásu. Góhan wa tabétaku nái deshō.
   3. Anáta wa tsukárete imásu. Nisampun yasúnde kudasai.
   4. Anáta wa máda okane ga irimásu. Watakushi ni itte kudasái.

5. Anáta wa watakushi yóri háyaku uchi e kaerimásu. Jochū ni kodomo o yobu yǒ ni itte kudasái.

6. Anáta ga Uehara-san o éki de machimásu. Watakushi wa uchi de machimásu.

7. Anáta ga yukkúri hanashimásu. Watakushi wa
   súgu wakarimásu.

8. Senséi ni aimásu. Sō iimashǒ.

9. Anáta ga Eigo de kakimásu. Tanaka-san wa wakaránai deshō.

10. Mō sukóshi isogimásu. Ma ni áu deshō.

11. Máinichi gyūnyū o nomimásu. Génki ni narimásu.

12. Anáta wa ano onná ni aitái desu. Goji góro ni
    toshókan no máe e kitára íi deshō.

13. Kodomo wa sono éiga o mí ni ikitái desu. Wata-
    kushi mo ikimashǒ.

14. Oténki ga warúi desu. Watakushi wa sampo ni
    ikitaku arimasén.

15. Sono tegami o yomimasén. Takayama-san ga ítsu
    kúru ka to iu kotó ga wakaránai deshō.

16. Anáta no tomodachi wa senkyǒshi desu. Bíiru o
    nománai hō ga íi deshō.

2. Under each item below, make the two sentences
   into one by changing the verb, adjective or copula
   of the first into the CONDITIONAL form with
   the meaning 'if...' or 'when...', translate the completed sentences.

1. Nisampun bákari machimáshita. Kinoshita-san
   ga kimáshita.

2. Watakushi ga Nihongo de hanashimáshita.

Ten-in wa taihen odorokimáshita.

3. Kóndō-san ni tegami o kakimásu. Ítsu ka asobi ni kúru yō ni to itte kudasái.

4. Sono hón wa Eigo de yomimáshita. Muzukashiku nákatta deshō.

.5. Jírō o yobimáshita. Tárō ga demáshita.

6. Kono kínjo de dáre ka shinimáshita. Súgu wakátta deshō.

7. Mō sukóshi isogimáshita. Ma ni átta deshō.

8. Kishá ni norimásu. Mádo no sóba no tokoro ni koshikakemashǒ.

9. Anáta wa mō sukóshi okane ga irimásu. Goenryo náku watakushi ni itte kudasái.

10. Nijíkan mo mátte imáshita. Kimura-san ga déte kimáshita.

11. Sore o tabemásu. Byōki ni narimásu yo.

12. Nisanjíkan benkyō shimásu. Asobi ni itté mo íi desu.

13. Kánai ga sampo ni ikitái desu. Watakushi mo ikú deshō.

14. Oténki ga íi deshita. Ensoku ni ittá deshō.

15. Okane ga arimásén. Eigákan e háiru kotó ga dekimasén.

16. Anáta deshita. Dǒ shita deshō ka?

3. Here are some sentences. Change each sentence so that it means (1) You have to, you must; (2) You don't have to, you need not; (3) You may; (4) You must not, Don't. For example, the first will be: (1)Soko e ikanákereba narimasén [ikanákereba ike-

masén, ikanákereba damé desu, ikanákute wa ikemasén, ikanákute wa narimasén, ikanákute wa damé
desu]; (2) Soko e ikanákute mo íi desu; (3) Soko e itté
mo íi desu; (4) Soko e itté wa ikemasén [itté wa narimasén, itté wa damé desu]. When there are several
possibilities, choose the most common one.

1. Soko e ikimásu.
2. Anó hito to hanashimásu.
3. Sono kotó o iimásu.
4. Máinichi éiga o mimásu.
5. Sono tegami o yomimásu.
6. Kono isu ni koshikakemásu.
7. Koko de yasumimásu.
8. Niwa no sóba de asobimásu.
9. Kono heya no náka e hairimásu.
10. Sono kusuri o nomimásu.

4.   Translate the following sentences into Japanese.

1. Whomever (I) meet, (I) speak (to) politely.
2. Whichever offices (you) enter, you see telephones.
3. Wherever (I) go, I have a good time.
4. It doesn't matter which book (of the two) I read.
5. In big department stores they have everything.
6. We have nothing.
7. It seems somebody had come for a visit.
8. Is there anybody (here) who knows English?
9. A policeman came from somewhere (or other).
10. I think I'd like to go to Enóshima for a picnic
    sometime.

D. COMPREHENSION.

[Yasuda-san wa Kodama-san ni denwa o kákete imasu.]

Kōkánshu.	Námban e okake désu ka?
Yasuda.	Ní yón ichi no nána kyū yón ní.
Áru hito.	Móshi moshi.
Yasuda.	Kodama-san désu ka?
Áru hito.	Iie, chigaimásu.
Yasuda.	241-7942 désu ka?
Áru hito.	Iie, chigaimásu.
Yasuda.	Dǒ mo shitsúrei.

[Yasuda-san wa juwáki o okimásu. Mō ichido juwáki o tótte, mimí ni atete, kōkánshu ga déru to, mō ichido onaji bangō o iimásu. Nidome ka sandome ní wa aité ga déte kúru deshō.]

Kodama.	Móshi moshi.
Yasuda.	Móshi moshi. Kodama-san désu ka?
Kodama.	Sǒ desu.
Yasuda.	Kochira wa Yasuda désu. Ano né. Kinō anáta no uchí e asobi ni itta tokí ně...
Kodama.	É.
Yasuda.	Tebúkuro o wasurete káetta n desu ga...
Kodama.	Á, anáta no déshita ka? Ano né. Arimásu yo. Kono kínjo e kúru yō na kotó ga áttara, ítsu de mo tóri ni kité kudasai.
Yasuda.	Anáta no uchi ni áru to iu kotó ga wakáreba, sore de íi desu. Sono uchi ni tóri ni

ikimashǒ. Sore ja, dǒ mo arígatō gozaimáshita.

Kodama. Iie. Dǒ itashimáshite.

Yasuda. Shitsúrei shimásu. Sayonára.

Kodama. Sayonára.

Note: Interrogative words and expressions used with indefinite
or generalized meaning often lose their accent: dáre de mo or dare
dé mo or dare de mo 'anybody at all'.

Footnotes to accompany p. 331:

*So that o-tégami may be 'your letter' or 'my letter to you',
and o-hanashi may be 'your story' or 'my story that I am telling
you'. Compare Káeru o-tsúmori desu ka? 'Do you intend to go
home?', O-suki désu ka? 'Do you like it?'

**But there are also conventional greetings like ohayō gozaimásu
'it is early=good morning', osamū gozaimásu 'it is cold', oatsū gozaimásu 'it is hot'.

Footnote to accompany p. 339:

*There is also the polite euphemism mésu, which is used as an
exalted form for (1) kiru 'wears', haku 'wears on feet or legs', kabúru
'wears headgear', (2) yobu 'calls', (3) kau 'buys', (4) noru 'rides',
(5) (kaze o) hiku 'catches (a cold)', and in a few other expressions
such as furo o mésu 'takes a bath' and kasa o mésu 'carries an
umbrella over one'. Note also o-ki ni mésu=ki ni ir-u 'is liked'.

LESSON 9.

A. BASIC SENTENCES. 'A Polite Conversation.'

1. Kinŏ wa Sátō-bokushi ni oai itashimáshita.

   Yesterday I met Reverend Sato.

2. Dóchira de oai ni narimáshita ka?

   Where did you meet him?

3. Kyōkai no máe de gozaimáshita.

   It was in front of the church.

4. Machí e kaimono ni irassháru to osshaimáshita kara, issho ni arúite mairimáshita.

   He said he was going to town for shopping, so I walked along with him.

5. Ítsu ka uchi e oasobi ni irasshátte kudasaimasén ka to watakushi wa osasoi itashimáshita.

   I invited him 'Won't you come to see us sometime?'

6. Bókushi-san wa kono goro oisogashikute irassháru deshō né.

   The pastor must be busy this time of year, I suppose.

7. Sayō de gozaimásu keredomo, raishū no Getsuyŏbi no ban, jíkan ga oari dá kara, uchi e asobi ni irasshátte kudasaimásu.

   Yes he is, however he has some time next Monday evening, so he's coming to our house to favor us with a visit.

8. Anatagáta mo irassháru kotó ga odeki ni narimáshitara, dózo onegai itashimásu.

If you people can come too, please do so.

9. Sekkakú de gozaimásu ga, Getsuyóbi wa háha no tanjóbi de gozaimásu no de, watakushidómo wa ryóshin to issho ni shibai e mairimásu kara...

Thank you very much, but Monday is Mother's birthday and we are going with our parents to a play, so...

10. Nán to iu oshibai de gozaimásu ka?

What play is it?

11. "Háha" to iu shibai e máiru no de gozaimásu.

We're going to a play called "The Mother".

12. Sore wa omoshiró gozaimashó né.

That should be enjoyable.

13. Kotoshi wa oyasumi ni dóchira e oide ni narimásu ka?

Where are you going on your vacation this year?

14. Miyanóshita e oide désu ka, Karúizawa e oide désu ka?

Are you going to Miyanoshita or to Karuizawa?

15. Kyónen yamá e mairimáshita kara, kotoshi wa úmi e mairitái to zonjimásu.

Last year we went to the mountains, so this year we think we would like to go to the sea.

16. Sayō de gozaimásu ka? Kamakurá e oide ni nátta kotó ga gozaimásu ka?

Oh? Have you ever been to Kamakura?

17. Máda de gozaimásu. A- soko no hamá wa yoroshū gozaimásu ka?

Not yet. Is the beach there good?

18. Hamá wa yoroshū gozaimásu ga, natsú wa daibu kónde imásu.

The beach is good, but in the summertime it's rather crowded.

19. Izu-hántō ni wa íi hamá ga takusan gozaimásu.

The are lots of good beaches on the Izu Peninsula.

20. Watakushi wa annaisho ga nisatsu gozaimásu kara, issatsu (sashi-) agemashó.

I have two copies of a guidebook so I'll give you one copy.

21. Arígatō gozaimásu. Kono chízu de Izu-hántō o omise ni nátte kudasaimasén ka?

Thank you. Won't you please show me on this map (where) the Izu Peninsula (is)?

22. Chotto haiken itashimashó.

Let me look at it [I'll just look at it] for a minute. [Let's see now.]

23. Goran nasái. Kochira wa Kamakurá de, sochira wa Izu-hántō de gozaimásu.

Look. This is Kamakura, and that's the Izu Peninsula.

24. Shōshō omachi kudasái. Kore yóri ōkíi chízu o

Please wait a little. I'll bring a bigger map

motté kite ome ni kakemashǒ.

than this one and show you (on it).

25. Itō to iu tokoró o gozónji desu ka?

Do you know a place called Ito?

26. Hái. Ítsu ka byōki ni nátta toki sankágetsu soko e yasúmi ni máitte orimáshita.

Yes, I was there for a rest once for three months when I had gotten ill.

27. Sono aida, náni o nasátte irasshaimáshita ka?

During that time, what did you do?

28. Máinichi kusuri o itadaite yasúnde bakari orimáshita.

Every day I just took medicine and rested.

29. Kono ōkíi chízu o haishaku itashitái n desu ga...

I'd like to borrow this big map.

30. Dǒzo, goenryo náku. Tatande sashiagemashǒ.

Please do. I'll fold it up for you.

VOCABULARY ITEMS.

NOUNS AND PHRASES

(o)jama	disturbance (of you); visit (to you)	okyaku	guest; customer
sekkaku	especially; making a great effort; going to the trouble of [Usually used as adverb.]	okamai (suru)	(go out of one's way to make) arrangements [for a guest]; (show proper) consideration [for a guest]
		setsumei	explanation

setsumci suru	explains	kangófu	nurse
(o)miyage	gift, souvenir	mé	eye
otsuri	change [money]	kóndo	this time;
komakái (okane)	small change		next time
omócha	toy	tsūyaku	interpreting

VERBS

tatamu	folds something up	kasu	lends
		yorokóbu	is glad, rejoices
sasou	invites, suggests	yakusu	translates
súmu	comes to an end	nokóru	gets left,
nokósu	leaves behind		remains

B. STRUCTURE NOTES.

9. 1. STATUS WORDS: HUMBLE, NEUTRAL, EX-
ALTED. A word or expression in Japanese may have one
of three connotations, indicating its reference to a social
status: humble, neutral, and exalted. Many textbooks
refer to the exalted forms as 'honorific'; in this book, the
latter term is used to refer to BOTH the humble and
exalted forms, and to the style of speech in which they
usually occur. Most of the words and expressions you
have learned so far are neutral. These are used in reference to anyone, provided you are not showing a special
deference. Ordinarily, however, Japanese use a more
polite level of speech—the honorific style—in speaking to
older people, officials, strangers, learned men, foreign
guests, and so forth. And even in the ordinary polite
level you use to a friend of your own age, it is customary
to show a deference to the other person and his family by
using exalted forms for kinship terms and certain other
words. Humble forms are only used when speaking of

yourself or members of your family to other people. When directly addressing a member of your family you use the exalted term if the person is older—**Okásan** 'Mother', **Níisan** 'Older Brother'; the given name if the person is younger—**Jíró** '[younger brother] Jiro'. For many expressions—including most nouns—there is no special humble form; instead, the neutral form is used for the humble situations in contrast with the exalted form. In speaking very politely to someone of equivalent social rank, you usually use the exalted forms for reference to him and his actions, and the simple neutral forms in reference to yourself and your own actions, unless your actions can be construed as involving him or his family or his property, or as involving someone else of higher social status than yourself, in which case you use the humble forms. If you are speaking to someone of much superior social rank—as a maid talking to her employer—you may use humble forms for yourself throughout.

9. 2. KINSHIP TERMS. The terms used to refer to members of a family come in pairs: one neutral [also used for the humble situations 'my...'] and the other exalted ['your...']. For 'his...' you would ordinarily use the exalted form, unless you consider the 'him' a member of your own in-group as contrasted with the person you are speaking to.

ENGLISH EQUIVALENT	NEUTRAL	EXALTED
father	chichí	otósan
mother	háha; ofukuro	okásan
parents	ryóshin	goryóshin
son	musuko	(o)musukosan; bótchan
daughter	musumé	(o)musumesan; ojósan

baby	akambō, áka-chan	—
child, children	kodomo	kodomosan; okosan
older brother	áni	(o)níisan
older sister	ane	(o)nēsan
younger brother	otōtó	otōtósan
younger sister	imōtó	imōtósan
brothers and sisters	kyōdai	gokyōdai
grandfather	sófu	ojíisan
grandmother	sóbo	obåsan
uncle	oji	ojisan
aunt	oba	obasan
nephew	oi	oigosan
niece	méi	méigosan
cousin	itóko	itókosan
husband	shújin; otto; danna	goshújin; dannasan
wife	kánai; tsúma	ókusan
family	kázoku; uchi	gokázoku; otaku

The words **ojisan** 'uncle' and **obasan** 'aunt' are also used in a general way by young people to refer to anyone of an older generation: **tonari no ojisan** 'the man next door', **byōki no obasan** 'a sick lady'.

9. 3. OTHER NOUNS. There are a few other nouns which come in pairs, with one neutral, the other exalted.

ENGLISH EQUIVALENT	NEUTRAL	EXALTED
house, home	uchi; ié	otaku
person	hito; monó	katá
he, she, they	anó hito	ano káta, ano katá
how	dô	ikága
where	dóko	dóchira
who	dáre	dónata; dóchira

The word **kochira** 'over here, this one' is often used as a sort of humble equivalent of **watakushi** 'me': **Kochira**

wa **Mōri** de **gozaimásu** 'This is (I am) Mr Mori'. **Kochira**
kóso '[The pleasure or the fault or the honor] is all mine.'
[**Kóso** is a particle meaning 'none other than, the very
one'.]

9. 4. HONORIFIC PREFIXES. There are two common
honorific prefixes **o-** and **go-**. There are also the less common
prefixes **on-** and **mi-**, and very occasionally compound
prefixes such as **o-mi-** and even **o-mi-o-**. Thus, a pair
of exalted feet may be called **o-ashi**, **mi-ashi**, **omi-ashi**, or
even **omio-ashi**.

Words containing an honorific prefix may indicate
an exaltation of the word itself, on its own merits—
watakushi no o-tomodachi 'my friend', **anáta no o-tomo-**
dachi 'your friend', or it may indicate the relationship
between the word and and an exalted person—**o-niwa** 'your
garden'.* Again, with nouns and verb forms, it may be just
generally honorific—used for both humble and exalted
situations. With adjective forms, the use of the honorific
prefix seems always to indicate an exalted relationship:
oisogashii toki 'at a time when YOU are very busy'.**

The prefix **go-** is attached to a number of nouns [often,
but not always, of Chinese origin] and to a few verb in
finitives: **goshújin** 'your husband', **goyukkúri** 'slowly', **go-**
zónji 'knowing'. The prefix **o-** is more widely used, and
is attached readily to nouns [including many of Chinese
origin: **obenjo** 'the toilet', **oshōyu** 'the soysauce', **odenwa**
'the telephone'], verb infinitives and many adjectives.

Some words by convention have the prefixes **o-** and
go-, particularly in the speech of women and children,
whether the situation calls for an honorific [humble or

---

*, **See p. 323.

exalted] form or not. This is an extension of the usage exalting the word itself, on its own merits. The present-day meaning of the prefix in many of these words is somewhat like that of the Chinese suffix -r, interpreted by Y. R. Chao as 'that familiar thing we often talk about'. Here is a list of some of these words with a conventional honorific prefix:

goén	relation, affinity	okome	rice (uncooked,
goenryo	reserve,reticence,		but harvested)
	hesitation	onaka	stomach
góhan	cooked rice,	osháberi	chatterbox
	meal, food	oshōyu	soysauce
gohóbi	reward, prize	oténki	weather
obon	tray	ohisama,	the sun [=hi]
ocha	tea	oténtosama	
ohashi	chopsticks	ótsukisama	the moon
okane	money		[=tsukí]
okáshi	pastry, sweets	otsuri	change

9. 5. HONORIFIC SUFFIXES. There are two honorific suffixes: **-san** and **-sama**. The latter is a formal variant of the former, usually restricted to certain set expressions. The suffix **-san** is widely used with names (= Mr, Miss, Mrs), kinship terms, occupations, and other nouns referring to people. In more formal speech, **-sama** sometimes replaces **-san** in these terms. In more intimate speech, **-chan or -tsan** is heard: **otóttsan** or **otótchan** 'Dad, Daddy'.

9. 6. VERBS: THE HONORIFIC INFINITIVE. The humble or exalted equivalent to a simple polite verb of neutral status is often an expression built around the

HONORIFIC INFINITIVE. For verbs, this form is usually made by prefixing o- to the regular infinitive.

The most common honorific usage for verbs is as follows. For the humble form, use the honorific infinitive + some form of the neutral verb **suru** 'does' or of the humble verb **itasu** 'does':

Okaeri itashimásu.	**Okaeri shimásu.**	I return.
Otabe itashimásu.	**Otabe shimásu.**	I eat.
Oyasumi itashimásu.	**Oyasumi shimásu.**	I rest.

The forms with **itasu** show greater deference [= are more humble] than the forms with **suru**.

For the exalted form, use the honorific infinitive + the particle **ni** + some form of the verb **náru** 'becomes'. Or, use the honorific infinitive + some form of the copula **dá** or of the honorific polite copula **de gozáimasu**, or of the exalted copula **de irassháru**. There is still another way to make an exalted verb form—the polite infinitive + the exalted verb **nasáru** 'does'—but this is rather old-fashioned.

Okaeri ni narimásu.
Okacri de irasshaimásu.
Okaeri de gozaimásu.   You return.
Okaeri désu.
(Okacri nasaimásu.)

Otabe ni narimásu.
Otabe de irasshaimásu.
Otabe de gozaimásu.   You eat.
Otabe désu.
(Otabe nasaimásu.)

Oyasumi ni narimásu.
Oyasumi de irasshaimásu.
Oyasumi de gozaimásu.   } You rest.
Oyasumi désu.
(Oyasumi nasaimásu.)

The first two forms—o- ... -i ni narimásu and o- ... -i de irasshaimásu—are about equally exalted, the other forms are a little less so.

Notice that an object preceding the verb retains its customary particle o:

HUMBLE   Kore o oyomi itashi-   (I) read this.
            máshita.
NEUTRAL   Kore o yomimáshita.   (Someone) read this.
EXALTED   Kore o oyomi ni na-   (You or he) read this.
            rimáshita.

If you want to make the expression negative, you use the negative forms of the final verb or copula:

Kore o oyomi itashimasén   I didn't read this.
deshita.
Kore o yomimasén deshita.   He didn't read this.
Kore o oyomi ni narima-   You didn't read this.
sén deshita.
Kore o oyomi de irasshai-
masén ka?
Kore o oyomi de gozaima-   } Aren't you going to read
sén ka?   this?
Kore o oyomi ja arimasén
ka?

9. 7. SPECIAL HONORIFIC VERBS. For many common verbs, in addition to (or to the exclusion of) regularly formed exalted and humble forms, Japanese use special verbs or special infinitives for either the exalted or the humble, or for both. In the Table of Special Verbs, you will find these listed in a systematic fashion. The verbs are arranged in three vertical columns—humble, neutral, and exalted; and the forms corresponding to each meaning given on the horizontal lines are included under the appropriate vertical column. For some of the meanings there are two or more possibilities given under a single large vertical column—this means there are synonyms [words meaning the same thing] for these categories. For example, the neutral of 'does' is either **suru** or **yaru**. The order in which these synonyms are placed in the horizontal line is not correlated with their frequency, but determined by the nature of the table itself. You will notice that verbs of identical shape appear in several columns or lines—this means there are homonyms [words sounding alike but meaning different things] for these categories. So far as possible, these homonyms are grouped together in the table, and they are recapitulated in an alphabetical list at the end for ready reference.

Where there are blanks in the table, it means there is no special verb for the humble or for the exalted, but that the form can be made in the regular way (honorific infinitive + **itasu**; honorific infinitive + **ni náru**, etc.). Even when special humble and exalted verbs do exist, it often happens that the regularly expected form from the neutral verb is also used—thus, **otabe ni náru** alongside **meshi-**

agaru 'you eat'. And sometimes a special honorific **verb** will be further put into one of the regular honorific phrases: **omeshiagari ni narimásu; oitadaki itashimásu.** The regularly formed humble expressions are less often used than the regular exalted expressions (partly because, in talking to a social equal very politely, you still use just neutral polite forms for your own acts when they do not involve the other person or his property), and some of the possibilities sound a bit odd to the Japanese ear unless the situation is built up just right.

The use of three dots after a word in the exalted column [**oide...**] indicates that the word is an honorific infinitive and must be followed by some other words [**...ni náru, ...de irassháru,** etc.] in order to be a complete expression. The use of parentheses around **suru** in the humble column indicates that the preceding word is a noun like **benkyō** of **benkyō suru** or **sampo** of **sampo suru,** and must be followed by some form of **suru** or **itasu** to make a complete expression.

TABLE OF SPECIAL HONORIFIC VERBS

MEANING	HUMBLE	NEUTRAL	EXALTED
I give	ageru sashiageru	*yaru	——
You or he gives	ageru (him)	*yaru (him) kureru (you, me, or mine)	kudasáru (you, me or mine)
Does	itasu -mŏsu	yaru suru	nasáru asobasu

*Instead of **yaru,** in colloquial speech you will sometimes hear **kureru** or **kurete** yaru for these categories.

MEANING	HUMBLE	NEUTRAL	EXALTED
Says	mōshiageru mōsu	iu	ossháru
Drinks	itadaku	nómu	agaru meshiagaru
Eats	itadaku	tabéru kuu [animals]	agaru meshiagaru
Receives	itadaku chōdai (suru)	morau	
Enters house		agaru	
Comes	máiru agaru	kúru	irassháru oide... miéru
Goes	máiru agaru	iku	irassháru oide...
Stays	oru	iru	irassháru oide...
Is ...ing	-te oru	-te iru	-te irassháru
Exists	gozáru	áru	gozáru
Is, equals	de gozáru	dá (de áru)	de gozáru de irassháru
Hears	ukagau uketamawaru	kiku	
Asks	ukagau	kiku tazunéru	
Visits	ukagau	asobu* tazunéru	
Knows	zonjíru	shiru	gozónji...
Feels, thinks	zonjíru	omou	oboshimesu
Looks at things	haiken (suru)	míru	goran...
Meets, sees people	ome ni kakáru	áu	
Shows	ome ni kakéru	miséru	
Borrows	haishaku (suru)	kariru	
Wears		kiru	omęshi...

*As in asobi ni iku (kúru) 'goes (comes) to visit.'

Here is an alphabetical recapitulation of those shapes with more than one meaning, together with verbs they are likely to be confused with. Synonyms are given in brackets.

agaru	HUMBLE of **kúru** 'comes' [syn: **máiru**]
	HUMBLE of **iku** 'goes' [syn: **máiru**]
	NEUTRAL 'enters house'
	EXALTED of **tabéru** 'eats' [syn: **meshiaga-ru**]
	EXALTED of **nómu** 'drinks' [syn: **meshi-agaru**]
ageru	HUMBLE of **yaru** 'I give' [syn: **sashiageru**]
	HUMBLE of **yaru** / **kureru** 'you or he gives (him / you, me)'
gozáru	(HUMBLE and EXALTED =) HONOR-IFIC of **áru** 'exists'
de gozáru	(HUMBLE and EXALTED =) HONOR-IFIC of **dá** [**de áru**] 'equals'
irassháru	EXALTED of **kúru** 'comes' [syn: **miéru, oide...**]
	EXALTED of **iku** 'goes' [syn: **oide...**]
	EXALTED of **iru** 'stays, exists [syn: **oide**]
de irassháru	EXALTED of **dá** [**de áru**] 'equals' when subject is a person
itadaku	HUMBLE of **tabéru** 'eats'
	HUMBLE of **nómu** 'drinks'
	HUMBLE of **morau** 'receives' [syn: **chō-dai (suru)**]
itasu	HUMBLE of **suru** 'does'
kudasáru	EXALTED of **kureru** 'you or he gives you, me, or mine'

kureru	NEUTRAL 'you or he gives you, me, or mine'
míru	NEUTRAL 'looks, sees'
miéru	NEUTRAL 'is seen'
	EXALTED of kúru [syn: irassháru, oide...]
mŏsu	HUMBLE of suru 'does' [syn: itasu]
	HUMBLE of iu 'says, tells' [syn: mōshiageru]
nasáru	EXALTED of suru 'does' [syn: asobasu]
oboshimesu	EXALTED of omóu 'thinks, feels'
oru	HUMBLE of iru 'stays, exists'
tazunéru	NEUTRAL 'asks' [syn: kiku]
	NEUTRAL 'visits' [syn: asobu]
ukagau	HUMBLE of kiku 'asks'
	HUMBLE of asobu 'visits'
	HUMBLE of kiku 'hears' [syn: uketamawaru]
yaru	NEUTRAL 'does' [syn: suru]
	NEUTRAL 'I give'
	NEUTRAL 'You or he gives...him'
zonjíru	HUMBLE of shir-u 'knows'
	HUMBLE of omóu 'thinks, feels'*

9.8. MŌSHIAGERU. A few verbs are made humble by prefixing the infinitive of the humble verb mŏsu 'does' [mōshi-]. or by suffixing the humble verb ageru 'I give' [-ageru]: mōshiukeru 'I accept, receive' from the neutral ukeru 'accepts, receives', sashiageru 'I offer, I give, present, hold up' from the neutral sásu 'indicates, points, shows'. The verb mōshiageru, though shown in the table only for 'says', is used as a humble form for either 'does' or 'says':

*See p. 323.

Mata oukagai mōshiagemásu =
Mata oukagai itashimásu = } I'll visit you again.
[neutral] Mata tazunemásu.

Mōshiagetai kotó ga gozaimásu =
Mōshitái kotó ga gozaimásu = } There's something I want to tell you.
[neutral] Iitai kotó ga arimásu.

9. 9. INFLECTION OF IRREGULAR EXALTED VERBS. The verbs nasáru, irassháru, kudasáru, and ossháru are irregularly inflected in similar ways:

PLAIN IMPERFECT	POLITE IMPERFECT	IMPERATIVE	GERUND	PLAIN PERFECT
nasáru	nasaimásu	nasái	nasátte or násutte	nasátta or násutta
irassháru	irasshaimásu	irasshái	irasshátte or iráshite	irasshátta or iráshita
kudasáru	kudasaimásu	kudasái	kudasátte	kudasátta
ossháru	osshaimásu	osshái	osshátte	osshátta

For gozáru (gozaimásu) see 9. 15.

9. 10. SPECIAL INFLECTIONS OF -MÁSU. The polite ending -másu is really itself a verb which is used only when attached to other verb infinitives. In ordinary polite speech it is inflected only for the imperfect -másu, the perfect -máshita, and the tentative -mashǒ. But in honorific speech, -másu is inflected for all categories except the infinitive. These polite forms are used at the end of sentence fragments, and also in the middle of sentences instead of the usual plain forms, to make the entire expression a bit more honorific:

Soko e oide ni narimá- You go there and...
shite...

Odeki ni narimáshitara...   If you could do it...
Yukkúri hanáshite kuda-   Please speak more slowly.
    saimáse.

Here are the inflections of the polite verb -másu:

Imperfect	–másu	Perfect	–máshita
Tentative	–mashó	Alternative	–máshitari[10.5]
Infinitive	——	Gerund	–máshite
Provisional	–máseba or	Conditional	–máshitara or
	–másureba		–máshitaraba
Imperative	–máse or –máshi		

You may also encounter **déshite**, a polite gerund for the copula 'is and': **"Sukíi-ō" to yobareta hitó deshite ne, Kánsai ni hajímete sukii-ba o hiraita hitó deshita** 'He was the man they called the "Ski King", you know, the one that opened the first ski resort in Kansai'.

9. 11. USE OF HUMBLE VERBS. In general, humble verbs are used of one's own acts when speaking to persons socially superior [they talk back in just polite or even plain speech]—as a maid to her employer. When two persons of approximately equal social status are talking, each may use the exalted forms in reference to the other person, but he generally uses just the simple polite forms in reference to himself, rather than the humble forms. An exception to this occurs when the verb implies participation of the other person or some person of higher social status as fellow-subject, indirect or direct object, possessor of something involved in the action, etc.; in this case, the humble form is customary. Sometimes, however, the humble forms may be used by both speakers.

ESSENTIAL JAPANESE

Examples, with all parties socially equal:

Ítsu Amerika e okaeri ni narimásu ka?	When are you returning to America?
Rainen kaerimásu.	I'm going back next year.
Uchi e kaerimáshŏ ka?	Shall we go home?
Tanaka-bókushi ni oai itashimáshita.	I met Reverend Tanaka.
Dóko de oai ni narimáshita ka?	Where did you meet him?
(Watakushi no) hón o oyomi ni narimáshita ka?	Did you read my book?
(Anáta no) hón o oyomi itashimáshita.	I read your book.
(Watakushi no) hón o yomimáshita.	I read my book.
(Tárō no) hón o yomimáshita.	I read Taro's book.
(Senkyŏshi no) hón o oyomi itashimáshita.	I read the missionary's book.
Shitsúrei itashimáshita.	I committed a discourtesy (to you).

Examples with the maid and the lady of the house:

Ókusan. Watakushi no yónde ita zasshi o dóko e okimáshita ka?	Lady. Where did you put the magazine I was reading?
Jochū. Tēburu no ue ni ooki itashimáshita. Íma	Maid. I put it on the table. I'm going out to

kaimono ni odekake ita-   do the shopping now.
shimásu.

You usually avoid adding the prefix **o-** to both the noun and the verb. 'I read your letter' will be either **Otégami o yomimáshita** or **Tegami o oyomi itashimáshita** The latter is more honorific.

9. 12. ADJECTIVES. An adjective used as a modifier before a noun or noun phrase either remains unchanged or just adds the honorific prefix **o-**: **kuroi obóshi** or **okuroi bóshi** 'your black hat', **oisogashii tokí** 'a busy time (for you)'. When an adjective is used at the end of a sentence as the main predicate, it may be treated in one of two ways: as an exalted expression, or as a general honorific [exalted or humble] expression. It is usually treated as an exalted expression IF THE REFERENCE IS DIRECTLY TO THE PERSON YOU ARE TALKING WITH OR TO SOMEONE ELSE OF HIGH SOCIAL STATUS; otherwise—if the reference is to one of his possessions, or to someone else of equal social status, or to yourself—it is treated as a general honorific.

The exalted expression is made by using the gerund [-kute] form of the adjective, with or without the honorific prefix **o-**, followed by some form of the exalted verb **irassháru** 'stays, exists' or the synonymous expression **oide ni náru**:

Oisogashikute irasshaimá-
su.   } You are busy.
Oisogashikute oide ni nari-
másu.

Kaerítakute   irasshaimásu
  ka?
Okaerı nı narítakute iras-
  shaimásu ka?
Okaeri ni narítakute oide   } Do you want to return?
  ni narimásu ka?
Okaeri ni naritái n desu ka?
(Kaeritái desu ka?)

To make the exalted expression negative, you make
the form of the final verb negative:

Oisogashikute   irassharánai
  yō de irasshaimásu ně.
Oisogashikute oide ni na-
  ránai yō de irasshaimásu   } You don't seem to be busy.
  ně.
(Isogáshiku nai yō desu ně.)
Okaeri ni narítakute irasshaimasén ka?
Okaeri ni narítakute oide   } Don't you want to return?
  ni narimasén ka?
(Kaerítaku arimasén ka?)

The general honorific expression, which may be
humble or exalted (but is generally not used when reference is directly to the person you are talking with) is
made by using the honorific infinitive of the adjective
[see 9. 13] + the honorific verb gozáru [see 9. 15]. The
prefix o- often occurs when the reference in any way involves someone other than oneself.

Isogáshū gozaimásu. (Iso- gashíi desu.)	I'm busy.
Oisogashū gozaimásu. (Iso- gashíi desu.)	He's busy.
Áō gozaimásu (Aói desu.)	It's blue.
Ốkyū gozaimásu. (Ōkíi de- su.)	It's big.
Chíisō gozaimásu. (Chiisái desu.)	It's little.

To make these expressions negative, you can just make gozáru negative:

Isogáshū gozaimasén. (Iso- gáshiku arimasén.)	I'm not busy.
Oisogashū gozaimasén. (I- sogáshiku arimasén.)	He's not busy.
Ốkyū gozaimasén. (Ốkiku arimasén.)	It's not big.
Chíisō gozaimasén. (Chíi- saku arimasén.)	It's not little.

Or, occasionally, you will hear the neutral infinitive followed by the negative of gozáru:

Isogáshiku gozaimasén. Oisogashiku gozaimasén. Ốkiku gozaimasén. Chíisaku gozaimasén.

9. 13. FORMATION OF THE ADJECTIVE HONOR- IFIC INFINITIVE. If we include the vowel which ap- pears before imperfect ending -i, Japanese adjectives are of four types: -ii, -ai, -oi, and -ui [ōkíi, akai, aói, warúi]. To produce the honorific infinitive form, we have to

change not only the ending, but also the vowel before the ending, as follows:

IMPERFECT	HONORIFIC INFINITIVE	NEUTRAL INFINITIVE
-ii, (-shii)	-yū, (-shū)	-iku, (-shiku)
-ai	-ō	-aku
-oi	-ō	-oku
-ui	-ū	-uku

Here are some examples of adjective expressions in the plain, polite, and honorific imperfect:

MEANING	PLAIN	POLITE	HONORIFIC
is big	ōkíi	ōkíi desu	ókyū gozaimásu
is satisfactory	yoroshii	yoroshíi desu	yoroshū gozaimásu
is delicious	oishii	oishíi desu	oishū gozaimásu
is red	akái	akái desu	ákō gozaimásu
is early	hayái	hayái desu	háyō gozaimásu
wants to return	kaeritái	kaeritái desu	kaerítō gozaimásu
is white	shirói	shirói desu	shírō gozaimásu
is good	íi, yói	íi desu, yói desu	yó gozaimásu
is slow, late	osói	osói desu	ósō gozaimásu
is bad	warúi	warúi desu	wárū gozaimásu
is thin	usui	usúi desu	usū gozaimásu
is old [not-new]	furúi	furúi desu	fúrū gozaimásu

Yoroshū gozaimásu is often substituted for **yó gozaimásu** as a more elegant honorific for **íi desu**.

9. 14. SUMMARY OF HONORIFIC PREDICATES.

	HUMBLE	GENERAL HONORIFIC	EXALTED

VERBS	1. Hon inf+ itasu
	   Hon inf + suru
		⟵⟶	1. Hon inf +
			   ni náru
			   (Hon inf +
			   nasáru)
			   Hon inf + dá
			   Hon inf +
			   de gozáru
			   Hon inf +
			   de irassháru

	2. Special verbs	⟵⟶	2. Special verbs

	3. Special verbs
	   treated as 1.
		⟵⟶	3. Special verbs
			   treated as 1.

VERB áru	⟶	special verb, gozáru	⟵
COPULA	⟶	de gozáru	de irassháru

ADJECTIVES	⟶	Hon inf+gozáru	Gerund +
			   irassháru
			Gerund +
			   oide ni náru
			Gerund +
			   oide dá
			Gerund +
			   oide de gozáru
			Gerund +
			   oide de
			   irassháru

9. 15. USES OF GOZÁRU. The verb gozáru is the honorific equivalent of the neutral verb áru 'exists'; it is neither specifically humble nor specifically exalted, just generally honorific. In modern speech it never actually

occurs in any plain forms—you don't hear gozáru, you hear gozaîmásu—even within a sentence: Okane ga gozai-máshitara 'If you have the money', Takusán gozaimásu kara 'Because there's lots', Tokei ga gozaimásu no de 'Since I have a watch'.

Neutral:	Zasshi ga nisatsu ari-másu.	There are 2 maga-zines.
Honorific:	Zasshi ga nisatsu go-zaimásu.	(I or you) have 2 magazines.
Neutral:	Watakushi wa kyő-dai ga sannin ari-másu. Anáta wa kyődai ga futari arimásu ně.	I have 3 brothers and sisters. You have 2 brothers and sisters haven't you.
Honorific:	Watakushi wa kyő-dai ga sannin go-zaimásu. Anáta wa gokyődai ga futari gozaimásu ně.	I have 3 brothers and sisters. You have 2 brothers and sisters, haven't you?

Gozaimásu is also used after the honorific infinitive form of the adjective to make an honorific equivalent of the final polite adjective in the neutral style [plain im-perfect + some form of the polite copula désu]:

Neutral:	Takái desu ně.	⎫ They're expensive,
Honorific:	Tákō gozaimásu ně	⎭ aren't they.
Neutral:	Isogashíi desu.	I'm busy.
Honorific:	Isogáshū gozaimásu.	I'm busy.
	Oisogashū gozaimásu.	He is busy.
[Exalted:	Oisogáshikute iras-shaimásu ně.	You're busy, aren't you.]

Just as gozaimásu [gozáru] is the general honorific equivalent of the neutral verb áru, the expression de gozamásu [de gozáru] is the general honorific equivalent of the copula dá. But there is also an exalted form of the copula de irassháru used in speaking of the second person directly.

Neutral:	Kore wa watakushi no hón desu ga, sore wa anáta no deshō.	}
Honorific:	Kore wa watakushi no hón de gozaimásu ga, sore wa anáta no de gozaimashŏ.	This is my book, and that must be yours.
Honorific + Exalted:	Watakushi wa Ueha-ra de gozaimásu ga, anáta wa Nishi-mura-san de iras-shaimásu ka?	I'm Uehara, and are you Mr Nishimura?

The negative of the honorific copula, corresponding to the plain ja nái and the polite ja arimasén, is either de gozaimasén or more often dé wa gozaimasén. Instead of ja arimasén in polite speech you will sometimes hear dé wa arimasén; ja is a contraction of dé wa.

Kore wa watakushi nó ja arimasén.	}
Kore wa watakushi nó de wa arimasén.	This isn't mine.
Kore wa watakushi nó de gozaimasén.	

Tanaka-san wa shachō dé wa gozaimasén. Watakushi mo shachō dé wa gozaimasén.	Mr Tanaka is not the president of the firm. I am not the president either.
Anáta wa shachō dé wa irasshaimasén ka?	Aren't you the president of the firm?

As in the last example, the negative of the exalted copula is similarly either de irasshaimasén or more often dé wa irasshaimasén.

Ogénki de (wa) irasshaimásén ka?	Aren't you feeling well?
Watakushi wa Táguchi de gozaimásu ga, anáta wa Nomura-san dé wa irasshaimasén ka?	I'm Taguchi; aren't you Mr. Nomura?

9. 16. USES OF IRASSHÁRU. The exalted verb irassháru corresponds to three different neutral verbs: kúru 'comes', iku 'goes', and iru 'stays, exists'. As with all homonyms, you can usually tell which meaning is intended by the context:

EXALTED	NEUTRAL	MEANING
Dóko kara irasshaimásu ka?	Dóko kara kimásu ka?	Where are you coming from?
Dóko e irasshaimásu ka?	Dóko e ikimásu ka?	Where are you going (to)?
Dóko ni irasshaimásu ka?	Dóko ni imásu ka?	Where are you (at)?
Donáta o mátte irasshaimásu ka?	Dáre o mátte imasu ka?	Who are you waiting for?

9. 17.   OIDE. The expected forms for the honorific infinitives of **kúru** 'comes', **iku** 'goes', and **iru** 'stays, exists'— **oki, oiki, oi**—rarely occur. Instead, for the exalted form you use either the special exalted infinitive **oide** [+ **ni náru**, etc.] or the exalted verb **irassháru**. For the humble form you use the special verbs **máiru** 'goes, comes' for **kúru** and **iku, oru** 'stays, exists' for **iru**.

Since there is no infinitive for the exalted verb **irassháru**, we can think of **oide** as an irregular infinitive for this verb. Thus **oide ni narimásu** 'you come, go, or stay' is equivalent in structure to **omeshiagari ni narimásu** 'you eat'; the phrases with **oide**, however, are much more common than the use of infinitives from other special exalted verbs.

Here are some examples:

Humble:	Ōsaka kara mairimáshita.	I came from Osaka.
Neutral:	Ōsaka kara kimáshita.	[Someone] came from Osaka.
Exalted:	Ōsaka kara oide ni narimáshita.	
	Ōsaka kara oide déshita.	
	Ōsaka kara oide de gozaimáshita.	[You or he] came from Osaka.
	Ōsaka kara oide de irasshaimáshita.	
	(Ōsaka kara oide nasaimáshita.)	
	Ōsaka kara irasshaimáshita.	

Humble:	Kóbe e mairimásu.	I'm going to Kobe.
Neutral:	Kóbe e ikimásu.	[Someone] is going to Kobe.

Exalted:	Kóbe e oide ni narimásu. Kóbe e oide désu. Kóbe e oide de gozaimásu. Kóbe e oide de irasshaimásu. (Kóbe e oide nasaimásu.) Kóbe e irasshaimásu.	[You or he] is going to Kobe.

Humble:	Éki ni orimásu.	I'm at the station.
Neutral:	Éki ni imásu.	[Someone]'s at the station.

Exalted:	Éki ni oide ni narimásu. Éki ni oide désu. Éki ni oide de gozaimásu. Éki ni oide de irasshaimásu. (Éki ni oide nasaimásu.) Éki ni irasshaimásu.	[You or he] is at the station.

Humble.	**Inaka ni súnde orimasu.**	I'm living in the country.
Neutral:	**Inaka ni súnde imasu.**	[Someone] is living in the country.
Exalted:	**Inaka ni súnde oide ni narimásu.**	
	Inaka ni súnde oide désu.	
	Inaka ni súnde oide de gozaimásu.	[You or he] is living in the country.
	Inaka ni súnde oide de irasshaimásu.	
	(Inaka ni súnde oide nasaimásu.)	
	Inaka ni súnde irasshaimásu.	

With adjectives, you find **oide** and **irassháru** for the 2d-person exalted, but a different sort of construction for the general honorific (which represents usual 3d-person and humble).

General Hon:	**Isogáshū gozaimásu.**	I am [he is] busy.
	Oisogashū gozaimásu.	He is busy.
Neutral:	**Isogashíi desu.**	[Someone] is busy.
2d Person:	**Oisogáshikute irasshaimásu né.**	
	Oisogáshikute oide ni narimásu né.	
	Oisogáshikute oide désu né.	You're busy, aren't you.
	Oisogáshikute oide	

de gozaimásu né.
Oisogáshikute oide
de irasshaimásu né.
(Oisogáshikute oide
nasaimásu né.)

9. 18. VERBS FOR GIVING. In addition to different
forms for humble, neutral, and exalted, there are two sets
of forms for the meaning 'give'. One set [yaru / ageru]
means 'somebody from the OUT-GROUP gives'. 'I, we,
and my family' are always in the IN-GROUP. 'You' are
in the OUT-GROUP unless you're giving to HIM [some-
one who isn't me or my family], 'he' is in the OUT-
GROUP unless he's giving to HIM [someone else who
isn't me or my family, or you or your family]. Here is
how it works out:

SOMEONE GIVES

SOMEONE	HUMBLE	NEUTRAL	EXALTED
I give you	ageru	yaru	——
I give him	ageru	yaru	——
You give him	ageru	yaru	——
You give me	——	kureru	kudasáru
He gives me	——	kureru	kudasáru
He gives you	——	kureru	kudasáru
He gives him	ageru	yaru	——

Notice that for each situation there are only TWO
POSSIBILITIES. The social status in the situations is
such that you can only have humble or neutral on the
one hand, and exalted or neutral on the other. In other
words, for any of these situations we have a NEUTRAL

way to say it, and an HONORIFIC way. Whether the honorific way is actually HUMBLE (using **ageru**) or EXALTED (using **kudasáru**) is determined by the ingroup-outgroup relationship of the giver and the recipient. Whether you use the NEUTRAL or the HONORIFIC depends on whether you want to show special deference with respect to the person you are talking about.

One of these rules of the thumb may prove useful:

1. If 'I' is the giver or if 'him' is the recipient, you use the set **yaru** / **ageru**.   In all other cases you use **kureru** / **kudasáru**.

2. You use **kureru** / **kudasáru** if 'HE gives YOU' or if ANYBODY 'gives ME'.   In all other cases you use **yaru** / **ageru**.

Remember that members of 'my family' are treated like 'me' if RECIPIENTS, like 'he' if GIVERS. And 'he, him' of course stand for 'he, she, they, them, Mr Tanaka, etc.'

The following diagrams sum up the situation. The numbers 1, 2, and 3 stand respectively for 'I, you, and he', 4 stands for another 'he'. The direction of the arrows indicates the direction of giving.

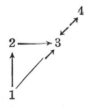

yaru / **ageru**

kureru / **kudasáru**

The particle used for the recipient is **ni**: **Watakushi wa Tanaka-san ni kono hón o agemashó** [yarimashó] 'I guess I'll give Mr Tanaka this book; I guess I'll give this book to Mr Tanaka.'

Here are some additional examples in sentences.

Otōtó ni hón o yarimáshita.	I gave my younger brother a book.
Jochū ni furúi kimono o yarimáshita.	I gave the maid an old kimono.
Senséi ni omiyage o agemáshita.	I gave the teacher a souvenir.
Otōsan ni waishatsu o agemáshita.	I gave my father a shirt.
Tomodachi ga atarashíi náifu o kuremáshita.	My friend gave me a new knife.
Yaoya ga otsuri o jūgoen kuremáshita.	The grocer gave me 15 Yen change.
Shachō-san ga atarashíi mannénhitsu o kudasaimáshita.	The president of the company gave me a new fountain pen.
Tonari no ojisan ga otōtó ni omócha o kudasaimáshita.	The man next door gave my younger brother a toy.
Ane wa obásan ni okáshi o agemáshita.	My older sister gave Grandmother some pastry.
Anáta ga otōsan ni tabako o ageru to, oyorokobi ni náru deshō.	Your father must be pleased when you give him cigarets.
Kore o sashiagetára, ikága deshō ka?	How about my giving him this?

9. 19. FAVORS. When you say 'someone does something FOR someone else' you are reporting a FAVOR. To do this in Japanese you use the gerund of the verb representing the action of the favor, and then add on the appropriate verb meaning 'gives'. In other words, to say 'I'll write the letter for you', the Japanese says something like 'I will give you [the favor of] writing the letter'— **Tegami o káite agemásu.** The person doing the favor is either the topic, followed by the particle **wa**, or the emphatic subject, followed by the particle **ga**. The person for whom the favor is done is indicated by the particle **ni**:

Tanaka-san wa Nakamura-san ni tegami o káite ya-rimásu.	Mr T. will write the letter for Mr N.

Notice the possible ambiguity here; the sentence could mean 'Mr Tanaka will write a letter to Mr Nakamura [for someone else]'. In such a sentence, you may want to indicate both the direction of reference of the verb **yaru** 'gives' [that is, the person TO whom you're giving, or FOR whom you're doing the favor] and the direction of reference of the verb **káku** 'writes' [that is, the addressee of the letter]. In such a case, the phrase nearest the gerund is most likely to refer to that verb:

Tanaka-san wa Nakamura-san ni Kimura-san ni te-gami o káite yarimásu.	Mr T. will write a letter to Mr K. for Mr N.

The verbs for giving are used just as they would be if you were giving some object instead of a favor.

Watakushi wa anáta ni shimbun o agemásu [yarimásu].	I'll give you a paper.
Watakushi wa anáta ni shimbun o yónde agemásu [yarimásu].	I'll read you the paper.
Watakushi wa Tanaka-san ni shimbun o agemásu [yarimásu].	I'll give Mr. T. the paper.
Watakushi wa Tanaka-san ni shimbun o yónde agemásu [yarimásu].	I'll read Mr. T. the paper.
Anáta wa Tanaka-san ni shimbun o agemásu [yarimásu].	You'll give Mr. T. the newspaper.
Anáta wa Tanaka-san ni shimbun o yónde agemásu [yarimásu].	You'll read Mr. T. the newspaper.
Anáta wa watakushi ni shimbun o kudasaimásu [kuremásu].	You'll give me the newspaper.
Anáta wa watakushi ni shimbun o yónde kudasaimásu [kuremásu].	You'll read me the newspaper.
Tanaka-san wa watakushi ni shimbun o kudasaimásu [kuremásu].	Mr. T. will give me the newspaper.
Tanaka-san wa watakushi ni shimbun o yónde kudasaimásu [kuremásu].	Mr. T. will read me the newspaper.

Tanaka-san wa anáta ni shimbun o kudasaimásu [kuremásu].	Mr T. will give you the newspaper.
Tanaka-san wa anáta ni shimbun o yónde kudasaimásu [kuremásu].	Mr T. will read you the newspaper.
Tanaka-san wa Nakamura-san ni shimbun o agemásu [yarimásu].	Mr T. will give Mr N. the newspaper.
Tanaka-san wa Nakamura-san ni shimbun o yónde agemásu [yarimásu].	Mr T. will read Mr N the newspaper.

Notice that each of the sentences involving the reading is possibly ambiguous, since it could mean 'somebody reads the newspaper TO somebody' or '...FOR somebody'. Ordinarily, it would probably mean both. But if Mr Nakamura were sick and Mr Tanaka relieved his nurse of the job of reading him the newspaper, then you might say something like Tanaka-san wa kangófu ni Nakamura-san ni shimbun o yónde agemáshita [yarimáshita] 'Mr. T. read the paper to Mr N. for the nurse.'

Now we can understand phrases like Mō ichido itte kudasái 'Please say it again'; itte kudasái means 'Please do me the favor of saying it.'

If you want to say 'I HAD someone do something or GOT someone to do something FOR me', you are reporting the RECEIPT OF A FAVOR. To say 'I had Jiro go buy me a paper' the Japanese says something like 'I received of Jiro [the favor of] buying the paper and coming' —Watakushi wa Jíro ni shimbun o katté moraimá-shita. The neutral verb for 'receives' [= 'has or gets some-one to do something for one'] is **morau**; the humble equiv-alent is **itadaku**. There is no special exalted form, but you can use the phrases **omorai ni náru, omorai de gozai-másu,** etc.

Notice that the person FROM whom the favor is re-ceived is indicated by the particle **ni,** the same one you use to indicate TO whom a favor is given when you use a verb of giving; there is no ambiguity, because the verb shows which meaning is called for. However, in the case of verbs of giving you always use **ni** (**Anáta ni hón o age-másu** 'I give you a book', **Anáta ni hón o yónde agemasu** 'I read you a book'), but with verbs of receiving, you use **ni** only if it is a FAVOR you have received (**Anáta ni hón o yónde itadakimáshita** 'I had you read me the book')— if it is an object of some sort, you use **kara** (**Anáta kara hón o itadakimáshita** 'I received a book from you'). Com-pare the following two sentences:

Ojíisan kara jiténsha o moraimáshita.	I got a bike from Grand-father.
Ojíisan ni jiténsha o naó-shite moraimáshita.	I got Grandfather to fix my bike.

There is possible ambiguity with verbs indicating ac-tions which ordinarily take an indirect object (like writ-ing, reading, saying, etc.), just as there is with the ex-pressions for doing a favor. **S[1]énsei ni tegami o káite mo-raimáshita** could mean either 'I had the teacher write the letter for me' or 'I got someone to write the letter to the teacher for me'; the former meaning is more likely. If you wanted to make the latter meaning explicit, you would probably say something like **Otŏsan ni senséi ni tegami o káite moraimáshita** 'I got my father to write a letter to the teacher for me.' This multiple use of the particle **ni** (each time with a different reference in the sentence) is similar to the sentence presented in diagrammatic form in note 7. 10: **Tárō ni Jírō ni Tanaka-san ni áu yō ni to iu yŏ ni (to) kakimáshita** 'I wrote Taro to tell Jiro to meet Mr Tanaka.' It is possible to make up even more complicated sentences—**Watakushi wa otŏsan ni Tárō ni Jírō ni Tanaka-san ni áu yō ni (to) káite itadakimáshita** 'I had Father write Taro to tell Jiro to meet Mr Tanaka'—but of course such clumsy sentences are seldom heard in real conversation.

If you say you WANT to do something for someone, or you WANT someone to do something for you, you use the same sort of construction as above, but change the verb of giving or receiving into a desiderative:

Watakushi wa anáta ni shimbun o agetái [yaritái] desu.	I want to give you the newspaper.
Watakushi wa anáta ni shimbun o yónde agetái [yaritái] desu.	I want to read you the newspaper.
Watakushi wa anáta kara shimbun o itadakitái [moraitái] desu.	I want to receive the newspaper from you.

Watakushi wa anáta ni shimbun o yónde itadakitái [moraitái] desu.	I want you to read the newspaper for me.

Here are some more sentences illustrating favors.

Kore wa otōtó ga kai ni itte kuremáshita.	My younger brother went to buy this for me.
Mé ga wárukereba, watakushi ga yónde agemashǒ?	If your eyes are bad, shall I read for you?
Jochū ni kutsúshita o issoku kashite yarimáshita.	I lent the maid a pair of stockings.
Tonari no ókusan ga góhan o tsukútte kudasaimáshita.	The neighbor's wife prepared the meal for us.
Watakushi ga káite yaréba, jōzú ni yomimásu.	If I write it for him, he reads it very well.
Katté kite yatté mo, súgu damé ni shimásu.	Even if I go and buy it for him, he immediately ruins it.
Hón o kárite kite agemáshita ga, ki ni iranai yǒ desu.	I went and borrowed a book for him, but it seems he doesn't like it.
Otosan ga watakushi ni katte kudasátta jiténsha wa, kyǒ níisan ga notte dekakemáshita.	(Big) Brother rode off today on the bicycle Father bought for me.
Kinǒ katté kite yatta zasshi	Where did you put the

wa dóko ni okimáshita
ka?

magazines I went and
bought for you yester-
day?

Íkura motte itte ageté mo,
máda hoshíi yō desu.

No matter how much of it
I take to him, it seems he
still wants more.

9. 20. REQUESTS. Japanese do not use imperative
forms so often as we do. There are several ways to make
a polite request in Japanese. The most polite of these
are (1) to use the INFINITIVE or more often the HON-
ORIFIC INFINITIVE + nasái [the imperative form of
the exalted verb nasáru 'does]; (2) to use the GERUND
+ kudasái [the imperative form of the exalted verb kudasáru 'you give the favor of']; (3) to use the HONORIFIC
INFINITIVE + kudasái; or, (4) to use the GERUND +
itadakimásu 'I will receive the favor of', itadakitái desu
or itadakitō gozaimásu 'I want to receive the favor of', or
itadakitái to zonjimásu 'I feel I should like to receive the
favor of.'

Kono tegami o oyomi nasái.
Kono tegami o yónde kuda-
sái.
Kono tegami o oyomi kuda-
sái.
Kono tegami o yónde itada-
kimasu.
Kono tegami o yónde itadakitái desu.
Kono tegami o yónde itadakitō gozaimásu.

Please read this letter.

Kono tegami o yónde itada-
    kitai to zonjimásu.   }

Another way, somewhat less common except in special phrases, is to use the imperative form of the polite auxiliary verb -másu attached to **kudasai-** or **nasai-**:

Kono tegami o oyomi kuda- saimáse (or nasaimáse).	Please read this letter.

A more indirect way to make a request is to frame it as a negative question:

Kono tegami o yomimasén ka?	Won't you read this letter?
Kono tegami o yónde ku- dasaimasén ka?	Won't you do me the favor of reading this letter?

Negative requests are not ordinarily made except in the form of prohibitions to inferiors: **Ítsu mo okáshi o tábete wa ikemasén yo** 'You mustn't eat sweets all the time.' To a social equal or superior, you suggest that 'it would be better not' to do something: **Sore o tabénai hō ga íi deshō** 'it would be better if you didn't eat that.' Or, given two alternatives, you emphasize the positive one: **Sore o tabenái de, kore o tábete kudasai** 'Please eat this one instead of that one.'

9. 21. ANSWERS TO NEGATIVE QUESTIONS. The words **hái** [or **ě**] and **iie** are used to mean 'what you've said is correct' and 'what you've said is incorrect'. So if you state a question in a negative way, the standard Japanese answer turns out to be the opposite of standard English 'yes' and 'no', which affirm or deny the FACTS rather than the STATEMENT of the facts.

Kumamoto e ikimasén de- Didn't you go to Kumamo-
shita ka? Hái, ikimasén to? No, I didn't. Yes,
deshita. Iie, ikimáshita I did indeed.
yo.

This usage strikes a more familiar note in the old
example from substandard English:

Bánana wa arimasén ka? Do you have no bananas?
Hái, bánana wa arima- Yes, we have no bananas.
sén.

Of course, if the negative question is really just an
oblique request, then you indicate assent with hái and your
and your refusal with iie, as you would in English.

Kaban o motté kite kuda- Won't you please bring the
saimasén ka? Hái, kashi- suitcase over here? Yes,
komarimáshita. gladly.
Mō sukóshi meshiagari- Won't you have a little
masén ka? Iie, mō kék- more [to eat]? No
kō de gozaimásu. (thanks), I've had ample.

9. 22. THE SPECIFIC PLURAL. In general, singular
and plural are not distinguished in Japanese: hón means
'book' or 'books', kore means 'this' or 'these', anó hito
means 'he' or 'they'. There are, however, ways to make
specific plurals for certain nouns, and these are in common
use, particularly for the equivalents of English pronouns,
There is the following set of suffixes:

HUMBLE	NEUTRAL	EXALTED
–dómo	-tachi	–gáta

These occur in the following combinations:

watakushítachi	we [neutral]
watakushidómo	we [honorific = humble]
anatátachi	you all [neutral]
anatagáta	you all [honorific = exalted]
ano hitótachi	they [neutral]
ano katágata	they [honorific = exalted]

The meaning of course excludes the possibility of an exalted 'we' or a humble 'you all' or 'they'.

About the only other word which occurs with -dómo for a suffix is jochūdómo 'maidservants'. The suffix -tachi is used frequently with nouns indicating people: shokkō-tachi 'factory hands', hyakushótachi 'farmers', suihéitachi 'Navy men', Tanakátachi 'Tanaka and his group', kodomó-tachi 'children'. Unless used impersonally, such expressions seem rather impolite; they can be made more polite by adding -san before -tachi: shokkō-sántachi, hyakushō-sántachi, suihei-sántachi, Tanaka-sántachi, kodomo-sán-tachi. If special deference is shown to the people discussed, the exalted suffix -gáta is used: senseigáta 'teachers', hyakushō-sangáta 'our friends the farmers [politician speaking]'. Both hitótachi and hitóbito are used to mean 'people'. Reduplications of the hitóbito type often include a connotation of variety or respective distribution 'various people'; other examples are kuníguni 'various countries', shimájima '(various or numerous) islands, island after island', sorézore 'severally, variously, respectively'.

The words **kore, sore,** and **are** refer to both singular and plural—'this' or 'these', 'that' or 'those'. They can be made specifically plural by adding the suffix **-ra: koré-ra** 'these', **soréra** 'these', **aréra** 'those over there'. But in a simple equational sentence like 'These are roses, and those are camellias' you just use the plain forms **Kore wa bara dé, sore wa tsúbaki desu.**

Another polite way to say 'you (all)' is **miná-san** or **mina-sángata.** The word **miná-san** is often heard at the beginning of a public talk, equivalent to English 'Ladies and Gentlemen:'. Sometimes it means just 'everybody [at your house]' as in **Miná-san** ni yoroshiku 'Please give my regards to everyone.'

C. EXERCISES.

1. Change each of the basic sentences from the honorific style to the ordinary polite style. For example, the first will be **Kinŏ wa Sátō-bokushi ni aimáshita.**

2. Here are some sentences in the polite style. Change each of them into the honorific style in two ways, first with the meaning 'I...' or 'my...', then as a question with the meaning 'You...?' or 'Your...?' For example, the first will be **Uchi no denwa wa námban de gozaimáshita ka?** 'What was the phone number at our place?' and **Otaku no denwa wa námban de gozaimáshita ka?** 'What was the phone number at your place?'

1. **Uchi no denwa wa námban deshita ka?**
2. **Senkyóshi desu.**

3. Okane ga áru deshō.
4. Amerika kara kimáshita.
5. Yokohama de shigoto o shite imásu.
6. Senséi ni kikimáshita.
7. Senséi no uchi e asobi ni ikimáshita.
8. Sono éiga o míta koto ga arimásu.
9. Shachō ni aitái desu.
10. Bokushi-san ni kono hón o misemáshita.
11. Kono empitsu o senséi ni karimáshita.
    [NOTE: 'borrow from' is either **ni kariru** or
    kara kariru.]
12. Tanaka Tárō to iimásu.
13. Táguchi-san o shitte imásu.
14. Atarashíi kimono o kite imáshita.
15. Náni ka tabetái to omoimásu.
16. Ashitá kara kusuri o nománakute mo íi desu.
17. Nijikan gúrai benkyō shimáshita.
18. Rainen Amerika e kaerimásu.
19. Takayama-san to hanashimáshita.
20. Kono goro isogashíi desu.

3. Say the following sentences in the honorific style.

1. Watakushi no jidósha wa kurói desu ga, anáta **no**
   wa aói desu né.
2. Kono tatémono wa ōkíi desu.
3. Anáta wa ítsu kaeritái desu ka?
4. Watakushi wa rokuji góro ni kaeritái desu.
5. Kyŏ wa oténki ga warúi desu né.
6. Kono kōen wa taihen íi desu né.
7. Sono éiga wa omoshírokatta desu ka?

8. Anáta wa dáre ni aimáshita ka?
9. Anáta wa watakushi ni shimbun o katté kite kure-máshita.
10. Tanaka-san wa ten-in ni jūénsatsu o nímai [two 10-yen bills] yarimáshita.

4. Translate the following sentences, first into the po-lite style, then into the honorific style.

1. I'll give you this book.
2. I gave my younger sister an umbrella.
3. My father gave me a bicycle.
4. Did your mother give your (younger) brother that pastry?
5. Did you give your uncle a shirt?
6. You gave me some gloves.
7. My older brother gave me these trousers.
8. Did your older sister give you anything?
9. I gave the clerk two hundred-yen bills.
10. The clerk gave me twenty-five yen change.

5. Each of the following sentences means somebody did something Make it mean (1) 'you did it for me', (2) I did it for you', (3) 'You did it for Mr Tanaka', (4)'Mr Tanaka did it for you' [in this case your choice of verbs depends on whether the speaker is more intimate with Mr Tanaka than with the person he is talking to—let's assume he's not], (5) 'Mr Tanaka did it for me', (6) 'Mr Tanaka did it for Mr Kimura'. Each time, say the sentence first with the neutral verb indicating the giving of a favor, then with the honorific verb.

1. Tegami o kakimáshita.
2. Jiténsha o naoshimáshíta.
3. Tokei o kaimáshita.
4. Hón o urimáshita.
5. Kaban o totte kimáshita.
6. Senséi ni hanashimáshita.
7. Shachō ni sore o iimáshita.
8. Shimbun o motte kimáshita.
9. Issho ni éki made arúite ikimáshita.
10. Kono kotoba no ími o setsumei shimáshita.

D. COMPREHENSION.

[Amerika kara oide ni nátta senkyóshi no Smith-san wa ókusan o tsurete Uchida-bóku-shi no otaku e oasobi ni irasshaimáshita.]

S.   Gomen kudasái. Uchida-bókushi no otaku de gozaimásu ka?

U.   Sayō de gozaimásu. Watakushi wa Uchida de gozaimásu ga, dónata-sama de irasshaimá-su ka?

S.   Smith to mōshimásu ga, Amerika kara máitta senkyóshi de gozaimásu.

U.   Smith-san to osshaimásu ka? Brown-san ka-ra otegami o itadaite, oide ni náru no o omachi itáshite orimáshita. Sá, dózo, oagari kudasái.

S.   Dé wa chotto ojama o itashimásu. Taihen kírei na oheya de gozaimásu né.

U.   Dó itashimáshite. Chiisái tokoro de gozái-másu ga... Dózo, kochira e ohairi kudasaimáse.

S.   Osóre irimasu. Kore wa kánai de gozaimásu.
        Dõzo yoroshiku.
U.   Kochira kóso. Ókusan mo Nihongo ga ode-
        ki ni narimásu ka?
S.   Iie, Eigo shika dekimasén. Nihonjin no káta
        to oai suru tokí wa watakushi ga tsūyaku o
        shite yarimásu.
U.   Oshígoto wa dóchira de nasáru n de gozai-
        másu ka?
S.   Nakayama to iu chíisa na tokoró e mairi-
        máshite, sochira no kyōkai de shigoto o suru
        kotó ni nátte imasu.
U.   Sayō de gozaimásu ka?. Anatagáta wa Ame-
        rika no katá de irasshaimásu kara, inaka ni
        osumi ni náru kotó wa fúben de gozaimashõ.
S.   Kánai wa nán de mo Nihonjin no yõ ni ita-
        shitai to mōshite orimásu kara, fúben de mo
        kamaimasén.
U.   Nakayama-kyōkai no Kuríhara-bokushi o yó-
        ku zonjite orimásu kara, goshōkai itashima-
        shõ.
S.   Osóre irimasu ga, onegai itashimásu. Móshi,
        ohima ga oari ni náttara, ítsu ka oasobi ni
        iráshite kudasaimasén ka?
U.   Ha, arígatō gozaimásu. Kánai no uchi wa
        Nakayama no tonari de gozaimásu kara, to-
        kidoki soko e tazunete ikimásu ga, kóndo wa
        Nakayama é mo oukagai itashimashõ.
S.   Dõzo. Tokí ni, myõban watakushidómo to

issho ni oshibai e oide ni narimasén ka?

U. . Sekkakú de gozaimásu ga, ashitá wa ane no tanjôbi de gozaimásu no de, ane no uchí e asobi ni ikimásu kara... A, kore wa kánai de gozaimásu ga...

U. no ókusan. Dôzo yoroshiku. Yóku irasshaimáshita. Ocha wa ikága de gozaimásu ka?

S. Arígatō gozaimásu.

U. Tabako wa ikága de gozaimásu ka?

S. Tabako wa itadakimasén.

U. no ókusan. Mō sukóshi ocha o sashiagemashô ka?

S. Mô kékkō de gozaimásu. Oisogashii tokí ni, ojama ni mairimáshite, sumimasén deshita.

U. Dô itashimáshite. Ítsu demo, machí ni oide ni nátta toki, oasobi ni oide kudasaimáse. Sekkaku iráshite kudasaimáshita no ni, nán no okamai mo itashimasén de, shitsúrei ita-shimáshita.

S. Dô itashimáshite. Ojama itashimáshita. Sayo-nára.

U. Mata, dôzo. Sayonára.

NOTE:

For more material on the honorific style, see Elizabeth F. Gardner and Samuel E. Martin, *Honorific and Familiar Speech in Japanese:* Institute of Far Eastern Languages, Yale University, 1952.

LESSON 10.

A. BASIC SENTENCES. 'Womantalk.'

1. Otaku no musukosan wa heitai ni onari ni naritái sō desu ně.

I hear your son wants to become a soldier.

2. Sō itte orimásu.

That's the way he's talking.

3. Daigaku ni háiru kotó ni nátte imáshita ga, benkyō ga kirai ná no de, heitai ni náru kotó ni shimáshita.

It had been arranged for him to enter the University, but he decided to become a soldier, because he doesn't like to study.

4. Oníisan no musukosan mo heitai ni nararemáshita ně.

Your older brother's son became a soldier too, didn't he.

5. Só desu. Oi no hanashí de wa ammari omoshirói seikatsu ja nái sō desu.

That's right. According to my nephew, it's not a very enjoyable life.

6. Hito ni yotte chigaimásu ga, gúntai no seikatsu no sukí na hito mo áru yō desu.

It all depends on the person, but there seem to be people who like Army life.

7. Jieitai no seikatsu ni tsúite sakúban no shimbun ni kíji ga

There was an article [came out] in last night's paper about life in the

déte imáshita.

8. Héisha de wa heitai ni kirai na shigoto o iro-iro sasemásu né.

9. Heya no sōji o sasetári, mádo o arawasetári, sentaku o sasetári, to-kidoki ryōri o sasetári suru só desu.

10. Musuko wa sentaku o saseraretára, hontō ni odoróku deshō.

11. Sore kara, ryōri nádo mo saseraretári shita-ra, miná ga shinde shi-maú ka mo shiremásen.

12. Nánni mo ryōri ga deki-nai wáke de wa nái n desu ga...

13. Táda, uchi no shigoto nádo wa shita kotó ga nái kara, gúntai ni háitte sonna kotó o saseraretára kitto ko-máru ni chigai ari-masén.*

14. Sore wa sō to, musuko-san wa itsu góro heitai

Defense Force.

In the barracks they make the soldiers do all sorts of unpleasant things, you know.

I hear they make them clean the rooms, wash the window, do the laundry, and sometimes cook.

If my son were made to do the laundry, he'd sure be surprised.

And then, if he were made to do the cooking and such things too, they might all end up dead.

I don't mean he doesn't know how to cook any-thing...

It's just that he's never done housework or the like, so if he is made to do such things when he joins [enters] the Army, I bet he sure will have a hard time.

By the way, [about] when [is it arranged that]

*or sázo komáru deshō (darō to omoimásu).

ni iku kotó ni náru
n deshō ka?

your son will go into
the service?

15. Mō súgu ka mo shire-
masén.

Maybe right away.

16. Kōkūtai ka náni ka ni
háiru kotó ni náru to
ka itte imáshita.

He was saying something
like he would like to
get into the aircorps or
the like. [to ka=nádo
(to) cf. pp. 193, 213].

17. Anó ko no otŏsan wa
rikusentai no gúnsō
datta n desv keredo-
mo...

His father was a Marine
sergeant, but...

18. Oi ni ataru kodomo wa
káigun ni hairitagátte
itá n desu ga, tōtō ri-
kúgun ni nátta n desu.

[The one who's] my neph-
ew had been eager to
get in the Navy, but he
finally ended up in the
Army.

19. Hohei wa yóku arukase-
raréru n de, heikō su-
ru sŏ desu nĕ.

I understand the infantry
are made to walk a lot,
and that's hard.

20. Dé mo, gunkan dá to,
shizumu osoré ga ari-
másu nĕ.

But if you're on [if it is]
a warship, there's the
danger of sinking, you
know.

21. Gunkan ga shizundára,
oborejini suru yóri
shikata ga arimasén
nĕ.

And if the warship sinks,
you're bound to get
drowned to death.

22. Kore wa, áme ga furisŏ

My, it looks like it's go-

desu ga, kasa o dóko ni oite oitá ka shira.

23. Sakúban wa furisó ni mo miénakatta no de, kasa o mótazu ni éiga o mí ni ikimáshita.

24. Éiga ga súnde kara, uchi e káeru tochū de áme ni furaremáshita.

25. Oténki no warúi hi ni wa kodomo o dóko de asobaserú ka to iú no wa mondai désu né.

26. Uchi no náka de térebi o misásetari, omócha de asobasetári suru kotó ga dekimásu ga...

27. Ryōri o shinagara kodomo o asobaseru kotó wa muzukashíi desu.

28. Okosan wa nánnin oari désu ka?

29. Futarí arimásu. Hitóri wa nanátsu de, mō hitóri wa itsútsu desu.

30. Futarí to mo otokó de yakyū ni nesshín desu.

ing to rain—I wonder where I put my umbrella.

Last night I went to the movies without [carrying] my umbrella, because it looked as if it weren't going to rain.

After the movie was over, on my way back home, I got rained on.

On bad-weather days it's a problem where to have the children play, isn't it.

You can have them watch television, play with toys and the like inside the house, but...

It's difficult to get children to play while you're cooking.

How many children do you have?

I have two. One is 7 and the other is 5.

They are both boys and wild about baseball.

VOCABULARY ITEMS.

NOUNS.

gúntai	Army (as opposed to civilians), Armed Forces	Nan-yō	South Seas [the Southwest Pacific]
rikúgun	Army (as opposed to Navy)	nesshín (na)	enthusiastic
		séito	student, pupil
káigun	Navy	jibun	oneself, one's own
rikusentai	Marines	(heya no) sōji	cleaning (a
kōkūtai	Air Force	(o suru)	room) up
hohei	infantry	nánni mo	
gunkan	warship	=náni mo	nothing
sensuikan	submarine	kikái	opportunity,
héisha	barracks		chance
shōkō	officer	kikái ga áru	has the chance to
gúnsō	sergeant	kobune	(small) boat
yobitai	Reserve (troops)	íken	opinion, view
osoré	danger; fear	bímbō (na)	(is) poor
mondai	problem, question (for discussion)	bimbōnin	poor people
		tokaku	likely, naturally
shitsumon	question (to be answered)	tó-ni-kaku	nevertheless, anyway
kippu	ticket		

VERBS

bakugeki suru	bombs	oboreru	drowns, is submerged
heikō suru [=komáru]	is in a fix, finds it tough, is hard-pressed	oborejini suru	drowns to death
		korosu	kills
shizumu	sinks	útsu	hits

B. STRUCTURE NOTES.

10. 1. SÓ DESU. When you want to report something you haven't actually witnessed yourself, you usually end the sentence with só desu which has the meaning 'I hear' or 'I'm given to understand' or 'what I've just said isn't something I myself observed'.* The part which goes in front of só desu ends in either the plain imperfect or the plain perfect. If the fact reported were from one's observation or knowledge, there would be no só desu and the sentence would end with a polite form. Here are some examples:

OWN OBSERVATION	HEARD FROM SOMEONE ELSE
Natsú wa oténki ga íi desu.	Natsú wa oténki ga íi sō desu.
In summer the weather's good.	In summer the weather's good, I hear.
Só desu.	Só da só desu ně.
That's right. It's so.	So they say [they say it's so].
Anáta no ojisan wa shachō désu ně.	Anáta no ojisan wa shachō dá sō desu ně.
Your uncle is president of the firm.	I understand your uncle is president of the firm.
Omusumesan wa taihen kírei desu ně.	Omusumesan wa taihen kírei da só desu ně.
Your daughter is very pretty.	They say your daughter's very pretty.
Senkyóshi wa rainen Ame-	Senkyóshi wa rainen Ame-

*Instead of só desu, you can use... tó no kotó desu or ...to iu kotó desu or just ...tte (cf. pp. 424-5).

rika e okaeri ni nari-
másu.

The missionary is return-
ing to America next year.

rika e okaeri ni náru sō
desu.

I hear the missionary is
returning to America
next year.

Táro wa kómban hachiji
góro ni kúru to iimá-
shita.

Taro said he is coming at
8 this evening.

Táro wa kómban hachiji
góro ni kúru to itta só
desu.

They say that Taro said
he is coming at 8 tonight.

10. 2. BOUND FORM -sō (na) 'appearance'. There is a
form -sō added to the infinitive of a verb, or the base of
an adjective, or to a copular noun, making a derived
copular noun with the meaning 'looking as if, having the
appearance of'. The resulting word, a copular noun, is
then followed by a form of the copula (dá/ná etc.) or by
the particle ni. Here are some examples:

MODEL

Máinichi áme ga furimásu.
It rains every day.
Oténki ga warúi desu.
The weather is bad.

Yasúmu kotó ga dekíru to-
koro désu.
It's a place you can rest at.

Génki na kodomo désu.
He's a lively child.

'LOOKING AS IF'

Ame ga furisó desu.
It looks as if it will rain.
Oténki ga warusó desu.
The weather looks as if it
were bad.

Yasúmu kotó ga dekisó na
tokoro désu.
It's a place that looks as
if you could rest at it.

Genki-só na kodomo désu.
He's a lively-looking child.

Two adjectives add -sasō instead of just -sō: yo-sasŏ 'looking as if it werc good', na-sasŏ 'looking as if it were non-existent'.

Sono sakana wa íi desu.	**Sono sakana wa yosasŏ desu.**
That fish is good.	That fish looks as if it were good.
Gyūniku wa arimasén.	**Gyūniku wa nasasŏ desu.**
They haven't any beef.	It looks as if they haven't any beef.
Nihonjín ja arimasén.	**Nihonjín ja nasasŏ desu.**
He isn't a Japanese.	He looks as if he weren't a Japanese.

Notice the difference in meaning between expressions with the form -sō and expressions ending sŏ desu:

Yukí ga fúru sō desu.	**Yukí ga furisō desu.**
They say it's going to snow.	It looks as if it were going to snow.
Yōniku ga nákatta sō desu.	**Yōniku ga nasasŏ deshita.**
I was given to understand they didn't have lamb.	It looked as if they didn't have lamb.

For the negative 'it doesn't look as if', the expression is usually followed by **ní wa** or **ní mo**, and either **nái** [arimasén] or **miénai** [miemasén] 'does not seem, does not appear'.

Sono éiga wa omoshirosǒ
ni wa arimasén.

Sono éiga wa omoshirosǒ
ni mo arimasén.

Sono éiga wa omoshirosǒ
ni wa miemasén.

Sono éiga wa omoshirosǒ
ni mo miemasén.

It doesn't look as if that
movie were interesting.

Compare the negative of the expressions with **sǒ desu**
'I hear that':

Áme ga furánai sǒ desu.	Áme ga furisǒ ni mo miemasén.
I hear it isn't going to rain.	It doesn't look as if it would rain.

10. 3. **RASHÍI**. The adjective **rashíi** means something
like 'seems to (be), gives every appearance of (being)' It
is used after nouns, and after verbs and adjectives in
the imperfect and perfect moods. [For accent, see p. 429.]

Sore wa anáta no jidōsha rashíi desu né.	That seems to be your car, doesn't it.
Anáta no tomodachi ráshikatta desu né.	It seemed to be your friend.
Kánai wa machí e kaimono ni itta rashíi desu.	My wife seems to have gone to town shopping.
Tanaka-san wa kómban asobi ni kuru rashíi desu né.	Mr Tanaka seems to be coming to see us this evening.
Kono kishá wa atarashii	This train gives every ap-

rashíi desu nĕ.	pearance of being new, doesn't it.
Táró wa sono tegami o kakanakatta rashíi desu.	Taro seems not to have written that letter.
Táró wa sono tegami o kaita ráshiku arimasén.	Taro doesn't seem to have written that letter.
Kodomo wa okáshi o tabetakatta rashíi desu.	The child seems to have wanted to eat the sweets.
Kodomo wa okáshi o tabetai ráshikatta desu.	The child seemed to want to eat the sweets.

The meaning of **rashíi** is very similar to the meaning of **yǒ desu** 'gives the appearance of'. For many situations, either one may be used. Sometimes **yǒ desu** means 'gives the appearance of being something else (other than what you know it really is)' as in **Ano heitai wa kodomo no yǒ ni miemásu** 'That soldier looks like a child', but **rashíi** always means 'gives every appearance of being (what you think it probably is)'—**Ano heitai wa Amerikajin rashíi desu** or ...**Amerikajin ráshiku miemásu** 'That soldier seems to be an American.' The difference in meaning between expressions with **-sǒ** 'appearance' and **rashíi** 'seems to be' is that the former refers to the looks of the situation, and the latter refers to the opinion of the person making the statement. **Áme ga furisǒ desu** 'It looks as tho it would rain [but perhaps I haven't made up my mind whether it really will or not]'—**Áme ga furu rashíi desu** 'It seems to be going to rain [I think it probably will].'

10. 4. EXPRESSIONS MEANING 'LIKE.' There are several ways to say 'A is like B, A looks like B, A seems as if it were B, A resembles B, etc.' Here is a list of some of these expressions:

A wa B no yǒ da	A is like B
A wa B no yǒ ni miéru	A looks (seems, appears) like B
A wa B no yǒ ni omowaréru	A is thought to be like B
A wa B no yǒ ni kangaeraréru	A is thought to be like B
A wa B to miéru	A seems (appears) to be B
A wa B rashíi	A seems to be B
A wa B-sǒ da	A looks as if it were B*
A wa B-sǒ ni miéru	A seems to look as if it were B*
A wa B da sǒ desu	They say A is B
A wa B ni nite iru	A resembles B

The verb **niru** means 'bears a resemblance'; **hito ni nite iru** 'resembles someone, looks like someone else'.

10. 5. THE ALTERNATIVE. The alternative is a mood indicated by the endings **-tari, -dari**. The alternative forms are made in the same way as the perfect or the conditional; but instead of ending in **-ta (-da)** or **-tara (-dara)**, they end in **-tari (-dari)**. For example:

---

*But with **-sǒ** B is limited to copular noun, adjective base, or verb infinitive.

IMPERFECT	PERFECT	CONDITIONAL	ALTERNATIVE
tabéru 'eats'	tábeta	tábetara	tábetari
ireru 'puts in'	ireta	iretára	iretári
iru 'stays'	ita	itára	itári
ir-u 'is needed'	itta	ittára	ittári
hanásu 'speaks'	hanáshita	hanáshitara	hanáshitari
kúru 'comes'	kitá	kitára	kitári
suru 'does'	shita	shitára	shitári
hayái 'is early'	háyakatta	háyakattara	háyakattari
awánai			
'doesn't meet'	awánakatta	awánakattara	awánakattari
dá 'equals'	dátta	dáttara	dáttari

Some sentences contain one alternative form; others contain several. The most frequent type of sentence using the alternative contains two. The last alternative, or the only one, is always followed by some form of the verb **suru** 'does'—working as a kind of dummy auxiliary.

The meaning of the alternative is either (1) actions in alternation [now doing this, now doing that], (2) simutaneous actions [doing this and that at the same time], or (3) representative or typical actions [doing things like this; doing things like this and that]. If there is only one alternative in the sentence, it is a representative or typical action. Here are some examples:

Tegami o káitari hón o yóndari shimásu.	I write letters and read books [in alternation, or typically].

Shimbun o mítari rájio o kiitári shite imáshita.

He was looking at the paper and listening to the radio [in alternation, or simultaneously, or typically].

Tōkyō e iku to, Ginza o sampo shitári shimásu.

When I go to Tokyo, I walk (along) the Ginza (and so on).

Kono-goro wa oténki ga yókattari wárukattari shimásu ně.

Lately the weather is good one day, bad the next, isn't it.

Áme ga futtári yandári shimásu.

It rains intermittently (off and on).

Táguchi-san wa shimbun-kísha dattari, senséi dattari shita kotó ga arimásu.

Mr. Taguchi has been at various times first a reporter, then a teacher.

Ítsu mo okáshi shika tabénakattari, bíiru shika nománakattari suréba, byoki ni narimásu yo.

If you eat nothing but pastry and drink nothing but beer all the time, you'll get sick.

Góhan o tábetari tabénakattari suréba, byōki ni narimásu yo.

If you eat irregularly [sometimes eat, sometimes don't eat], you'll get sick.

10. 6. -NÁGARA. To describe two simultaneous actions by a single person, you can use the infinitive of a verb + **-nágara** [**-nagara,** if the verb is atonic] 'while ...ing' for the subsidiary action. **Rájio o kikinagara hón o yomi-**

máshita 'I read the book while listening to the radio'. If the two simultaneous actions are performed by different people, you have to say it another way: **Watakushi ga rájio o kiite iru aida ni tomodachi wa hón o yomimáshita** 'While I was listening to the radio, my friend read a book.'

The difference in meaning between …**kikinagara** …**yomimáshita** and …**kiitári** …**yóndari shimáshita** is that in the former case the one action is SUBORDI- NATED to the other—the emphasis is on reading the book, and the fact that this took place while you were listening to the radio is supplied as supplementary in- formation. In the latter case, using alternatives, the two actions are treated with equal emphasis—you be- haved [shimáshita] in a way such that the two actions were going on at the same time […-tari …-tari]. Using the alternatives, there are also two other possible interpre- tations—'doing the two things alternately' and 'doing such things as these'.

There is also another possible interpretation for the expressions with -nágara. Just as English 'while' means either 'during the same time as' or 'although', Japanese -nágara (or -nágara mo) sometimes means 'though':

Rájio o kikinagara, hón mo yomimáshita.	While [though] I listened to the radio, I also read a book.
Jidósha o kashite kureru to	While he said he'd lend me

iinagara, kasánakatta n   a car, he didn't.
desu.

The copular infinitive appears in a zero alternant,
leaving nágara standing as if a particle: Byōki nágara
génki ni shigoto o shite imásu 'Though ill he is working
hard', Génki nagara náni mo shimasén 'Though healthy
he does nothing.' And, with abbreviation of the noun no,
nágara sometimes appears after an adjective: Chiisái nagara chikara ga arimásu 'He may be small but he's got
strength.'

10. 7. ARU WITH PEOPLE. The verb iru means
'someone (or some animal) stays, someone exists (in a
place)' or, after a gerund, 'someone or something is doing
something'. The verb áru means either 'something exists
(in a place)' or 'something or someone exists (as an abso-
lute thing, as a relative, as a role), something or someone
is available, we have something or someone'. So, to say
'I have three brothers and sisters' you say Kyōdai ga san-
nin arimásu. To say 'My three brothers and sisters are
at home' you say Sannin no kyōdai ga uchi ni imásu.
Here are some other examples:

Kono gakkai ní wa kaichō   Our society does not have
to iu monó wa arimasén.   (such a thing as) a pres-
                                ident.

Inú ga arimásu (or imásu)   Do you have a dog (at your
ka?   house)?

Inú wa dóko ni imásu ka?   Where is the dog?

Gokyŏdai ga nánnin oari désu ka?	How many brothers and sisters do you have?
Níisan ga arimásu ka?	Do you have any older brothers?
Chichí wa imasén.	My father isn't here.

10. 8. KOTO NI SURU. KOTÓ NI NÁRU. After a modifying clause ending in the plain imperfect form, the expression **kotó ni suru** means 'decides to [do something]'; after a noun **ni suru** means 'decides on'. **Éiga o mí ni iku kotó ni shimáshita** 'We decided to go see a movie.' **Éiga ni shimáshita** 'We decided on the movies.' To say 'let's go see a movie' you can say either **Éiga o mí ni ikimashŏ** or **Éiga o mí ni iku kotó ni shimashŏ**— you would be more likely to say the latter if there are other things you might decide on instead. And you can just say **Éiga ni shimashŏ** 'Let's decide on the movie; let's make it the movies.' To say 'Let's not do something' you say **yamemashŏ** 'let's give it up, let's forget the idea' if the suggestion has already been made; but if just deciding from scratch, you say something like **Éiga o mí ni ikanai kotó ni shimashŏ** 'Let's decide not to go to the movies.' The verb **yameru** means 'stops something, gives something up'—**Kusuri o nómu no o yameté mo íi desu ka?** 'May I stop taking my medicine?' **Sono kŏbá de hataraku kotó o yamemáshita** 'I stopped working at that factory.' **Sono shigoto o yamemáshita** 'I gave up that job.'

The expression **kotó ni náru** means 'it is decided or settled that', **kotó ni nátte iru** means 'it has been decided or settled or arranged that.' **Senkyŏshi to shite Nihón e iku kotó ni nátte imasu** '[It's been decided or arranged that] we are to go to Japan as missionaries.' **Musukosan wa sono gakkō de benkyō suru kotó ni nátta sō desu.** 'I hear it was arranged for your son to study in that school.'

10. 9. SHIMAU AND OKU. The verb **shimau** means 'finishes up': **Shigoto o shimatté kara, yasumimáshita** 'After finishing the job, I rested [or, went to bed].' A gerund + **shimau** has the meaning 'finishes up doing, does completely or thoroughly; does and ends up=ends up doing'. **Hón o yónde shimaimáshita** 'I read the book through, I finished the book.' **Góhan o tábete shimaimasén deshita** 'I didn't finish (eating) dinner.' **Uchi no inú wa nagái aida byōki dátta keredomo, kinŏ shinde shimaimáshita** 'Our dog was sick for a long time, but yesterday it died.'

The verb **oku** means 'puts, places, puts aside'. **Kono empitsu o hón no sóba ni okimashŏ** 'I'll put (leave) this pencil by the book.' A gerund + **oku** has the meaning 'does something and puts it aside; does something in preparation; does something for later on; does something in advance.' The idea is that the action is done and then put to one side, with the expectation of some consequence or result at a later time rather than immediately. **Kono hón o yónde okimashŏ** 'I'll get this book read (and then I'll have it done when the teacher asks us about it).' **Raishū no shibai e ikitái kara, kippu o katte oite kudasái** 'I want to go to the play next week, so please buy tickets (in advance).' **Yōfuku o tēburu no ue ni oite oita kaban ni iremáshita** 'I put my clothes in a suitcase I had placed on the table (before—in anticipation).'

Notice the difference in meaning between the gerund + shimau and the gerund + oku—shimau suggests completion and thoroughness, oku suggests preparatory action in anticipation of later consequences or benefits.

Tegami o káite shimaimáshita.	I got the letter (all) written. I finished (writing) the letter.
Tegami o káite okimáshita.	I got the letter written (so that it would be done, for some later consequence). I wrote the letter and put it aside. I wrote the letter in advance.

The English verb 'get' is quite ambiguous: 'I got the letter written' can mean either of the Japanese sentences above, or it can also mean **Tegami o káite moraimáshita** 'I received the favor of someone writing the letter for me, I had someone write the letter for me.' [It could also mean **Tegami o kakasemáshita** 'I ordered someone to write the letter, I made someone write the letter.']

10.10. WÁKE. The noun **wáke** has several meanings— 'meaning; reason; explanation; case; special circumstances.' It is often used in explaining a situation.

Dó iu wáke desu ka?	What do you mean? What does it mean?

Kono wáke o oshiete kudasái.	Please explain the meaning of this.
Dố iu wáke de shigoto o yamemáshita ka?	Why [with what reason] did he quit his job?
Sono tegami o káku wake o tazunemáshita.	I asked his reason for writing that letter.
Inaka e iku wáke o iroiro hanashimáshita.	He gave all sorts of reasons for going to the country.
Shachō wa sonna ni isogashíi wake wa arimasén.	There's no reason the president of the firm should be so busy. He can't be so busy.
Sō iu wáke nara, dố shimashố ka?	If that's the case, what shall we do?
Tárō wa wáke ga wakátte imásu.	Taro is sensible. Taro knows what's what.
Oyogí wa wáke mo nái kotó desu.	Swimming is no trick at all; swimming is easy. [There are no special circumstances involved.]
Sō iu wáke de, iku kotó ga dekimasén deshita.	Because of that, I couldn't go.

10. 11. DOUBLE NEGATIVES. In English, we sometimes hear two negative words in a sentence where one would be enough—'Nobody never does anything' with the same meaning as 'Nobody ever does anything.' In Japanese when two negatives are used, the meaning is always changed. Notice the translations of the following sentences.

Kutsú o haita mama uchi e háiru hito mo nái koto wa arimasén.

It isn't that there aren't also people who enter the house with their shoes on = Some people also enter the house with their shoes on.

Nihongo mo dekínai wake ja arimasén ga, máda kotobá ga ammari wakarimasén.

It isn't (the case) that I can't talk Japanese, it's (just) that I can't understand too many words yet.

Kono kusuri o nomitái kotó wa arimasén ga, nománakereba yóku narimasén.

It isn't that I want to take this medicine, it's just that unless I do, I won't get well.

Éiga o mítaku nái to iu wáke ja arimasén ga, kyǒ wa isogashíi n desu.

I don't mean to say I don't want to see the movie, it's just that I'm busy today.

Kono hón o kómban yónde shimawanákereba naránai kotó wa nái wake ja arimasén.

I don't mean (to say) it isn't a fact that I have to finish this book tonight = I don't mean I don't have to finish this book tonight.

Kono hón o kómban yónde shimawanákereba naránai wake ja arimasén.

There's no reason you need to finish this book tonight.

10. 12. **NI CHIGAI NÁI**. The noun **chigai** 'discrepancy, error' is made from the infinitive of the verb **chigau**

'is different'. The expression **chigai nái** is based on the
construction **chigai wa nái** 'there is no error'. After a noun
or an imperfect or perfect verb or adjective, the expression
ni chigai nái means 'without a doubt, no doubt, certainly,
surely.' It is often translated 'must have done, must be,'
etc., but of course this is not the 'must' of obligation [='has
to'] which is equivalent to Japanese **-(a)nakereba narimasén** 'unless you do, it won't do.' Cf. **hazu dá** (pp. 151-2).

Kore ni chigai arimasén.	It must be this one. I'm sure this is it.
Okamoto-san ga kúru ni chigai arimasén.	Mr Okamoto will surely come.
Ojíisan wa Tárō-san ni tegami o káite oita ni chigai nái n desu.	Your grandfather has no doubt written to Taro (about the matter, in anticipation).

10.13. NI TSÚITE AND NI YOTTE. The verb **tsukú**
has the basic meaning 'comes in contact with'; the expression noun + **ni tsúite** has the meaning 'with respect to,
regarding, about'.

Gakkō no kotó ni tsúite obásan ni tegami o kakimáshita.	I wrote Grandmother a letter about school.
Andō-san no tokoró ni tsúite júnsa ni kikimáshita.	We asked the policeman about Mr. Ando's place.
Tanaka-san ni chigai nákatta desu. or **Tanaka-san dátta ni chigai nái desu.**	It must have been Mr. Tanaka.

Sensō (no kotó) ni tsúite   We were talking about the
hanáshite orimáshita.   war.

The whole expression is usually treated as an adverb, modifying the following predicate, but it sometimes occurs also as a noun phrase modifying a noun (and linked to it by the particle **no**):

Kéizai ni tsúite kíji o ka-   I wrote an article about
kimáshita.   economics.
Kéizai ni tsúite no kíji o   I wrote an article about
kakimáshita.   economics.

Compare **Keizai no kotó o kakimáshita** 'I wrote about economics'; **Tanaka-san no kotó o iimáshita** 'I told about Mr. Tanaka.'

The verb **yoru** has the basic meaning 'leans on, relies on'. The expressions noun + **ni yoru to** and noun+**ni yoréba** mean 'if you rely on... =according to...' **Shimbun ni yoru to, áme ga fúru sō desu** 'According to the paper, I see it's going to rain.' But 'according to SOMEONE' is more commonly ...**no hanashí de wa. Táro no hanashí de wa, okane ga nákute mo háiru kotó ga dekíru sō desu** 'According to Taro, you don't need money to get in.' [The phrase telling what the person said need not be followed by **só desu.**]

The expression noun + **ni yotte** means 'according to, depending on (its being)':

Tokoro ni yotte oténki ga   The weather varies from
chigaimásu.   place to place; depend-
**   ing on the place, the**
**   weather is different.**

Hito **ni** yotté wa, íken ga chigaimásu.	Opinions differ with people; different people have different views.
Tomodachi ga kúru ka, kónai ka ni yotte, ensoku ni shimásu.	We'll let the picnic [it's being a picnic] depend on whether my friend comes or not.
Ensoku wa tomodachi ga kúru ka, kónai ka ni yorimásu.	The picnic depends on whether my friend comes or not.

10. 14. CAUSATIVE, PASSIVE, AND PASSIVE CAUSA TIVE VERBS. Most Japanese verbs have corresponding CAUSATIVES, PASSIVE, and PASSIVE CAUSATIVES.

The causative verbs are made, for the most part, by adding the ending **-sase-ru** to vowel stems [-sasé-ru if the verb is tonic], the ending **-ase-ru** to consonant stems [-asé-ru if the verb is tonic]. Some of the meanings of such a verb are 'causes someone to do something; makes someone do something; lets someone do something'. The forms **kosaséru** 'lets someone come, makes someone come' (from **kúru** 'comes') and **saseru** 'lets someone do, makes someone do' (from **suru** 'does') are irregular.

The passive verbs are made by adding the ending **-rare--ru** to vowel stems [-raré-ru if the verb is tonic], the ending **-are-ru** to consonant stems [-aré-ru if the verb is tonic]. Some of the meanings are 'is affected by another person's action; undergoes the action; is adversely affected by the action'. Japanese passives can be made both from transitive verbs [those which take a direct object—like tabéru 'eats'] and intransitive verbs [those which do not ordinarily take a direct object—like shinu 'dies', iru 'stays']. The forms koraréru 'has someone come, is affected by someone's coming' and sareru 'gets done, is affected by someone's doing' are irregular.

There is also a passive formation made from causatives; this consists of adding the ending -rare-ru to the causative stem which ends in -(s)ase-, so that the complete ending for the passive causative is somewhat formidable— -(s)ase-rare-ru. There is a shortened form of this ending, alongside the longer form: -(s)asare-ru, that is -sasare-ru after a vowel stem, -asare-ru after a consonant stem. This shortened form may be visualized as -(s)as[e-r]are-ru; in other words, the last sound of the causative ending and the first sound of the passive ending are dropped. The meaning of the passive causative is something like 'is made to do, has to do.'

Of course the final -ru in these various endings is just the regular ending for the imperfect mood of vowel verbs—compare tabé-ru 'eats'. And these causatives, passives, and passive causatives can be inflected for all the usual moods: kosáseta, kosaseyǒ, kosásetara, kosásetari, kosásereba, kosasemásu, etc.; sareta, sareyō, saretára, saretári, saretárí, saretárí, saretárí, saretárí, saretárí, saretárí, saretárí, saretárí, sareréba, saremásu, etc.; tabesáseta, tabesaseyō, tabesásetara, tabesásetari, tabesásereba, tabesasemásu, etc.

Here is a list of some typical verbs together with the causative, passive and passive causative forms. All the forms are imperfect.

MEANING	SIMPLE VERB	CAUS.	PASS.	PASSIVE-CAUSATIVE LONG FORM	SHORT FORM
VOWEL STEMS }-ru		-sase-ru	-rare-ru	-sase-rare-ru	-sas-are-ru
eats	tabéru	tabesaséru	taberaréru	tabesaseraréru	tabesasaréru
looks at	míru	misaséru	miraréru	misaseraréru	misasaréru
stays	iru	isaseru	irareru	isaserareru	isasareru
CONS. STEMS }-u		-ase-ru	-are-ru	-ase-rare-ru	-as-are-ru
is needed	iru	iraseru	irareru	iraserareru	irasareru
rides	noru	noraseru	norareru	noraserareru	norasareru
waits	mátsu	mataséru	mataréru	mataseraréru	matasaréru
speaks	hanásu	hanasaséru	hanasaréru	hanasaseraréru	hanasaréru
meets	áu	awaséru	awaréru	awaseraréru	awasaréru
writes	káku	kakaséru	kakaréru	kakaseraréru	kakasaréru
swims	oyógu	oyogaséru	oyogaréru	oyogaseraréru	oyogasaréru
calls	yobu	yobaseru	yobareru	yobaserareru	yobasareru
reads	yómu	yomaséru	yomaréru	yomaseraréru	yomasaréru
comes	kúru	kosaséru	koraréru	kosaseraréru	kosaréru
does	suru	saseru	sareru	saserareru	sasareru

10. 15.   USE OF THE CAUSATIVE.   The basic meaning of the causative is 'someone causes someone else to do
something.' The person who does the causing is indicated by the particle ga or wa. The person caused to
perform the action takes either the particle o or ni if the
verb is intransitive; the particle ni if the verb is transitive,
since the particle o is used to indicate the object of the
verb itself.   Compare the following:

Cuchí wa áni o ikasemá-
  shita.   My father had my older
Chichí wa áni ni ikasemá-   brother go.
  shita.

Chichí wa áni ni tegami o kakasemáshita.	My father had my older brother write a letter.

If the object of the transitive verb is not mentioned, however, you sometimes hear the particle **o** used to indicate the person caused to perform the action:

Chichí wa áni ni kakase-máshita.	My father had my older brother write (it).
Chichí wa áni o kakasemá-shita.	

Once again there is the possibility of a sequence of clauses each marked off by the particle **ni**, with the **ni** of the clause nearest the verb referring to the meaning of the underlying simple verb and the more remote one referring to the causative meaning.

Chichí wa áni ni itoko ni tegami o kakasemáshita.	My father had my older brother write a letter to our cousin.

The causative is largely limited to situations in which a person is in a position to order or permit an action on the part of another person; for an act done as a favor, you use an expression with **morau** or **itadaku**. So, while you might say 'my father had my older brother write the letter' with the causative, you probably wouldn't say 'my older brother had my father write the letter' with the causative, since the social situation would indicate this was a favor: **Áni wa chichí ni tegami o káite moraimáshita.**

Here are some additional examples of uses of the causative:

Anáta wa máinichi kodomo ni nanjíkan benkyō sasemásu ka?

Dónna monó o kodomo ni tabesasemásu ka?

Tomodachi o mataséru kotó wa yóku arimasén né.

Jochū o isha no tokoró e mashố ka?

Ma ni áu yō ni, jidốsha o isogasemashố.

Jochū o isha no tokoró e isogasemáshita.

Anáta wa kodomo ni niwa de asobasemásu ka, uchi no náka de asobasemásu ka?

Tokidoki é ya jí o kakasemásu ka?

Sensếi wa tokidoki séito ni jibun no taiken o hanasasemásu.

Ryốshin ni awasetái tomodachi ga áru n desu.

Kodomótachi o kono heyá e kosasénai de kudasai.

Kono kotó o háha ni shirasemashố.

How many hours a day do you have the children study?

What do you feed the children?

It isn't good to keep friends waiting, you know.

Shall we have the maid call a cab?

I'll step on the gas so we'll get there in time.

I had the maid rush to the doctor's.

Do you have the children play in the garden or in the house?

Do you have them draw pictures and write characters sometimes?

The teacher sometimes has the students tell their own experiences.

I have a friend I'd like to introduce to my folks.

Please don't let the children come in this room.

We'll let our mother know about this.

10. 16. USES OF THE PASSIVE. If the underlying verb indicates an action that can be done to a person, the meaning of a passive expression is 'someone has something done to him, someone undergoes the action.' The person undergoing the action is indicated by the particle **wa** or **ga**; the person responsible for the action [the agent] is indicated by the particle **ni**.

Kodomo wa okăsan ni yobaremáshita.	The children were called by their mother.
Musumé wa dorobō ni korosaremáshita.	The girl was killed by a burglar.
Tárō wa Jírō ni utaremáshita.	Taro was struck by Jiro.

But if the underlying verb indicates some action that can't be done directly to a person—like 'dies, quits, comes, writes'—the meaning of the passive expression is 'someone is unfavorably affected by another person's action'.

Tonari no musumesan wa kyónen otōsan ni shinaremáshita.	The girl next door had her father die [suffered the death of her father] last year.
Watakushi wa sakúban, góhan o tabeyǒ to shita toki tomodachi ni koraremáshita.	Last night just as I was about to eat dinner, I had a friend drop in on me (unexpectedly) .

If the underlying verb takes an object, indicated by the particle **o**, this object may be retained in the passive expression.

Watakushi wa hón o tora-remáshita.	I had my book taken [swiped].
Hyakushǒ wa umá o nusu-máreta n desu.	The farmer had his horse stolen (on him).
Watakushi wa áni ni ame o minna taberaremáshita.	I had my candy all eaten up by my older brother.

The passive is usually used only to refer to *people* undergoing or suffering actions, but sometimes inanimate things are referred to also: **Tabako wa tsukuraremásu** 'Tobacco is [gets] grown.' To refer to an object being in a certain state resulting from someone's action, you use the gerund + áru: **Tegami wa mǒ káite (oite) arimásu** 'The letter is already written.' To say a person is in a state resulting from some other person's action, you use the passive construction: **Tárō wa Jírō ni utaremáshita** 'Taro was hit by Jiro.' To say a person or thing is in a state resulting from his own action, provided the verb is intransitive, you use the gerund + iru: **Tsukárete imásu** 'I'm tired [I'm in a state resulting from getting tired]', **Sóra ga hárete imásu** 'The sky is cleared [is in a state re-sulting from clearing up]', **Tomodachi ga kité imasu** 'My friend is here [is arrived]', **Mǒ itte imásu** 'They've gone [they are gone] already.'

The passive is also used just as an EXALTED FORM—with no special passive meaning—especially in the hon-orific speech of men.

Kómban otomodachi ga koraréru no de, ashitá ni itashimashǒ ka?	Since you have a friend coming tonight, shall we make it tomorrow?

402 ESSENTIAL JAPANESE

Tanaka-sensei wa otaku máde arúite ikaremáshita.	Dr Tanaka walked to his house.
Bokushi-san wa iroiro o-moshirói kotó o iware-máshita.	The pastor said all sorts of interesting things.
Musukosan wa heitai ni nararemáshita ně.	Your son became a soldier, didn't he?

Here are some more examples of passives.

Néko ni sakana o tabera-remáshita.	The cat ate our fish up.
Gakkō e iku tochū de, áme ni furaremáshita.	On the way to school, I got rained on.
Benkyō shite iru tóki ni, tomodachi ni korárete, komarimáshita.	I had a friend drop in on me in the midst of my studying, darn it.
Dénsha no náka de okane o toraremáshita.	I had money swiped on the streetcar.
Senséi ni yobarete, shikara-remáshita.	I was called and scolded by the teacher.
Kodomo ni jama o saretá no de, kono tegami o káite shimau kotó ga dekimasén deshita.	I couldn't get this letter finished because I was disturbed by the children.
Kinō osoku káettara kánai ni nakarete komarimá-shita yo!	When I was late getting home last night I was bothered by having my wife burst into tears.

10. 17. USE OF THE PASSIVE CAUSATIVE. Expressions with the passive causative mean things like 'someone was made to do something by someone else'. The person made to perform the action is indicated by the particle wa or ga, the person by whom he is made to perform the action is indicated by the particle ni.

Watakushi wa isha ni ku-suri o nomas(er)aremá-shita.

I was ordered to take medicine by the doctor = The doctor had me take medicine.

Chichí ni shimbun o katte kosas(er)aremáshita.

I had to go buy a newspaper for my father = My father had me go buy a newspaper.

Watakushidómo wa senséi ni sono éiga o mí ni ikas(er)arerú deshō.

I bet the teacher will have us see that movie [we'll be made to see that movie by the teacher].

Gúntai de wa heitai wa kirai na shigoto mo sase-raremásu.

They make the boys in service do disagreeable things.

Heya no sōji o saseraretári, mádo o arawaseraretári sentaku o saseraretári tokidoki ryōri mo sase-raretári shimásu.

They're made to clean rooms, wash windows, do the laundry, and even cook sometimes.

Nagái michí o arukas(er)a-réru koto ga ichiban kírai da só desu.

I hear the thing they hate most is being made to make long marches [walk long roads].

Watakushítachi wa senséi ni máinichi hón o yoma-seráretari, jí o kakaserá-retari, hanashí o sasera-retári shimásu.	We have the teacher have us read [books], write [characters], and give talks every day.

10. 18. THE POTENTIAL. Any Japanese verb can be made into a potential verb with the meaning 'is able to be done'. For vowel verbs, the potential is always exactly the same as the passive. **Tabe-raré-ru** means either 'someone gets something eaten on them, someone suffers someone else's eating something' or 'something can get eaten = someone can eat something.' **Ko-raré-ru** means 'someone has someone else come [to their disadvantage]' or 'someone can come.' For consonant verbs, too, the full passive forms may be potential: **yob-are-ru** 'gets called' or 'can be called'. There is also a SHORT POTENTIAL for CONSONANT verbs only, made by adding **-e-ru** [**-é-ru** if the verb is tonic] to the stem: **yob-e-ru** 'can be called', **yom-é-ru** 'can be read', **aruk-é-ru** 'can walk', etc.* This SHORT POTENTIAL is just an abbreviation of the longer potential which is identical with the passive: **-[ar]é-ru.** Compare the short form of the passive causative: **-(s)as[e-r]aré-ru.**

Since the polite forms of the short potential differ from the polite forms of the ordinary verb only by having the vowel **e** instead of **i** before the endings **-másu, -máshita,** etc., it is very important to pronuonce these vowels clearly and distinctly so that **kaemásu** 'can buy' will not sound like **kaimásu** 'will buy', or **nomemásu** 'can

---

*Some Tokyo speakers use short potentials from vowel verbs too: **tabe-ré-ru** 'can be eaten; can eat'.

drink' like nomimásu 'will drink.' Occasionally, the potential of one verb will sound just like the ordinary form of some other verb: kakéru can be either kak-é-ru 'can be written' or kaké-ru 'hangs; makes a phone call, etc.'

The meaning of the potential verbs is 'something can be done', and the something itself takes the particle ga: Kono jí ga kakemásu 'This character can be written = I can write this character.' You're already familiar with this process—Kono musumé ga sukí desu 'This girl is liked = I like this girl.' The person who can do something is marked by either wa or ga depending on the emphasis; sometimes, the person can be explicitly marked by ni:

Watakushi wa [or Watakushi ní wa] Nihongo ga yomemásu.	I can read Japanese.
Nihongo wa watakushi ga [or watakushi ni] yomemásu.	It's I that can read Japanese.

The potential of suru 'does' is the same as its passive sareru. But instead of sareru, the verb dekíru 'is possible' is often substituted. So for the potential of expressions involving verbal nouns like benkyō 'study', sampo 'walk', you say Benkyō dekimásu ka? 'Can you study?' Ame ga futtá kara, sampo dekimasén deshita 'It rained, so we couldn't take our walk.'

The meaning of any potential is about the same as the meaning of the ordinary verb imperfect + kotó ga dekíru: Nihongo ga yomemásu ka? = Nihongo o yómu kotó ga dekimásu ka? 'Can you read Japanese?'

Instead of kikareru (or kikeru) and miraréru for kiku 'hears' and míru 'sees', you often hear the derived verbs kikoeru 'is heard, can be heard', and miéru 'is seen, can be seen, appears.'

Here are some examples of the potential in sentences:

Ano mizu wa nomaremásu [nomemásu] ka?
Can that water be drunk— Is that water drinkable?

Náni ka taberaremásu ka?
Can you eat something?

Nihongo no shimbun ga yomaremásu [yomemásu].
I can read a Japanese newspaper.

Hitóri de koráretara, hitóri de kité kudasai.
If you can come by yourself, please do so.

Anáta wa asoko máde arukaremásu [arukemásu] ka?
Can you walk over to that place?

Minna taberarénakattara, nokóshite mo íi desu.
If you can't eat it all, you may leave (some).

Shikóku made hikóki de ikaremásu [ikemásu] ka?
Can you go to Shikoku by plane?

Kono tegami wa yoménakatta kara, yónde moraimáshita.
I couldn't read this letter, so I had it read for me.

Tegami ga kakénakatta kara, dcnwa o kakcmáshita.
I couldn't write a letter, so I telephoned.

Kono jí ga kakaremásu [kakemásu] ka?
Can you write this character?

Hitóri de koraremásu ka?
Can you come by yourself?

You will recall that the negative of the short potential of **iku** 'goes' —**ikemasén**—is also used with the special meaning 'it's no good, it won't do.' **Kō káite wa ikemasén** 'You mustn't write this way.' Sometimes it means 'that's too bad'—when someone has told you some ill that has befallen him, you may sympathize with **Sore wa ikemasén deshita ně** 'That was too bad, wasn't it?'

10. 19. **KA MO SHIRENÁI.** The form **shirenái** [**shiremasén**] is the negative of the short potential of **shir-u** 'knows', and means 'can not be known'. **Ka mo shirenái** means something like 'it can't be known even whether', and is added after a predicate in the plain imperfect or perfect or after a noun [with the plain copula **dá** dropping before **ka** as usual] with the meaning 'maybe, perhaps, it may be that.' Sometimes the sentence may be introduced by the adverb **kitto** 'I bet; like as not' or by the lively phrase **hyotto shitára** 'by some chance; just'. Here are some examples of **ka mo shirenái**:

Jitsugyōka ká mo shiremásén.	He may be a businessman.
Áme ga fúru ka mo shirenái kara, kasa o motte ikimashǒ.	It may rain, so I'll take an umbrella.
Ashitá wa tegami ga kúru ka mo shiremasén.	Maybe a letter will come tomorrow.
Kómban wa áme ga fúru ka mo shiremasén.	It may rain this evening.
Gogo ní wa harerú ka mo shiremasén ně.	In the afternoon, it may clear up, you know.

Áme wa furánai ka mo shi-renái keredomo tó-ni-ka-ku kasa o motte ikima-shō.

It may not rain, but any-way [nevertheless] I'll take my umbrella.

Kitto Ōsaka e ittára, Ma-tsumoto-san ni aéru ka mo shiremasén.

I bet when you go to Osa-ka you may be able to see Mr Matsumoto.

Hyotto shitára, ma ni awá-nai ka mo shirenái kara, kuruma de ikimashō.

We might just happen not to be on time, so let's take a taxi.

Kippu o moraenái ka mo shirenái keredomo, tó-ni-kaku kiite mimashṓ.

We may not be able to get tickets, but anyway let's find out.

Osoku ittára hairénai ka mo shirenái kara, háya-ku ikimashṓ.

If we go late, we may not be able to get in, so let's go early.

10. 20. **KA SHIRA**. The expression **ka shira** is added to predicates in the same sort of way as **ka mo shirenái** but the meaning is a little different—'I wonder if.' This is very similar to the meaning of **ka né** at the end of a sentence. The difference is that you are really talking to yourself with **ka shira**, whereas with **ka né** you're half-way talking to someone else.

Kómban áme ga fúru ka shira.

I wonder if it's going to rain tonight.

Mádo o shímeta ka shira.

I wonder if I closed the windows.

Sonna ni Nihón e ikitái ka

I wonder if they really

shira.	want to go to Japan so much.
Sonna ni okane ga hoshíi ka shira.	I wonder if they want money that much.

10. 21. DESIDERATIVE VERBS. You have learned that each verb can underlie a desiderative adjective with the meaning 'wants to'—**tabéru** 'eats', **tabetái** 'wants to eat'; **iku** 'goes', **ikitai** 'wants to go'. There is also, for each verb, a DESIDERATIVE VERB made by adding **-ta-gar-u** [**-ta-gár-u** if the verb is tonic] to the infinitive. So, alongside the adjective **tabetái** 'wants to eat', we have the verb **tabetagáru** 'is eager to eat, desires to eat'; alongside the adjective **ikitai** 'wants to go', we have the verb **ikitagaru** 'is eager to go, desires to go'. [The **-ta-** element is the same in the forms with **-ta-i** and the forms with **-ta-gar-u**.]

These desiderative verbs are often used in expressions consisting of the gerund **-te + iru** with little difference in meaning or English translational equivalent from the ordinary forms. **Kamakurá e ikitagarimásu** and **Kamakurá e ikitagatte imásu** both mean about the same thing— 'He wants to go to Kamakura'—and another way to say it is **Kamakurá e ikitai yō desu.** The desiderative verbs seem to be a bit stronger in meaning than the desiderative adjectives and you seldom use them of yourself.

Here are some examples:

Kono-goro no hitó wa son-	People nowadays don't

na hón wa yomitagari-
masén.

want to read that sort
of book.

Íma Nihon no wakái hitó-
tachi wa Beikoku no éi-
ga o mitagarimásu.

Japanese young people are
now eager to see Amer-
ican films.

Eigo o naraitagátte imásu.

They're eager to learn
English.

Nihón ni iru watakushi no
tomodachi wa Nihonjin
no uchí e asobi ni ikita-
gatte imásu keredomo,
nakanaka iku kikái ga
nái n desu.

My friend who's in Japan
is eager to visit Japa-
nese homes, but he never
has the opportunity.

Notice that the desiderative verbs take direct objects
with the particle o—Eigo o naraitagátte imasu, but the
desiderative adjectives take either direct objects with o
or emphatic subjects with ga—Eigo o naraitái desu or
Eigo ga naraitái desu [latter usage preferred].

10. 22. MONÓ DESU. You have learned that the noun
monó means 'a thing that you can touch or feel' —as contrasted with kotó, an abstract thing you talk about. You
have also learned it sometimes means 'guy, fellow', a
slightly less polite term than hito 'person'. There is a
special use of monó desu in which the noun does not
have a concrete meaning but means something like 'in
the nature of things...', 'it's characteristic that...', 'it
happens that...', 'such is life'. Often the adverb tokaku
'likely, naturally' [do not confuse with tó-ni-kaku 'anyway, nevertheless'] is added somewhere in the sentence.

For example, **Tokaku bimbōnin ní wa kodomo ga ōi monó desu** 'Poor people always seem to have lots of children.' **Kodomo wa yóku sonna tokoró e ikitagaru monó desu** 'Children just naturally seem to want to go such places.' **Monó** is often abbreviated **món** in these expressions: **món desu**. Here are additional examples:

Ikenai to iu to, kodomo wa tokaku yaritagaru monó desu.	If you say they mustn't [do something], children always want to do it.
Toshiyori wa sonna monó o tabetagáru món desu.	It's natural for old folks to be eager to eat that sort of thing.
Jūgorokusai no kodomo wa yóku sonna kotó o iitagáru mon desu.	Children of 15 and 16 years naturally want to say such things a lot.

When the expression **monó desu** is preceded by the perfect the meaning is something like 'used to' [that is, it used to be characteristic for someone to do something].

Tōkyō ni súnde ita tokí ni wa, yóku Ginza c asobi ni itta monó desu.	When I was living in Tokyo, I often used to go to the Ginza [for amusement].
Gakkō ni ita tokí ni wa, yóku sonna hón o yónda món desu.	When I was in school, I used to read such books a lot.
Kodomo no tokí ni wa, yóku sonna kotó o shite asonda món desu.	When I was a child, I used to play a lot at such things.

| Gúntai ni ita tokí ni wa, yóku sake o nónde sawáida món desu. | When I was in the Army, I used to drink liquor and raise hell. |
| Okane ga nákute komátte ita tokí ni wa, yóku ane no uchí e góhan o tábe ni itta monó desu. | When I was in a fix without any money, I used to go to my brother's house to eat a lot. |

C. EXERCISES.

1. Make each of the following sentences mean 'I hear that...' or 'They say that...' by changing the predicate to the appropriate plain form and adding sŏ desu. Then make each one mean 'It seems that...' by adding rashíi desu. For instance, the first one will be Káigun ni háitta sō desu 'They say he joined the Navy,' and Káigun ni haitta rashíi desu 'He seems to have joined the Navy.'

   1. Káigun ni hairimáshita.
   2. Gúntai ni ita tokí ni wa, yóku sake o nónde sawáida monó desu.
   3. Kippu o moraemasén.
   4. Sakana wa tábezu ni nokoshimáshita.
   5. Omúsukosan wa jiténsha o toraremáshita.
   6. Heitai wa sentaku o saseraremásu.
   7. Jochū wa kodomo o uchi no sóba de asobasemáshita.
   8. Sensō ni tsúite no kíji ga sakúban no shimbun ni déte imashita.
   9. Júnsa ni kiite imásu.
   10. Gúntai ni háitta ni chigai arimasén.

11. Sono gunkan wa shizumimáshita.
12. Súihei wa oborejini suru osoré ga arimásu.

2. For each of the following items there are two or three sentences. Combine these into one sentence that means 'somebody does this and that (and that)' by using the alternative forms. For instance, the first will be Hataraitári yasúndari shimásu 'We work a while, then rest a while.'

1. Hatarakimásu. Yasumimásu.
2. Hanashimásu. Kikimásu. Hón o yomimásu.
3. Úmi e háitte oyogimásu. Hamá de asobimásu.
4. Nihongo de hanáshite imáshita. Eigo de hanáshite imáshita.
5. Héisha ni ite kirai na shigoto o saseraremáshita. Machí e itte sake o nónde sawagimáshita.
6. Áme ga fútte imásu. Yukí ga fútte imásu.
7. Góhan o tábete imáshita. Ocha o nónde imáshita.
8. Umá o nusumaremásu. Kodomo o korosaremásu.
9. O'kásan ni shikararemáshita. Tonari no kodomo ni utaremáshita. Ammari okáshi o tábete byōki ni narimáshita.
10. Rájio o kikimáshita. Térebi o mimáshita.

3. For each of the following items there two sentences. Combine the two into one sentence meaning 'while I did something else'. For instance, the first will be Dénsha ni notte kinágara shimbun o yomimáshita 'While riding on the streetcar, I read the paper.'

1. Dénsha ni notte kimáshita. Shimbun o yomimá-shita.
2. Óngaku o kikimáshita. Tegami o kakimáshita.
3. Tanaka-san to hanáshite imáshita. Sono jimúsho o míte imáshita.
4. Ryōri shimásu. Rájio o kikimásu.
5. Sentaku o shimásu. Kodomo o uchi no sóba de asobasemásu.

4. Make each of the following sentences mean 'some-body can do something'. Do it first with the ex-pression kotó ga dekimásu; then with a potential. verb. If the verb has a consonant stem give both the longer potential and the short form.

1. Yūbínkyoku de wa, dempō o uchimásu.
2. Kono denwáshitsu de wa, chōkyoridénwa o kake-másu.
3. Sono tegami wa Nihongo de kakimásu ka?
4. Kono sentaku o háyaku shimásu ka?
5. Dáre ka ni mádo o arawasemásu ka?
6. Dóko de shimbun o kaimásu ka?
7. Okosan wa hitóri de arukimásu ka?
8. Mō sukóshi isogimásu ka?
9. Okinawa máde hikóki de ikimásu ka?
10. Kono mizu wa nomimásu ka?

5. Make each of the following sentences mean 'I had the maid do it' by adding Jochū ni... at the begin-ning, and making the verb causative.

1. Mádo o araimáshita.

2. Kaimono ni ikimáshita.
3. Tegami o dashimáshita.
4. Oishii tabemóno o tsukurimáshita.
5. Kono kíji o mimáshita.
6. Háiyā o yobimáshita.
7. Tonari no hitó ni sō iimáshita.
8. Mō sukóshi isogimáshita.
9. Júnsa ni kikimáshita.
10. To o shimemáshita.

6. Make each of the following sentences mean 'I suffered from someone's doing something—I had someone do something to me or to my disadvantage' by changing the particle after the subject to ni and making the verb passive.

1. Jochū ga tegami o yomimáshita.
2. Senséi ga shikarimáshita.
3. Isogashíi toki ni okyaku ga kimáshita.
4. Góhan o tabeyó to shita tokí ni, kodomo ga uchi o demáshita.
5. Dáre ka okane o torimáshita.
6. Chichí ga shinimáshita.
7. Dorobō ga jidōsha o nusumimáshita.
8. Néko ga sakana o tabemáshita.
9. Musumé ga kasa o naku-shimáshita.
10. Ten-in wa shitsúrei na kotó o iimáshita.

D. COMPREHENSION.

[Yamamoto-san wa Haraguchi-san to hanáshite
iru tokoró desu.]

Y.   Musukosan wa heitai ni nátta sō desu nĕ.

H.   Só desu. Kōkūtai ni hairitagátte itá no ni, tōtō hohei ni nátta n desu.

Y.   Watakushi ga heitai dátta toki ni wa, ammari arukaserárete, heikō shita món desu. Anáta wa káigun deshita nĕ.

H.   Chigaimásu. Rikusentai no gúnsō deshita. Senzen wa káigun no shōkō ni naritákute, daigaku ni hairimáshita ga, benkyō ga ammari sukí ja nákatta no de, yamete, sensō ni nátte kara rikusentai ni háitta n desu.

Y.   Sore dá kara, gunkan ni notta kotó ga átta n desu nĕ.

H.   Yóku arimáshita. Áru toki, Nan-yō ni imáshita ga, rikusentai no notte ita gunkan wa bakugeki sarete shizunde shimaimáshita. Oborejini suru to iu tokoró ni kobune ga míeta no de, soko máde oyóide ikō to shitá kedo, ashí ga tsukárete soko máde oyogemasén deshita.

Y.   Hontō ni komarimáshita nĕ. Sore kara, dó shimáshita ka?

H.   Tomodachi ni mirárete tasukeraremáshita. Anáta mo Nan-yō déshita ka?

Y.   Iie, Shína deshita. Yonen gúrai soko ni imáshita.

H.   Shína de mo taihen déshita nĕ.

Y.   Só desu. Omoshirói kotó mo nákatta to iu wáke ja arimasén ga, futsū wa hito o korosaseraretári, shōkō ni shikararetári shite itá

kara, sensō ga dáikirai ni narimáshita. Shan-
hai [Shanghai] no héisha ni ita tokí ni wa,
ban ni náru to machí e itte sake o nónde sawáida monó desu. Áru tokoró de ammari
sake o nomi-súgite nisanjíkan neta áto de
ókite míru to, pokétto ni irete oita okane o
nusumárete imáshita.

H. Sore wa ikemasén deshita nế.

Y. Okane dake toráreta no ja arimasén deshita.
Ryốshin kara moratta kín no tokei mo toraremáshita.

H. Dorobō ni monó o torarerú no wa baka rashíi
desu nế. Tokaku heitai wa sensō ga kirai
ni nátte sake o nónde sawáidari suru món
desu nế.

Y. Số desu. Sore kara sake o nónda otokó wa
onná ni aitagátte, iroiro warúi tokoro de
asondári surú no de, okane ya tokei nádo o
nusumárete shimau monó desu.

H. Sore wa số to, Amerika no gúntai ni tsúite no
kíji ga shimbun ni déte imáshita ga, sono
kíji ni yoru to, Amerika no gúntai ni wa
onna no hitó mo hairaréru số desu.

Y. Số desu ka? Watakushi no héisha ni onna
no heitai ga háitte itára, omoshírokatta ni
chigai arimasén.

APPENDIX I.

OTHER STYLES OF SPEECH.

1. THE IMPERSONAL STYLE. In lectures, radio announcements, and the like, Japanese often use the impersonal style. It is also seen in books and articles. Here are the principal ways in which this style differs from the usual polite style of speech (See also p. 142 fn.):

1. Polite forms are not used; instead, the plain forms are used even at the end of sentences. Sometimes, however, a Japanese will end his explanatory sentences with ...no de arimásu instead of ...no de áru 'it is a fact that...' Here are some examples:

MEANING	POLITE	IMPERSONAL
He was born in 1900.	1900-nen ni umaremá-shita.	1900-nen ni umareta.
There is no explana-tion.	Setsumei wa arimasén.	Setsumei wa nái.

2. Colloquial words, lively particles like yo and né, and contractions like ja for dé wa and n for no, are avoided.

3. The copula dá is replaced by the phrase de áru or de arimásu. The phrase is inflected just like áru:

Imperfect	de áru	=dá [na, no]	de arimásu	=désu
Perfect	de átta	=dátta	de arimáshita	=déshita
Tentative	de arŏ	=darō	de arimashŏ	=deshŏ
Gerund	de átte	=dé	de arimáshite	=déshite
Infinitive	de ári	=ni, dé		

Provisional   de áreba =nára
Conditional   de áttara=dáttara de arimáshitara=déshitara
Alternative   de áttari =dáttari de arimáshitari =déshitari

Here are some examples:

MEANING	POLITE	IMPERSONAL
China is Japan's neighbor.	Shína wa Nihon no tonari désu.	Shína wa Nihon no tonari de áru.
That was before the war.	Sore wa senzen déshita.	Sore wa senzen de átta.
Prices have risen.	Nedan wa agattá n desu.	Nedan wa agattá no de áru.

4. Instead of a gerund, an infinitive is often used at the end of a clause meaning 'does and, did and' or 'is and, was and'. This is just a stylistic variant of the use of the gerund.

Japan is a Pacific nation, and England is an Atlantic nation.	Nihón wa Taihéiyō no kuni dé, Igirisu wa Taiséiyō no kuni désu.	Nihón wa Taihéiyō no kuni de ári, Igirisu wa Taiséiyō no kuni de áru.
The older brother became a doctor, and the younger a teacher.	Níisan wa isha ni nátte, otōtosan wa senséi ni narimáshita.	Níisama wa isha ni nári, otōtosama wa senséi ni nátta (no de áru).
They have no money and can't buy food.	Okane ga nákute, tabemóno o kau kotó ga dekimasén.	Okane ga náku tabemóno o kau kotó ga dekínai.

5. Nouns are sometimes strung together in a series without a connecting particle [we would expect to or ya in the polite style]. There is often, but not always, a pause after each item except the last, which is usually followed by the appropriate particle to link the entire phrase up with the rest of the sentence.

Kyoto, Osaka, and	Kyóto ya Ōsaka ya	Kyóto Ōsaka Kóbe wa
Kobe are all in	Kóbe wa minna	mina Kánsai de áru.
Kansai.	Kánsai desu.	

2. THE PLAIN STYLE. The most down-to-earth way of talking in Japanese is that of the plain style [also called the familiar style, the intimate style, the ordinary style]. This sort of speech is used among workmen, servicemen, waitresses and geisha-girls, students, and others in a situation where a certain amount of camaraderie is inherent. It is also often used within the family, with truly intimate friends, and in certain set phrases (like proverbs) which are inserted into otherwise polite-style speech. The foreigner seldom has occasion to use much of this style himself, but he hears a good deal of it around him. Here are some of the characteristics of this style of speech:

1. DIFFERENCE BETWEEN WOMEN'S SPEECH AND MEN'S SPEECH. In the polite style, there is very little difference between the way women talk and the way men talk. Women will sometimes choose a more elegant expression—such as **tearai** or **gofujō** for 'toilet', where men would not avoid more plain-spoken terms such as **benjó** or **habakari**. Women are expected to use the honorific style more than men, and they often attach the honorific prefix **o-** to nouns even when speaking in the polite or plain styles.

Certain constructions are more common with one sex or the other; the use of the passive in the exalted sense is largely confined to the speech of men. In the plain style, women often use the plain forms of the honorific verbs—like **irassháru, máiru, oide ni náru, itasu, nasáru**— but men usually use the plain forms of the neutral verbs.

Women seem to leave more of their sentences dangling with non-finite verbal expressions that men do, although sentence fragments are widespread in the plain style for both sexes. Japanese often turn a finite verb expression into a noun expression with the noun **no** or **kotó** 'fact', which is frequently followed by the particle **yo**, or just ends the sentence itself: **Ikú no yo** 'I'm going.' **Kore ná no yo** 'It's this one.' **Tadáima kitá no?** 'Did you just get here?'

Women often use **atashi** for **watashi** or **watakushi** 'I' in plain or sometimes in polite speech, and men often substitute **boku** [or **bóku**] for **watakushi**. The explicit plural of **boku** is **bókura**. Men also use **kimi** (explicit plural **kimítachi** or **kimíra**) for **anáta** 'you'. There are other impolite pronouns such as **ore** 'I' which are considered vulgar; and the condescending word **omae** 'you' is rather insulting except when used in talking to children.

2. USE OF PARTICLES. The particles **wa, ga,** and **o** are freely dropped. The question particle **ka** is often dropped. The meaning is carried by the context:

Tabako áru (ka)?=**Tabako ga áru ka?**	Do you have any cigarettes?
Okáshi tábete iru (ka)?= **Okáshi o tábete irú ka?**	Are you eating sweets?

Dóko e iku? = **Dóko c ikú**   Where are you going?
ka?
Náni tábete iru? = **Náni o**   What are you eating?
tábete irú ka?

In the speech of men, the question particle **ka** is often replaced by **ká ne** [contraction **kai**] or **dá ne** [contraction **dai**]. If the sentence contains an interrogative word, **dá ne** [**dai**] is more likely to occur.

Nán dai? = **Nán desu ka?**   What is it?
Omoshirói kai? = **Omoshi-**   Is it interesting?
rói desu ka?

The plain copula **dá** usually drops before **ka**:

Tomodachi kai? or **Tomo-**   Is it your friend?
dachi ka? = **Tomodachi**
désu ka?
Kírei kai? or **Kírei ka?**   Is she pretty?
= **Kírei desu ka?**

The final intensive particle **yo** occurs more commonly in the plain-style for both men and women. Women often end a plain-style sentence with **wa** (or **wa yo!**); you will occasionally hear men use final **wa**, but only after a polite-style sentence. Men sometimes use final **zo!** or **ze!** to be forceful. Both men and (especially) women freely punctuate their relaxed speech with the particle **né!** ('you see, you know, I mean'); in Tokyo, the more vigorous **sa!** ('I tell you, you see, mind you!') is often used instead.

3. USE OF CONTRACTIONS. Contractions occur

in all styles of speech, but they are more common in the plain style. Some contractions are peculiar to individual words—like the women's form **atashi** for **watashi**, and **ánta** for **anáta**; others are more widespread shortenings or modifications of certain sound sequences.

The topic particle **wa** is often shortened to just **a**. We find **jidósha-a** [= **jidóshā**] alongside **jidósha wa** 'as for the car', and **kinó-a** alongside **kinó wa** 'as for yesterday'. A front vowel—i or e—at the end of a word preceding **wa** may be replaced by **y**: **kory-a** for **kore wa**, **áky-a** for **áki wa**. Or it may be replaced by nothing: **kor-a** for **kore wa**, **okásh-a** for **okáshi wa**. The shortened form of **wa**, **a**, is then sometimes lengthened before a pause to **ā**: **koryā** or **korā** = **kore wa**.

This explains the contraction **já** [or **jā**] from **dé wa**. The sequence **d-y** does not occur in modern Japanese, so **j** is substituted for it. A gerund ending in **-de** followed by the particle **wa** becomes **-ja** in the same way: **Kono mizu o nónja ikenai yo** = **Kono mizu o nónde wa ikenai yo** 'Don't drink this water.' This contraction is paralleled by the contraction of **-cha** [or **-chā**] for **-te wa** [ch since the sequence **t-y** does not occur in modern Japanese]: **Soko e itcha ikenai yo** = **Soko e itté wa ikenai yo** 'You mustn't go there.' **Máinichi sakana o tabénakucha ikenai** = **Máinichi sakana o tabénakute wa ikenai** 'Every day we have to eat fish.' **Shitsúrei ni hanáshicha damé da** = **Shitsúrei ni hanáshite wa damé da** 'It's no good to talk rudely.'

The provisional endings **-(r)eba** and **-kereba** are often contracted to **-(r)ya** [or **-(r)yā**] and **-kerya** [or **-keryá**]: **Kono** kusuri nománakerya narán = Kono kusuri o nománakere-ba naránai 'I have to take this medicine.' Kore tabérya byōki ni náru yo = Kore o tabéreba byōki ni náru yo 'If you eat this, you'll get sick.'

A gerund + the verb shimau 'finishes, does complete-ly' is contracted in the following way: -te shimau becomes -chimau or -chau; -de shimau becomes -jimau or -jau. Shinjimatta or Shinjatta=Shinde shimatta 'He died.' Tábechimatta or Tábechatta = Tábete shimatta 'He ate it all up.'

The initial i of the verb iru 'stays, is ...ing' often drops after a gerund: Náni shite-ru? = Náni o shite irú ka? 'What are you doing?' The final e of the gerund form is often dropped before the verb oku 'puts away, does for later': Koko ni oit-oita empitsu wa dóko e itta? = Koko ni oite oita empitsu wa dóko e ittá ka? 'Where did the pencil go I put here?' Kippu katt-oita = Kippu o katte oita 'I bought the tickets (in advance).'

The particle keredomo is often shortened to keredo or kedo. Shortenings of monó to món and of no to just n have already been noted; the use of these, like the use of ja for dé wa, is common in polite speech, too.

The plain negative ending -(a)nai is often contracted to -(a)n: Wakarán desu nĕ = Wakaránai desu ne 'I don't know, you see.' Wakarán yo = Wakaránai yo 'I don't know.' [The polite negative ending -masén also ends in -n, as if it were from a form -mas-ena-i.]

The word tte is said to be a contraction of to itte 'saying thus', but it is perhaps best treated as just another particle. The word has two uses: one is the same as the

quoting particle **to** [or **to itte**], the other is the same as
the topic particle **wa**.* The gerund and conditional forms
of the copula, **dé** and **nára**, are also often used with about
the same meaning as **wa** and **tte**—singling out a topic for
consideration:

Kono éiga nara, íi desu.	
Kono éiga de, íi desu.	This movie'll be OK.
Kono éiga wa, íi desu.	
Kono éiga tte, íi desu.	
Sayonára tte, itchatta =	He said goodbye and left.
Sayonára to itte, itte	
shimatta.	

In addition to **tte,** some speakers use **ttára** and **tcha**—from
to ittára, to itté wa—in a similar fashion, as a sort of lively
substitute for the drab particle **wa.**

  In addition to these and other more-or-less standard-
ized contractions, some speakers tend to *underarticulate*
many of their sounds, particularly certain consonants.
The expression **Só desu ně** 'Let me see now' frequently
sounds as if the d were completely dropped, and the **e** is
also difficult to distinguish: **Só-s-ně.**

  4. CHOICE OF FORMS. In the polite style, plain
forms of verbs, adjectives and the copula are usual in
all positions except at the end of the sentence, and sometimes in the middle before loosely connective particles
like **ga, keredomo.** Occasionally, polite forms are used
within the sentence to give an extra-polite flavor. In
plain speech, the plain forms are usual in all positions.
The plain copula is often omitted, especially in questions.

---

*For a third use (=... **só desu**) see p. 378.

5. THE PLAIN IMPERATIVE. In the polite style, you usually make commands in a round-about way. If a genuine imperative form is used, it is from one of the exalted verbs: **nasái** from **nasáru, kudasái** or **kudasai-máse** from **kudasáru.** In plain speech, too, oblique commands are common: **Shimbun katté kite kurén ka=Shimbun o katté kite kurenái ka** 'Won't you go buy me a newspaper, please?' Often, you use the simple gerund: **Chótto mátte (yo)!** 'Wait a minute!'

In addition there is a plain imperative form, but you seldom use it except when showing extreme impatience, or when quoting rather impersonal commands. For vowel verbs, there are two endings: **-yo** (more common in quotations) and **-ro;** and the **-ro** imperative may be followed by the particle **yo!** For consonant verbs, **-e** is added to the stem, and the form is often followed by the particle **yo!** [When **yo!** follows, an atonic imperative picks up a final accent: **akero** but **akeró yo!, ike** but **iké yo!**] **Kúru** and **suru** are irregular in their forms. Study the following examples:

VOWEL VERBS

MEANING	IMPERFECT	IMPERATIVE	
	-ru	**-yo**	**-ro**
looks	**mí-ru**	**mí-yo**	**mí-ro**
leaves	**dé-ru**	**dé-yo**	**dé-ro**
opens it	**ake-ru**	**ake-yo**	**ake-ro**
stays	**i-ru**	**i-yo**	**i-ro**
does	**su-ru** [Irreg.!]	**se-yo** [Irreg.!]	**shi-ro**
comes	**kú-ru** [Irreg.!]	——	**kói** [Irreg.!]*

*And put with the **-ro** forms because it can be followed by the particle **yo!**

CONSONANT VERBS

MEANING	IMPERFECT -u	IMPERATIVE -e
waits	mát[s]-u	mát-e
returns	káer-u	káer-e
buys	ka[w]-u	ka-e
talks	hanás-u	hanás-e
listens	kik-u	kik-e
rushes	isóg-u	isóg-e
calls	yob-u	yob-e
reads	yóm-u	yóm-e
goes	ik-u	ik-e

The plain NEGATIVE IMPERATIVE is made by adding the particle **na!** 'do not!' to the plain imperfect: **Kúru na** 'Don't come', **Mátsu na** 'Don't wait', **Tabako nómu na** 'Don't smoke', **Akerú na** 'Don't open it'. Avoid confusing this with another type of plain command (rather "talking down") which consists of the infinitive [minus accent]+**ná,** a shortening of **nasái** 'please do', and often followed by the particle **yo!: Ki ná (yo)** 'Come', **Machi ná (yo)** 'Wait', **Kore nomi ná (yo)** 'Drink this', **Ake ná (yo)** 'Open it'.

3. THE MODERN LITERARY STYLE. The modern literary style is seldom heard except in the form of set expressions quoted, as it were, from written sources. It is not even often used in contemporary writing, but many things written a generation ago were in this style. The grammar of the literary style is different from that of colloquial Japanese in many ways, and its structure should be studied separately. If you are reading something

which contains literary passages, the quickest way to understand the material is to get some Japanese to 'translate'
the passages into colloquial Japanese. For a scientific
analysis of the forms of the modern literary style, see
Elizabeth F. Gardner's excellent treatment The *Inflections
of Modern Literary Japanese*, Language Dissertation No.
46, Language 26. 4, Suppl. (Linguistic Society of America,
Baltimore, 1950.)

ADDED NOTE ON ACCENT TO ACCOMPANY p. 433:

The following atonic nouns acquire a final accent
WHEN MODIFIED: **hi** 'day', **hito** 'person' (but **anó hito**
'he, she' is a special case), **uchi** 'house; midst', **ue** 'above',
shita 'below', **tokoro** 'place'. Compare **hi ni yotte** 'depending on the day', **onaji hí ni** 'on the same day'; **hito wa**
'as for (other) people', **koko ni iru hitó wa** 'as for the
people who are here'; **uchi e** 'to the house', **watakushi no
uchí e** 'to my house'; **ue ní mo shita ní mo** 'both above
and below', **sono ué ni mo sono shitá ni mo** 'both above
it and below it'; **tokoro ni yotte** 'depending on the place',
iru tokoró ni yotte 'depending on where we are'.

APPENDIX II.

ACCENT PATTERNS.

Japanese accent consists of pitch patterns found in words or phrases. The syllable marked with an acute accent ′ in this book is the LAST SYLLABLE BEFORE A FALL IN PITCH. [In the case of the long vowels, the accent is on the first of the two syllables represented by the vowel symbol with the long mark: ǎ = áa, ě = ée, ǒ = óo, ǔ = úu. However, some speakers treat the word ǒi 'is much' as oói.]

Japanese words may be divided into TONIC and ATONIC. A tonic word is one which has a basic accent, although this accent may disappear in certain contexts. An atonic word is one with no basic accent, although it may acquire an accent in certain contexts.

An accent may occur on any syllable of a word, from first to last. But within any given word, or any accent phrase, only one accent occurs. When two or more tonic words are said as one accent phrase, the first usually retains its accent, and the following words lose their accents. In Tokyo speech, accent phrases are often quite long, so that many words seem to have lost their accent when you hear them in positions other than near the beginning of a sentence.* As an exception, some words—for example, the adjective rashíi, the particle gúrai—retain their accent and cause any tonic words preceding them in an accent

---

*But you will head a reduced "secondary" accent on some parts of a long sentence. Cf. E. H. Jorden, The Syntax of Modern Colloquial Japanese; E. H. Jorden and H. Ito, Beginning Japanese.

phrase to lose their accents; kōbá desu 'it's a factory', but kōba rashíi desu 'it seems to be a factory'; yojíkan kakarimasu 'it takes 4 hours', but yojikan gúrai kakarimasu it takes about 4 hours'. Cf. p. 190.

Many 4-syllable nouns are atonic: sensō 'war' [se-n-so-o], heitai 'soldier', yōfuku 'Western-style clothes', tēburu 'table', gekkyū 'monthly salary'. A goodly number of 3-syllable nouns are also atonic: denwa 'telephone', jigyō 'enterprise', kaisha 'company', jishin 'earthquake'.

Most nouns of 1, 2, or 3 syllables are unpredictably atonic or tonic, with the accent on any syllable. There are a number of tonic 4-syllable nouns. For nouns of more than 4-syllables, the vast majority are not only tonic but have a THEMATIC accent—one that can be predicted. The rule for the thematic accent is: on the 3d from the last syllable, unless this is the 2d vowel in a vowel sequence, or is a syllabic consonant—in which cases, on the 4th from the last. Following this rule, we find the following to be examples of thematic accent: hóteru 'hotel', tatémono 'building', káigun 'Navy', óngaku 'music', chōkyori-dénwa 'long-distance telephone (call)', Nippon-Bōeki-Kabushiki-Gáisha 'The Japan Trade Company, Inc.'

Just as some Americans say AUtomobile and others say automoBILE, or ICE-cream and ice-CREAM, there are words which will have one accent pattern for some speakers of Standard Japanese and another pattern for other speakers. For 'preacher', some speakers say bókushi, others say bokushi. For the masculine 'I, me', older speakers say bóku, younger speakers say boku.

From the imperfect form, the accent of adjectives and verbs is predictable for each inflectional category. Some apparent inconsistencies occur because of the tendency for the accent to avoid syllables containing a voiceless vowel: we hear **kité kudasai** 'please come' where we might expect **kíte kudasai** by analogy with **míte kudasai** 'please look', and **motté kite** 'bringing' where we might expect **motte kíte**. A verb or adjective is said to be atonic if the imperfect form has no accent; other forms in the paradigmatic set may have an accent. For atonic verbs, the imperfect [**kau** 'buys'], perfect [**katta**], gerund [**katte**], and infinitive [**kai**] have no accent. For atonic adjectives only the imperfect [**akai**] 'is red' and the infinitive [**akaku**] lack an accent. The unaccented forms often acquire a final accent in certain contexts.

Most particles do not have an accent when they occur alone after an atonic word, but when two or more of these unaccented particles occur in sequence after an atonic word, the first is usually accented: **koko ni** 'at this place', but **koko ní wa** 'as for at this place'.

Atonic inflected forms—like **kau** 'buys', **katta** 'bought', **katte** 'buys and', **kai** 'buying'; **akai** 'is red', **akaku** 'being red'—acquire a FINAL accent before many particles (but not before the particles **to**, **yo**, **ne**), before the noun **no**, and before the copula. [But the verb infinitive acquires this accent only before the particles **wa** and **mo**.] The FINAL accent is on the LAST syllable, unless this is the second member of a vowel sequence, in which case it is on the next-to-last syllable; the combinations **a-u**, **a-i**, **a-e** of consonant verbs with the 'disappearing **w**' do not count as vowel sequences for this purpose. Examples:
Akai 'is red', **akai hón** 'a red book', **akai to** 'when(ever) it's red', **akái no wa** 'as for a red one', **akái ka** 'is it red?', **akái desu** 'it is red', **akái n desu** 'it is red' or

'it's a red one', **akái nara** 'if it's red', **akái keredomo** 'it's red, but', **akái ga** 'it's red, but', **akái shi** 'it's red and also', **akái kara** 'it's red, so'.

Osoku kimáshita 'came late', **osokú made benkyō shimáshita** 'studied till late', **osokú wa arimasén** 'it's not late', **osokú mo nái** 'it's not late either'.

Kau 'buys', **kau hito** 'the man who'll buy', **kau hón** 'the book he'll buy', **kaú no wa** 'as for the one he'll buy' or 'as for the one who'll buy' or 'as for the fact of buying', **kaú n desu** 'he will buy', **kaú ka** 'will he buy?', **kaú keredomo** 'he'll buy, but', **kaú ga** 'he'll buy, but', **kaú shi** 'he'll buy and also', **kaú kara** 'he'll buy, so', **kaú deshō** 'he'll probably buy'; I think he'll buy'.*

Itta 'went', **itta hito** 'the man who went', **itta tokoro** 'the place he went', **ittá no wa** 'as for the one who went' or 'as for the one he went to' or 'as for the fact of his having gone', **ittá n desu** 'he went', **ittá ka** 'did he go?', **ittá keredomo** 'he went, but', **ittá ga** 'he went, but', **ittá shi** 'he went and also', **ittá kara** 'he went, so', **ittá deshō** 'he probably went'.

Itte 'saying', **itte imásu** is saying', **itte kudásai** 'please say', **itté kara** 'says and then', **itté mo íi** 'it's OK to say', **itté wa ikemasén** 'must not say'.

Hataraku 'working', **hataraki ni ikimáshita** 'he went to work', **hatarakí mo shimasén** 'he doesn't do any work', **hatarakí wa shimasén** 'he doesn't work'.

Nouns with a FINAL accent [on the last syllable, or on the next-to-last, if the last is the second of a vowel sequence, or is syllabic n] lose that accent when followed by the particle **no** [or the copula-alternant **no**]. After

*Cf. **kau deshó** '*maybe* he will buy'. This subtle distinction is limited to atonic verbs: **ushi o káu deshō** means both 'He will probably raise cattle' and '*Maybe* he will raise cattle'.

one of these accent-deprived words or after a basically atonic word, the particle **no** itself has an accent if followed by some other particle or by the copula.

Kōbá wa 'as for the factory', **kōbá desu** 'it's the factory', **kōba no shigoto** 'factory work', **kōba nó wa** 'as for the factory one', **kōba nó desu** 'it's the factory's'.

Nihón wa 'as for Japan', **Nihón desu** 'it's Japan', **Nihon no gakkō** 'schools of Japan', **Nihon nó wa** 'as for the ones in Japan', **Nihon nó desu** 'it's the ones in Japan'.

Senséi wa 'as for the teacher', **senséi desu** 'it's the teacher', **sensei no hón** 'the teacher's book', **sensei nó wa** 'as for the teacher's', **sensei nó desu** 'it's the teacher's'.

Watakushi wa 'as for me', **watakushi nó wa** 'as for mine', **watakushi nó desu** 'it's mine'.

There are some exceptions to this rule: words of 1 syllable (like **té** 'hand', **mé** 'eye', **kí** 'tree') and words of 2 syllables with the last syllable the 2d of a vowel sequence or syllabic **n**; numerals and quantity words (like **futatsú** 'two' and **takusán** 'many much'); and a few isolated items like **tsugí no** 'the next', **yosó no** alien', **otokó no ko** 'boy', **onná no ko** 'girl':

> **Kí no shita** 'under the tree', **hón no nedan** 'the price of the book', **méi no gakkō** 'my niece's school', **kyô no oténki** 'the weather today'; **futatsú no kaban** 'two suitcases', **takusán no jidōsha** 'lots of cars'; **tsugí no búnshō** 'the next sentence'.

There are a number of special cases where the context occasions a loss of accent. The most important is the loss before pause of a final accent or an accent on the next-to-last syllable when the last syllable is voiceless (as in **arimásu** and **désu** before pause).

Cf. footnotes on pp. 177, 190, 195. See also note on p. 428.

KEY TO EXERCISES

Lesson 1. 1. (a) 2. (b) 3. (b) 4. (c) 5. (b) 6. (d) 7. (d) 8. (a); (f) 9. (c) 10. (c) 11. (a) 12. (d)

Lesson 2. 1. , wa, ka 2. no, ka, no, ka 3. wa, ni, ka 4. ga, no, ka 5. ga, nó 6. wa, no, ga 7. wa, no, ga 8. no, wa, ka 9. wa, [or ga], ni, ka 10. no, ni [or ga], ka

2. 1. désu, désu 2. désu 3. imásu 4. désu 5. arimásu 6. imásu 7. désu 8. imásu 9. arimásu 10. arimásu

Lesson 3. 1. 1. de 2. de, de 3. ni 4. ni 5. ni 6. ni 7. de 8. ni 9. de 10. ni

2. 1. ga 2. o 3. ga 4. ga 5. o 6. o 7. ga 8. o 9. ga, o 10. ga

3. 1. Watakushi wa sakana o tabemasén deshita 'I didn't eat fish.' 2. Watakushi wa kyō, benkyō shimasén 'I won't study today.' 3. Íma wa, hataraite imasén né 'You're not working now, are you?' 4. Rainen Yamanóshita e (wa) ikimasén 'Next year I'm not going to Yamanoshita.' 5. Sakúban sono hón o yónde imasén deshita 'Last night I was not reading that book.' 6. Anó hito wa byōki ja arimasén deshō 'He probably isn't sick.' 7. Só ja arimasén ka? 'That's right, isn't it? Isn't that right?' 8. Ano jitsugyōka wa Amerika e kaerimasén deshita 'That businessman did not return to America.' 9. Kono yadoya wa kirai ja arimasén 'I don't dislike this inn.' 10. Issho no dénsha de kimasén deshita ka? 'You didn't come by the same streetcar?

Lesson 4. **1.** 1. tábete 2. míta 3. oyógu 4. áu
5. háyakatta 6. notte 7. yobi 8. kai 9. arúku 10. dá,
itte, asobu 11. súnde ita, hanásu 12. iru, tomaru 13.
tomatte 14. kité 15. káki
  2. 1. (c) 2. (b) 3. (d) 4. (d) 5. (d) 6. (c)
7. (a) 8. (d) 9. (a) 10. (a)
  3. (b) (c) (d), (e), (i), (j), (k), (m), (p), (q),
(r), (t), (x), (y)
  4. shímeta, níta, koshikáke, yande, tonda, núide,
haita, sótte, káchi, omótta, dáshi

Lesson 5. **1.** (a), (b), (d), (f), (g), (h), (j), (l), (m), (p),
(q), (r), (s), (t), (v), (w), (y), (z)
  2. 2. **Kinō asobi ni kitá tomodachi désu** 'He's
my friend who came to visit yesterday.' 3. **Ueno-kŏen
no sóba ni áru eigákan desu** 'It's the movie theatei
alongside Ueno Park.' 4. **Jimúsho de tsutómete iru
Tanaka-san désu** 'It's the Mr Tanaka who works in the
office.' 5. **Oyógu koto no dekínai kodomo désu** 'It's the
child who can't swim.' 6. **Ashita háyaku Kyóto e tsukú kishá desu** 'It's the train that will arrive in Kyoto
tomorrow morning.' 7. **Kitanái heyá desu** 'It's a dirty
room.' 8. **Éiga o mí ni ikanákatta onná desu** 'It's
the girl who didn't go to see the movie.' 9. **Byŏki
no jimúin desu** 'It's the office-worker who is sick.' 10.
Shízuka de kírei na kōen désu 'It's a park that's quiet
and (is) pretty.' 11. **Sakúban okane ga nákatta hito désu**
'It's the man who didn't have money last night.' 12.
Kono kōbá de hataraku shokkō no Tanaka-san désu
'It's the Mr Tanaka who is a factory-hand working at

this factory.'

3. 2. **Kore wa watakushi ga tomodachi ni kái-ta tegami désu** 'This is the letter I wrote my friend'. 3. **Kore wa byōki no hito no nónda kusuri désu** 'This is the medicine the sick man took'. 4. **Kore wa ano hito no yonda kodomo désu** 'This is the child the man called'. 5. **Kore wa watakushi no míta éiga désu.** This is the movie I saw.' 6. **Kore wa anáta no shita shigoto désu** 'This is the job you did.' 7. **Kore wa watakushi no yóku shitte iru isha désu** 'This is the doctor I know very well.' 8. **Kore wa watakushi ga késa yónde ita zasshi désu** 'This is the magazine I was reading this morning.' 9. **Kore wa sensei no mō ichido itta kotobá desu** 'This is the word the teacher repeated.' 10. **Kore wa shiháinin no ókiku shita kōbá desu** 'This is the factory the manager enlarged.'

4. 2. **Asoko wa watakushi mo Eigo o benkyō shita gakkō désu** 'That's the school where I studied English too.' 3. **Asoko wa mainen yasumí ni iku yama no tokoro désu** 'That's the mountain place we go for our vacation.' 4. **Are wa máinichi góhan o tabéru shokudō désu** 'That is the restaurant where I eat every day.' 5. **Asoko wa watakushi no kitá machí désu** 'That's the town I came from.' 6. **Asoko wa tomodachi no súnde iru inaka no tokoro désu** 'That's the country place where my friend is living.' 7. **Are wa shiháinin no isóide arúite itta ginkō désu** 'That's the bank the manager rushed off to.' 8. **Are wa musumé ga kimono o katta misé desu** 'That's the store where the girl bought the kimono.' 9. **Are wa senséi ga sóto o**

míte íta mádo desu 'That's the window from which the
teacher was looking outside.' 10. Are wa watakushi no
itta fúne desu 'That's the ship I went on.'

5. 2. Shimbun o yómazu ni, sampo shimashǒ.
Shimbun o yománai de, sampo shimashǒ 'Instead of
reading the paper, I think I'll go for a walk.' 3. Koko
e asobi ni kózu ni, eigákan e ittá deshō. Koko e asobi
ni kónai de, eigákan e ittá deshō 'He probably went to
a movie instead of coming here to visit.' 4. Inoue-san
wa yamá e ikazu ni, úmi e ikú deshō. Inoue-san wa
yamá e ikanái de, úmi e ikú deshō 'Mr Inoue will probably go to the sea(shore) instead of mountains.' 5. Kuríhara-san wa máinichi góhan o tábezu ni, kusuri o nomimásu. Kuríhara-san wa máinichi góhan o tabénai
de, kusuri o nomimásu 'Mr Kurihara takes medicine
every day, instead of eating.' 6. Jidǒsha ni norazu ni,
arúite ittá n desu. Jidǒsha ni noranái de, arúite ittá
n desu 'Instead of taking the car, we walked.' 7. Uchi
e káerazu ni, kōen e itte osokú made sampo shite imáshita. Uchi e kaeránai de, kōcn e itte osokú made
sampo shite imáshita 'Instead of returning home, we
went to the park and strolled about till late.' 8. Shiháinin ni tegami o kákazu ni, dcnwa o kakemáshita.
Shiháinin ni tegami o kakánai de, denwa o kakemáshita
'I phoned the manager instead of writing him a letter.'
9. Machi no shokudō de tábezu ni, uchi e kaerimashǒ.
Machi no shokudō de tabénai de, uchi e kaerimashǒ
'Instead of eating at a restaurant in town, let's go home.'
10. Watakushi wa kómban shigoto o sezu ni, kodomo
to asobimashǒ. Watakushi wa kómban shigoto o shi-

nái de, kodomo to asobimashǒ 'This evening I'll play
with the children instead of working.'
   6.   1. mí, iku   2. owatté   3. tábete   4. míta   5.
dekakeru   6. súnde irú, itta   7. káku   8. déru   9. nománai   10. kau
      7.   2. Góhan o tábete kara, uchi e káetta no desu.
3. Éki de watakushi no kōbá de hataraku shokkō ni
átta no desu.   4. Yukí ga fúru to, yamá ga shíroku
náru no desu.   5. Okane ga sukúnakatta no ni, iroiro
asondá no desu.   6. Wakaránai kotobá wa ǒi no de,
jibikí ga irú no desu.   7. Shimbun o yómu no ni mo
jibikí ga irú no desu ka?   8. Úmi de oyóida kotó ga
aru no desu ka?   9. Íma dekakerú no desu ka?   10.
Kyónen Kanázawa e shutchō shitá no desu.

Lesson 6.   3. (a) sánjū yón, (b) nanájū nána, (c) hyakú rokú, (d) sámbyaku nanájū, (e) kyǔ, (f) roppyakú jǔ, (g) nihyakú jǔsan, (h) ichimán nisén, (i) hya-
kumán, (j) issén roppyakú yonjūmán, (k) nanáhyaku
sánjū gomán rokusén nihyakú, (l) ichíoku sámbyaku
níjū sammán hassén yónhyaku jūrokú, (m) jūkyǔ.
      4.   (a) gohyakúen, (b) sanzén gohyakúen, (c)
ichíman nisén gojǔen, (d) níman gosén-en, (e) san-
jūmán-en, (f) níjū góen gojissén, (g) nihyakú jūgo-
mán yónhyaku níjū góen nanajǔ gosén, (h) gohyakú
kyǔjū gódoru, (i) nisén gohyakúdoru.
      7.   1. (d) 'I drank two or three cups of tea.'   2.
(g) 'I have 10 fountain pens.'   3. (b) 'We saw two or
three steamships.'   4. (f) 'I wonder who wrote those
two letters?'   5. (l) 'From the three buildings, lots of

people came out.' 6. (c) 'I just bought one automobile.'
7. (k) 'I need 4 or 5 sheets of paper.' 8. (h) 'Have you
read the two books he wrote?' 9. (j) 'There was only
one dog there.' 10. (m) 'The two teachers know English.' 11. (a) 'I expect it would take a couple of days
to go to Kumamoto.' 12. (e) 'Three birds were perched
on top of the tree.' 13. (i) 'The girl ate only one
serving of fish.'

8. (a) Níjū yón ni sánjū rokú o tasu to, rokujū
ni narimásu. (b) Yónjū hachí o yón de waru to, jūní
ni narimásu. (c) Nána kara ní o hiku to, gó ni narimásu. (d) Rokú ni nána o kakéru to, yónjū ní ni narimásu. (e) Nána ni hachí o tasu to, jūgo ni narimásu.
(f) Ippyakú gojū yón kara kyūjū san o hiku to, rokujū
ichí ni narimásu. (g) Gohyakú sánjū ni nihyakú níjū
o tasu to, nanáhyaku gojū ni narimásu. (h) Kyūhyaku
kyūjū o san de waru to, sámbyaku san ni narimásu.
(i) Rokú kara rokú o hiku to, réi ni narimásu.

9. (a) jittō, (b) hattsū, (c) gojissén, (d) íkken,
(e) hasshakú, (f) jítchō, (g) sámmai, (h) námpeiji,
(i) yoen, (j) sámbon, (k) sámpun, (l) sambiki, (m)
sambai, (n) sámbai, (o) íppai, (p) jíppun, (q) yóm-
pun, (r) yonen, (s) sángen, (t) sanzún, (u) sansén,
(v) sanzén, (w) nánjaku, (x) yojíkan, (y) yómbyō,
(z) hyákkcn, (aa) sanzeki, (bb) sánjū íssai, (cc) ip-
pyaku yoen, (dd) hyakú yónjū yonen.

10. (a) jūji (b) jūji-hán (c) gógo sánji (d)
gózen hachiji-hán (e) kyūji jūgófun (f) góji níjū na-
náfun (g) rokúji jíppun (h) gógo yoji góro (i) kyūji yónjū gófun (or jūji jūgófun máe) (j) gógo ichíji
jíppun máe (k) ichiji-han góro.

Lesson 7. 1. 1. Tárō wa mố sono éiga o míta to iimá-shita. 2. Tárō wa yūbínkyoku wa dóko ka (to) kiki-máshita. 3. Tárō wa Jírō ni tegami o kírei ni káku yō ni (to) iimáshita. 4. Tárō wa Jírō ni kómban hachiji góro ni kúru yō ni (to) iimáshita. 5. Tárō wa wata-kushi ni iitai kotó ga áru to iimáshita. 6. Tárō wa senkyốshi wa dáre ka (to) kikimáshita. 7. Tárō wa Kyốto wa Tōkyō to chigau tokoró ga ối to iimáshita. 8. Tárō wa shōji wa ichímai no kamí de tsukúru to ii-máshita. 9. Tárō wa Nihonjín wa geta ka kutsú o núide uchi e agaru to iimáshita. 10. Tárō wa Jírō ni shízuka ni suru yố ni (to) iimáshita.

2. 1. bōshi [all others are 'worn' with the verb haku] 2. ichido [all others are kinds of doors] 3. za-búton [all others are names of rooms] 4. furobá 'bath-room', semmenjo 'lavatory' [all others are words for 'toilet'] 5. tebúkuro, yubiwa [all others are 'worn' with the verb kiru]

3. 1. ikō 'I think I'll go see that movie.' 2. da-rō 'I think they must be living in the suburbs.' 3. yasumố 'When it gets to be four o'clock, my friend suggests we rest awhile.' 4. dekakeyō 'Just as I had been about to go out, the boss [or my husband] tele-phoned.' 5. koyō 'This morning just when I was about to come here for a visit, Mr Inoue came to my house for a visit.' 6. shiyō 'I was just on the point of study-ing.' 7. kakố 'I think I'll write my wife a letter this evening.' 8. aố 'I think I'll meet Mr Tanaka.' 9. ka-erố 'Jiro was tired so he suggested we go back home.' 10. yobō 'I think I'll call the children before it gets

late.' 11. tabeyǒ 'I suggested we eat at a restaurant.'
12. miyǒ 'Just when I had been about to ask the policeman, you came.'
  4. 2. iretai 3. kaeritái desu 4. tabétaku 5.
kakitái 6. aitái 7. kiritái desu 8. kitái desu 9. netai
10. Iitai 11. asobitai 12. ikitái desu
  5. 2. (a) Nágoya datta ka, Shizúoka datta ka,
shirimasén. (b) Nágoya datta ka, Shizúoka datta ka,
wasuremáshita. (c) Nágoya datta ka, Shizúoka datta
ka, kiite mimashǒ. (d) Nágoya datta ka, Shizúoka
datta ka shitte imásu ka? 3. (a) Ano tatémono wa ōkíi
ka, chiisái ka, shirimasén. (b) Ano tatémono wa ōkíi ka,
chiisái ka, wasuremáshita. (c) Ano tatémono wa ōkíi
ka, chiisái ka, kiite mimashǒ. (d) Ano tatémono wa
ōkíi ka, chiisái ka, shitte imásu ka? 4. (a) Hóngō ni
súnde itá ka, sore tó mo Asákusa ni súnde itá ka, shirimasén. (b) Hóngō ni súnde itá ka, sore tó mo Asákusa ni súnde itá ka, wasuremáshita. (c) Hóngō ni
súnde itá ka, sore tó mo Asákusa ni súnde itá ka, kiite
mimashǒ. (d) Hóngō ni súnde itá ka, sore tó mo Asákusa ni súnde itá ka, shitte imásu ka? 5. (a)Íma hataraite irú ka, hataraite inái ka, shirimasén. (b) Íma
hataraite irú ka, hataraite inái ka, wasuremáshita. (c)
Íma hataraite irú ka, hataraite inái ka, kiite mimashǒ.
(d) Íma hataraite irú ka, hataraite inái ka, shitte imásu
ka? 6 (a) Ashita kúru ka, asátte kúru ka, shirimasén.
(b) Ashita kúru ka, asátte kúru ka, wasuremáshita. (c)
Ashita kúru ka, asátte kúru ka, kiite mimashǒ. (d)
Ashita kúru ka, asátte kúru ka, shitte imásu ka? 8.
(a) Éiga o mí ni ittá ka, dǒ ka, shirimasén. (b) Éiga o

mí ni ittá ka, dǒ ka, wasuremáshita. (c) Éiga o mí ni ittá ka, dǒ ka, kiite mimashǒ. (d) Éiga o mí ni ittá ka, dǒ ka, shitte imásu ka? 9. (a) Monó o minna hitótsu no kaban ni iretá ka, dǒ ka, shirimasén. (b) Monó o minna hitótsu no kaban ni iretá ka, dǒ ka, wasuremáshita. (c) Monó o minna hitótsu no kaban ni iretá ka, dǒ ka, kiite mimashǒ. (d) Monó o minna hitótsu no kaban ni iretá ka dǒ ka, shitte imásu ka? 10. (a) Heyá wa kírei ka, dǒ ka, shirimasén. (b) Heyá wa kírei ka, dǒ ka, wasuremáshita. (c) Heyá wa kírei ka, dǒ ka, kiite mimashǒ. (d) Heyá wa kírei ka, dǒ ka, shitte imásu ka? 11. (a) Íma hataraite irú ka, dǒ ka, shirimasén. (b) Íma hataraite irú ka, dǒ ka, wasuremáshita. (c) Íma hataraite irú ka, dǒ ka, kiite mimashǒ. (d) Íma hataraite irú ka, dǒ ka, shitte imásu ka? 12. (a) Ashita kúru ka, dǒ ka, shirimasén. (b) Ashita kúru ka, dǒ ka, wasuremáshita. (c) Ashita kúru ka, dǒ ka, kiite mimashǒ. (d) Ashita kúru ka, dǒ ka, shitte imásu ka?

6. 2. Néko ga sakana o tábeta yō désu. 3. Kono mizuúmi wa ōkíi yō desu. 4. Kono misé wa depǎto no yō désu. 5. Asoko wa hóteru datta yō desu ně. 6. Ano rōdǒsha wa íma hataraite iru yǒ desu. 7. Tanaka-san no tomodachi wa inaka ni súnde iru yō desu. 8. Osoku nátta yō desu ně. 9. Dénsha wa kónde iru yō desu ně. 10. Kono nikú wa totemo íi yō desu.

7. 2. Kono tegami wa káite arimásu. 3. Watakushi no hón mo kaban ni irete arimásu. 4. "Sakanaya" to iu jí ga káite arimásu. 5. Kusuri wa nónde arimásu. 6. Gyūniku wa mǒ minna tábete arimásu.

8. 1. Ginkō wa tokeiya yori ōkíi desu. 2. Rin-

ₐgó wa míkan hodo takái desu ka? 3. Kore wa Nihón
de ichiban ōkíi depáto desu. 4. Anáta wa anó hito hodo wákaku arimasén ně. 5. Ringo to míkan to kaki
no uchí de, dóre ga ichiban sukí desu ka? 6. Aói no
yori, kuroi hǒ ga yasúi to iimáshita. 7. Ōkíi hō ga kaitai to omoimásu. 8. Ichiban ōkíi no ga kaitai to omoimásu. 9. Ōkíi no ga kaitai to omoimásu. 10. Nihongo
o hanásu hō ga, káku yori yasashíi desu. 11. Hón to
zasshi de, dóchira ga takái desu ka? 12. Sono nikú yori
wa, kono niku no hǒ ga íi yō desu.

Lesson 8. 1. 1. Watakushi wa nijikan gúrai shika ne-
nákereba, mō sukóshi benkyō suru kotó ga dekimásu
'If I sleep for just a couple of hours, I'll be able to
study a little more.' 2. Kodomo wa ammari okáshi o
tabéreba, góhan wa tabétaku nái deshǒ 'If the children
eat too much pastry, they won't want to eat their dinner.'
3. Anáta wa tsukárete iréba, nisampun yasúnde kudasai 'If you're tired, rest for two or three minutes.' 4.
Anáta wa máda okane ga iréba, watakushi ni itte kudasái 'If you still need money, please tell me.' 5. Anáta wa watakushi yóri háyaku uchi e káereba, jochū ni
kodomo o yobu yǒ ni itte kudasái 'If you get home before I do, please tell the maid to call the children.'
6. Anáta ga Uehara-san o éki de máteba, watakushi wa
uchi de machimásu 'If you'll wait for Mr Uehara at
the station, I'll wait at home.' 7. Anáta ga yukkúri
hanáseba, watakushi wa súgu wakarimásu 'If you speak
slow, I understand right away.' 8. Senséi ni áeba, sō
iimashǒ 'If I see the teacher, I'll tell him,' or 'If we see

the teacher, let's tell him.' 9. **Anáta ga Eigo de kákeba, Tanaka-san wa wakaránai deshō** 'If you write in English, Mr Tanaka won't understand.' 10. **Mō sukóshi isógeba, ma ni áu deshō** 'If you [we] hurry a little more, you [we] will be on time.' 11. **Máinichi gyūnyū o nómeba, génki ni narimásu** 'If you drink milk everyday, you'll get healthy.' 12. **Anáta wa ano onná ni aítakereba, goji góro ni toshókan no máe e kitára íi deshō** 'If you want to meet that girl, you better come to the front of the library around 5.' 13. **Kodomo wa sono éiga o mí ni ikitákereba, watakushi mo ikimashǒ** 'If the children want to go see that movie, I guess I'll go too.' 14. **Oténki ga wárukereba, watakushi wa sampo ni ikitaku arimasén** 'If the weather's bad, I don't want to go for a walk.' 15. **Sono tegami o yománakereba, Takayama-san ga ítsu kúru ka to iu kotó ga wakaránai deshō** 'Unless you read that letter, you won't know when Mr Takayama is coming.' 16. **Anáta no tomodachi ga senkyǒshi nara, bíiru o nománai hō ga íi deshō** 'If your friend's a missionary, we better not drink beer.'

    2. 1. **Nisampun bákari máttara, Kinoshita-san ga kimáshita** 'When I waited for two or three minutes, Mr Kinoshita came.' 2. **Watakushi ga Níhongo de hanáshitara, ten-in wa taihen odorokimáshita** 'When I spoke in Japanese, the clerk was very much surprised.' 3. **Kóndō-san ni tcgami o káitara, ítsu ka asobi ni kúru yō ni to itte kudasái** 'When you write to Mr Kondo, tell him to come visit us sometime.' 4. **Sono hón wa Eigo de yóndara, muzukashiku nákatta deshō** 'If you

had read that book in English, it wouldn't have been (so) hard'. 5. **Jírō o yondára, Tárō ga demáshita** 'When I called Jiro, Taro came out.' 6. **Kono kínjo de dáre ka shindára, súgu wakátta deshō** 'If someone had died in this neighborhood, we would have known about it right away.' 7. **Mō sukóshi isóidara, ma ni átta deshō** 'If we had hurried a little more, we would have made it on time.' 8. **Kishá ni nottára, mádo no sóba no tokoro ni koshikakemashô** 'When we get on the train, let's sit next to the window.' 9. **Anáta wa mō sukóshi okane ga ittára, goenryo náku watakushi ni itte kudasái** 'When [If] you need a bit more money, don't hesitate to tell me.' 10. **Nijíkan mo mátte itára, Kimura-san ga déte kimáshita** 'When I had been waiting all of two hours, Mr Kimura came out.' 11. **Sore o tábetara, byōki ni narimásu yo** 'If you were to eat that, you'd get sick.' 12. **Nisanjíkan benkyō shitára asobi ni itté mo íi desu** 'When you've studied for 2 or 3 hours, you can go out and play.' 13. **Kánai ga sampo ni ikitákattara, watakushi mo ikú deshō** 'If my wife should want to go for a walk, I'd go too.' 14. **Oténki ga yókattara, ensoku ni ittá deshō** 'If the weather had been nice, we'd probably have gone on a picnic.' 15. **Okane ga nákattara, eigákan e háiru kotó ga dekimasén** 'If you hadn't any money, you wouldn't be able to get in the movie theater.' 16. **Anáta dattara, dô shita deshō ka?** 'If you were me [If it were you], what would you have done?'

3. 2. (1) **Anó hito to hanasánakereba narimasén.** (2) **Anó hito to hanasánakute mo íi desu.** (3) **Anó hito**

to hanáshite mo íi desu. (4) Anó hito to hanáshite wa
ikemasén. 3. (1) Sono kotó o iwanákereba narimasén.
(2) Sono kotó o iwanákute mo íi desu. (3) Sono kotó
o itté mo íi desu. (4) Sono kotó o itté wa ikemasén.
4. (1) Máinichi éiga o mínakereba narimasén. (2) Máinichi éiga o mínakute mo íi desu. (3) Máinichi éiga o
míte mo íi desu. (4) Máinichi éiga o míte wa ikemasén.
5. (1) Sono tegami o yománakereba narimasén. (2) Sono tegami o yománakute mo íi desu. (3) Sono tegami
o yónde mo íi desu. (4) Sono tegami o yónde wa ikemasén. 6. (1) Kono isu ni koshikakénakereba narimasén. (2) Kono isu ni koshikakénakute mo íi desu. (3)
Kono isu ni koshikákete mo íi desu. (4) Kono isu ni
koshikákete wa ikemasén. 7. (1) Koko de yasumána-
kereba narimasén. (2) Koko de yasumánakute mo íi
desu. (3) Koko de yasúnde mo íi desu. (4) Koko de
yasúnde wa ikemasén. 8. (1) Niwa no sóba de asoba-
nákereba narimasén. (2) Niwa no sóba de asobaná-
kute mo íi desu. (3) Niwa no sóba de asondé mo íi
desu. (4) Niwa no sóba de asondé wa ikemasén. 9.
(1) Kono heya no náka e hairánakereba narimasén. (2)
Kono heya no náka e hairánakute mo íi desu. (3) Kono heya no náka e háitte mo íi desu. (4) Kono heya
no náka e háitte wa ikemasén. 10. (1) Sono kusuri o
nománakereba narimasén. (2) Sono kusuri o nománakute mo íi desu. (3) Sono kusuri o nónde mo íi desu.
(4) Sono kusuri o nónde wa ikemasén.

    4. 1. Dáre ni átte mo, téinei ni hanashimásu.
2. Dóno jimúsho [or Dóko no jimúsho] no náka e háitte mo, denwa o mimásu. 3. Dóko e itté mo, yóku aso-

bimásu [or omoshirói desu]. 4. Dóno hón o yónde mo, kamaimasén. 5. Ōkíi depáto de wa, nán de mo arimásu. 6. Náni mo arimasén. 7. Dáre ka asobi ni kitá yō désu. 8. Dáre ka Eigo no dekíru hito ga imásu ka? 9. Dóko ka kara [or Dókosoko kara] júnsa ga kimáshita. 10. Ítsu ka Enóshima e ensoku ni ikitai to omoimásu.

Lesson 9. 1. 2. Dóko de aimáshita ka? 3. Kyōkai no máe deshita. 4. Machí e kaimono ni iku to ittá kara, issho ni arúite ikimáshita. 5. Ítsu ka uchi e asobi ni kité kudasai to watakushi wa sasoimáshita. 6. Bókushi-san wa kono goro isogashíi deshō ně. 7. Só da keredomo, raishū no Getsuyóbi no ban, jíkan ga áru kara, uchi e asobi ni kité kuremásu. 8. Anatátachi mo kúru kotó ga dékitara, dózo. 9. Sekkakú desuga, Getsuyóbi wa háha no tanjóbi na no de, watakushítachi wa ryóshin to issho ni shibai e ikimásu kara... 10. Nán to iu shibai désu ka?. 11. "Háha" to iu shibai e ikú no desu. 12. Sore wa omoshirói deshō ně. 13. Kotoshi wa yasumí ni dóko e ikimásu ka? 14. Miyanóshita e ikimásu ka, Karúizawa e ikimásu ka? 15. Kyónen yamá e ittá kara, kotoshi wa úmi e ikitai to omoimásu. 16. Só desu ka? Kamakurá e itta kotó ga arimásu ka? 17. Máda desu. Soko no hamá wa íi desu ka? 18. Hamá wa íi desu ga, natsú wa daibu kónde imasu. 19. Izu-hántō ni wa íi hamá ga takusan arimásu. 20. Watakushi wa annaisho ga nisatsu áru kara, issatsu yarimásu. 21. Arígatō gozaimásu. Kono chízu de Izu-hántō o mísete kuremasén ka? 22. Chotto [watakushi ga] mimashǒ. 23. Míte kudasai. Kore wa Kamakurá de, sore wa Izu-hántō désu. 24. Shōshō mátte kudasai. Kore yóri ōkíi chízu o motté kite mísete yarimashǒ. 25. Itō to iu tokoró o shitte imásu ka? 26. Hái. Ítsu ka byōki ni nátta toki sankágetsu soko e yasúmi ni itte imáshita. 27. Sono aida, náni o shite imáshita ka? 28. Máinichi kusuri o moratte yasúnde bakari imáshita. 29. Kono ōkíi chízu o karitái n desu ga.....30. Dǒzo, goenryo náku. Tatande yarimashǒ.

2. 2. (a) Senkyǒshi de gozaimásu. (b) Senkyǒshi de irasshaimásu ka? 3. (a) Okane ga gozaimashǒ. (b) Okane ga gozaimashǒ? or Okane ga oari deshǒ? 4. (a) Amerika kara mairimáshita. (b) Amerika kara irasshaimáshita [oide ni narimáshita] ka? 5. (a) Yokohama de shigoto o itashite orimásu. (b) Yokohama de oshígoto o nasátte irasshaimásu ka? [nasátte oide ni narimásu ka?] 6. (a) Senséi ni ukagaimáshita. (b) Senséi ni otazune ni narimáshita ka? 7. (a) Sensei no otaku e ojama ni mairimáshita. (b) Sensei no otaku e oasobi ni oide ni narimáshita ka? [oasobi ni irasshaimáshita ka?] 8. (a) Sono éiga o haiken itashita [míta] kotó ga gozaimásu. (b) Sono éiga o goran ni nátta kotó ga gozaimásu ka? [kotó ga oari désu ka?] 9. (a) Shachō ni ome ni kakaritō gozaimásu. (b) Shachō ni aítakute irasshaimásu ka? [or ...oai ni naritái desu ka?] 10. (a) Bokushi-san ni kono hón o ome ni kakemáshita [or omise itashimáshita]. (b) Bokushi-san ni kono hón o omise ni narimáshita ka? 11. (a) Kono empitsu o senséi ni haishaku itashimáshita. (b) Kono empitsu o senséi ni okari ni narimáshita ka? 12. (a) Tanaka Tá-

rō to mōshimásu. (b) Tanaka Tárō-san to osshaimásu
ka? 13. (a) Táguchi-san o zónjite orimásu. (b) Táguchi-san o gozónji desu ka? 14. (a) Atarashíi kimono
o kite orimáshita. (b) Atarashíi kimono o omeshi ni
nátte irasshaimáshita ka? 15. (a) Náni ka itadakitai
to zonjimásu. (b) Náni ka meshiagaritai to oboshimeshi-
másu ka? or: Náni ka meshiagaritai to oomoi ni narimásu ka? [More often: Náni ka meshiagaritákute irasshaimásu ka?] 16. (a) Ashitá kara kusuri o nománakute
mo yǒ gozaimásu. (b) Ashitá kara okúsuri o meshi-
agaranákute mo yoroshū gozaimásu ka? [Or: Ashitá
kara kusuri o onomi ni naránakute mo yoroshū gozaimásu ka?] 17. (a) Nijikan gúrai benkyō itashimáshita.
(b) Nijikan gúrai (go)benkyō nasaimáshita ka? 18. (a)
Rainen Amerika e okaeri itashimásu. (b) Rainen Amerika e okaeri ni narimásu ka? 19. (a) Takayama-san to
ohanashi itashimáshita. (b) Takayama-san to ohanashi
ni narimáshita ka? 20. (a) Kono goro isogáshū gozaimásu. (b) Kono goro oisogáshikute irasshaimásu ka?
3. 1. Watakushi no jidósha wa kúrō gozaimásu
ga, anáta no wa áō gozaimásu ně. 2. Kono tatémono
wa ōkyū gozaimásu. 3. Anáta wa ítsu okaeri ni naritái desu ka? 4. Watakushi wa rokuji góro ni kaerítō
gozaimásu. 5. Kyó wa oténki ga wárū gozaimásu ně.
6. Kono kōen wa taiheu yoroshū gozaimásu ně. 7. Sono éiga wa omoshírō gozaimáshita ka? 8. Anáta wa
dónata ni oai ni narimáshita ka? 9. Anáta wa watakushi ni shimbun o katté kite kudasaimáshita. 10. Tanaka-san wa ten-in ni jūénsatsu o nímai oyari ni narimáshita. [Notice avoidance of agemáshita, which

would put the clerk on a higher plane.]
4. 1. **Kono hón o yarimashǒ.** Kono hón o age-
mashǒ. 2. Watakushi wa imōtó ni kōmorigása o íppon
yarimáshita. **Watakushi wa imōtó ni kōmorigása o
íppon agemáshita** [But would probably not be used
because of the sister's inferior status.] 3. **Chichí wa
watakushi ni jiténsha o kuremáshita.** Chichí wa watakushi ni jiténsha o kudasaimáshita. 4. **Okǎsan wa
oimōtosan ni sono okáshi o yarimáshita ka?** [But would
probably not be heard because of social status of
your relatives.] Okǎsan wa oimōtosan ni sono okáshi o agemáshita ka? Or ...oage ni narimáshita ka?
5. **Ojisan ni waishatsu o yarimáshita ka?** Ojisan ni
waishatsu o agemáshita ka? Or ...oage ni narimáshita
ka? 6. **Tebúkuro o kuremáshita.** Tebúkuro o kudasaimáshita. 7. **Áni wa watakushi ni kono zubon o kuremáshita.** Áni wa watakushi ni kono zubon o kudasaimáshita. 8. **(O)něsan wa náni ka anáta ni kuremáshita ka?** (O)něsan wa náni ka anáta ni kudasaimáshita ka? 9. **Watakushi wa ten-in ni hyakuénsatsu
o nímai yarimáshita.** Watakushi wa ten-in ni hyakuénsatsu o nímai agemáshita [see note to 2 above]. 10.
Ten-in wa watakushi ni otsuri o níjū goen kuremáshita.
Ten-in wa watakushi ni otsuri o níjū goen kudasaimáshita [see note to 2 above.]
5. 1. (1) **Tegami o káite kudasaimáshita.** (2)
Tegami o káite agemáshita. (3) Tanaka-san ni tegami
o káite agemáshita [or: káite oage ni narimáshita].
(4) Tanaka-san wa anáta ni tegami o káite kudasaimáshita. (5) Tanaka-san wa watakushi ni tegami o káite

kuremáshita [kudasaimáshita]. (6) Tanaka-san wa Ki-mura-san ni tegami o káite yarimáshita [agemáshita]. 2. (1) Jiténsha o naóshite kudasaimáshita. (2) Jiténsha o naóshite agemáshita. (3) Tanaka-san ni jiténsha o naóshite agemáshita [oage ni narimáshita]. (4) Tanaka-san wa anáta ni jiténsha o naóshite kudasaimáshita. (5) Tanaka-san wa watakushi ni jiténsha o naóshite kuremáshita [kudasaimáshita]. (6) Tanaka-san wa Ki-mura-san ni jiténsha o naóshite yarimáshita [agemáshita]. 3. (1) Tokei o katte kudasaimáshita. (2) Tokei o katte agemáshita. (3) Tanaka-san ni tokei o katte agemáshita [oage ni narimáshita]. (4) Tanaka-san wa anáta ni tokei o katte kudasaimáshita. (5) Tanaka-san wa watakushi ni tokei o katte kuremáshita [kudasaimáshita]. (6) Tanaka-san wa Kimura-san ni tokei o katte yarimáshita [agemáshita]. 4. (1) Hón o utte kudasaimáshita. (2) Hón o utte agemáshita. (3) Tanaka-san ni hón o utte agemáshita [oage ni narimáshita]. (4)Tanaka-san wa anáta ni hón o utte kudasaimáshita. (5) Tanaka-san wa watakushi ni hón o utte kuremáshita [kudasaimáshita]. (6) Tanaka-san wa Kimura-san ni hón o utte yarimáshita [agemáshita]. 5. (1) Kaban o totte kudasaimáshita. (2) Kaban o totté kite agemáshita. (3) Tanaka-san ni kaban o totté kite agemáshita [oage ni narimáshita]. (4) Tanaka-san wa anáta ni kaban o totté kite kudasaimáshita. (5) Tanaka-san wa watakushi ni kaban o totté kite kuremáshita [kudasaimáshita]. (6) Tanaka-san wa Kimura-san ni kaban o totté kite yarimáshita [agemáshita]. 6. (1) Senséi ni hanáshite kudasaimáshita. (2) Senséi ni hanáshite agemáshita. (3)

Tanaka-san ni senséi ni hanáshite agemáshita [oage ni narimáshita]. (4) Tanaka-san wa anáta ni hanáshite kudasaimáshita. (5) Tanaka-san wa watakushi ni hanáshite kuremáshita [kudasaimáshita]. (6) Tanaka-san wa Kimura-san ni senséi ni hanáshite yarimáshita [agemáshita]. 7. (1) Shachō ni sore o itte kudasaimáshita. (2) Shachō ni sore o itte agemáshita. (3) Tanaka-san ni shachō ni sore o itte agemáshita [oage ni narimáshita]. (4) Tanaka-san wa anáta ni shachō ni sore o itte kudasaimáshita (5) Tanaka-san wa watakushi ni shachō ni sore o itte kuremáshita [kudasaimáshita]. (6) Tanaka-san wa Kimura-san ni shachō ni sore o itte yarimáshita [agemáshita]. 8. (1) Shimbun o motté kite kudasaimáshita. (2) Shimbun o motté kite agemáshita. (3) Tanaka-san ni shimbun o motté kite agemáshita [oage ni narimáshita]. (4) Tanaka-san wa anáta ni shimbun o motté kite kudasaimáshita. (5) Tanaka-san wa watakushi ni shimbun o motté kite kuremáshita [kudasaimáshita]. (6) Tanaka-san wa Kimura-san ni shimbun o motté kite yarimáshita [agemáshita]. 9. (1) Issho ni éki made arúite itte kudasaimáshita. (2) Issho ni éki made arúite itte agemáshita. (3) Tanaka-san ni issho ni [= with someone else, Tanaka-san to issho ni = with Tanaka] éki made arúite itte agemáshita [oage ni narimáshita]. (4) Tanaka-san wa anáta ni issho ni [anáta to issho ni] éki made arúite itte kudasaimáshita. (5) Tanaka-san wa watakushi ni issho ni [watakushi to issho ni] éki made arúite itte kuremáshita [kudasaimáshita]. (6) Tanaka-san wa Kimura-san ni issho ni [Kimura-san to issho ni] éki made arúite itte yarimáshita [agemáshita]. 10. (1) Kono kotoba no

ími o setsumei shite kudasaimáshita. (2) Kono kotoba no ími o setsumei shite agemáshita. (3) Tanaka-san
ni kono kotoba no ími o setsumei shite agemáshita [o-
age ni narimáshita]. (4) Tanaka-san wa anáta ni kono
kotoba no ími o setsumei shite kudasaimáshita. (5)
Tanaka-san wa watakushi ni kono kotoba no ími o setsumei shite kuremáshita [kudasaimáshita]. (6) Tanaka-san wa Kimura-san ni kono kotoba no imi o setsumei shite yarimáshita [agemáshita].

Lesson 10. 1. 2. Gúntai ni ita tokí ni wa, yóku sake o
nónde sawáida monó da sō desu. Gúntai ni ita tóki
ni wa, yóku sake o nónde sawáida mono rashíi desu.
3. Kippu o moraenai sô desu. Kippu o moraenai rashíi
desu. 4. Sakana wa tábezu ni nokóshita sō desu. Sakana wa tábezu ni nokoshita rashíi desu. 5. Omúsukosan wa jiténsha o toráreta sō desu. Omúsukosan wa
jiténsha o torareta rashíi desu. 6. Heitai wa sentaku
o saserareru sô desu. Heitai wa sentaku o saserareru
rashíi desu. 7. Jochū wa kodomo o uchi no sóba de
asobaseta sô desu. Jochū wa kodomo o uchi no sóba
de asobaseta rashíi desu. 8. Sensō ni tsúite no kíji ga
sakúban no shimbun ni déte ita sô desu. Sensō ni tsúite no kíji ga sakúban no shimbun ni déte ita rashíi desu.
9. Júnsa ni kiite iru sô desu. Júnsa ni kiite iru rashíi
desu. 10. Gúntai ni háitta ni chigai nái sō desu. Gúntai ni háitta ni chigai nai rashíi desu. 11. Sono gunkan
wa shizunda sô desu. Sono gunkan wa shizunda rashíi
desu. 12. Súihei wa oborejini suru osoré ga áru sō
desu. Súihei wa oborejini suru osoré ga aru rashíi

454 ESSENTIAL JAPANESE

desu.

2. 2. Hanáshitari, kiitári, hón o yóndari shimásu. 3. Úmi e háitte oyóidari, hamá de iroiro asondári shimásu. 4. Nihongo de hanáshitari, Eigo de hanáshitari shite imáshita. 5. Héisha ni ite kirai na shigoto o saseraretári, machí e itte sake o nónde sawáidari shimáshita. 6. Áme ga futtári, yukí ga futtári shite imásu. 7. Góhan o tábetari, ocha o nóndari shite imáshita. 8. Umá o nusumáretari, kodomo o korosaretári shimásu. 9. Okăsan ni shikararetári, tonari no kodomo ni utáretari, ammari okáshi o tábete byōki ni náttari shimáshita. 10. Rájio o kiitari, térebi o mítari shimáshita.

3. 2. Óngaku o kikinagara, tegami o kakimáshita. 3. Tanaka-san to hanáshite inagara, sono jimúsho o míte imáshita. 4. Ryōri shinagara, rájio o kikimáshita. 5. Sentaku o shinagara, kodomo o uchi no sóba de asobasemásu.

4. 1. Yūbínkyoku de wa, dempō o útsu kotó ga dekimásu. Yūbínkyoku de wa, dempō ga utaremásu. Yūbínkyoku de wa, dempō ga utemásu. 2. Kono denwáshitsu de wa, chōkyoridénwa o kakéru kotó ga dekimásu. Kono denwáshitsu de wa, chōkyoridénwa ga kakeraremásu. 3. Sono tegami wa Nihongo de káku kotó ga dekimásu ka? Sono tegami wa Nihongo de kakaremásu ka? Sono tegami wa Nihongo de kakemásu ka? 4. Kono sentaku o háyaku suru kotó ga dekimásu ka? [Or: Kono sentaku ga háyaku dekimásu ka?] Kono sentaku ga háyaku saremásu ka? [Or: Kono sentaku ga háyaku dekimásu ka?] 5. Dáre ka ni

mádo o arawaseru kotó ga dekimásu ka? Dáre ka ni mádo ga arawaseraremásu ka? 6. Dóko de shimbun o kau kotó ga dekimásu ka? Dóko de shimbun ga kawaremásu ka? Dóko de shimbun ga kaemásu ka? 7. Okosan wa hitóri de arúku kotó ga dekimásu ka? Okosan wa hitóri de arukaremásu ka? Okosan wa hitóri de arukemásu ka? 8. Mō sukóshi isógu kotó ga dekimásu ka? Mō sukóshi isogaremásu ka? Mō sukóshi isogemásu ka? 9. Okinawa máde hikǒki de iku kotó ga dekimásu ka? Okinawa máde hikǒki de ikaremásu ka? 10. Kono mizu wa nómu kotó ga dekimásu ka? Kono mizu wa nomaremásu ka? Kono mizu wa nomemásu ka?

5. 1. Jochū ni mádo o arawasemáshita. 2. Jochū ni kaimono ni ikasemáshita. 3. Jochū ni tegami o dasasemáshita. 4. Jochū ni oishii tabemóno o tsukurasemáshita. 5. Jochū ni kono kíji o misasemáshita. 6. Jochū ni háiya o yobasemáshita. 7. Jochū ni tonari no hito ni sō iwasemáshita. 8. Jochū ni mō sukóshi isogasemáshita. 9. Jochū ni júnsa ni kikasemáshita. 10. Jochū ni to o shimesasemáshita.

6. 1. Jochū ni tegami o yomaremáshita. 2. Senséi ni shikararemáshita. 3. Isogashíi toki ni okyaku ni koraremáshita. 4. Góhan o tabeyǒ to shita tokí ni, kodomo ni uchi o deraremáshita. 5. Dáre ka ni okane o toraremáshita. 6. Chichí ni shinaremáshita. 7. Dorobō ni jidōsha o nusumaremáshita. 8. Néko ni sakana o taberaremáshita. 9. Musumé ni kasa o naku-saremáshita. 10. Ten-in ni shitsúrei na kotó o iwaremáshita.

ADDITIONAL ACCENT PRACTICE

Here are some place names in Tokyo for accent pronunciation practice:

(1) Train stations on the Yamaté line (the "outer loop"): Tōkyō (Tōkyố-eki), Yūrakú-chō, Shímbashi, Hamamatsú-chō, Támachi, Shinagawa, Gotanda, Méguro, Ébisu, Shibuya, Harájuku, Yoyogi, Shinjuku (Shinjukúeki), Shin-Ōkubo, Takada-no-bába, Mejiro, Ikebúkuro, Ōtsuka, Súgamo, Komagome, Tábata, Nippori, Uguisudani, Ueno (Uenó-eki), Okachí-machi, Akihábara, Kanda.

(2) The Chūō line from Akihábara to Mitaka: Ochanomizu, Suidōbashi, Iidábashi, Ichígaya, Yotsuya, Shinano-machi, Sendágaya, Yoyogi, Shinjuku, Ōkubo, Higashi-Nákano, Nakano, Kốenji, Asagaya, Ogikubo, Nishi-Ogíkubo (Nishi-Ogi), Kichijōjí, Mitaka.

(3) The Ginza subway line: Asakusa, Tawará-machi, Inarí-chō, Ueno, (Ueno-) Hirokốji, Suehiró-chō, Kanda, Mitsukoshí-mae, Nihombashi, Kyōbashi, Ginza, Shímbashi, Toranomon, Akasaka-mítsuke [Akásaka], Aóyama itchōme, Gaiém-mae, Jingū-mae, Shibuya.

(4) The Marunóuchi subway line: Ikebúkuro, Shin-Ōtsuka, Myōgá-dani, Kōrakúen, Hóngō sanchōme, Ochanomizu, Awají-chō, Ōté-machi, Tōkyō, Nishi-Gínza, Kasumi-gá-seki, Gijidố-mae, Akasaka-mítsuke, Yotsuya, Yotsuya sanchōme, (Shinjuku-) Gyoém-mae, Shinjuku sanchōme, Shinjuku.

(5) Landmarks: Tōkyō-táwā (T. Tower), Shiba-kốen (Shíba Park), Hibiya-kōen (H. Park), Ueno-kōen (U. Park), Kyūjō (Imperial Palace), Surugá-dai (Súruga Heights), Yasukuni-jínja (Y. Shrine), Meiji-jíngū (Méiji Shrine), Gijidō (Diet Building).

INDEX TO STRUCTURE NOTES

[References are to pages. Japanese words are in bold face.]

accent.... 26, 177, 190, 195,
.......428, 429, 456
accompaniment 69
adjectives 83, 94, 343
   honorific infinitive 345
   honorifics 343
   modifier clauses 132
   plain negative 102
adverbs 112
advice 305
alternative mood (-tari) 383
alternative questions 228
-(a)nai *see* negatives
'and' 67, 71, 314
answers to negative questions 364
'appearance' 379
arithmetic 179
áru with gerund 241
áru with people 387
'as soon as' 76
asobu 117, 337
áto de 155
-(a)zu 149

bákari 254
'because' 105, 144–45

causative verbs 395, 397
clothing, wearing 257
comparisons 244
   negative with **hodo** 252
   with questions 250
compound correlatives 317

conditional mood (-tara) 297, 299
consonants 14–23
contractions 422
copula (**dá, désu,** etc.) ... 48, 94
   modifier clauses 135
   plain & polite 85, 94, 147
copular nouns (*see also*
   mítai, -sō, yó) 42, 135, 149
   in modifier clauses 135
   with **-sō** 379
   with **-sugíru** 100
correlative compounds 317
counters 180
   for birds 187
   for days 187
   for people 186
   secondary 186
   and sound changes 182

dá *see* copula
daké 195
-dasu 100
dates 190
de 65, 94
   with imperfect negative .. 150
denial of permission 292
denial of obligation 293
deshō with verb 141
desideratives (**-i-tai, -i-tagaru**)
.... 224, 409
désu *see* copula

e 62

-eba *see* provisional

errands 113

exalted status words 328, 330, 343

F, pronunciation of 17

favors 357

flapped **R** 21

fractions 198

G, pronunciation of 17–19

ga 44, 130, 133

gerund (-te) 70, 71, 88

  expressions 113

  +**áru** 241

  +**iru** 115, 401

  +**kara** 105, 156

  +**míru** 223

  +**mo** 282

  +**mo** (after interrogative) 284

'giving', verbs for 354

go- (honorific prefix) 331

going in vehicles 76

góro 190, 191

góto ni 190, 201

gozáru 347

gúrai 190, 191

H, used for **F** 17

'had better' 307

-**hajimeru** 100

'has to' 291

hazu 151

hearsay 378

hitótsu 194

hǒ 243

hodo 252, 313

honorifics 328, 330–32, 347

  adjective infinitive 345

  adjectives 343

infinitive 332

predicates 347

  use of humble verbs 341

  verbs 335

'hotel', words for 52

humble status words .. 328, 343

humble verbs, use of 341

ichiban 251

imperative 426–27

imperfect mood (-**u**) 73, 96

  imperfect negative+**de** ... 150

infinitive (-**i**) 98

  adjective honorific 345

  honorific 332

  negative 149

inflected words 49

  irregular exalted verbs ... 340

  -**másu** 340

interrogatives with **ka**

  and **mo** 274, 284

iru 115, 387

irassháru 350

'is' 48

J, pronunciation of 17

-**ja** (=-**de wa**) 423

-**jatta, -jau** 423

ka 46

  with interrogatives 274

  meaning 'or' 193

  +**mo shirenái** 407

  +**ně** 144

  +**shira** 408

-**kaeru** 100

kara 62, 105

-**káta** 101

-**katta** (adjective perfect) ... 94

kikoeru 240
kinship terms 329
(k)kirí 195, 256
'know' 159
kóso 331
kotó 108
+ni náru/suru 388
-ku (adjective infinitive) 94
-kute (adjective gerund) 94

'leaving', verbs for 154
'let's' 73, 388
'like' 383

máde 62, 158
máe ni 155, 190
mamá 256
-másu, special inflections of 340
'may (not)' 292
-me 252
mi- (honorific prefix) 331
miéru 240
míru, with gerund 223
mítai (na) 234
mo 103
    with gerund 282, 284
    with interrogatives ... 274, 284
    with yóri 246
modifiers 127
    adjective clauses 132
    copula clauses 135
    copular nouns 135
monó 108, 330, 410
months, names of 189
'more' ('the more/the more') 313
mōshiageru 339
multiples 199
'must' 291
'must not' 292

N, pronunciation of 23-6
n (=no) 141
ná (copula alternant) 135
nádo 192
-nágara 385
(-)nai see negatives
nán (=náni) 53
ná n (=ná no) 141
nán- (=iku-) 174, 182
nánka 192-3
naruhodo 254
nasal sounds 23-6
né 64, 144, 422
negatives 74
    answers to negative
        questions 364
    comparisons with hodo ... 252
    double 391
    imperfect negative+de ... 150
    infinitive 149
    plain negative 102, 147
neutral status words 328, 330
ni 47, 149, 311, 360
    explicit use 311
    +chigai nái 392
    infinitive 98
    +shite 223
    +tsúite 393
    +yotte 393
    with copular nouns 136
    with pronouns 241
no, as particle 46, 130, 133
    as copula-alternant 135
    as noun 138
    +de 144
    +desu 139
    +ni 145
nouns 41
    copular 42, 135, 149

derived from infinitive ... 101
no 138
+**to (ni) shite** 223
verbal 75
with and without particles 61
see also **hazu, kotó, mamá,
monó, onaji, tamé, tokoro,
tsumori, uchi, wáke, yatsu**
numbers 174
approximate 197
fractional 198
multiples 199
ordinals 252
percentages 199
use of 176
numerals 174
primary 178
primary & secondary 177
secondary 185
and sound changes 182

o (particle) 66, 130, 154, 194
o- (honorific prefix) 331
-ō *see* tentative
obligation 291, 293
oide 351
óki ni 201
oku 389
on- (honorific prefix) 331
onaji 256
'only' 195
'or' 193
ordinal numbers 252

particles 44, 61, 130, 421
bákari 253–4
de 65, 94, 360
e 62, 153
ga 44, 130, 133

góro 190, 191
góto ni 190, 201
gúrai 190, 191, 253
hodo 252, 313
ka 46, 144, 193
kara 62, 105, 156
kéredomo 85, 282
(k)kirí 195, 256
kóso 331
máde 62
mo 103, 246, 274, 282, 284
multiple 106
nádo 192
nánka 192–3
nē, né 64, 144, 422
ni 47, 98, 241, 311, 360
no 46, 128, 130, 133
o 66, 130, 154, 194
sa 422
sáe 308
shi 314
to 67, 103, 212, 257
tte 424–5
wa 44, 130, 194, 422
ya 191
yo 239, 422, 426–7
yóri 245
ze, zo 422
zútsu 190, 199
passive causative verbs.. 395, 403
passive verbs 395, 400
percentages 199
perfect mood (**-ta**) ... 73, 88, 96
permission 292, 294
place words 41
plain forms: of adjectives .. 85
of copula 85
negative 102, 147
shapes of 86

tentative 219
uses of 96
of verbs 85
plural, specific 365
polite moods 69, 85
potential verbs 404
predicates, honorific 347
prefixes, honorific 331
prenouns 41
+ni 241
prohibition 292, 294
pronouns 43
pronunciation 3
check points 34
provisional mood (-eba) 288

quantity words 175-6
questions, alternative 228
answers to negative 364
with comparisons 250
quotations 212, 237

R, pronunciation of 21-3
rashii 381
related reference, words of.. 50
requests 237, 363
'restaurant', words for 52
rhythm 4

sa 422
sáe 308
-sama, -san 332
sentence types 50
shi 314
shika 195
shimau 389
'since' 105
-só (na) (appearance) 379
só desu (hearsay) 378

sound changes 182
'speaks' 161
status words 328
styles of speech 418
impersonal 418
modern literary 427
plain 420
suffixes, honorific 332
sugí 190
-sugíru 100
sumimasén 56
syllabic nasal 23
syllables 5

-ta see perfect
'talking' a language 161
-tai, -tagaru see desideratives
ta(m)bí ni 201
tamé 146-7
-tara see conditional
-tari see alternative
-te see gerund
tentative mood (-ō).. 73, 141, 219
+to suru 222
time, telling 190
words for 59
to 67, 103, 212, 257, 378
+ka 193, 213
+iu 210, 378
+shite 223
+suru, with tentative 222
'toilet', words for 53
tokoro 152
tokoró ga 282
tóri (ni) 237, 256
tsumori 111
-tsuzukeru 99
tte 378, 424

uchi 158
untranslated English words.. 43

vehicles, going in 76
verbs, alternative mood 383
  causative 395, 397
  conditional mood 297, 299
  desideratives 224, 409
  forms, learning of 90
  gerund, uses of 71
  honorific 335
  honorific infinitive 332
  honorifics, irregular 340
  humble verbs, use of 341
  imperfect mood 73, 96
  infinitive, negative 149
  infinitive, uses of 98
  irregular 92, 340
  negative, plain 102, 147
  obligation 291, 293, 294
  passive 395, 400
  passive causative 395, 403
  perfect mood 73, 96
  permission 292–4
  polite moods 69, 85
  potential 404
  plain & polite forms 85

plain imperative 426–27
plain form, shapes of 86
provisional mood 288
tentative mood 73
tentative, plain 219
verbal nouns 75
voicing 6
vowels, pronunciation of .. 8–14

wa 44, 130, 194, 422
  infinitive+ 98
wáke 390
'what' 53
'with' 67
'work' 75

ya 191
yátsu 108
yo 239, 422, 426–7
yŏ (na) 233
-yŏ *see* tentative
yóri 245

ze, zo 422
-zu 149
zútsu 190, 199